# Douglas SBD Dauntless

# DOUGLAS
## SBD DAUNTLESS

## Peter C. Smith

AVIATION CROWOOD SERIES

First published in 1997 by
The Crowood Press Ltd
Ramsbury, Marlborough
Wiltshire SN8 2HR

**British Library
Cataloguing-in-Publication Data**

A catalogue record for this book is
available from the British Library.

ISBN 1 86126 096 2

To Patricia M. McGinnis,
with gratitude and appreciation.

Typeset by Phoenix Typesetting, Ilkley,
West Yorkshire

Printed and bound in Great Britain by
Butler and Tanner

# Contents

# Reflections

The Navy has its classy planes, their names on every lip,
The newest Grumman fighter needs a three-mile landing strip,
Those boys in Fighting Squadron Eleven may make America free,
But give me the Douglas DAUNTLESS pal, yeah – that's the plane for me!

See, I'm not one for flips and frills, I never beat the mat,
You'll never see me showing off; and zooming like a gnat,
The British have their victory roll, when they have 'popped a blighter',
But I don't do that in my SBD, I ain't no bloody fighter!

I watch the boys in F4Fs as they go roaring by,
In baseball caps and earphones, making runs on lesser fry,
They'll return as conquering heroes, while the whole damn nation shouts,
But they still lose all their money to the Bombers and the Scouts!

I never was a glamour boy, I never posed for Arrow,
I haven't got a slick physique, like Joseph Louis Barrow,
I'm not an ace, I'm not in Life, I'm not a daring hero,
And I'd rather run in my SBD than climb to fight a Zero!

Maybe my butt gets sore and stiff from a tough six-hour patrol,
While the fighters sit in the ready room and gamble away their roll,
But it's worth it all when the chips are down and you're roaring into your dive,
And you're aiming at the biggest one, with a thousand-pound beehive!

Of course, you're not thinking 'bout it then, but, just the same, its true,
That they've got to shoot down the F4Fs, before they can get to you,
So here's the latest dope boys, every Admiral agrees,
That ALL the fighters are good for – is to protect the SBDs!

So, let them prance and let them boast, and let them hog the sky,
And let the natives dance and cheer, as they go flashing by,
Yes, let the fighters have their fling, as they zoom our poor tent city,
For they're Air Group Eleven's cannon fodder – boy…ain't THAT a pity!

Anon

# Introduction

The story of the Douglas SBD Dauntless, and its Army Air Force counterpart, the A-24 Banshee, is a fascinating one and has long held my attention during my decades-long research into dive bombers and dive bombing. Much of the information that I had unearthed about this aircraft had been cut from other books due to lack of space, which for any historian is a frustrating experience. I was therefore particularly pleased to be asked to contribute this volume, and subsequent volumes on the Curtiss SB2C Helldiver and Junkers Ju 87 Stuka, to the outstanding Aeroclassics series which Crowood have so happily initiated and where the emphasis is on quality and comprehensiveness. As such they deserve the backing of enthusiasts and historians alike.

I have made much use of orginal documentation, both from the Douglas archives and the US Navy, Marine Corps and Army Air Force documentation held at various centres in the USA. Secondly, I have been fortunate in that I have been able to make several research trips to centres of aviation history excellence where I have been afforded every facility and help by their historians, archivists and curators who have, without exception, made me welcome and given me valuable direction and advice. My third good source has been friends and fellow historians in both the UK and the USA who have also generously allotted me time, assistance and sensible comment, in particular in the search for good quality and original photographs. From the vast number examined, I hope that the final selection does the subject the merit it deserves. Fourthly, the eye-witness comments of those who flew the Douglas dive bomber have been incorporated, for a unique viewpoint. I have utilized previously published sources as little as possible to avoid duplication; some books however, although flawed by being written with wartime propaganda in mind do contain much very valuable comment from combat flyers and their aircrew, and deserve selected quotation.

I would therefore like to extend my sincere and deep gratitude to the following individuals and organizations: Don Hanson and especially Pat McGinnis, both of the Douglas Aircraft Company (Boeing-McDonnell) at Lakewood, Long Beach, California, for their warm hospitality on my visit and for throwing open the extensive archives and files to me during my stay, an invaluable source; Hill Goodspeed, Emil Buehler Naval Aviation Library, National Museum of Naval Aviation, Pensacola, Florida, for wise counsel and great help in researching photographs and archives and for making my stay at Pensacola such a pleasant and rewarding one; Ray Wagner, archivist, Tim Cunningham, Restoration Manager, Bob Ratlieff, Docent; Jim Woodward, Docent, Jim Caldwell, Docent, San Diego Aerospace Museum, San Diego, California, for access to the archives (which include the Ed Heinemann papers) and the restoration facility, and for their kindness to me and their generous allocation of their time and making my visit such a valuable one; Ron Hinrich at the same facility, and Escondido, California, for the loan and use of his personal service papers relating to his training in the SBD; Vernon R. Smith, Textual Reference Division, National Archives at College Park, Maryland, for his patience and dedication in producing for me all the various combat reports and war diaries of the various US units involved.

Dr Steve Ewing, historian, USS *Yorktown* Patriots Point & Maritime Museum, Mount Pleasant, Charleston, South Carolina, a mine of information and good ideas; Bill Tunnell, Executive Director, USS *Alabama* Battleship Memorial Park, Mobile, Alabama; T. J. Zalar, Curator, Lone Star Flight Museum, Galveston, Texas; Robert L. North, New England Air Museum, Windsor Locks, Connecticut; Danny J. Crawford, Head, Reference Section, History and Museums Division, Marine Corps Historical Center, Washington DC; Michael E. Starn, aviation specialist, Museums Branch, Marine Corps History and Museums Division, Quantico, Virginia; Paula Ussery, curator, Admiral Nimitz Museum, Fredericksburg, Texas; James W. Robinette, project assistant, American Airpower Heritage Museum Inc, Midland, Texas; Dan Hagedorn, reference team leader, Archives Division, Smithsonian Institution, National Air and Space Museum, Washington DC; Cindy J. Keller and Frank R. Mormillo, Planes of Fame Aviation Museum, Chino, California; Wendy Vandervort, *Air Power History*, Lexington, Virginia; M. Vincent Mollet, conservateur des archives centrales, le chef du Service Historique de la Marine, Marine Nationale, Vincennes, France; M. Jean Cuny, historian, Soignolles-en-Brie, France, for invaluable help in unearthing little-known documents on the French purchasing commission in the USA.

Nick Williams, historian, AAHS, Waverly, Iowa, for the loan and the permission to use some of his considerable documentation and some rare photographs accumulated during his own research into the A-24 twenty years ago but never used; Walter Walsh, historian 27th Fighter Bomber Squadron, Desert Hot Spings, California, for records and eye-witness reports in his excellent archives; Arthur Pearcy, historian and friend, Sharnbrook, Bedford, for his guidance and wise words; Thomas M. Alison, curator, Aeronautics Department, National Air & Space Museum, Washington DC; Edwin R. Walker, historian, Great Bookham, Surrey, my old friend of long standing, for his encouragement and advice while I was researching extensively in obscure documents at the Public Record Office, Kew, London; Air Commodore T. J. MacLean de Lange, Rotorua, New Zealand; Meg Campbell, Wellington, New Zealand; Colonel Elmer Glidden, Canton, Massachusetts; Ken R. Scadden, National Archives, Department of Internal Affairs, Wellington, New Zealand for detailed documentation on No 25 Squadron, RNZAF.

Richard K. Smith, historian, Wilmington, North Carolina, for his views on various aspects of aircraft design and dive bombers in particular, and for his encouragement and example; Vice Admiral William I. Martin, USN, Alexandria, Virginia; Admiral Paul A. Holmberg, USN, Arlington, Virginia; David A. Wilson, historian, Narrubundah ACT, Australia, for documents on the 8th Dive Bomber Squadron, USAAF in New Guinea; Captain Claude Huan, historian, French Navy, Paris, for helping me decipher the various French combat reports and combat diaries; Teruaki Kawano, Military History Department, National Institute for Defense Studies, Tokyo, for once again guiding me through the Japanese combat reports, helping me research the Japanese archives in the accuracy of various battle claims and reports.

Barbara Cooper, USS *Lexington* Museum on the Bay Association, Corpus Christi, Texas; Frank B. Mormillo, The Air Museum, Planes of Fame, Chino, California; Therese of The Society of Experimental Test Pilots, Lancaster, California; Kevin R. Smith, Dauntless Aviation, Fredericksburg, Virginia; Colonel Tom Barnes, Confederate Air Force, Marietta, Georgia; The Curator, RNZAF Museum, Air Force World, Wigram AFB, Christchurch, New Zealand; Frank A. Tinker, Pearce, Arizona for memoirs of the 351st Fighter–Bomber Squadron, Richard H. Best, Santa Monica; Barton N. Hahn; and Simon Volpe.

To all these fine people my sincere thanks for helping me tell the Dauntless story.

Peter C. Smith, Riseley, Bedford, UK
May 1997

## A Note on Ranks

British readers are probably unfamiliar with many of the ranks of personnel serving in the US Navy, Marine Corps and Army Air Force and the French Navy and Air Force as recorded in this book, although the ranks of the Royal New Zealand Air Force, being based on the RAF, will be familiar. Often no direct comparisons with British ranks are possible and the following is for general guidance only. In the US Navy the rank of lieutenant is sub-divided further as lieutenant and lieutenant (jg). The 'JayGees' (standing for lieutenant, junior grade) form the bulk of the young naval pilots who flew the SBD in combat, with full lieutenants above them and ensign (which has no British equivalent) below them. Roughly, Royal Navy ranks would be midshipman, sub-lieutenant and lieutenant. In the US Marine Corps and USAAF the same seniority ranks of the Dauntless or Banshee flyers would be colonel, 1st lieutenant, 2nd lieutenant. In the French Navy these ranks would be *enseigne de vaisseau 2ème classe*, *1ère classe* and *lieutenant de vaisseau*. Higher ranks stepping up were *capitaine de corvette*, (lieutenant commander), *capitaine de frégate* (commander) and *capitaine de vaisseau* (captain). Rear-seat men were aviation radiomen (ARs) of various classes in the USN; sergeants or staff sergeants in the USAAF and wireless operator/rear gunner (WOAGs) in the RNZAF.

## A Note on Aircraft Names

It was not until 1 October 1941 that US Navy aircraft were 'officially' allocated names, although 'Dauntless' had been used unofficially before then. The USAAF followed this practice even later, in April 1942, when the 'Banshee' name was allocated to the A-24. In neither service did these names really have much currency among the aircrew themselves who, with the brashness of their youth, were mainly disdainful of using anything 'official'; so arose the many nicknames of the SBD, ranging from 'The Barge' to 'Speedy D', always with a wry mockery relating to its performance. Army flyers never adopted the name at all, always referring to their mounts as A-24s, but more often more derogatory, again because of their lack of speed – they were awaiting (vainly) the much hyped and heralded Brewster Buccaneer and Curtiss Shrike which were destined never to appear! The official designations therefore remained predominant, SBD being the composite of the aircraft's two main functions, S = scout and B = Bomber, plus the manufacturers' designation, D = Douglas, followed by various mark numbers. On the Army side the lateness and reluctance with which they came to the dive bomber caused them to range these aircraft in the A for 'Attack' bracket, plus their number. To this was added D = Douglas, followed by the plant of construction, E = El Segundo and T = Tulsa.

# CHAPTER ONE

# The Dive Bomber Concept 1917–35

The Douglas SBD Dauntless United States Navy dive bomber of World War II, and its United States Army Air Force equivalent, the A-24 Banshee, carried more than its fair share of nicknames given to it by its aircrew, none of them very complimentary. The SBD[1] was translated acronymically as 'Slow But Deadly' by many airmen – and indeed, the Dauntless was no racehorse. The army flyers who took the A-24 into combat in the South Pacific at the same time christened their mounts more derisively, as the 'Blue Rock Clay Pigeons'. Other epithets applied to the Dauntless and the Banshee included 'The Barge', 'Clunk' and 'Speedy D' and all of them were ironic statements about the speed of the aircraft. But if not the speediest of aeroplanes, the 'Deadly' part of the title became very apt, for, as with most dive bombers – none of which were very fast warplanes – the SBD shared the one attribute that was more valuable than any other: the ability actually to hit the target it aimed at.

The British had originally invented dive bombing in 1917 and first used it on combat missions and demonstrated its effectiveness.[2] Moreover it had been the British Royal Air Force that had first tested the method scientifically[3], while it had been the United States Army Air Corps that had kept dive bombing as a practical method of aerial combat in the early 1920s when everyone else had abandoned it.[4] Both later discarded it in favour of the heavy bomber concept which, they trumpeted, would win all future wars unaided!

It was not until the late 1920s that the United States Navy and Marine Corps had taken up dive bombing as a serious tool in their armoury. This followed trials and tests with Navy Curtiss F6C fighters of VF-2 flying from the Naval Air Station at North Island under the auspices of Captain Joseph Mason Reeves. This was followed by a practical demonstration by the same unit flying from Long Beach, California, in October 1926, when diving attacks were made from 12,000ft (3,647m) against a force of battleships of the US Pacific Fleet. Admiral F. D. Wagner wrote of this attack:

> This was the first dive bombing, as such, that we had ever heard of and the reactions of the battleship commanders were most interesting . . . the general consensus was that there was no defence against it.[5]

At around the same time similar experiments were taking place on the east coast of the USA under Rear Admiral A. C. Davis. As Lee M. Parsons was to record later[6]:

> Early tests proved that this kind of attack gave unparalleled accuracy to machine-gun and bombing attacks. Where there had been great reluctance to interrupt scheduled training to experiment with the new tactics, now there was enthusiasm.

It was this enthusiasm that soon led the United States Navy and Marine Corps to be in the forefront of dive bomber development. It was the United States Navy and

A view of a Martin BM-1 dive bomber taking off from the USS *Lexington* (CV-2) in 1934. The BM-1 was one of the first *true* dive bombers designed from the outset to carry a bomb load effective against small warships. (US Navy official).

Perhaps the most successful of the new breed of single-engined monoplane attack bombers developed in the USA in the mid-1930s for ground attack work was the Northrop A-17A. Fitted with a 750 hp Pratt & Whitney 1535-13 engine, this model is shown on 12 November 1936. Designed by Northrop, it is clearly one of the SBD's ancestors. (McDonnell Douglas, Long Beach)

Marine Corps that took the development of dive bombers into the era of the monoplane, and it was American designers and manufacturers who came up with some of the most innovative designs in the late 1920s and throughout the following decade.

The Bureau of Aeronautics, with Lieutenant Commander Davis, set up a series of tests designed to improve the bomb racks and associated equipment to better enable the fleet's fighter aircraft to carry out the new role of dive bombing; this followed further demonstrations against destroyer targets off the East Coast in which Lieutenant O. B. Hardison employed a gun camera to record results. At around the same time the Navy fighter squadrons VF-1 and VF-2 made the film *Hell Divers* which featured the technique – it brought it to the attention of a whole new audience, among them young pilots of the Imperial Japanese Navy!

The aircraft that the US Navy aviators initially employed in the dive-bombing role was the Curtiss F6C fighter. This was a rugged and reliable mount, but in the haste to adapt the method of all Navy pursuit types, including the Boeing F4B-1, the Chance Vought O2U-1 seaplane, and the Boeing F2B and F3B, it was quickly found that the stresses and strains of dive bombing on airframes was considerable, and that not every type proved capable of withstanding them. After several aircraft had disintegrated attempting the dive method some concern was being expressed within the Bureau, not all of whom shared Wagner's and Reeves' enthusiasm.

The reservations held by some led to a further series of detailed trials, during which all manner of fighters were used in shallow dives of 45 degrees from 1,000ft (305m) to 400ft (122m) in order not to push them beyond their limits. Even with such restrictions the results of the

dive-bombing tests were conclusive: dive bombing gave 'unprecedented results', and although the maximum size of bomb utilized, the 500lb (225kg) SAP[7], would obviously not penetrate the armoured decks of battleships, they were sufficiently powerful to make the dive-bombing method of attack against more lightly protected warships, wooden-decked aircraft-carriers, lightly armoured light cruisers and destroyers, a very worthwhile proposition.

Indeed, so successful were these trials employing standard fighter-type aircraft that there was a feeling in 1927 that there was no need to develop any special dive bombing-type aircraft at all, and that the standard pursuit-type would prove adequate for the job. Had that view prevailed there would have been no story to tell, but it did not. Further tests were conducted by VF-FS under Lieutenant Wallace M. Dillon in October 1927. They made dives against a target platform towed at a speed of 20 knots behind a destroyer in Hampton Roads. Again, the accuracy of the method was undeniable, and fully confirmed earlier trials. A detailed examination into the potential of dive bombing against an enemy fleet was conducted by the Taylor Board, and their final recommendation was quite firm: that a specialized dive bomber *was* a requirement; the 'general-purpose' type was roundly condemned by Commander Newton White as '. . . an inefficient hybrid'.

As a result, 1928 saw the first experimental aircraft types designed specifically for the US Navy, with dive bombing as their principal role; thus strength, lifting capacity and ruggedness were emphasized.[8] The Curtiss XF8C-2 was evolved to see whether a specially designed aircraft would be better at the job than an adapted fighter plane. This aircraft was powered by a 450hp Pratt & Whitney Wasp R-1340-B engine and had a maximum speed of 149mph (240km/h), again carrying a 500lb (225kg) bomb into action. This aircraft (serial number 7673) had the then-conventional biplane configuration, and was the prototype of the first and original 'Helldiver' series; in fact it was often called the ancestor of all real American dive bombers. The XF8C-2 had a steel and aluminium tubing fuselage, and fabric-covered wings.

This aircraft proved very successful, and a second prototype was built as the XF8C-4 (serial number 8314). From these modest beginnings sprang a whole series of Curtiss F8C marks, starting with twenty-five production model F8C-4s and twenty F8C-5s (serial numbers 8446/8456 and 8589/8597). But of even greater potential, the same year saw the development of the XT2M-1 which could carry a 1,000lb (450kg) bomb and drop it in a dive-bombing attack. Now even battleships could be hurt badly, if not sunk outright. Once the concept had been enthusiastically embraced, the pace of design was, in two short years, stunning.

A contemporary account made the following observations on the proven superiority of the diving attack method:

Bombs are released at an altitude of 1,500 feet (457m) or less. Target practice conducted against targets towed at a speed of twenty knots in the open sea, indicate an accuracy of about 30 per cent hits on a destroyer target, in

The near-rival to the SBD was the Vought SB2U-1 Vindicator, here seen on the flight deck of the USS *Saratoga* (CV-3) on 8 February 1938. By the outbreak of the war they had been phased out of carrier work, but served with the US Marine Corps at Midway as late as 1942, and briefly with the naval air arms of both France and Great Britain in 1940. (US Navy official)

the neighbourhood of 50 per cent on light cruiser targets and approximately 60 per cent on battleship targets.[9]

The same source added the pertinent fact that:

The diving form of attack is now being extended to use of heavier bombs up to 500lb weight. We are now putting into the fleet a new type of two-seater machine to replace the old two-seat observation machines.[10]

The real starting point for purpose-built specialized dive bombers in the US Navy was the Martin machine, described as '. . . the first airplane specifically developed for a dive-bombing mission'[11] (in the USA). The same source also described the BM-1 as '. . . a nondescript biplane of about 6,500lb Mtow[12] and capable of delivering a 1,000lb bomb': the BM-1 etc was indeed a conventional-looking biplane of the period, but one which was stressed to take a force of 9G in a 90-degree dive[13] (remember that the majority of current 1990s 'state-of-the-art' aircraft will *not* survive 9G).

Not surprisingly, such an original concept was not without teething troubles because in the late 1920s it was a case of 'into the unknown'. During an initial test programme in October 1929 with the XT5M-1, the huge stresses badly damaged the aircraft's wings. When the tests were resumed with a strengthened structure in March 1930 under three different conditions, minor distortions of the wings were again encountered, and the first production model BM-1 crashed during its acceptance trials.[14] Yet further strengthening was required before the BM-1 joined the fleet for deck trials aboard the aircraft-carriers Lexington and Saratoga.

Nor was strength of airframe the only problem associated with the development of a satisfactory dive bomber. Releasing a bomb at a steep angle of dive, when utilized with adapted fighter aircraft like the XF6C-4, the F3B and the F6C-4, had often resulted in the missile hitting the fixed landing gear. Similar problems had been encountered ten years earlier by the RAF when testing the Sopwith Camel fighter as a dive bomber at the Orfordness proving grounds in Suffolk,[15] and in addition,

**Dauntless Men: Designer Ed Heinemann**

The brilliant designer of a magnificent aeroplane, Ed Heinemann belonged to first the Northrop and then the Douglas team. He was born in Saginaw, Michigan, on 14 March 1908; when he was six his family moved to California. His formal education was completed at the age of seventeen and he joined the Douglas Aircraft Company in 1926 as draughtsman, becoming the chief draughtsman for international aircraft the following year.

Ed Heinemann first left Douglas in 1927 and spent time with several aircraft companies honing his skills. In 1928 he moved to Moreland's as assistant chief engineer, soon becoming chief engineer. He joined the Northrop company in September 1930. At first at Burbank, he moved to the El Segundo plant in January 1932. After his wartime work, of which his dive bombers the Dauntless, the Destroyer and the Skyraider were but a part, he went on to make his mark in the post-war aviation field in a big way.

Among the famous aircraft with which his name will always be associated are the Douglas DC-airliner, the A-20 Havoc and A-26 Invader light bombers, and the D-558-1 Skystreak, D-558-II Skyrocket, F3D Skynight, A2D Skyshark, A3D Skywarrior, F4D Skyray (for which he was awarded the Collier Trophy in 1953), the F5D Skylance and A4D Skyhawk. In 1958 Ed Heinemann was appointed vice president at Douglas, and in 1960 became executive vice president of Guidance Technology. In 1962 he joined General Dynamics as their corporate vice president of engineering, finally retiring in 1973 and writing his autobiography. He suffered a stroke, and on 26 November 1991, he passed away, having made his mark on four decades of aviation history. (McDonnell Douglas)

engine failures which resulted in crashes which almost killed the test pilot, Captain Oliver Stewart. These results had turned the RAF away from dive bombing; with the US Navy, however, these same results only spurred them on to find a solution.

Carrying the bombs outboard under the wings was one answer, but this was only practical with the smaller fragmentation bombs, acceptable for use against infantry in the open, but useless against warships which would be the 'heavy' dive bombers' principal role.

Theoretical studies showed that the bomb released from beneath the fuselage would *always* hit the landing gear when released in a vertical dive, but practical results showed that, in fact, this only occurred occasionally.[16] Further trials were therefore conducted at the Dahlgren naval proving grounds, during which cine photography was utilized to record the trajectory of the bombs as they left the aircraft at different diving angles. This revealed that the average pilot miscalculated his angle of dive by between 15 to 30 degrees, thus rendering relatively ineffectual any theoretical maximum angle at which a bomb could be released safely. To overcome this human error an automatic device was required, and a team comprising Lt Cdr A. C. Miles of the Bureau of Aeronautics and Cdr C. L. Schuyler and

Mr George A. Chadwick of the Bureau of Ordnance invented a simple displacing gear arrangement.[17]

This dive-bombing crutch had two pivoted arms which were fixed to the fore end of the aircraft under-fuselage. When released, the mechanism instantly swung the bomb down and out from the aircraft itself, clear of both the propeller and the fixed undercarriage. After static testing at the Martin plant, actual aerial trials of the new dive-bombing crutch were conducted at Dahlgren by Lt Cdr Ostrander on 7 and 8 January 1931, utilizing the XT5M-1; these proved entirely satisfactory. This device was therefore made standard equipment and was widely copied abroad, including in Japan and Germany. Strangely enough, although the Germans took the automation of dive bombing much further, incorporating the Ascania automatic pull-out device[18], no such aide was actually employed operationally on US Navy dive bombers, mainly because the dive bomber pilots themselves did not want it.[19]

Another useful invention was the fitting of a slow-arming fuse to the 500lb and 1,000lb bombs; this meant that the bomb was not 'live' until after it was well clear of the aircraft, and thus reduced the risk of chance ignition on release. By April 1931 the Martin company had demonstrated the excellence of their product and the BM-1 was ordered for the service. As so often befalls the innovators, Martin were destined not to capitalize very much on their pioneering work, and not until 1948 did another Martin dive bomber join the fleet, the mighty Martin AM-1 Mauler.

By the time the twelve original BM-1s were aboard the aircraft-carriers in July 1932, followed by twenty-one of the improved BM-2s, the Bureau of Aeronautics was already looking ahead to its replacement.[20] Already by 1932 the one specialized type had become several sub-types – but the one that concerns our story here is the 'heavy' dive bomber.

The 'heavy' dive bomber definition at that time was a two-seater airplane for dive bombing, requirements for which were the ability to haul a 1,000lb (450kg) bomb for

a range of 400 miles (644km) and a 500lb (225kg) bomb for 750 miles (1,207km).[21] Into this category came the Great Lakes XBG-1 and the Consolidated XB2Y-1. When the Great Lakes company was taken over by Martin in October 1932, many features of the latter's TG-2 torpedo bomber were incorporated into the design. They were ordered as the BG-1 for the US Marines and Navy and sixty were constructed, first entering service in October 1934. They were smaller than the BMs and thus easier to handle aboard the carriers where deck and hangar space was always at a premium. They had 43mph (69km/h) extra speed at 188mph (302km/h) and a 3,700ft (1,128m) advantage in service ceiling at 20,100ft.

This was considered totally inadequate for the future needs of the fleet however, for the 1934 Bureau design competitions called for two types, the scout (VSB) with a total all-up weight of 5,000lb (2,268kg) and able to carry 500lb (225kg) bombs, and the dive bomber (VB) with a Mtow of 6,000lb (2,722kg) and capable of carrying 1,000lb (450kg) bombs. Both were to be equipped with the new dive brakes, bomb crutches and other refinements, and were to have stalling speeds of 65mph (105km/h) for carrier landings.

By 1935 a host of differing experimental types were being tested and evaluated, including the Northrop XBT-1, Chance-Vought XSB2U-1, XSB3U-1, Brewster XSBA-1, Curtiss XSBC-2 and the Grumman XSBF-1. Different companies responded in different ways: the Chance-Vought design was a re-worked biplane type with a fully retractable undercarriage, and the SBU-1 was, in fact, the first to carry the SB designation, illustrating how the Bureau of Aeronautica hoped to combine the scouting and bombing requirements within one airframe. Brewster's answer was the revolutionary XSBA-1, a mid-wing monoplane with fully retractable undercarriage, and a concept which altogether held out great promise.[22] Unfortunately the company was unable actually to construct and test the aircraft design it had submitted, and it was later developed by the Naval Aircraft Factory as the SBN-1;

thirty of these were subsequently built. Grumman never got around to submitting their design at all. Meanwhile Curtiss replaced the crashed XSBC-1 with the XSBC-2, with greater performance, to meet the new specification.[23] Great Lakes tried the same approach with their biplane XB2G-1, but it was clearly yesterday's technology.

Another monoplane design was the Vought SB2U-1, later known as the Vindicator to the US Navy and Marines, and 'Wind Indicator' to its wartime aircrew five years later when, old as it was, it was thrown into combat. The aircraft had a top speed of 257mph (414km/h) at 11,000ft (335m) when it first flew in January 1935, and could carry a bomb load of 1,500lb (675kg). Drop tanks could give it a range of 700 miles (1,127km). Some 240 Vindicators were built, including fifty-seven 3s of a special long-range batch for the US Marine Corps; all saw much service aboard pre-war carriers, while others went into combat at Midway as late as 1942.

The Vought suffered from major problems with its power plant, and the self-same problems also caused much grief to its contemporaries the SBC-3 and the BT-1, almost bringing the entire dive-bombing programme to a premature end. The trouble lay with the Wright R-1535-94 radial engine with which all these aircraft were equipped: engines were failing in the dive, and testing revealed that the master rod bearings were the culprits. Not until two years had elapsed was a satisfactory solution found by Pratt & Whitney, with the fitting of silver-lead bearings; later on, indium was added.

In 1935 one other company saw the answer to the Navy's dive bomber needs as a combined function (scout and dive bomber) airframe of the monoplane form, but they combined this with a whole host of new and original features which made their design outstanding. That company was Northrop, and the aircraft was the XBT-1. Their technology was very much 'state-of-the-art' and beyond, and with their arrival on the scene the final piece of the essential jigsaw that resulted in the Dauntless was in place.

# CHAPTER TWO

# Design and Prototype Testing

The family tree of the Dauntless is a diffuse one, like Topsy, in that 'it just grew'; but the line of US Navy dive bomber research that had begun in the mid-1920s had gradually evolved the necessary adjuncts, know-how and technology to blossom into the SBD. What was then required was a touch of genius, and at this point it appeared on the scene in triplicate, the following names standing out in this final line of development: the young and innovative aircraft designers John K. Northrop and Donald Douglas, and the famed young designer who worked for both these dynamic new companies whose fates became entwined, one Edward Henry Heinemann.

Ed Heinemann was born in Saginaw, Michigan on 14 March 1908; at the age of six his family moved to California. His formal education was completed at the age of seventeen, but '... he gained a thorough knowledge of aeronautical engineering through study and experience'.[24] He joined the Douglas Aircraft Company in 1926 as a draughtsman, and promotion was rapid: he became chief draughtsman for International Aircraft the following year, and this was followed in 1928 by his appointment as Moreland's assistant chief

Rear view of the XBT-1 at El Segundo on 17 August 1935. Note the two-bladed propeller and no radio mast yet fitted. (McDonnell Douglas)

engineer, and then chief engineer.[25]

Donald Douglas had originally set up his own small aviation group in 1920, with a total staff of ten people. In 1924 the Douglas company achieved fame by building the first aircraft to circumnavigate the globe. Under the guidance of chief engineer James H. ('Dutch') Kindelberger, Douglas started a series of commmercial transport aircraft which continued almost non-stop for the next fifty years: by 1937 it was employing 6,550 at the Clover Field plant, with three machine shops in Los Angeles.

In January 1932 John K. Northrop, with the backing of the Douglas Aircraft Company, organized, along with A. K. Jay and associates, the Northrop Corporation. It was first established in the old Moreland aircraft building at Inglewood, located opposite the then Los Angeles municipal airport. The first aircraft built by the new company were the 'Alpha' and 'Beta' types, followed by the mail planes of the 'Gamma' series which were revolutionary in concept, reaching a speed of 220mph (355km/h). Moving to the former Pickwick Coach building at Mines Field, now the site of LAX, by March 1934, by 1937 the plant was employing 1,000 people with $4,500,000 worth of business in hand.

In 1927 Ed Heinemann left Douglas and spent time with several aircraft companies honing his skills; he joined the Northrop company in September 1930. At first at Burbank, he moved to the El Segundo plant in January 1932. Considering that Heinemann and Northrop had 'basically different design philosophies'[26] the new team worked remarkably well. Northrop, for ever pushing at the boundaries of known aeronautical engineering, was counter-weighted by Heinmann's basic, down-to-earth practicality, and between them they transformed the US Navy dive bomber from a wings-and-struts biplane not much different from its Great

The final view of the XBT-1 (Bu No 9745) at El Segundo on 17 August 1935. The perforated flap/dive brakes extend the whole admidships' length of the wing section. (McDonnell Douglas)

War ancestors, into a sleek but rugged monoplane incorporating state-of-the-art manufacturing technology.

Continuing from the Northrop-designed, experimental Army attack aircraft with fixed undercarriages, the XA-13 and the XA-16, the company had come up with the A-17 for the USAAC. This was a two-seater, low-winged monoplane powered by a single 750hp Pratt & Whitney R-1535 radial engine which gave it a top speed of 206mph (332km) and which could carry a 650lb (295kg) bomb load externally. The new Navy dive bomber was to employ the same power plant and the basic design was similar, but with a 41ft 6in (12.6m) wingspan rather than one of 48ft (14.5m)[27] in order to accommodate the aircraft on aircraft-carrier hangars, for the XBT-1 was not designed with folding wings since Heinemann was principally seeking strength in his design. The aircraft's other dimensions – a length of 31ft 6in (9.5m) and a height of 12ft 6in (6.4m) reflect the same considerations.

The XBT-1 (No 9745) first flew on 19 August 1935, and had an all-up weight of 1fitons, carrying a 1,000lb (450kg) bomb.

The final view of the XBT-1 at El Segundo on 4 December 1936. This shows how the retractable wheel gear fitted the large underwing fairings. (McDonnell Douglas)

Powered by the R-1535-66 Twin Wasp, it had a maximum speed of 184mph (296km/h). It was also an all-metal, low-wing, two-seat monoplane, but the fixed undercarriage of the A-17 had been replaced by a compromise undercarriage arrangement that partially retracted the wheels into a large underwing fairing described as a 'bathtub', which left the underside of the type exposed. This was due to the adoption of the Northrop method of the sparless, multi-cellular wing structure that had been a feature of the Alpha design. This enabled the abandon-

Rear view of the Northrop XBT-1 at El Segundo on 4 December 1936. Compare this view of the dive flaps with that of the earlier photograph taken on 17 August. (McDonnell Douglas)

ment of braces and struts without loss of strength, although it precluded at this time a fully retractable landing gear.

For its defensive fire-power the XBT-1 was built with only a single, fixed, forward-firing pilot-controlled 0.50in (12.5cm) machine gun, although for production provision had been made for an observer-gunner swivel mounting with a 30-cal in the rear cockpit.

The aircraft's speed was obviously inadequate, and in December 1935 the prototype was re-engined with a 825hp -94 Twin Wasp instead of the -66, which pushed speed up to a more respectable 212mph (341km/h). Surface ceiling was now 22,500ft (6,858m) with the maximum external bomb. The new fitting resulted in a shortened engine cowling, and for better handling the tailplane was enlarged and given a more rounded profile.[28]

For dive bombing, the aircraft's whole *raison d'être*, Heinemann had incorporated very large, hinged split-flaps attached to the trailing edge of both wings, another original Northrop feature. A minimum 60-knot stalling speed was the Navy's limitation here, and the flaps had to take this factor into consideration as well as dive-attack requirements. As Heinemann later recorded: 'I designed a double,

concentric-cylinder, hydraulic-control mechanism which permitted either the lower flap to be extended for take-off and landing, or both upper and lower flaps extended for the dives. Both sets of flaps had to be carefully sychronized to avoid negative effects on longitudinal trim during extension in dives.'[29] To make this system work better, Heinemann based his linkage system on the Scott Russell linkage '... coupled with some of my own ideas ...' and he also acknowledged the invaluable assistance of Walt Cerny and Dick Cooper in the overall dive brake design.

Indeed the system worked well, and initially no problems showed themselves as trials were mainly concerned with level flights. Ed Heinemann personally took part in these trials, which were held at Mines Field, taking the observer's seat behind famed test pilot, Vance Breese. Once diving tests began, they began to encounter buffeting problems on the horizontal tail surfaces when the trailing edge flaps were extended. Shallow dives were acceptable, but the steeper the angle of attack attempted by Breese, the worse the problem became, with the outer edges of the tail flapping themselves more than 2ft (60cm). Heinemann frankly recorded that this 'scared the hell' out of him.

The XBT-2 (Bu No 0627) in its final assembly, seen here at the Douglas El Segundo plant on 24 August 1938. Now a three-bladed propeller drives a Wright cyclone engine, the wheels are fully retractable and their housings have been eliminated. The shape of the SBD Dauntless has become established. (McDonnell Douglas)

The problem was caused by the vortex effect from the air flowing over the extended flap surfaces. Although it was a tribute to Heinemann's 'strength before all' basic building of the aircraft that the tail assembly had taken such stresses without collapsing and causing a fatal accident, an urgent solution was obviously required, because yet another dive bomber unable to dive, after the Vindicator, was a liability and an embarrassment. Over in England, RAF 'experts' were proclaiming that dive bombing could *not* be done with modern monoplane aircraft.[30] Northrop and Heinemann knew this was rubbish,

Northrop BT-1 (Bu No 0606) final assembly, with flaps open, pictured on 10 May 1938. She carries the markings 5-B-10 as allocated to VB-5 aboard the new carrier *Yorktown*. (McDonnell Douglas)

but how to rectify the problem was baffling.

Fortunately, help was at hand in the form of Charles Helm, of the government-sponsored National Advisory Committee for Aeronautics. Mr Helm was seconded on loan to Northrop's El Segundo site. He examined all the evidence and proposed that the 'altering vortex theory' was maybe the answer. In order to reduce the vortex problem, a series of 3in (76mm) diameter holes was cut through the inner section of the flaps; with one-third of their length perforated thus, further diving tests were conducted. The eddies set up through these holes reduced the major vortices, and much less buffeting was encountered. Progressively this series of holes was extended until the whole length of the flaps was perforated and looked like ' . . .a slab of Swiss cheese'.

The final tests were made before both Mr Helm and Mr Tripolitis, a US Navy flight inspector, and proved totally satisfactory; in fact they enabled the flaps to be extended even more in the dive, while when shut the holes made no difference to the lift. The perforated dive flaps were to become almost the trademark of the SBD. Although the Bureau of Aeronautics were 'sold' on this idea, it did result in a one-knot excess of stalling speed over their absolute minimum requirement, but they

turned a Nelsonic blind eye to it in the case of this aircraft.

Nor was this the only problem encountered by the Northrop team with the XBT-1. Again, the difficulties were a by-product of the vertical dive on a modern system, in this case the carburettor which was unable to cope with the changes in barometer pressures. As the machine sped earthwards, globules of unburned fuel were pumped out of the exhaust manifolds and ignited as they left the exhaust ports below the fuselage; flames stretched back under the aircraft for some thirty feet (9m) or more, and so intense was the heat thus generated that the paintwork in the vicinity of the dummy practice bombs was scorched off. The whole phenomenon was named 'engine torching'. It took Vance Breese over one hundred very courageous dive trials from 15,000ft (4,570m) before the problem was isolated and solved.

Perfected in the Californian sun, the XBT-1 reacted rather differently when exposed to winter in Anacostia Naval Air Station, Washington, and trials at the US Navy test field found yet more problems, including the landing gear refusing to lower until parts had heated up at low altitude, and cracks in the new plastic cockpit coverings also caused by the low temperature. These too were rectified.

Finally it became a straight choice between the Northrop product and Chance-Vought's XSBU-1, and in the end both won out, both Vindicator and BT-1 being ordered for fleet use, the Northrop company receiving an order for fifty-four aircraft on 18 September 1936.

The production line BT-1s were engined with the Pratt & Whitney R-1535-94 which developed 825bhp at sea level and were fitted with a two-blade, 10ft (3m) diameter propellor. It had a gross weight of 6,966lbs (3,160kg) and it had a top speed of 222mph (357km/h) with a 1,000lb (450kg) bomb. The range was 1,150 miles (1,850km), and when it entered service with VB5 and VB6 aboard the aircraft-carriers *Enterprise* and *Yorktown* in 1937–8, it became the Navy's only *designated* dive bomber. The maximum number of BT-1s in service was attained in 1940 with forty machines, and it was a non-combatant type by the time of Pearl Harbor. But if its numbers were small, then its influence and the problems it had overcome were enormous: Without the BT-1 there would have been no SBD.

However, the many problems encountered by their first dive bomber had been a considerable drain on Northrop's resources. This culminated in the sale of the company to Douglas on 1 September 1937. Douglas already held 51 per cent of the Northrop stock, and on purchasing the rest, the El Segundo plant became the Northrop Division of Douglas Aircraft[31] and John K. Northrop became its manager. Fortunately Ed Heinemann continued as chief engineer so continuity of design was maintained as the switch from Northrop BT-1 to Douglas SBD took place. This continuity continued when a year later 'Jack' Northrop tired of this arrangement and again left Douglas in January 1938 to set up his own company once more, and Ed Springer took over at El Segundo.

Of the fifty-four production line BT-1s, the final two produced were experimental aircraft. One of these was used in trials of a nose-wheel-type landing gear, which was ultimately rejected. The other BT-1 became the XBT-2 (No 0627) and utilized funds allocated by the Navy for a second prototype. Dive bombers were needed as part of a much-expanding American fleet, and as both the SB2U-1 and the BT-1 were experiencing more than their share of teething troubles in service, there was an urgent requirement for an improved and more reliable dive bomber as soon as possible.

Ed Heinemann has revealed[32] how the Navy itself – in the form of the Bureau of Aeronautics project officer Commander Ed Caxton – helped Northrop and then Douglas to short-cut the usual protracted experimental aircraft procedures to get such a dive bomber operational in a record time of sixty days. This was a great tribute to the very hard work put in by both the designer and the test pilots, the latter of which included the indefatigable Breese and another outstanding pilot, Frank Sinclair, who did mainly roll examination tests. In one intensive period, twenty-one different types of tail and rudder configurations were tried to get the correct elevator settings, and a dozen alternate lateral control settings were trialled exhaustively before the optimum performance was attained. Flight testing was aided by the Navy's recommendation of the fitting of adjustable control, fore-and-aft surface hinges to monitor the flights which enabled the individual adjusting of aileron, elevator and rudder

The final assembly of the XBT-2 seen from above, 24 August 1938. (McDonnell Douglas, Long Beach)

controls to narrow down the options.

The XBT-2 first flew on 22 April 1938, and was then still powered by the 825 hp Pratt & Whitney R-1535-94 engine; but Heinemann took advantage of a belly landing by this machine to negotiate a change in the contract, dated 21 June 1938, which enabled him to fit a 950hp Wright R-1820-G133 engine and the three-bladed propeller and catapult hooks. Indeed for the new XBT-2, only the dive brakes and the gunner's seat remained of the original, at least according to Heinemann. The chief difference was the power-plant, with the Wright Cyclone being substituted for the R-1534 as described, which gave the aircraft far greater power (and it was known to be the Bureau's choice of future engine, so its adoption was a sound marketing move also!). This larger engine necessitated a redesigned nose. Although Jack Northrop objected to the switch, it went ahead anyway, and in addition the propeller was also replaced, the new 10ft 9in (3.3m) diameter, three-bladed, adjustable pitch being selected. Other modifications included an improved control panel with superior instrumentation designed to overcome some of its stalling deficiencies.

With the new engine in place, the XBT-2 was put through its paces from 25 April 1938, however prolonged tests showed that these modifications had not

resulted in more than very minor improvements in performance. The aircraft was taken to the NACA testing site at Langley Memorial Aeronautical Laboratory, Virginia, to be further trialled in the full-scale wind tunnel there. Here the Bureau's specialists, including Ed Claxton and Walter Diehl, were also on hand to give advice and let Heinemann know exactly what the Navy was looking for in their new dive bomber.

The revised tail surfaces of the XBT-2 shown at El Segundo on 7 October 1939. (McDonnell Douglas, Long Beach)

## Dauntless Men: Vance Breese - Test Pilot

One of the greatest test pilots of his era, Vance Breese diced with death many times in his long and illustrious career. He took the SBD Dauntless, and its immediate ancestors, through all the trials and tribulations of test flying with the Douglas company, and thanks to his diligence the Dauntless turned out to be one of the most versatile and successful dive bombers of all time. It also enjoyed the lowest casualty loss rate of any American front-line combat aircraft of World War II. In light of this, Breese can be considered one of the key 'Dauntless Men'.

Vance was born at Keystone, Washington, on 20 April 1904, the son of Lee Humbert and Anna Edria (Dixon) Breese. At the tender age of just thirteen (!) he learnt how to fly, at Seattle. From then on the air was his life, although he did finally marry Loudell Stephens of Los Angeles on 3 December 1940. His commercial pilot licence (Certificate No. 1331), in all aircraft class ratings, was obtained and by 1942 he had logged more than 11,400 flying hours.

His early days as an aviator were spent, as one would expect, barnstorming his way around the States between 1919 and 1923. He then moved on to operate his own flying school and aerial photographic service, as well as sky-writing, at San Francisco between 1925–26. He organized operations for Pacific Air Transport and Ryan Airlines, doubling up as test pilot and sales rep. In 1927 he formed the Breese Aircraft Company with himself as President. This company manufactured aircraft, including the Trans-Pacific 'Aloha'. When this venture ended Vance became the Chief Test Pilot to the Detroit Aircraft Corporation, and then assistant to the President, supervising design and engineering work and sales, a position he held between 1930 and 1932. This in turn led to him becoming the Vice-President, in charge of operations, at the Air Express Corporation in 1933.

Much in demand, Vance was employed as consulting engineer and test pilot with a whole succession of companies: Bell Aircraft; Douglas; Lockheed; the Morrow Aircraft Corporation; and, between 1933–34, Northrop, where he flew demonstrations of their Navy fighter and test flights for A. H. G. Fokker. In 1937 he became Vice-President and test pilot at the Bennett Aircraft Corporation, before moving on to Douglas, Vultee and many

others utilizing his skill and experience at the cutting edge of pre-war and then wartime aerial developments. One famous story which demonstrates his quick-thinking concerned a passenger flight on which the aircraft's engine dropped off. Among the passengers was a woman with a baby in her arms but it is reputed that Breese calmly asked her to 'please step forward', along with some others. The plane managed to land safely on a hillside near San Francisco Bay and everyone aboard walked away. Afterwards, Breese attributed their miraculous survival to the fact that by shifting the weight of the passengers forward they compensated for the loss of the engine's weight and helped restore the balance of the aircraft sufficient for him to retain enough control to put her down in one piece.

On several more occasions he almost paid with his life, as in October 1937 when, coming in to land at Mines Field in Los Angeles in a new Navy fighter aircraft, he was in collision with another aircraft flown by student instructor Ross Seeley. Both aircraft were gliding in to land when they struck wing-tip to wing-tip and both crashed. Amazingly both men walked away from the wrecks. According to the local Times newspaper, it was Seeley's first such accident. 'Breese, however, has figured in so many it appears his skill is backed by a charmed life.'

By 1942 he was living on Amestoy Avenue, in Encino, California, in easy reach of the mushrooming production lines and was a member of the Institute of Aeronautical Sciences and the Quiet Birdmen, while his clubs included the County, Hollywood Athletic and Deauville Beach, Los Angeles.

Among the many unique aircraft that Vance flew was Howard Morrow's 'plastic-bonded' training aircraft, the so-called 'Victory Trainer' which was essentially a plywood trainer with mili-

tary-type retractable landing gear, which Vance flew at the San Bernadino airport in November 1941. It was an attempt to use non-strategic materials in a simple design which could be mass-produced by furniture makers and the like with no aeronautical engineering skills. It had a doubled-shelled fuselage, was powered by a 175hp six-cylinder Lycoming engine and had a top speed on 165mph. This was a very tame beast compared with what Vance had flown previously. Earlier he had tested another 'plastic' trainer, the Timm PT-160-K 'Aeromoid' from the L.A. Metropolitan airport at Van Nuys. This was built by Walter A. Hite with pre-formed spruce plies 1/24in thick which were impregnated with phenolic resin plastic developed by the Timm company in a similar attempt to produce a cheap training aircraft without impinging on essential materials need for combat machines. It was powered by a 160hp Kinner engine with a top speed of 140mph.

Vance was hired to do the XBT-1 testing at Mines Field and flew on a part-time basis. Ed Heinemann recalled that Vance, '...was a superb aviator, one of the finest I every knew.' They paid him $2,000 for the test flying; a few years later Lockheed paid him $65,000 to do a similar job on the P-38 fighter. As Heinemann also recorded, 'I don't think there is anyone who has made more 9g pullouts than Vance Breese and myself.'

Vance continued his flying career with the same charismatic flair that had marked his early years and became an distinguished member of The Society of Experimental Test Pilots, Lancaster, California. He finally passed away in 1978, much honoured and revered among his contemporaries as one of the 'greats'.

Among the many further alterations which resulted from the exhaustive tests at this time were the abandonment of the 'bathtub' fairings and the making of the landing gear fully retractable and inward-folding. The tail and rudder were increased to balance changes to the fuselage, centre and outer wing forms, and a new cockpit canopy was adopted (with the Aldis telescopic sight being fitted to aid dive bombing). The forward-firing and ground-strafing armament was doubled and became two fixed .50 cal machine guns mounted in the fuselage in front of the cockpit with their breeches protruding back into it, and a flexible .30 cal machine gun on a swivel mounting (later to be twinned) carried aft. One recommendation which NACA made was *not* carried out, and this was the removal of the perforated dive flaps!

The fuselage was constructed in four water-tight sub-assemblies of stressed-skin configuration, all-metal, aluminium alloy, semi-monocoque. The wings were likewise of stressed-skin construction, all-metal and multi-cellular, with anti-stall 'letterbox' slots next to the leading edges, forward of the aileron, designed to reduce the risk of stalling at the optimum 60 knots. The tail assembly was also an all-metal cantilever structure, with fabric movable surfaces and metal-covered stablizers. A NACA 2415-2409 airfoil gave the machine lift boosted by the trailing edge flaps. The aircraft's all-metal ailerons were fabric-covered and of ribbed construction. The left aileron had a metal trim tab inserted. The trailing edges of all the tail assembly's moving surfaces were also fitted with tabs to aid trim.

The aircraft cockpit was redesigned as a continuous transparent canopy, with one fixed and three sliding segments to enclose pilot and radio operator/tail gunner seated in tandem. As yet there was no proper armoured plate to give either men any head protection, nor was the front windshield built of laminated, bullet-proof plastic; these very desirable combatant qualities did not arrive until the SBD-3 some time later. The pilot's controls were duplicated in the rear cabin. The bomb-carrying crutch was modified, and when fully swung out below the fuselage, allowed a 1ft (30cm) clearance of the new three-bladed propeller.

The landing gear was fully hydraulic, with the wheels, when fully retracted into the wheel wells, housed flush with the lower wing surface; the wheel remained on outward display without covering, but the wheel strut itself retracted into a fairing. The solid rubber rear wheel was fixed at the base of a short fairing but had full swivel performance. The standard arrestor hook was provided for carrier landings, but after problems encountered in the fleet with the BT-1, this had been made longer and larger to compensate for 'bounce'. The Northrop-type flaps proved difficult to fit, and there were changes made here by Douglas, with a 1ft (30cm) half-round rod attached to the leading edges of the wings positioned 3ft (90cm) away from the fuselage as an alternate spoiler. The trailing-edge flaps were split, and when engaged, the upper was raised 37fi degrees while the lower was dropped 42 degrees.

The weights of the XBT-2 came out at 5,093lb (2,310kg) empty and 7,593lb (3,444kg) fully laden. The wing area was 320sq ft (29.6sq m). Cruising speed was a mere 155mph (249km/h), with a maximum speed of 265mph (426km/h), a 35mph (56km/h) improvement. Rate of climb was 1,450ft (442m) per minute and the service ceiling was listed as 30,600ft (9,327m). In the dive bomber configuration with a maximum bomb load of 1,200lb (544kg) up, range was 604 miles (972km), which the Navy considered totally inadequate; the Bureau of Aeronautics was promising further improvement on this as a high priority. They wanted at least 1,400 miles (2,253km) and eventually Douglas came up with a solution which gave the aircraft, while in the scouting mode (and the XBT-2 was still expected to perform both functions) a range of up to 1,485 miles (2,389km) – but this was not until the SBD-2.

Meanwhile, for some time after Jack Northrop's abrupt departure and Douglas's takeover, the machine still retained its T designation; but later that year it was redesignated, just before the final trials, as the XSBD-1, SB being the new designation of all US Navy *single-engined* dive/scout bombers. It was therefore under its new title that the prototype SBD received its final blessing from the Bureau of Aeronautics in February 1939.

Despite continuing work to achieve ever-changing and more demanding Navy requirements, as an interim measure to get some modern SBDs into the fleet and evaluated by Navy and Marine aircrew in operational conditions, the government went ahead and purchased limited numbers. On 8 April 1939 firm orders were placed for 144 SBD-1s. In the event only eighty-seven improved versions (the SBD-2) reached the US Navy, and the first fifty-seven off the production line (as the SBD-1) were assigned to the US Marine Corps. The aircraft also received its name for the first time from the Naming Committee, and a more apt choice could hardly have been made: the Dauntless had arrived!

# CHAPTER THREE

# Into Service

From the time the XSBD-1 appeared in August 1938 to the first SBD-1 (c/n 549, BU.No 1596) leaving the El Segundo production line in April 1940, was not an enormous time-scale for the development of an aircraft. The power plant was now the 1,000hp Wright R-1820-32 engine, and fuel capacity had been increased by the fitting of two auxiliary 15-US gallon tanks, which gave a total fuel load of 210 US gallons (795 litres). Another change incorporated was the fitting of a second 0.5in machine gun fixed firing forward. This aircraft first flew on 1 May 1940 and was delivered on 6 September 1940. But, speedy as development was by Douglas and acceptance was by the US Marines, events on the world stage were moving at a greater pace. In Europe, September 1939 had seen the German invasion of Poland, the declaration of war by Great Britain and France, the Soviet Union's ruthless stabbing in the back of a Polish army already totally shattered by the Junkers Ju 87 Stuka dive bomber in combination with fast-moving tank columns, and the first public demonstration of the *Blitzkrieg*. The dive bomber had altered ground warfare for all time. In case people thought this was a fluke the

*(Above)* The same SBD-1 2-MB-1, airborne in 1940. (McDonnell Douglas)

same deadly combination of dive-bomber and *Panzer* smashed through the sluggish Allied armies in France and the Low Countries in May 1940, with equal ease and, at the time the first Dauntless was joining the US armed forces, France,

Belgium, Holland, Luxembourg, Norway and Denmark had been totally defeated and the British Army chased from the continent minus most of its equipment; and the RAF was penned into its home airfields, its policy of low-level bombing and half-hearted army support totally discredited. Equally the dive-bomber was influencing sea warfare also, with the Stuka causing unexpectedly high losses among French and British warships operating off Norway and in the English Channel.

Not surprisingly such momentous events had a great influence on contemporary thinking elsewhere. The Japanese Navy had already invested heavily in dive bombers, its Aichi D3A1 'Val' being a two-seater monoplane with a fixed undercarriage closely resembling the dreaded Stuka. They had *no* doubts of the value of dive bombing, at sea or on land,

*(Above)* Two Marine Corps SBD-1s warming up in 1940. That closest to the camera – 1-2-MB-1. (McDonnell Douglas Photo)

*(Above)* Rear quarter view of US Marine Corps' SBD-1 in flight. (San Diego Aerospace Museum)

*(Below)* A classic aerial view of the SBD-1 in flight in USMC markings. (McDonnell Douglas, Long Beach)

having tested the latter theory extensively in China and found it valid. The US Army was aghast at the cheap and easy victories of the Germans, for the tiny American army had hardly any tanks and the Army Air Corps likewise had no dive bombers, or even ideas about dive bombers, at all![33] The type of expensive long-range bomber they and the RAF favoured had proven singularly useless at influencing all the rapid Allied defeats by one iota! The *only* thing that had saved London going the same way as Paris had been 26 miles (42km) of salt water. Suddenly the USAAC ideas of warfare seemed very outmoded indeed.

We shall return to examine the response of the US Army to this new form of land warfare. The US Navy and Marine Corps, by strict contrast, needed no reminding just how potent the dive bomber was; they had been converted in the late 1920s and, once convinced, had been dedicated and enthusiastically practising and developing tactics and skills, as well as the proper aircraft, to utilize the dive attack to its maximum.[34] This learning curve continued as the SBD arrived with the fleet.

The differences between the XSBD-1 and the first production SBD-1s were not physically large, but several of the Navy's required improvements resulted in a slightly different configuration. Perhaps most obviously to the outward observer was around the nose area. The radio mast which was fitted well forward on the XSBD-1 was moved aft of the fire wall in the SBD-1, and the engine cowling had a pronounced carburettor air intake added on top which made for an instant identification pointer. The twin, fixed machine guns forward fired through troughs in this cowling.

Less obvious was that the overall height of the SBD-1 and -2 increased to 13ft 7in (4m) and the wing area increased by 5sq ft (0.4sq m). While empty weight remained the same, the loaded weight increased to 9,790lb (4,441kg). The range was increased from 604 miles (972km) to 860 miles (1,384km), but the 210 gallons[35] (954l) of fuel was carried in two fixed tanks, with a further two 15-gallon (68l) auxiliary tanks, which were *not* self-sealing. The weight penalties of Mtow (fuselage, wings, landing gear, empennages, nacelles, equipment, fuel and oil, cockpit fittings, fixed armaments, bomb load, crew) were unforgiving and resulted in a slower aircraft, with maximum speed reduced

# US Navy/Marine Corps Units Equipped with SBDs

| US Marine Corps | Unit | Areas | Dates |
|---|---|---|---|
| | VMB-1 | East Coast USA – Cuba | 1940–41 |
| | VMB-2 | West Coast USA – Hawaii | 1940–41 |
| | VMS-3 | St. Thomas, Virgin Islands | 1942–44 |
| | VMSB-132 | Guadalcanal & Solomons | 1942–43 |
| | VMSB-133 | Torokinda – Solomons – Philippines | 1944–45 |
| | VMSB-141 | Guadalcanal – Solomons | 1942–43 |
| | VMSB-142 | Guadalcanal – Emirau – Solomons – Philippines | 1942–45 |
| | VMSB-144 | Guadalcanal – Solomons | 1943–44 |
| | VMSB-151 | Tutuila – Gilbert Islands, Engebi – Marshall Islands | 1943–45 |
| | VMSB-231 | Espiritu Santo – Guadalcanal – Marshalls | 1942–44 |
| | VMSB-232 | Pearl Harbor – Guadalcanal | 1941–42 |
| | VMSB-233 | Solomons | 1943–44 |
| | VMSB-234 | Solomons | 1943–44 |
| | VMSB-235 | Solomons | 1943–44 |
| | VMSB-236 | Philippines | 1945 |
| | VMSB-241 | Midway – Solomons – Emirau – Philippines | 1942–45 |
| | VMSB-243 | Efate – Green Island – Philippines | 1944–45 |
| | VMSB-244 | Solomons – Green Island – Philippines | 1943–45 |
| | VMSB-245 | Marshalls – Ulitihi | 1944–45 |
| | VMSB-331 | Samoa – Nukufetau – Gilberts – Marshalls | 1943–45 |
| | VMSB-333 | Boca Chica – Hawaii – Midway | 1943–44 |
| | VMSB-341 | Gilberts – Efate – Green Island – Philippines | 1943–45 |
| | VMSB-342 | Boca Chica | 1943–44 |

| US Navy | Unit | Base | Dates |
|---|---|---|---|
| | VB-1 | Yorktown II (CV-10) | 1944 |
| | VB-2 | Lexington (CV-2), Hornet II (CV-12) | 1941–42, 1944 |
| | VB-3 | Saratoga (CV-3) | 1941–42 |
| | VB-5 | Yorktown II (CV-10) | 1943–44 |
| | VB-6 | Enterprise (CV-6) | 1942–44 |
| | VB-8 | Hornet (CV-8) | 1942 |
| | VB-9 | Essex (CV-9) | 1943–44 |
| | VB-10 | Enterprise (CV-6) | 1942–44 |
| | VB-16 | Lexington II (CV-16) | 1943–44 |
| | VB-17 | Bunker Hill (CV-17) | 1943 |
| | VB-98 | Solomons | 1944 |
| | VB-305 | Solomons | 1943–44 |
| | VB-306 | Solomons | 1943–44 |
| | VC-22 | Independence (CVL-22) | 1943 |
| | VC-28 | Solomons | 1943–44 |
| | VC-29 | Santee (CVE-29) | 1943 |
| | VC-40 | Solomons | 1943–44 |
| | VGS-26 | Sangamon (CVE-26) | 1942–43 |
| | VGS-29 | Santee (CVE-29) | 1942–43 |
| | VS-2 | Lexington (CV-2) | 1941–42 |
| | VS-3 | Saratoga (CV-3) | 1941–42 |
| | VS-5 | Yorktown (CV-5), Saratoga (CV-3) | 1942–43 |
| | VS-6 | Enterprise (CV-6) | 1942 |
| | VS-10 | Enterprise (CV-6) | 1942–44 |
| | VS-41 | Ranger (CV-4) | 1942–43 |
| | VS-51 | San Jacinto (CVL-30), Solomons | 1943–44 |
| | VS-71 | Wasp (CV-7) | 1942 |
| | VS-72 | Wasp (CV-7) | 1942 |
| | TNG | Charger (CVE-30) | 1942–45 |

from 265mph (426km/h) to 253mph (407km/h), and cruising speed down from 155mph (249km/h) to 142mph (228km/h). The service ceiling was also reduced by 1,000ft (305m).

The lack of range alone was enough to bring about the decision that the initial batch of fifty-seven SBD-1s (Nos 1596–1631 and 1735–1755) should equip Marine Corps squadrons and not be embarked for carrier operations. Thus it was that the first of these aircraft, twenty-two in all, were allocated to Marine Air Group Eleven (MAG 11). Although most books state that they were, at that

The Douglas Production Team. Left to right: T. E. Springer, Plant Manager, El Segundo, BAGR West Division; Rear-Admiral E. M. Pace Jr; Chief Engineer Ed Heinemann BAR-DES; and Commander B. J. Connell. (McDonnell Douglas, Long Beach)

*(Above)* The first SBD-1s, 1603 and 1605, in the markings of 1-MB-1. (McDonnell Douglas, Long Beach)

*(Below)* SBD-1 1628 of 2-MB-1 airborne. (McDonnell Douglas, Long Beach)

time, based at Quantico, Virginia, Ed Heinemann himself was to recall that '. . . the first batch of bombers were assigned to Marine Bombing Squadron Two (VMB-2) at North Island.'[36]

A US Marine Corps history confirms that VMB-2 was based at San Diego at this time.[37] Here the first SBD-1s equipped Marine Bombing Squadron Two (VMB-2) briefly, but the aircraft had to be returned to the Douglas plant at El Segundo for 'painting modifications'; after this was done, these same aircraft were sent to VMB-1, commanded by Major Joe Smith, serving on the East Coast with MAG-1. During November 1940, this unit transferred to McCalla Field, Guantanamo Bay, Cuba, and practised simulated carrier landings with their new mounts. The final SBD-1 was delivered on 18 December 1940.

This training showed up other problems in the SBD-1 very quickly, in particular some aircraft after a series of dives starting to show the ominous signs of stress, with wrinkles developing at the wing roots. The Bureau of Aeronautics was informed of the problem by MAG-1, and they in turn cabled Donald Douglas to send an expert to sort out the problem. Naturally the man sent was Ed Heinemann himself, who arrived at the Marines' Cuban airbase on 12 December 1941.

Here, Heinemann worked closely with Smith and Captain Carson Roberts, the units engineering officer, Colonel William Manley of MAG-1, and First Lieutenant George Beard, and his personal observation and camera pictures revealed that the problem was not caused by the dives but by the landings. The low speed approach and heavy sink rate before the wheels touched were causing very heavy impact, which, constantly repeated, had affected the wing root structure causing the skin to flex and ripple. The solution was the fitting of an extra set of pre-cut aluminium stiffeners. Trials showed that, although this resulted in a heavier landing effect, it solved the problem. Existing SBDs were retro-fitted accordingly and the new stiffeners were introduced to the production line SBD-2s.

Later batches of SBD-1s were sent to VMB-1 early in 1941, and also equipped MAG-21 which found itself in Hawaii at the beginning of December of that year.

Meanwhile, work was continuing on making the remaining Dauntless aircraft of the first order up to Navy requirements, especially with regard to range requirements. Starting with the 58th aircraft of the production line (Nos 2102–2188), the range with full bomb load (one 1,000lb (450kg) on crutch under fuselage, two 100lb (45kg) on underwing racks) was increased to 1,125 miles (1,810km), while in scouting mode the range was 1,370 miles (2,204km). This was accomplished by replacing the two small auxiliary fuel tanks with fixed tanks in the outer wing panels, each having a capacity of 65 gallons (296l), giving a new total fuel load of 310 gallons (1,409l). An autopilot was another extra fitting, essential for the long cross-ocean navigation this device now made possible.

Dimensions, armament and power-plant were unchanged, and so the extra weight of fuel embarked inevitably had to result in a loss of other performance due to the inexorable law of the Mtow. Thus, even though the SBD-2 still carried no armour protection, top speed dropped by one knot, although cruising speed increased slightly. The rate of climb fell away to 1,080ft (329m) per minute, and service ceiling was now down to 26,000ft (7,925m). In order to somehow redress the balance, one of the fixed forward-firing .50 calibre machine guns was sometimes omitted.

For the purpose of visual recongnition, the -2 was just about identical to the -1, save for the fact that the bulbous carburettor scoop atop the engine cowling was slightly less prominent.

So the SBD-2 was still not the dive bomber that the US Navy required, but the Bureau of Aeronautics accepted the eighty-seven machines in order for the service to get some aboard the aircraft-carriers for evaluation, while the work continued to find improvements. The first of the SBD-2s was delivered on 18 December 1940, but the second SBD-2 crashed while undergoing acceptance trials, and later was replaced by an early production SBD-3 (c/n 1003). The eighth suffered the same fate, also being replaced by an SBD-3 (Bu No 2109). The rest soon joined the fleet, with Bombing Squadron Two (VB-2) commanded by Lieutenant Commander H. D. Felt aboard the *Lexington* in November 1941, then Scouting Squadron Two (VS-2) aboard the same ship just a month before Pearl Harbor. Others joined VS-6 and VB-6 aboard the *Enterprise* shortly afterwards, replacing BT-1s and SB2Us. The remaining SBDs had all become operational by May 1941.

The *Lexington's* air group took its new dive bomber to participate in the annual Army manoeuvres at Lake Charles, Louisiana to demonstrate the potency of

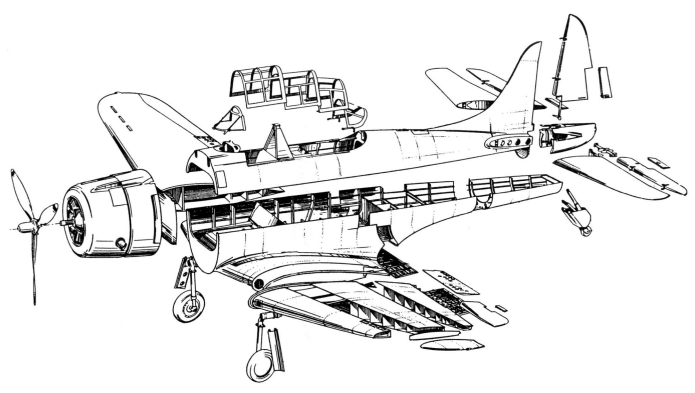

*Exploded view of the SBD.*

the weapon to sceptical USAAC chiefs. Equally ironically, Felt's SBD-2s participated in a mock two-day air attack on Oahu, Hawaii, in May 1941.

Back at the Douglas plant, an early problem with the SBD-2 at first caused some head-scratching when Vance Breese found one airplane of this batch stalling at a much higher speed than previously encountered. Nothing in the specification had changed, and it was two days before the problem was solved: it transpired that the aircraft had been painted (yellow on top, aluminium below), and where the paint from the upper edge had met the lower along the leading edge, a minute ridge had formed, and this was sufficient to change the airflow over the wing and cause the earlier stall. By eliminating this blemish the problem was removed and the aircraft performed normally.[38]

On 18 November 1941, Ed Heineman patented the SBD (design no 130,473), and before the war ended, no fewer than 5,936 of these, and the Army's A-24, would be produced at an average fly-away cost of $55,000 each.

As the first SBD-2s joined their units at sea, the hitherto bright and colourful squadron markings of the 1930s were giving way to a more realistic camouflage scheme. In the autumn of 1940, US Navy aircraft were repainted an overall sea grey broken only the white star and red 'meat-ball' on the circle of dark blue of the national insignia, and the white identity numbers.

Meanwhile a third mark of Dauntless was being produced to meet the growing need and the growing danger. The Navy had already decided that the Douglas was only to be an interim stop-gap, and that the dive bomber that they really required was to be a much larger and more potent machine. They had fixed their eyes on the Curtiss SB2C Helldiver as incorporating their ideals, and had ordered this 'straight off the shelf' as it were. However, constantly changing specifications, lessons of war and difficulties in setting up production lines almost from scratch, continually delayed the entry of the Helldiver in action,[39] and thus, perforce, it was upon the SBD that the Navy had to rely to fight its sea/air war in the Pacific between 1941 and 1943.

In June 1940, at the time of the cataclysmic collapse of France, a further order had been given to Douglas for 174 aircraft[40] (Nos 4518–4691): this became the SBD-3 to the US Navy who placed orders in September 1940. Delivery commenced in March 1941, and these were later followed by a further 500, of which 410 (Nos 03185–03384 and 06492–06701) were of the same specification.

Combat lessons from Europe had shown the need for such refinements as self-sealing fuel tanks, and crew protection in the form of steel armour and bullet-proof windscreen, and these refinements were all incorporated, along with the reinstating of the second forward-firing .50 calibre machine gun and the twinning of the rear-firing defensive .30 calibre machine gun, utilizing belt-fed instead of drum-fed weapons. The new fuel tanks were wing-mounted, bladder-type with a 260 gallon (1,182l) capacity. The new Wright R-1820-52 became the power-plant, while the 12-volt electrical system remained, although this was soon to change.

At the same time it was realized that the weight envelope was again creeping up and adversely affecting performance, so lighter clad skinning was adopted and floatation equipment went by the board as well, resulting in a 180lb (82kg) airframe weight loss. Even so gross weight now reached 10,400lb (4,717kg) and speed dropped another 2mph (3.2km/h). Rate of climb improved to 1,190ft (363m) per minute, and range was now 1,345 miles (2,164km) fully laden. Visually there was virtually no identification feature, other than the slightly larger fixed-opening ventilation slot abaft the engine cowling.

The first SBD-3 (c/n 751, Bu No 4518) was delivered on 18 March 1941, and it was with this aircraft that the US Navy dive bomber crews fought their greatest battles.

*(Left)* US Marine Corps' SBD-1 in flight. (San Diego Aerospace Museum)

# CHAPTER FOUR

# The Wail of the Banshee

We have seen how the USAAC had cold-shouldered the dive bomber concept ever since the 1920s, but the spectacular success of the Stuka brought them back to reality very fast. As early as 1 June 1940 General George C. Marshall had requested information on converting the A-20 type for dive bombing.[41] On 8 June 1940, Brigadier General B. K. Young of the Plans Division had been asked for an investigation into whether the A-20 could be modified so that it could perform as a dive bomber.[42] The plan was considered, but it was found on study that a complete re-design would have been necessary, and as there was no time for this, the Material Division in Washington DC therefore recommended that dive bombers be procured either by purchase of the latest Navy machines, or as a result of new design competitions.[43]

On 8 June the Bureau of Aeronautics had been requested to furnish the Air Corps with one of each of their latest design dive bombers for pilots' observations and a check on their diving characteristics. General George H. Brett, Material Division, stated that:

This will permit the Air Corps to take advantage of the years of research and development that have been conducted by the Navy on this

SBDA (A-24) 41-15747 (the second A-24) at El Segundo on 6 June 1941. (McDonnell Douglas)

type of airplane. In addition to this, delivery schedules and prices for a quantity of twenty-five of the SBD-2 Douglas diver (sic) bombers have been requested. The Navy has a contract for 114 of these airplanes with the Douglas Company, which will be completed in February 1941.[44]

At a staff conference held on 19 June 1940, Brigadier General H. H. ('Hap') Arnold, Chief of the Air Corps, said that the Air Corps would have to furnish two groups of dive bombers to operate with armoured divisions. It was revealed that the '2181 program' had originally contained provision for 200 SBD-2 dive bombers, and that this was later changed to seventy-eight A-20s.[45]

In order to get some dive bombers quickly, the former cause was adopted, and on 26 June it was decided to procure seventy-eight Navy SBD-2s instead of the A-20s, which were to be modified to use Army-type bombs and other equipment.

These seventy-eight airplanes (Nos 41-15746–15823) were given the 'Army Attack' designation A-24-DE (DE = Douglas El Segundo, likewise -DT = Douglas Tulsa) and were included in the Navy's purchase of 252 airplanes from the Douglas Aircraft Company, under contract N-77114 of 27 September 1940.[46] These machines were to be delivered by 1 October 1941, although on 13 July a detailed procurement specified delivery starting with one machine in October 1940, rising steadily to ten per month by March 1941, with the final batch being delivered by August 1941.[47]

Even then the Army was lukewarm about full-blooded dive bombing, the A-24 being described as '. . . a modification of the Navy SBD-2 type airplane, purchased through the Navy in an effort to procure as expeditiously as possible planes capable of performing dive bombing at a 30-degree angle or more and glide bombing up to a 30-degree angle.'[48]

A-24 in flight on 3 February 1942. (US Air Force via Nick Williams)

Three A-24s on a training flight on 14 October 1942, no rear-seat men embarked. (US Air Force via Nick Williams)

On 19 July 1940, the list of Army modifications included deletion of the carrier arrestor gear and the provision for catapult launching, also of the floatation gear, the barrier crash hook installation '. . . and as much as can be eliminated without changing the basic structure or causing redesign'. This meant that the actuator fairing remained. The Army wanted leakproof tanks, armour protection for the crew, and two fixed and one swivel defensive machine-gun mountings. Design changes required included a slightly larger, pneumatic tail wheel, the Marine Corps type being acceptable. The Model DU rotating loop direction finder was to be deleted, and although Navy-type radio equipment was accepted, because it '. . . does not meet the needs of the tactical employment of this airplane, it is probable that Air Corps equipment will be installed at a later date.'[49]

In order to evaluate the type quickly, a number of SBD-1s were borrowed from the Marines and put through their paces by the 24th Bombardment Squadron. They performed well in their designed role, although after twenty years of neglect the Army had nothing against which to judge them as aircraft, and no expertise in dive bombing itself. Nonetheless there was sufficient potential revealed to ensure that the orders went ahead.

The name allotted to the A-24A by the USAAC was the Banshee,[50] a particularly appropriate one for the howl of a diving aircraft, and the first machine (c/n 802, serial number 41-15746) arrived at Wright Field on 18 June 1941. The project officer, Major P. W. Timberlake, reported that its flight characteristics were excellent '. . . insofar as could be determined while ferrying the aircraft'.[51] He added the fact that aircraft were on a Navy contract and it was necessary to install Army radio equipment at the Sacramento Air Depot but that trial installation would be made on this first aircraft at Wright. A shortage of carburettors had been cleared up, and a further five machines had been accepted in California at this date; this was increased by eight by 1 August. A further batch of ninety of the Navy's SBD-3s were appropriated (as SBD-3As) for the Army's needs and similarly modified (Nos 42-6682–6771); they were delivered from July to October 1942. Meanwhile the earlier deliveries were being allocated to operational units, the first fifty-four machines to the 27th Bombardment Group (Dive), commanded by Colonel Guy McNeil; this unit was based at Savannah, Georgia, and comprised the 16th, 17th and 91st Squadrons, commanded by Captains William Hipps, Render D. Denson and Lieutenant William Burbanks respectively. As well as equipping these three squadrons of the 27th, a start was made

next to equip the 3rd Bombardment Group with the Banshee, starting with the 8th Squadron. They familiarized themselves with their new aircraft, which arrived in July 1941, and took part in the Lake Charles combined manoeuvres in September.[52]

On 1 November, the air and ground crew of the 27th Bombardment Group embarked from San Francisco for the Philippines, their aircraft to follow later. However, due to the Japanese attack on Pearl Harbor and the Philippines on 7 December 1941, the ship carrying the 27th's aircraft was diverted to Australia for safety; meanwhile almost the entire unit was lost fighting as infantry. A party of pilots under the group's new commander Major John H. Davies, left the islands on 18 December and reached Darwin, Australia, four days later, hoping to get their A-24s which they had learned were undocked in Brisbane. As Major Davies himself was to record:

When our dive bombers did arrive in Australia they were lacking parts that prevented their assembly for combat activity until the opportunity to get them against the advancing enemy in the Philippines had gone. The persons in America responsible for sending our dive bombers over without gun mounts, trigger motors, sights etc, in my opinion are subject to trial for criminal negligence.[53]

The idea was to assemble the A-24s at Amberley and Archerfield airfields: this was done with all crews working three shifts twenty-four hours a day. The first was flying by 29 December, followed by others – but still without armaments. Once assembled, the A-24s were formed into a dive-bomb school, and the veteran flyers of the unit taught the new techniques to fresh US pilots from West Coast flying schools in the States. Once enough were proficient, the idea was then to ferry the Banshees back to the Philippines to join in the fight. On 23 January, Captain Ed Backus, the 27th's Group Material Officer, moved to Archerfield to organize and take command of the 91st Bomb Squadron.

Meanwhile back in the United States a defence committee under the directorship of Senator Harry S. Truman had examined the Army's needs, and reached the startling conclusion that dive bombers were not a high priority: they recommended a cut-back in the funding of such aircraft. General Orvil A. Anderson also took a

# Principal AAF Units Equipped with the A-24 1941–43

| Unit | Designated | Task/Squadrons | A-24 Usage |
|---|---|---|---|
| 1st Air Force | 1941 | 2nd Tow Target Sqdn | 1943–45 |
| 3rd Bombardment Group (Dive) | Sept 1942 | 8th/13th/89th/90th | 1942–43 |
| 22nd Bomb Training Wing | Aug 1943 | Tactical Air Training | 1943 |
| 24th Bombardment Squadron | June 1940 | Evaluation Tests | 1940–41 |
| 27th Bombardment Group (Light) | Feb 1940 | 15th/16th/17th/91st | 1941–42 |
| 48th Bombarment Group (Dive) | Sept 1942 | 55th/56th/57th/88th | 1942–3 |
| 58th Bombardment Squadron (Dive) | April 1943 | 58th | 1942–3 |
| 84th Bombardment Group (Dive) | July 1942 | 305th/306th/307th/308th | 1942–43 |
| 85th Bombardment Group (Dive) | July 1942 | 305th/306th/307th/308th | 1942–43 |
| 86th Bombardment Group (Dive) | Sept 1942 | 309th/310th/311th/312th | 1942–43 |
| 311th Bombardment Group (Dive) | July 1942 | 382nd/383rd/384th/385th | 1942–43 |
| 312th Bombardment Group (Dive) | July 1942 | 386th/387th/388th/389th | 1942–43 |
| 339th Bombardment Group (Dive) | Aug 1942 | 482nd/483rd/484th/485th | 1942–43 |
| 404th Bombardment Group (Dive) | Jan 1943 | 620th/621st/622nd/623rd | 1943 |
| 405th Bombardment Group (Dive) | Feb 1943 | 624th/625th/626th/627th | 1943 |
| 406th Bombardment Group (Dive) | Feb 1943 | 628th/629th/630th/631st | 1943 |
| 407th Bombardment Group (Dive) | Mar 1943 | 632nd/633rd/634th/635th | 1943 |
| 408th Bombardment Group (Dive) | Mar 1943 | 636th/637th/638th/639th | 1943 |
| 415th Bombardment Group (Dive) | Feb 1943 | 465th/667th | 1943 |
| 531st Fighter Bomber Squadron | Dec 1943 | 531st | 1943–4 |

similar view and ordered that the sixteen planned dive bomber groups be replaced by fighter aircraft. General Marshall disagreed and reinstated the dive bombers in the budget.[54] Although the A-24s were proving not quite what was required, the plan was to replace these with the Army version of the Curtiss Helldiver, the A-25 Shrike, and the new Vultee A-31 and A-35 Vengeance, then being built under contract for the RAF. However, both these dive bombers, theoretically superior in every way to the A-24, were experiencing production problems and none were yet in sight. Meanwhile the war was not going well and combat aircraft were required, and in numbers!

The only way to resolve the problem appeared to take yet more Navy SBDs, and on 7 March 1942, Lieutenant General Arnold informed the Bureau of Aeronautics that:

It is desired to activate additional dive bomber squadrons in the Pacific combat area. Most of the SBD-3A (A-24) airplanes procured on contract No 77114 are now in that theatre. To

An overhead view of an A-24 in flight on 3 February 1942. (US Air Force via Nick Williams)

activate the new squadrons and provide a minimum amount of replacement, it is imperative that airplanes of this type be available before those set up for the Army on contract No 91397 are delivered. In view of the above, it is requested that consideration be given to the release of one hundred and seventy (170) SBD-3 airplanes to the Army, in addition to the one hundred and fifty (150) on contract, and prior to the present scheduled delivery.[55]

Rear Admiral J. H. Towers, Chief of BuAer, replied that the Bureau was proceeding to extend the present contract for SBD-3 airplanes by one hundred and seventy additional airplanes and that efforts were being directed towards obtaining a revised schedule of delivery which would further accelerate production.[56]

These 170 machines became the A-24A-DEs (Nos 42-6772–6831 and 42-60772–60881)[57] and were modifications of the new Navy type SBD-4, and although again superficially almost identical to the -3, some significant internal changes were incorporated. They were delivered from October 1942 through to March 1943. They were the equivalents of the Navy's SBD-4, which also adopted the 24-volt electrical system. The first of these was delivered to the fleet on 18 October 1942, and it was followed by 779 more (Bu Nos 06702–06991 and 10317-10806).

Obviously new to the eye on both the SBD-4 and the A-24A-DE (or SBD-4A as one batch were also to be later known), and an immediate identifying feature, was the fitting of the new Hamilton standard hydromatic constant speed propeller which was spinnerless. Inside the aircraft the main electrical system was upgraded from the 12-volt to the 24-volt system. This permitted the fitting of up-to-date radio navigation and airborne radar equipment (ASB), which greatly increased the SBD's potential. Other electronic additions included an electric fuel pump and emergency fuel pump. Of course, not all this new equipment was immediately available in quantity for production line assembly to incorporate it, and many aircraft had to be retro-fitted.

Weights naturally increased again to 6,360lb (2,885kg) empty, 10,400lb (4,717kg) fully laden, and maximum speed slipped back up to 245mph (394km/h), but service ceiling was reduced again to 26,700ft (8,138m). Range was also reduced by a few miles, to 1,300

A side view of an A-24 in flight on 3 February 1942. (US Air Force via Nick Williams)

(2,092km) with full bomb load.

Production was now gearing up to wartime needs at El Segundo, reaching a peak of eleven SBDs a day compared to only twenty a month at the time of Pearl Harbor. Like all aircraft manufacturers at this time, a huge expansion of production facilities was called for, only limited by lack of basic tooling, armour and other vital parts. To cope with ever-increasing demands, the Douglas Aircraft Company opened a second major production plant at Tulsa, Oklahoma. Even this increased capacity was threatened to be swamped with the new orders that came from a request from Brigadier General Meyers on 17 April 1942, for the authority to purchase 1,200 A-24A dive bombers. This was approved by Lieutenant General 'Hap' Arnold on 20 April, and five days later the Douglas Company was given a letter of intent to this effect. The original memorandum stated that Wright R-1820-40 engines were to be installed on these airframes, and further, that ten were to be assembled at the Tulsa plant prior to February 1943, from parts supplied by El Segundo and using the Wright R-1820-52 engine.[58] From that date the airframes '. . . will be equipped with an R-1829-G200 engine of the same type as being installed

in Navy aircraft . . .';[59] provision was also to be made for Army-type radio equipment. Production was to rise from six in February 1943, through to seventy machines in July and to reach 130 per month by October 1943 and thereafter.

Heavy combat usage in the South Pacific was already leading to complications regarding the Navy/Army share-out of the 170 aircraft ordered earlier. On 16 May, Captain H. B. Sallada, USN, at the BuAer was writing to the commanding general, Army Air Force (USAAF as the Air Corps had now become) that: 'The US Navy faces very serious shortages of carrier dive bombers in

A-24 landing at El Segundo. (McDonnell Douglas)

the immediate future . . .'. He stated that a readjustment of the delivery schedule was required to rectify the situation. As things stood, El Segundo was to have produced, '. . . for delivery by the Navy to the Army Air Force . . .', seventy-seven machines in July 1942, seventy-three in August, ninety-three in April 1943 and seventy-seven in May. The remaining production was to be of SBD-3 carrier-type aircraft for the Navy.[60] The new proposal for the A-24 Army type was twenty machines in July 1942, and thirty per month thereafter. This was agreed to.[61]

On 1 June 1942, further elucidation was made when the Chief of BuAer informed the Chief of the Bureau of Ordnance that '. . . thirteen hundred and twenty-five (1325) Model SBD-5 airplanes have been released by this Bureau for procurement.' He went on:

It will be noted that the Army and Navy planes on contract 91397 will be delivered concurrently. The change from 12 to 24 volts will still be effective on the three hundred and first (301st) airplane of this contract, and at this point the designation will change from model SBD-3 to SBD-4. The last seven hundred and fifty (750) airplanes on contract 91397 will have been reduced to six hundred (600), and the one hundred and fifty (150) will be put on a new contract with the subject thirteen hundred and twenty-five (1,325), making a total of fourteen hundred and seventy-five (1,475) on the new contract. An engine

change will make the designation of these fourteen hundred and seventy-five (1,475) airplanes become model SBD-5.[62]

To get this programme under way, a conference was held at the Douglas plant on 21 May 1942, when it was agreed that every effort should be made to keep the SBD and the A-24 types identical (save for the radio equipment) so production could be expedited through standardization.[63]

## Production Schedule SBD/A-24 as at June, 1942

| Number | Type Number | Contract | Voltage | Service | May-42 | Jun-42 | Jul-42 | Aug-42 |
|---|---|---|---|---|---|---|---|---|
| 200 | SBD-3 | 89641 | 12 | Navy | 54 | 70* | | |
| 220 | SBD-3 | 91397 | 12 | Navy | – | 2 | 73 | 7 |
| 80 | SBD-3 | 91397 | 12 | Army | – | – | 20 | 3 |
| 280 | SBD-4 | 91397 | 24 | Navy | – | – | – | – |
| 70 | SBD-4 | 91397 | 24 | Army | – | – | – | – |
| 490 | SBD-4 | 91397 | 24 | Navy | – | – | – | – |
| 110 | SBD-4 | 91397 | 24 | Army | – | – | – | – |
| 1,415 | SBD-5 | New Contract | 24 | Navy | – | – | – | – |
| 60 | SBD-5 | New Contract | 24 | Army | – | – | – | – |
| 2925 | *76 Delivered | | | | 54 | 78 | 93 | 1C |

The engineering for the A-24A model was released from the El Segundo plant from July 1942 onward, while the A-24B with revised power-plant was still on the drawing boards. The Tulsa plant proceeded to build five A-24As up to the stage preparatory to engine installation, but the R-1820-52 was not available. In November 1942, Tulsa was informed that there would not be any R-1820-52 engines and that all 1,200 airplanes would be A-24B models with the R-1820-60 engine installed.[64]

It was tentatively agreed at the 2 June conference that model numbers would be used as follows: -52 engine, 12-volt electrical system: A-24 SBD-3; -52 engine, 24-volt electrical system: A-24A SBD-4; -40 engine, 24-volt electrical system: A-24B SBD-5.

On 1 July it was agreed that of the 1,200 A-24 type airplanes to be built at Tulsa, the first fifty-five would be A-24s and the remaining 1,145 would be A-24Bs, the difference being the R-1820-40 engine for the latter. The items of equipment to be furnished by the AAF were engines, radios and .50 calibre guns.[65] In the event this was not the end of the story.

By November 1942 the El Segundo plant was still in the development stage on the -60 engine, and Tulsa had to develop the power-plant in parallel. The five completed airframes had to undergo considerable redesign before A-24B production could commence there.

A-24 in flight. (San Diego Aerospace Museum)

| Sep-42 | Oct-42 | Nov-42 | Dec-42 | Jan-43 | Feb-43 | Mar-43 | Apr-43 | May-43 | Jun-43 | Jul-43 | Aug-43 | Sep-43 | Oct-43 | Nov-43 | Dec-43 |
|---|---|---|---|---|---|---|---|---|---|---|---|---|---|---|---|
| 72 | | | | | | | | | | | | | | | |
| 30 | | | | | | | | | | | | | | | |
| 11 | 100 | 115 | 54 | | | | | | | | | | | | |
| – | 30 | 30 | 10 | | | | | | | | | | | | |
| – | – | – | 76 | 145 | 160 | 109 | | | | | | | | | |
| – | – | – | 20 | 30 | 30 | 30 | | | | | | | | | |
| – | – | – | – | – | – | 61 | 170 | 170 | 200 | 200 | 175 | 160 | 150 | 80 | 49 |
| – | – | – | – | – | – | – | 30 | 30 | | | | | | | |
| 113 | 130 | 145 | 160 | 175 | 190 | 200 | 200 | 200 | 200 | 200 | 175 | 160 | 150 | 80 | 49 |

Although it had been agreed that standardization was most desirable, the Tulsa plant found that most of the equipment delivered into it was of the Army type, and not the Navy type as ordered by the contractor. A complete engineering revision for installation of the instruments, electrical equipment, radio equipment and hydraulic systems was therefore required. Tulsa asked El Segundo for a block of drawing numbers to use for these design changes. Initially this was turned down, and project sketch numbers had to be used on all new drawings. Later, after considerable contract changes had been accomplished by this method, a block of drawing numbers was allocated; however, they had to use a quantity of drawings already completed. More complications were found still later when it was found necessary definitely to identify certain SBD-5 drawings that were being used for A-24B airplanes but had certain changes to AAF requirements. This was done by adding the prefix 'A' to all the drawing numbers this affected.

The differing requirements of the Army over the Navy, which included Army-type radio in lieu of Navy, a demand-type oxygen system in lieu of Navy rebreather type, deletion of the Sperry auto pilot and substitution of equivalent gyro instruments, further added to the complexity of the standardizing of the SBD-5 and the A-24B. Both the Navy and the Army, as well as Douglas itself, came to the belated conclusion that such standardization was impossible.

The Army stated that they did not have any aircraft-carriers and were not interested in carrier-board equipment, that they in turn operated over airfields which were frequently quite dusty and therefore carburettor air filters were necessary; whereas the Navy operated

Security guards watch as an A-24-A undergoes engine maintenance at the Douglas Plant. (McDonnell Douglas, Long Beach)

over water and did not encounter the dust problems.[66]

Complete provisions were retained in the airplanes for subsequent installation of carrier-board equipment in the A-24Bs, but no such equipment was furnished. Eventually El Segundo furnished Tulsa with a complete set of ozalid originals reproduced from master ink tracings prepared in California; but even then '. . . considerable discrepancies and continual problems have arisen caused by tracing errors', and it was found necessary to ask for a complete set of reference drawings from the original vellums for comparison. Once the development of the R-1820-60 – with the various Army 'deviations' as above, totalling some 100 master changes to the airplanes – was complete, production finally got under way in earnest, and the first airplane of the contract flew on 16 March 1943.

Eventually the rest of the A-24As (Nos 42-60772–60881) and some 675 A-24B-DTs (Nos 42-54285–54899) were built for the Army. Only 615 actually joined the Air Force. On 28 April 1943, Captain B. Lester of the AAF wrote to Colonel Seasums that:

Wright Field has verbal information that there is a move to delay the delivery of sixty (60) A-24 airplanes from El Segundo until later in the summer. These are airplanes being produced by the Navy on contract NXS-6970 and thirty (30) are scheduled to be delivered to the Army in April and thirty (30) in May. These are the last of the A-24s to come from the Navy production at El Segundo and the delay is involved because this production was far behind schedule.

Lester added that:

Since Tulsa production is now getting started and El Segundo A-24s must first go to the modification center (sic) after they are accepted, Wright Field is of the opinion that the contract for the above sixty (60) might just as well be cancelled if the above delay is involved. This seems logical in view of the limited use of these airplanes.[67]

He got his answer in a teletype message three days later which informed him that, 'Pending final action by higher authority, deliveries of the sixty A-24Bs to the Army . . . are to be deferred. Until further notice, all A-24Bs from Navy contracts will be delivered to the Navy.'[68] And on 3 August 1943, Colonel S. R. Brentnall, chief, Production Engineering Section, AAF, advised that:

This office has been advised that the allocation of the sixty A-24B airplanes on contract N-6970, which were to have been delivered to the Army from the Navy, has been cancelled. Therefore, no action will be required on these airplanes insofar as the AAF is concerned.[69]

In fact, after being redesignated as RA-24B-DEs by the Army, they were delivered to the Navy and were turned straight over to the US Marine Corps (as the SBD-5A),[70] and given the BuAer numbers 09693–09752 inclusively. The first was delivered to the Marine Corps on 29 April 1943.

Meanwhile the equivalent Dauntless aircraft delivered to the Navy were 780 SBD-4s (Nos 06702–06983 and 10317–10906); these arrived between October 1942 and February 1943. The first SBD-5 (c/n 2236, Bu No 10807) was delivered on 21 February 1943, and no fewer than 2,963 SBD-5s were subsequently delivered, out of more than 3,000 ordered (Nos 10807–11066; 28059–29213; 35922–36421; 36433–36932 and 54050–54599) with the 1,200hp Wright R-1820-60 cyclone power-plant. This mark therefore became easily the most numerous of the Dauntless types to see service; these aircraft were delivered between February 1943 and April 1944.

Once again, visually there was little outward difference between the -4 and the -5. The obsolete three-power telescopic sight that fogged up with altitude changes in the dive was replaced, very late indeed, by the modern Mk VIII reflector gun-sight, and this was the most obvious change coupled with the deletion of the carburettor air-intake scoop atop the engine cowling. More subtle was the reduction of the cowl flaps to one each side, and the moving aft of the engine ventilation slot, which became slightly larger.

Much of the advantage of the improved power-plant was immediately offset by the increased load of equipment the SBD-5 was expected to haul into combat. The -5 was also fitted with a windscreen heater, to help overcome the persistent 'fogging up' problems in dives. With the failure of the SB2C Helldiver to enter service in 1943, as hoped for by the Navy, the -5s continued to carry the main weight of the Navy's and the Marine's new offensives in the Pacific, where a new ascendancy over the Japanese was daily being demonstrated. As the over-water battle range increased, so did the need for yet more range, and there was provision on the -5 for two 58-gallon (264l) drop tanks to be carried under the wings. With these in place, the aircraft's scouting range increased to 1,340 nautical miles (normal bombing strike range without the tanks remained at 1,115 nm).

The Mtow continued to dictate the weight envelope limitation as before, and with the all-up weight increasing to 10,700lb (4,854kg) with only a 7mph (11.3km/h) increase in the top speed of the -5, to 252mph (405km/h), was gained, while the cruising speed fell from 150mph (240km/h) to 130mph (210km/h). Service ceiling also decreased again, to 24,300ft (7,407m).

One production aircraft (c/n 4177, Bu No 28830) was utilized as an experimental prototype model, the XSBD-6, in July 1943. We shall return to this mark later in our story.

# CHAPTER FIVE

# A Detailed Description

Pilot's cockpit, front. (McDonnell Douglas, Long Beach)

The Dauntless was, from all accounts, both a simple and a pleasurable aircraft to fly, although it is certainly true, as Ed Heineman himself freely admitted, that it had some failings: for instance, 'Some early versions were under-powered, and the plane was inherently noisy and draughty. Many considered it under-armed.'[71] These, however, were small things compared to its merits; moreover of other points that he made, some are questionable. For example, while it was also true that because the Dauntless had fixed wings it meant that it could only operate in limited numbers from light carriers, in fact such ships did not exist and nor were they planned at the time the Dauntless was designed and built. The *Independence* class only came about as a wartime expediency of converting the hulls of *Cleveland* class cruisers into such carriers to help supplement the *Essex* class main fleet units, and the Douglas team can hardly be faulted for not foreseeing such an event five years earlier! Fixed wings also gave the Dauntless extra strength as a bonus.

While it is debatable whether or not the

Pilot's cockpit, left side. (McDonnell Douglas, Long Beach)

Dauntless was '. . . the best dive bomber ever built', it is certainly *not* the case that '. . . the Dauntless was considered the only true master. . .'[72] at dive bombing at 80 degrees or more. The Junkers Ju 87 Stuka, the Aichi 'Val' and the Vultee Vengeance (in RAF and RAAF combat service) dived vertically on their targets, as attested by many pilots of each to this author.[73] Nonetheless the Dauntless had, without any doubt, one of the very best dive-bomber operational records, and its combat achievements were unsurpassed. What Ed Heinemann had done was come

Pilot's cockpit, right side. (McDonnell Douglas, Long Beach)

up with the right plane at the right time, and in a war situation that was what really counted.

To its pilot, the primary controls, secondary controls and the landing and diving flaps were easy to identify and use. Let us briefly describe each in turn.[74]

## Primary Controls

These were the rudder, the elevators and the ailerons.

The rudder control system consisted of a set of rubber pedals in each cockpit and the necessary cables to connect the pedals to the rudder horn, located aft of frame –7 below the rudder surface. This horn was enclosed in the tail fairing. The front rudder pedals were adjustable fore and aft and were also equipped with adjustable toe pedals for brake operation. The rear pedals were similar but lacked the toe pedals.

The elevator control system consisted of a control stick in each cockpit, the one in

Pilot's cockpit, rear. (McDonnell Douglas, Long Beach)

| | XBT-2 | SBD-1 | SBD-2 | SBD-3 |
|---|---|---|---|---|
| Wingspan (Ft/Ins) | 41-6 | 41-6 | 41-6 | 41-6 |
| Wingspan (Metres) | 12.65 | 12.66 | 12.66 | 12.66 |
| Length (Ft/Ins) | 31-9 | 32-1 | 32-1 | 32-8 |
| Length (Metres) | 9.68 | 9.79 | 9.79 | 9.96 |
| Height (Ft/Ins) | 12.10 | 13.7 | 13.7 | 13.7 |
| Height (Metres) | 3.91 | 4.14 | 4.14 | 4.14 |
| Wing Area (Sq/ft) | 320 | 325 | 325 | 325 |
| Wing Area (Sq/Metres) | 29.73 | 30.00 | 30.2 | 30.00 |
| Empty Weight (Lbs) | 5,037 | 5,903 | 5,652 | 6,345 |
| Empty Weight (Kg) | 2,285 | 2,690 | 2,564 | 2,878 |
| Maximum Weight (Lbs) | 7,560 | 9,790 | 10,360 | 10,400 |
| Maximum Weight (Kg) | 3,429 | 4,440 | 4,699 | 4,717 |
| Engine Type | XR-1820-32 | R-1820-32 | R-1820-32 | R-1820-52 |
| Take-off power (H.P.) | 1,000 | 1,000 | 1,000 | 1,000 |
| Take-off power (kW) | 746 | 746 | 746 | 746 |
| Maximum speed (M.P.H.) | 265.5 | 253 | 256 | 250 |
| Maximum speed (Km/H) | 427 | 407 | 412 | 402 |
| Cruising Speed (M.P.H.) | 155 | 142 | 148 | 152 |
| Cruising Speed (Km/H) | 249 | 228 | 238 | 245 |
| Climbing Speed (FPM) | 1,450 | 1,730 | 1,080 | 1,190 |
| Climbing Speed (M/min) | 442 | 527 | 329 | 363 |
| Service Ceiling (Ft) | 30,000 | 29,600 | 27,260 | 27,100 |
| Service Ceiling (Metres) | 9,175 | 9,022 | 8,310 | 8,260 |
| Range as Dive Bomber (Miles) | 604 | 860 | 1,225 | 1,345 |
| Range as Dive Bomber (Kilometres) | 972 | 1,384 | 1,970 | 2,164 |
| Range as Scout Bomber (Miles) | 1,485 | 1,165 | 1,370 | 1,580 |
| Range as Scout Bomber (Kilometres) | 2,345 | 1,875 | 2,205 | 2,543 |
| Forward-firing fixed machine guns (Cal) | 2 ˇ 30 | 2 ˇ 30 | 2 ˇ 30 | 2 ˇ 50 |
| Rear-cover flexible machine guns (Cal) | 1 ˇ 30 | 1 ˇ 30 | 1 ˇ 30 | 2 ˇ 30 |
| Maximum Bomb load (Lbs) | 1,200 | 1,200 | 1,200 | 1,200 |
| Maximum Bomb load (Kilograms) | 544 | 544 | 544 | 544 |
| Number of Type Completed | 1 | 57 | 87 | 584 |
| Serial Numbers (BuNo- Navy-Serial Army) | 0627 | 1596-1631 1735-1755 | 2102-2188 | 518-4691 (Ex-French) 03185-03384 06492-06701 |
| Contract (Contract Nbr (Quantity/Type) | 50517 | 65969 | 65969 | 77114 (174 French) 89641 (200) 91397 (210) |
| c/n | 330 | 549/584 585/605 | 628/714 1003(2109) | 751/801 803/955(odd) 957/1002 1007/1206 1229/1282 1314/1358 1376/1403 1434/1516 |
| Delivery commenced: | February 1939 | June 1940 | November 1940 | March 1941 |

# Charts for SBD/A–24

| A-24-DE | SBD-4 | A-24A-DE | SBD-5 | A-24B-DT | SBD-6 |
|---|---|---|---|---|---|
| 41-6 | 41-6 | 41-6 | 41-6 | 41-6 | 41-6 |
| 12.66 | 12.66 | 12.66 | 12.66 | 12.66 | 12.66 |
| 32-8 | 32-8 | 32-8 | 33.1 | 33.1 | 33.1 |
| 9.96 | 9.96 | 9.96 | 10.09 | 10.09 | 10.09 |
| 13-7 | 13-7 | 13-7 | 13-7 | 13-7 | 13-7 |
| 4.14 | 4.14 | 4.14 | 4.14 | 4.14 | 4.14 |
| 325 | 325 | 325 | 325 | 325 | 325 |
| 30.00 | 30.00 | 30.00 | 30.00 | 30.00 | 30.00 |
| 6,181 | 6,182 | 6,182 | 6,404 | 6,330 | 6,554 |
| 2,803 | 2,804 | 2,804 | 2,905 | 2,871 | 2,975 |
| 10,200 | 10,200 | 10,200 | 10,700 | 10,500 | 10,882 |
| 4,627 | 4,627 | 4,627 | 4,853 | 4,763 | 4,936 |
| R-1820-52 | R-1820-52 | R-1820-52 | R-1820-60 | R-1820-60 | R-1820-66 |
| 1,000 | 1,000 | 1,000 | 1,200 | 1,200 | 1,350 |
| 746 | 746 | 746 | 895 | 895 | 1,007 |
| 250 | 245 | 250 | 255 | 255 | 262 |
| 402 | 394 | 402 | 410 | 410 | 422 |
| 173 | 173 | 173 | 185 | 185 | 143 |
| 278 | 278 | 278 | 298 | 298 | 230 |
| 1,429 | 1,150 | 1,316 | 1,700 | 1,639 | 1,710 |
| 435 | 350 | 401 | 518 | 500 | 521 |
| 26,000 | 26,000 | 26,000 | 25,530 | 27,000 | 28,600 |
| 7,780 | 7,780 | 7,780 | 7,780 | 8,230 | 8,717 |
| 950 | 1,300 | 950 | 1,115 | 950 | 1,230 |
| 1,529 | 2,092 | 1,530 | 1,794 | 1,529 | 1,979 |
| 1,300 | 1,450 | 1,300 | 1,565 | 1,250 | 1,700 |
| 2,092 | 2,333 | 2,092 | 2,518 | 2,012 | 2,736 |
| 2 ˇ 50 | 2 ˇ 50 | 2 ˇ 50 | 2 ˇ 50 | 2 ˇ 50 | 2 ˇ 50 |
| 2 ˇ 30 | 2 ˇ 30 | 2 ˇ 30 | 2 ˇ 30 | 2 ˇ 30 | 2 ˇ 30 |
| 1,200 | 1,200 | 1,200 | 2,250 | 2,250 | 2,250 |
| 544 | 544 | 544 | 1,020 | 1,020 | 1,020 |
| 78 + 90 SBD-4 | 780 | 170 | 2,965 + 60 SBD-5A | 615 | 450 |
| 41-15746-15823<br>42-6682-6771<br>(SBD-3As) | 06702-06991<br>10317-10806 | 42-6772-6831<br>42-60772-60881<br>(QF-24A)-48-044 | 10807-11066<br>28059-29213<br>35922-36421<br>36433-36932<br>54050-54599<br>(5As-09693/09752)<br>(ex-42-60882-60941) | 2-54285/54399 (-1)<br>2-54400/54459 (-5)<br>2-54460/54649 (-10)<br>2-54650/54899 (-15)<br>8-045 (DF-24B-DT) | (XSBD-6)-28830<br>54600-55049 |
| 77114 (78-3A)<br>91397 (90-3A) | 91397 (780) | 91397 (170)<br>NXs 6970 (1,265) | 91397 (150)<br>N0a(s)-3563<br>NXs(a)-17618<br>Noa(s) 269 (1550) | NXs 6970<br><br>(60 retained Navy)<br>28716 (615) | D. 1853-44 (45) |
| 802/956 (evens)<br>12091/1228<br>1284/1313<br>1404/1433<br>1517/1526 | 1547/1651<br>1682/1801<br>1832/1875<br>2221/2235<br>2241/2246<br>2247/2324<br>2355/2518<br>2549/2646<br>2657/2698<br>2729/2732<br>2753/2786<br>2807/2830<br>2861/2884<br>2915/2934<br>2969/2970 | 1527/1831<br>1652/1681<br>1802/1811<br>1812/1831<br>2325/2354<br>2519<br>2548<br>2699/2728 | 1283 (10957)<br>2236/2240<br>2647/2656<br>2733/2752<br>2787/2806<br>2831/2860<br>2885/2914<br>2935/2968<br>3236/3265(5As)<br>3266<br>3267/3360<br>3361/3390(5As)<br>3391/3405<br>3406/4176<br>4178/4560<br>4561/5060<br>5061/5560<br>5564/6113 | 17124/17238 (-1)<br>17239/17298 (-5)<br>17299/17488 (-10)<br>17489/17738 (-15) | 4177 (XSBD-6)<br>6114/6563 |
| June 1941 | October 1942 | October 1942 | May 1943 | May 1943 | March 1944 |

Pilot's instrument panel. (McDonnell Douglas, Long Beach)

Pilot's seat installed. (McDonnell Douglas, Long Beach)

rudder pedal was locked by a bellcrank which was connected to the yoke assembly by an adjustable rod; the rudder pedals and sticks could thus all be locked with one simple operation. There was also a parking brake which was operated by depressing the toe pedals which were then locked by means of a pull handle located near the instrument panel.

The elevator's range of travel was 20 degrees down and 30 degrees up (5flin (14.6cm) and 8⅝in (21.9cm) respectively measured at root) and the rudder movement was 30 degrees right and left of neutral (15flin (39.2cm) measured at root). The aileron travel was 17 degrees up and 10 degrees down (5in and 3in (12.7 and 7.6cm) respectively). The elevator tab travel was 12 degrees up and 6 degrees down (1in and fiin (2.5 and 1.3cm) respectively), the rudder tab travel was 10 degree right and 15 degrees left (1⅛in and 1⅞in (3.1 and 4.7cm) respectively) and the aileron tab travel 15 degrees up and down (1in (2.5cm)). The load conditions on the Dauntless were such that only a single aileron tab was found necessary instead of the usual two.

The wing flaps were fitted with dual operation facility. The wing-flap actuating cylinder was located close to the trailing edge of the wing in the centre section; this also operated the dive flaps. To open the wing flaps the pilot pushed the valve-operating lever into the forward position, then had to press down on the manually operated control valve; this shut off the return line to the reservoir from the hydraulic pump and directed the oil to the wing-flap operating cylinder. Once the wing flaps were opened to the desired amount, the manually operated control valve was released.

the rear cockpit being removable, plus the necessary tubes and cables to connect and effect proper working on the elevator horns, which were located aft of Frame -17 and also enclosed in the tail fairing. The pilot's fixed stick was connected to the rear stick by a torque tube and a push-rod, and both were fitted with canvas control boots at their bases which prevented any small object jamming the system. As a safety measure, a dual set of cables was provided to connect the control column to the elevator horns.

The aileron control system consisted of a lever arm, or horn, attached to the control column. This rotated laterally about the cockpit torque tube which was controlled by either control stick. A push-pull tube connected the arm to the bellcrank located in the outer wing. Cables connected this crank with a differential bellcrank located at wing station -192 near the aileron. The differential bellcrank was connected to the aileron horn by a push-rod.

## Secondary Controls

These included the rudder, the elevator and the aileron tab control systems.

The tab control wheels were mounted in a group on a panel assembly which was located on the left-hand side of the front cockpit, close to the pilot's seat. There was no duplication in the after cockpit. Each

tab unit was of irreversible cable-operated design, with stops to provide a limit to the travel.

The aircraft used two flap systems, as mentioned earlier: one operated as a diving flap, and the other as a landing flap. Both systems were operated by a single hydraulic unit, which was a combination of two cylinders. The flaps had mechanical synchronization, and a mechanical position indicator was located in the front cockpit on the hydraulic control panel.

A control locking device was provided for when the aircraft was stowed at sea, consisting of a yoke with an attached locking pin. In use, this yoke assembly rotated about a supporting bracket located on the centre-section, and locked the control stick in the neutral position. Each

Rear cockpit, left side. (McDonnell Douglas, Long Beach)

Rear cockpit, right side. (McDonnell Douglas, Long Beach)

# List of Equipment Required to Equip one SBD-4/SBD-5

| EM | Name of Item | DRG.Nbr. | Per A/C | Cost | Per A/C |
|---|---|---|---|---|---|
| | **Synchronised Gun Equipment** | | | | |
| 1 | MG Gun, .5 Cal, M-2 Basic | 297034 | 2 | A/F | - |
| 2 | Operating Slide Group Assembly | 189790 | 2 | A/F | |
| 3 | Control Unit Assembly Mk 2 Model | 284464 | 1 | $14.00 | $14.00 |
| 4 | Impulse Cable Assembly Mk. 1 | 163658 | 2 | $8.00 | $16.00 |
| 5 | Trigger Motor Unit Mk 1 Mod 1 | 227622 | 2 | $14.00 | $28.00 |
| 6 | Trunnion Bolt Assembly Mk 1 for Gun Camera | 179008 | 3 | $8.70 | $26.10 |
| 7 | Rear Mounting Post Assembly Mk 1 ditto | 179007 | 3 | $9.31 | $27.93 |
| 8 | Illuminated Gun Sight Mk. 8 | 238545 | 1 | £225.00 | $225.00 |
| 9 | Bracket for Illuminated Gun Sight Mk 8 | - | 1 | $2.50 | $2.50 |
| | **Flexible Gun Equipment** | | | | |
| 10 | MG Gun, .30 Cal. M-2 flexible, fixed back plate | - | 2 | A/F | |
| 11 | Gun Mount Adapter Mk 11 Mod 2 | - | 1 | $225.00 | $225.00 |
| 12 | Illuminted Sight Mk. 9 | 281777 | 1 | $75.00 | $75.00 |
| 13 | Fore Post Sight Mk 1 Mod 1 | 114077 | 1 | $0.50 | $0.50 |
| 14 | Rear Ring Sight Mk. 11 | - | 1 | $10.00 | $10.00 |
| 15 | Bolt Handles | 147212 | 2 | A/F | - |
| | **Bombing Equipment** | | | | |
| 16 | Bomb Rack Mk. 81 Mod 3 (24 volt) | - | 1 | $90.00 | $90.00 |
| 17 | Bomb Rack Mk 80 Mod 1 (24 Volt) | - | 2 | $90.00 | $180.00 |
| 18 | Bomb Rack Mk 43 | 182990 | 1 | £80.00 | £80.00 |
| 19 | Bomb Release Handle Mk 4 Mod 1 | 179000 | 1 | $15.00 | $15.00 |
| 20 | Portable Bomb Hoist AN-Mk 7 | 300172 | 1/3 | $17.36 | $52.08 |
| | **Hydraulic Equipment** | | | | |
| 21 | Pyrotechnic Projector, M-8 | - | 1 | A/F | - |
| 22 | Flare Release Handle, M-2 | 120437 | 1 | $5.00 | $5.00 |
| | **Gun Camera Equipment** | | | | |
| 23 | Gun Camera AN-N4 | 294389 | 2 | A/F | - |
| 24 | Camera Mk 2 (fixed) | 300522 | 1 | $3.00 | $3.00 |
| 25 | Ditto Mk 7 (fixed) | - | 1 | $0.50 | $0.50 |
| 26 | Camera Mount Mk 3 (flexible) | (a) | 1 | $20.00 | $20.00 |
| | | | | Total | $1095.62 |

Rear cockpit, rear. (McDonnell Douglas, Long Beach)

Surface controls, rear cockpit. (McDonnell Douglas, Long Beach)

Instrument panel, rear cockpit. (McDonnell Douglas, Long Beach)

The dive flaps had the four-way valve, but here the operating lever (marked 'D' for 'dive') was positioned forward for closed, and aft for open. The reason for this was that when coming in to make a landing, the pilot then had *all* levers in the forward position, thus preventing mistakes; the dive flaps were therefore always safely closed and the landing flaps always open when making a landing.

The wing flaps could operate on their own, but the dive flaps always operated *in conjunction* with the wing flaps. In summary:

1: Wing-flap operating lever in open position (forward) = wing flaps *down*. (The dive-flap lever in forward position is not touched.)
2: Dive-flap lever in open position (aft) = dive flaps *and* wing flaps open. 'Wing-flap lever must be in closed position (aft)'.[75]

A dive-flap operating check valve was fitted because of the enormous wind pressure exerted in the diving attack. This condition created a much higher pressure than in the hydraulic system, and the dive flaps would start creeping in a closing direction. The check valve stopped the return flow when the four-way valve was in the open position, and the stainless-steel tubes prevented leakage. When the operating lever was put back to the forward position, the valve was reversed and the fluid could flow back to the reservoir.

## Instruments

Facing the pilot of a Dauntless or Banshee would be a typical 1940s instrument layout. In addition to the magnetic compass (mark VIII or IX), there were three instrument panels;[76] the components for each panel are listed below.

### The Main Panel

1 Air speed indicator

2 Turn and bank – gyro

3 Climb indicator

4 Altimeter – barometer

5 Check-off switch

6 Directional gyro: bank and climb; auto pilot

7 Engine gauge unit: oil temp: inlet thermometer 70–80°C (158–176°F); oil pressure: 65lb (29kg)/in; fuel pressure: 6–7lb (about 3kg)/in; cylinder head temperatures were:
max for take-off (5 min) – 250°C (482°F);
max allowed continuous – 230°C (446°F);
max allowed cruising – 200°C (392°F)

8 Manifold press: evacuated capsule in sealed case. Rates were:

sea level – take-off: 41.0in (104cm) high;
climb sea level to 2,000ft (610m): 38.8in (98.6cm) high;
climb 2,000 to 4,000ft (610 to 1,219m): 38.6in (98cm) high;
climb 4,000 to 5,000ft (1,219 to 1,524m): 37.3in (94.7cm) high;
full throttle 5,000ft (1,524m)

9 Tachometer

### The Lower Panel

1 Clock

2 Thermometer

3 Suction gauge

4 Auto pilot press gauge

5 Fuel level indicator

### The Rear Cockpit

1 Altimeter

2 Clock

## Radio

There was a fixed antenna which was 21ft (6.3m) long and had a 24in (60.8cm) minimum clearance and a trailing antenna for long wave – low frequency. An ADV direction-finding loop was fitted. The

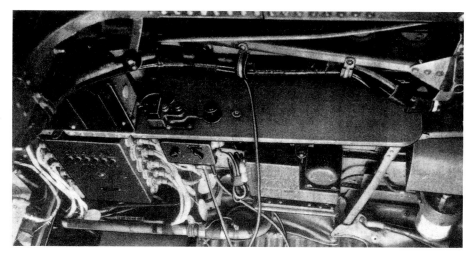

Gunner's compartment, right side (top) and gunner's compartment, left side. (McDonnell Douglas)

5  When clear signal given, move mixture control into 'full rich' position.

6  Pull out the starter engaging handle, and at the same time move the magneto switch to 'both' position.

7  When the engine starts, run between 700 and 780 RPM until the oil pressure builds to 50psi, then increase throttle to 1,000 RPM.

8  Check all instruments working satisfactorily.

9  Set oil and fuel pressures.

On conclusion of a mission and after a safe landing, the engine close-down routine was:

1  Move throttle forwards until engine turning up 1,600 RPM.

2  Move prop. Pitch control from 'low' to 'high pitch', and when engine loses 450 to 500 RPM, pull mixture control back to 'idle cut-off' position.

3  When propeller stops turning over, move the magneto switch to 'off' position.

4  Move battery and generator switches to 'off' positions.

SBDs had the Navy-type GP series radio mounted in the rear cockpit. The Army had their own fitted, with a throttle switch for the microphone.

## Engine Start Procedure

The normal procedure for starting the SBD/A-24 engine was as follows:[77]

1  Check-off procedure: all ignition switches to be in 'off' position. The propeller pulled through three complete revolutions. The blower control in 'low blower' setting. Throttle and mixture controls in closed position. Fuel selector to left-hand main tank. Open cowl flaps (checking nothing lodged in carburettor scoop). Open oil cooler scoop. Move propeller pitch control to high pitch (low RPM). Check all instruments in neutral position.

2  Engine start: manipulate the wobble pump so as to build up 6 or 7psi fuel pressure as the engine is cranked. Check fuel-pressure gauge. At the same time prime the engine with two or three full strokes of primer control.

3  Put battery and generator switches to on.

4  Open throttle approximately ³/₈in here (10mm) to turn engine up 700 to 800 RPM.

# CHAPTER SIX

# Operation and Tactics

## Training

The Navy and the Army had very different requirements for their respective aircraft of course, and even though the Banshee was, in all but a few respects, the same as the equivalent mark of Dauntless, attitudes and methods were very different. As we have seen, the Navy had thought, dreamed, practised, rehearsed, improved, refined and above all totally *believed* in dive bombing. By contrast, the Army had all but ignored it for two decades, they were only converted to it reluctantly by the example and the belief of one man, and they had to make up for that lack of awareness and commitment in very short order.

That fact in no way belittles the bravery of the Army flyers who took the Banshee into combat against impossible odds. They were as dedicated as their Navy counterparts in wanting to utilize their new-found skills against the enemy, and we have already seen how the men of the 27th Group did all in their power to get their aircraft to the front line after supply mess-ups had deprived them of their A-24s at a vital time.

The best way of describing the methods of the two services at this period is to allow the pilots to relate their own experiences. Thus, Ron W. Hinrichs was a Navy pilot who later flew both the Dauntless and the Helldiver in World War II. He flew with VB4, and then from the carriers *Bunker Hill* and *Essex*, and so his expertise is unchallenged:

My acquaintance with the SBD was my transition from flight school to combat-type aircraft. One thing that comes to mind was the reaction of one of my flight instructors to the SBD-5. He was a Marine lieutenant who had just returned from a tour of duty in the South Pacific flying an SBD-3. He knew that the -5 was an improved model with a more powerful engine and was expecting great things from it. He complained that they had loaded the new model with so much additional equipment that there seemed to be no difference from the -3.[78]

However, for our group of eight students in Squadron 42 at Naval Air Station De Land, Florida, the SBD seemed a great plane to fly. Seven of us were Navy ensigns and one a Marine 2nd lieutenant, all newly commissioned with approximately 250 hours of flight time. The changeover from the SNJ with which we were all familiar was an easy one, and we completed the operational training with no mishaps of any sort.

This period of training took place from 27 January 1944 to 1 April 1944, followed in my case by two days at NAS Glenview, Illinois, where I qualified in carrier landings aboard the USS *Sable*.

One of the more thrilling training flights was night dive bombing. While I was at De Land, one of the students crashed straight into the ground on a dive-bombing run; it was one of several such occurrences in the Florida training area at that time. It was finally determined that the cause was loss of fabric in the elevators, which in turn was the result of a different stitching pattern in manufacturing. We had a stand-down until all of our planes were inspected and okayed for flight.

On studying the various flight logs and reports, a good picture of a Dauntless pilot's training at this time can be seen. From 27 January to 18 February 1944, Ensign Hinrichs was flying both the SNJ-3 and -4 (eight flights) and the SBD-4 and -5 (nineteen flights) almost alternately at first, and then almost exclusively on the latter. From the 21 February until 1 April, the SNJ faded out fast (five flights) and the Dauntless became the almost exclusive mount (fifty-six flights). The duration of each flight varied, with the majority being of about 1.5 hours, and totalling over 102 hours in the Dauntless.

The hours of classroom lectures were as follows:

A Marine Corps SBD Dauntless in 1942 markings. (NASM)

| Subject | Hours | Grade |
|---|---|---|
| Aircraft Familiarization (1) Engines | - | - |
| Aircraft Familiarization (2) Accessories | 2 | Lecture |
| Aircraft Familiarization (3) Plane and Equipment | 3 | Lecture |
| Night and Instrument | 1 | Training Film |
| Navigation | 26 | Excellent |
| Aerology | 3 | Excellent |
| Communications (1) Code, Blinker, Semaphore | 12 | Good |
| Communications (2) Procedures, Reports, Etc. | 4 | Good |
| Communications (3) Radar | 6 | Good |
| Fighter Direction | - | - |
| Gunnery (1) Ammunition | 2 | Lecture |
| Gunnery (2) Guns | 2 | Good |
| Gunnery (3) Drills | 3 | Good |
| Gunnery (4) Other Equipment | 3 | Excellent |
| Gunnery (5) Bombing | - | - |
| Gunnery (6) Torpedoes | - | - |
| Operations | - | - |
| Air-Combat Information | 6 | Lecture |
| Recognition and Identification | 10 | Excellent |
| Administration | - | - |
| Anti-Submarine Warfare | 1 | Lecture |

Interestingly there was little or no classroom theory on bombing as such, which is surprising, although the lack of similar theory on torpedoes, fighter direction and administration was more understandable.

The actual flight training to be a dive bomber pilot was a little more comprehensive, again as one would have expected at this stage of the war. It was divided up as indicated in the table below.

At this stage of the war the average USN Dauntless pilot had over 300 training hours flight time under his belt before joining his carrier group, just about double that of his Japanese opposite number flying a Val.

A similar attitude was expressed by another Navy aviator, a flight instructor at Pensacola Naval Airfield, after watching practice dive bombing at the ranges at Norfolk, Virginia, pre-war. He accurately conveys the sheer enthusiasm of the Navy pilots of that time (1940) for the dive-bombing method of attack:

> Many of the pilots, considering that the bombs were released when the target was over a quarter of a mile below, achieved considerable accuracy. If they had ever come down out of the sun-lane at any vulnerable target, even though it was protected by gunfire, most of them would have made direct hits.[79]

The US Army Air Corps took a *very* different view. For instance, when in 1940 General Marshall had wished to include the dive bomber in the newly contemplated support units, he met stiff resistance: 'Arnold told Marshall that the Air Corps had tested the dive bomber concept years earlier, rejecting it as dangerous and potentially ineffective because of enemy fighters.'[80]

Even with the acquisition of the A-24, full-blooded dive bombing was not embraced; moreover, far from 80 degree-plus angles of attack, the Army only wanted a machine '. . . capable of performing dive bombing at a 30-degree angle or more'[81] – which most Navy pilots would say was *not* dive bombing at all, but glide bombing, a much less accurate and more vulnerable approach.

| Phases | Hours Required | Hours Flown | Flights Required | Flights Flown |
|---|---|---|---|---|
| Familiarization | 9.5 | 10.2 | 7 | 8 |
| Instrument | 10.0 | 14.8 | 10 | 13 |
| Tactics | 4.0 | 4.6 | 4 | 4 |
| Navigation | 9.0 | 8.8 | 4 | 4 |
| Dive Bombing | 28.5 | 24.0 | 19 | 14 |
| Glide Bombing | 2.0 | 4.4 | 2 | 3 |
| Anti-Sub Bombing | 2.0 | 3.4 | 2 | 3 |
| Fixed Gunnery | 16.0 | 8.3 | 10 | 6 |
| Night Flying | 20.0 | 17.5 | 16 | 13 |
| Field Carrier Landings | 8.0 | 15.4 | 8 | 16 |
| Combat Tactics | 8.0 | 2.5 | 4 | 2 |
| Supplementary | 9.0 | | | |
| Total | | 113.9 | 86 | 86 |

This underside view of an Aéronavale SBD clearly shows the perforated flaps and the slotted leading edge in front of the aileron that helped give the SBD its fine handling.

Initially then, the Army had to rely on experienced Navy and Marine Corps flyers to impart the new skills; later they undertook their own training. Just what this meant to the 27th Bomb Group squadrons marooned in Australia early in 1942, and eager to get back into battle, was spelt out by their commanding officer's report:

On 1 January, the 27th Group started its official training operations in the new theatre of war. With much careful planning, a training schedule was made out. The new pilots were given transition time, formation, night flying, and finally practice in bombing and gunnery. An island south of Southport was used as a target, and was riddled with Aussie practice bombs during the next few weeks.

As the days passed rapidly by, the boys became better and better until finally it was decided that they were ready to be placed into individual squadrons. The squadrons were formed, and soon the 91st was making itself ready for the push north. They based at Archerfield, and the 16th and 17th Squadrons continued training at Amberley. After a few more days the 16th moved out to the rolling prairie called Lowood, leaving the 17th at Amberley; the Group plans and training office were then dissolved.

## Tactics

Right from the start, Army dive-bombing combat missions in the Banshee were made against ship targets. The 27th had no opportunity to try its hand at land or sea targets in the Philippines, and all of the fighting in the South Pacific was at this time against Japanese ship-borne convoys landing and quickly conquering Australian, Dutch and British islands around the strategic Java/Sumatra/New Guinea chain. Therefore Navy dive bomber tactics and procedures dominated all the SBD/A-24s' early battle experience.

Ironically, in the same period Navy dive bomber combat attacks in the Dauntless were, as often as not, made against land targets, reversing the expected roles of the two services – it was, of course, against *naval* targets that these dive bomber crews were principally trained to operate.

The ideal was for a combination attack in which fighter aircraft provided protection against defending aircraft, the dive bombers attacked from on high against enemy carriers and battleships in order to damage them severely and suppress (or divert) their AA fire, while the torpedo bombers came in at sea level to deliver the *coup de grâce*. The synchronized attack was the ideal, always aimed for but rarely achieved until later in the war when sufficient aircraft were available to swamp any defence. Differences in speed and range between all three types made co-ordination difficult: too long in orbiting a target while the various squadrons formed up and all surprise would be lost, the defences alerted and casualties high. Conversely, attacks in 'penny packets' as by the various US efforts against the Japanese fleet at Midway, would enable the enemy to deal with each section successively and destroy them piecemeal.

Accordingly, the typical composition of an Air Group aboard a US aircraft carrier in 1941 would be a mix of initially all four types: fighters (VF), scouts (VS), dive bombers (VB) and torpedo bombers (VT). In the Dauntless the same aircraft doubled for two of the roles, scout and dive bomber, eventually resulting in the merging of the two types as VB. Both VS and VB units were organized in squadrons of eighteen aircraft, plus spares if the carrier could accommodate them, a handy number which could be sub-divided into tactical units of pairs (on scout missions), or three divisions of two three-plane sections. Thus each dive-bombing assault could be made *en masse*, from a position out of the sun, or split into separate converging attacks from differing points of the compass to take advantage of the wind conditions and the speed of the target, and to further confuse and split the defensive fire.

# CHAPTER SEVEN

# The SBD Battle Scenario

A Dauntless mission from a carrier at the height of the Pacific war would follow roughly a scenario which could be broken up into small segments. Let us examine each in turn as it would apply to a typical SBD mission.[82]

## Scouting Mission

As already noted, the pre-war tactic called for a squadron of scouting aircraft armed with light bombs (500lb (227kg)), but with greater fuel capacity for range. The SBD fulfilled this function. The scout version of the Dauntless had, as we have seen, a range of over 1,300 miles (2,092km), but the Japanese used specially equipped float planes carried on their heavy cruisers for this self-same task, which they termed multi-phase air searches; they had no carrier-operated counterparts to the SBD scout squadrons. This left their main carrier striking forces free to operate against the enemy fleet. But later, a new high-speed dive bomber, the Yokosuka D4Y1-C Judy, was adapted as a carrier-borne reconnaissance aircraft; in particular it had a range of 2,417 miles (3,889km) which made it outstanding.

Far from improving its own techniques, the US Navy continued to down-grade the importance of scouting, and by 1944 the VS squadrons had merged with the VB. As a result the Japanese were better at locating targets, usually did it first, and could therefore both surprise and out-range the Americans. On their side, the US Task Forces had superior numbers, defensive armaments, fighter protection and radar, which in the end outweighed the Japanese scouting advantage.

The standard SBD search between 1941 and 1943 was based on the two-plane patrol. A typical scouting deployment would see ten search sectors, marked 'A' through to 'T', allocated in the expected direction of the Japanese fleet. Each sector comprised a triangular segment of the search arc, with its point the carrier and its outer edge a 10-degree base. Each pair of SBDs would fly in company on an outward 'leg' of anything between 150 to 250 miles (240 to 320km) in length. Usually the scouting legs were flown at relatively low altitudes, 1,000-2,000ft (305 to 610km) depending upon expected weather conditions, both in order to conserve fuel and to ensure correct identification of any shipping sighted[83]. On reaching the furthest point on the initial leg the aircraft would make a 90-degree turn and carry out a 'cross-leg' search for anything from 20 to 50 miles (32 to 65km). The final segment of the search would be the return leg to the carrier.

Pre-flight planning would find the pilots plotting the legs and plotting the bearings and exact distances over the featureless Pacific on their portable individual flight navigational chart boards kept below the instrument panel in the cockpit. Headings were read off from a compass rose visible through a clear plastic top, on which the settings were written with a grease pencil.

As the base ship would itself have moved a considerable distance between the time of launching the search mission and the SBDs' return, a pre-ordained rendezvous position was laid down, known as 'point option'. In combat the unforeseen movements that a fleet, and therefore the carrier itself could be called on to perform would often mean that point option was not always a possible meeting point. To aid them in finding their home base, the scouts would rely on a homing beacon. This

The SBD-3A production line at El Segundo showing 102–114 under construction. (McDonnell Douglas, Long Beach)

# Actual Combat Loading Details SBD/A-24

| Model | Gross Dive | Weight Bomber | Max Speed Scout | (MPH) Bomber | Max Range Dive Bomber | Miles Scout | Bomb Load | Fuel Capacity |
|---|---|---|---|---|---|---|---|---|
| SBD-1 | 8194 | 7652 | 247 | 256 | 545 | 1130 | 1-1,000 + 2-100 | 210 |
| SBD-2 | 8139 | 8429 310 Gals | 247 | 256 | 550 | 1850 | Ditto | 310 260 Self-Seal tanks |
| SBD-3 | 8933 | 8889 260 Gals | 243 | 253 | 500 | 1430 | Ditto | 260 Self-Seal tanks |
| A-24 | 9252 | 9209 260 Gals | 242 | 252 | 480 | 1378 | Ditto Ditto | Ditto |
| SBD-4 | 9137 | 9094 260 Gals | 242 | 252 | 485 | 1395 | Ditto | Ditto |
| A-24A | 9259 | 9216 260 Gals | 242 | 252 | 482 | 1363 | Ditto | Ditto |
| SBD-5 | 9359 | 9328 260 Gals | 247 | 257 | 506 | 1450 | 1-1600 or 1-1000 + 2-500 or 3-500 | Ditto |
| A-24B | 9505 | 9474 260 Gals | 246 | 255 | 499 | 1429 | Ditto | Ditto |
| SBD-6 | 9493 | 9461 260 Gals | 255 | 265 | 520 | 1522 | Ditto | 284 Self-Seal tanks |

rotating aerial sent out a signal at regular intervals, based on a 30-degree scan, the signal usually being the broadcast of a signal letter in Morse code. This letter related to the pre-arranged code letters of the search segments so that returning aircraft could identify quickly by the code letter received whether they were on the right course for home or not. This device only had a range of about 35 miles (56km).

## Location of the Enemy

Once sighted and confirmed, the location of the enemy fleet would be transmitted by the rear-seat man in Morse code, and although standing orders were for these reports to be encoded, in practice and the heat of battle this was frequently not done. An ideal report would be brief and concise and contain the number and type of enemy ships sighted, their bearing, distance, course and estimated speed. In pre-radar days the scouts would have to rely on visual sighting and confirmation of course, and ship recognition was an essential factor.

It would normally be the duty of any two-plane team locating the enemy target to maintain a watch on it for as long as possible, this dependent upon the amount of fuel remaining and the enemy fighter reaction. It also gave scouts in the vicinity a chance to join in the watch. But early in the war it became the practice to subject 'targets of opportunity' to bombing attack: this was because the Japanese radar was unable to pick up these small formations either during their scouting orbits or during their subsequent climb to an attack height, However, although several very successful attacks were made in this way, the damage two SBDs could in fact inflict with just a single 500lb (227kg) bomb apiece was in most instances limited; moreover, even their vastly more important function of homing the larger striking forces to the target to do real damage was considerably compromised, as these depended on a steady stream of updated and corrected reports, rather than a single signal and silence.

Back at the task force, once the target was confirmed, there would be an initial briefing followed by the launch of the air striking force. The mix of types (fighter, dive bomber and torpedo bomber) varied considerably from one battle to another, since there was always a balance to be struck regarding how many fighters were sent off as escorts, and how many were retained to protect the ships. In the early days this latter concern was taken to extreme lengths, and in some instances even SBDs were held back for air defence duties; in this they ably acquitted themselves, but of course their true potential was thrown away.

From the scouts, accurate information was what was required, for in the carrier war more than any other type of combat, very often the victor was 'the firstest with the mostest', regardless of overall numbers, as Midway graphically demonstrated. The standard of contact reports varied widely, and the Admiral controlling the battle was very much at the mercy of the scouts as to whether or not the composition of the

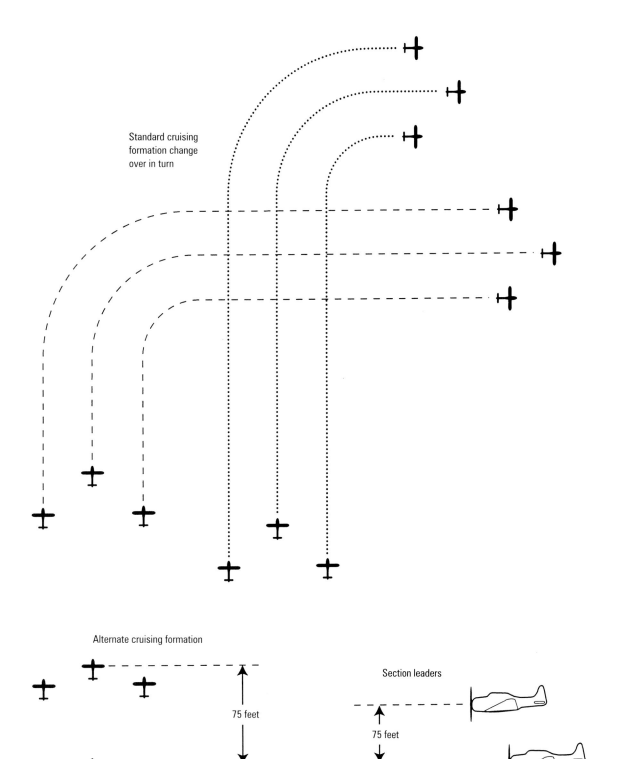

Standard cruising
formation change
over in turn

Alternate cruising formation

75 feet

Section leaders

75 feet

# US Navy Dive Bomber Formation Details

forces that they spotted, and their location and heading, was correct.

## Initial Rendezvous

Once all the dive bombers had been launched they would be vectored out to their own segment of sky above the Task Force to form up in flights. At times of maximum all-out effort all eighteen Dauntless dive bombers would be airborne in three groups of six aircraft; the more normal wartime strike however would be twelve SBDs in two divisions of six aircraft each, each division composed of two three-plane sections. Here the dive bombers differed from the two-plane sections of the fighters and scouts, the third aircraft providing a strong defensive box. Strict discipline was maintained to hold the formation tight so as to present any intercepting Zero fighter with a mass of defensive fire-power, and this was often a sufficient deterrent. However, tight boxes, suitable though they were as a defence against fighters, gave long-range anti-aircraft guns a good solid target to engage. Nonetheless this flight formation was strictly maintained for as long as possible after initial form-up until just before the attack phase.

## Climb to Cruising Altitude

Once the appropriate formation had been achieved, the squadron climbed together slowly, in order to conserve precious fuel, to the desired cruising altitude, which could be up to 18,000ft (5,500m) but was more usually in the 14,000 to 16,000ft (4,300 to 5,000m) range. At such an altitude oxygen masks did not have to be worn, but it was high enough to avoid most short-range AA fire. However, at this height near to the enemy fleet, the SBDs would still meet bursts of long-director-controlled barrage AA fire, for the Japanese 5in (127mm) 40 cal. weapon had a range of about 12,500 yards (11,500m), though it lacked radar control. In addition the imperial Japanese Navy developed the *sanshiki-dang* (incendiary shrapnel) projectile, fitted with time fuses, for the main batteries of their battleships (16in (406mm) and 18.1in (460mm) guns) and heavy cruisers (8in (203mm) guns).

If long-range AA had been the sole factor affecting the formation adopted, a

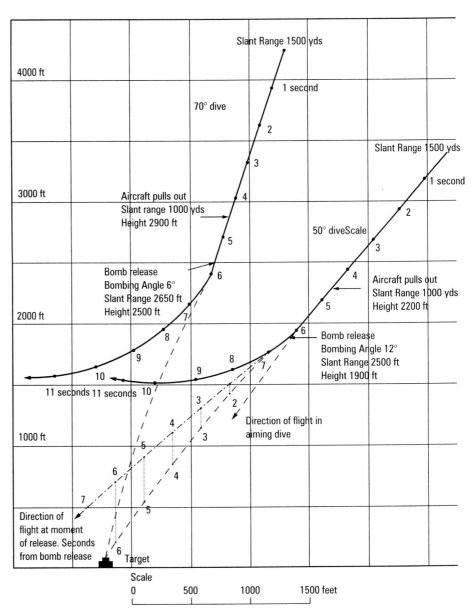

## Typical Path of a Dive Bomber in Dives of 50 and 70 Degrees with 'Pull-Out' Acceleration of 4G. Air Speed 200 Knots for both Attacks

line-astern attack sequence would have been ideal, but there were other factors to be considered, such as defending fighters and the need to maintain defensive formation for as long as possible; therefore sub-formations were adopted, each comprising three to six aircraft flying in line astern at intervals of at least 300 yards (270m), in the shape of an inverted V with wingmen slightly astern and to either side of the section leader. Each sub-section would be stacked *en échelon* below the one before, thus enabling each to deploy freely when the time came without 'wooding' the view of the section behind it. As Dickinson observed, in *The Flying Guns*:

That step-down formation has a further purpose concealed in its design. Starting with the highest step, as each man peels off in a dive-bombing attack, he does not impede the forward flight of the others. Thus when the last man in the squadron begins his dive, all have been spaced over a line perhaps 1500 feet long. From that line of starting points the dive courses may converge, thus tracing a pattern like the sticks of a lady's collapsible fan. We would arrive, not together in confusion, but in a nicely timed succession at a point (where the bombs are to be dropped) possibly 1500 feet above the deck of a target, even though it be a ship moving thirty knots or more. During such a dive the rear seat gunners still have clear, unhampered sweep of the sky, ready to shoot at enemy fighters without risk of hitting a squadron mate. We had drilled ourselves in this manoeuvre ceaselessly, never quite satisfied with our performance but sure that, given an opportunity, we would get some bombs on our target.[84]

It was considered that long-range anti-aircraft fire was not the best defence against dive bombing, for two reasons: firstly, before the SBDs were committed to the attack phase they were free to manoeuvre and were therefore not easy targets to lock-on to, unlike high-level formations forced to fly straight and true. Secondly, once the SBDs were committed to the dive, the speed of their approach was so great that the fuse-prediction gear of the AA weapons could not function. The Japanese fleet lacked the proximity fuses that were later widely used by Allied Naval defences, and which effectively removed much of the dive bombers' 'immunity envelope' in this respect. Also, although later in the war the Japanese Navy acquired and fitted radar control to aid their gunnery, the fact that they did not have suitably trained operators reduced its effectiveness to near-zero.

## Approach to Target

On visual contact being made with the target ships, normally at ranges of between 25 and 40 miles (40 and 65km) distant, the Dauntless flight would use all its commanding officers' skills and expertise in 'stalking' its quarry, with care but without delay, to achieve the maximum degree of surprise. Radar eliminated much of this skill as the war went on, but it was still an essential element, to the very end.

The approach to the target would therefore be affected by the desirability of carrying out the attack with as little delay as possible, the use of the sun, and to a lesser extent cloud cover, and the proposed relative direction of attack with regard to defence encountered and wind conditions.

While still several miles from the target, the attack formation – having kept its tight discipline as far as it could under barrage fire from the enemy warships or attacks by their combat air patrol (CAP) – would begin to loosen up and change direction slightly in preparation for attack, and steadily to reduce its altitude, all the time taking advantage of any cloud cover available. This had the dual effect of increasing the flight's speed and presenting the defences with a complex set of equations to solve involving varying speed, height and direction, thus minimizing still further the effect of heavy barrage fire.

## Approach Dive

During the approach or initial dive, the object of the SBD flight leader would be to position his unit so that every one of his pilots had a good view of the target while descent was being made at high speed down to a height of 10,000 to 12,000ft (3,000 to 3,600m). Normally the attacking flight would assume line astern, or sections in line astern formation, the individual aircraft or sections opening out at intervals of about 500 yards (450m) to obtain increased immunity from long-range gunfire. But if Zero fighters were present in numbers the tight-knit formation would have to be maintained to the last minute, the rear gunners with their cockpit sections slid open and guns deployed for defence. Once into the actual terminal dive, however, the Dauntless was practically immune from fighter interception until the attack was completed.

The initial part of the dive could be commenced from the side of the ship *opposite* to that which it was intended to attack; the crossing to the attacking position could then be delayed to as late a phase of the dive as was consistent with good aiming. In this way the dive bomber came within the defensive field of fire at the latest possible moment.

The flight leader would indicate the exact moment he intended to launch his final attack dive by kicking his rudder as a visual signal to his flight. The commander would then lead the wing-over off the top of the stack, and he would be followed down by the whole formation in succession, the onus of individual marksmanship thus devolving onto each pilot in turn.

Each one would then throttle back and lift the nose of his Dauntless to slightly above the horizon into a stall position, and then the break was made from formation into the final attack dive.

## Final Attack Dive

From this point every Dauntless pilot was master of his own particular attack, and it was up to the skill and judgement of each individual as to how successful the dive was. He had about forty seconds to carry out all the permutations and checks required to keep his fast-swing target in his sights, to release at the correct altitude and to get clear. Checks would include the throttle settings, propeller pitch and opening the dive brakes.

The normal optimum angle of attack was 70 degrees or just over. Although in theory the greater the angle of dive, the greater the accuracy, very few dive bomber forces actually went in at 90 degrees; the early Stuka attacks in Europe were the most frequent exponents of this, and later the Vengeance in Burma. The Royal Navy in its pre-war dive-bombing tests against the target vessel *Centurion* concluded that: 'Steeper angles of dive give a far greater degree of accuracy, and it is suggested that an angle of not less that 65 degrees would be most advantageous.' The US Navy Dauntless pilots mainly attacked with a 70–75 degree parameter during the Pacific war; a shallower angle and the aircraft was subject to a longer period of close-range AA fire which was distracting, even if not lethal. It also meant far less accurate bomb aiming, and less terminal velocity on impact of the bomb, this latter being a vital requirement when attacking heavily armoured targets like battleships.

For most of the Pacific war it was the Japanese carriers that were the priority targets for the SBDs. They were considered the most suitable for several reasons: firstly, they posed the most immediate threat to the US Task Forces and the carriers themselves. Eliminate the Japanese carriers, and the American fleet had nothing much to fear, for it was protected from all else by its own battleships, cruisers and destroyers force which could then dispose of the enemy at leisure. Secondly, the Japanese carriers were vulnerable, being both vast and easy-to-identify targets with their great wooden decks (as against successive decks or

An SBD behind an A-24 on the same production line at El Segundo. (McDonnell Douglas, Long Beach)

inches-thick armour on the enemy battleships), and they could be opened up easily by dive bombing alone, whereas the battleships would only sink if torpedoes were utilized to open them up below. The vast areas of open hangar space, as against hundreds of integral watertight compartments in a battleship, added to this vulnerability and made them highly sought-after targets. 'Get the carriers!' was the only operation instruction that the SBD pilot wanted to hear prior to take-off.

Japanese close-range weapons were mainly based on the 1in (25mm)/60 cal. cannon carried in single twin and triple mountings, and were director controlled. This weapon, designed in France, fired a 9oz (250g) shell at 220 rounds per minute and had a range of 5,500 yards (5,000m) at 80-degree elevation. It was estimated that an SBD diving at 70 degrees would be under fire from such weapons for about twelve seconds. Not long, it would seem, but the gunners on the target ship would have nil-deflection shot and there would be scores of such guns on each ship, plus a covering barrage from ships in the immediate vicinity, with battleships carrying a hundred such guns and heavy cruisers forty

or more – thus a veritable hail of fire would be encountered in those twelve seconds.

Accuracy of the defending fire would also depend on the avoiding action of the ship itself. Japanese carriers tended to turn in full-helm 360-degree circles at high speed when attacked by dive bombers, thus causing great difficulties for the SBD pilot in lining up.

Between the approach and the final dive there was always a short period during which the flight could take note of the target ship's heading and select the point from which the final dive was to be made. If sufficient height was available this period would embrace the approach dive, during which time the SBDs would arrange themselves in the order of the final dive and cross the bow or stern of the ship.

Since the relative movement of a ship during a turn was to port or starboard, it was better for that reason to attack across her beam than along her fore and aft line. However, a fore-and-aft attack gave a greater length of target at which to aim and tended to reduce the quantity of AA fire met, especially if attacks were made from dead astern. This brought into account also the other factors that a Dauntless pilot

had to allow for in his final plunge, such as speed of the target, angle of attack (which influenced track lag from the point of bomb release), wind speed and strength, and optimum height release for the ordnance carried – in other words, was the bomb a general purpose (GP), or a semi-armour piercing (SAP) designed to destroy flak batteries and so on and causing mainly superficial damage so as to weaken the defence for the torpedo bombers, or an armour piercing (AP) designed to penetrate the target vessel and cause more serious harm.

The pilot had to arm the bomb before the attack. The fuse was threaded through with 'arming wires', and these had to be pulled out physically from it; this moved the two parts of the fuse into position so the 'vanes' on the fuse could rotate properly, and the bomb would then explode on impact. In the USN the rear-seat man had the job of tactfully reminding his skipper to do this, or of checking that he had done so. Depending on the relationship between the two men, this might require a lot of tact from the gunner/radio man to his officer.

The 'point of aim' had to take into account the ship's movements (and in a tight turn a ship would skid as well), the wind drift affecting the pilot's own aircraft (which would also skid if any violent movement was made on the controls) and his speed of approach. Thus the pilot, on entering his final dive, would select a point of aim off the target and then allow the wind to drift him towards it, making the essential longitudinal corrections on the way down but all the time flying his aircraft and remaining in control of events right up to the moment of bomb release.

Relative wind – obtained by combining vectorially the true wind and the ship's course and speed – could cause considerable error in the trajectory of the bomb, as much as 10ft (3m) for every knot of wind vector error.

Only constant and continual practice could ensure that a Dauntless pilot had the ability and composure coldly to calculate all this during a dive into enemy fire. Only by keeping the plummeting SBD stable and true by controlling it with tab and rudder could 'skidding' be avoided. In the final analysis, 'down-wind and up-sun' was the best combination of approach, coupled with an ice-cold judgement and a steady eye.

Use of the three-power telescope was considered an aid to dive bombing, but not a panacea. Lieutenant Clarence E. Dickinson has left us this description of a Dauntless pilot's eye view through this device, which Dickinson himself used at the Battle of Midway in 1942 to good effect:[84]

> The only bombsight we use in a dive bomber is an optical tube about two feet long, mounted so that the axis of the tube coincides more or less with the axis of the plane. Coming in we get what we call a position angle. The whole of the dive is really an aiming period, but you do not put your eye to the sight until near the end of the dive; that is when you make minute corrections in the course of your plane, striving to keep the pipper at the middle of the optical sight just short of the target until the instant when you are going to drop. Then, allowing for the wind, you get the pipper right on the target. You are pointing the plane.

Squinting down through the sights the target was kept in the crosshairs while concentrating on maintaining the ball centrally in its groove: this indicated that his machine was flying true in its descent. The early problem of fogging-up of this sight when dives were made from 16,000 to 18,000ft (5,000 to 5,500m) usually seemed to take place at around 7,000ft (2,000m) and this led to miscalculation and to too high a bomb release height. One solution was to approach at lower altitude, between 12,000 and 15,000ft (3,600 and 4,500m); later, special coatings of both telescope glass and windshield eliminated the problem for good, but the introduction of the Mark VIII reflector sight was a great step forward in 1943.

## Bomb Release and Pull-out

Bomb release was usually made at around 2,500ft (750m), although attacks could be made higher or lower than this. At this height a bomb would take about six seconds to hit the target. The best height of release was always a compromise between the increased accuracy bestowed by a lower height of release, and the increased risk of being shot down by defending gunfire which that lower height brought with it. It was obviously more desirable to press a diving attack home to a lower altitude against a small, fast and highly manoeuvrable and comparatively lightly armed warship such as a destroyer to ensure its destruction, than against a battleship,

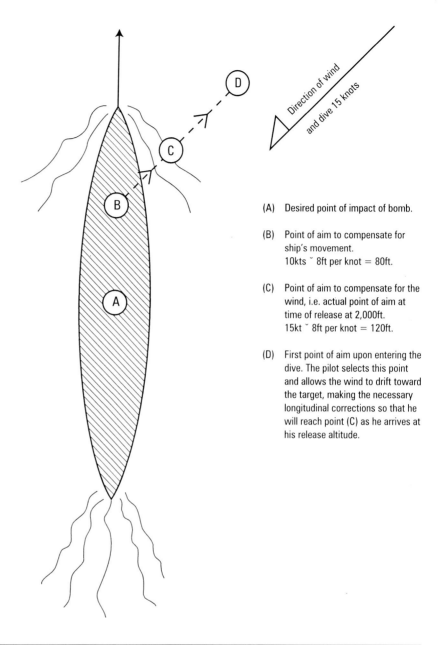

(A)  Desired point of impact of bomb.

(B)  Point of aim to compensate for ship's movement.
10kts ˇ 8ft per knot = 80ft.

(C)  Point of aim to compensate for the wind, i.e. actual point of aim at time of release at 2,000ft.
15kt ˇ 8ft per knot = 120ft.

(D)  First point of aim upon entering the dive. The pilot selects this point and allows the wind to drift toward the target, making the necessary longitudinal corrections so that he will reach point (C) as he arrives at his release altitude.

## Illustrating the 'Point of Aim' and wind drift

which was a larger target and much more heavily armed with defensive weapons. The 'balance height' between the expectation of scoring a direct hit on the target ship and being shot down by it was estimated at about 2,200ft (650m) initially, but this increased as warships adopted efficient tachometric control systems for their close-range weapons and the numbers of such weapons mushroomed.

It was found that probable errors of line and range in steep dive bombing were

approximately the same, and that the permissible errors for both were therefore the same. Once the Dauntless was put into the aiming dive the subsequent conditions of bomb release were more or less fixed, and correct selection of the moment of tip-over was important. The actual path of the bomb after its release could be plotted with some accuracy if the bomb was assumed to fall away from the direction of flight at the moment of release at a gravity acceleration measured vertically of

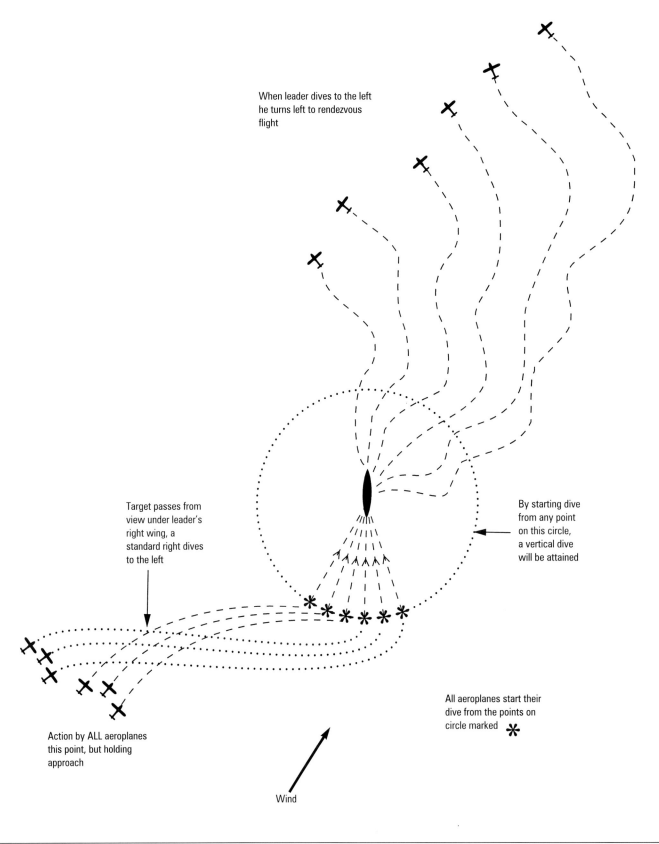

When leader dives to the left
he turns left to rendezvous
flight

Target passes from
view under leader's
right wing, a
standard right dives
to the left

By starting dive
from any point
on this circle,
a vertical dive
will be attained

Action by ALL aeroplanes
this point, but holding
approach

All aeroplanes start their
dive from the points on
circle marked ✳

Wind

# Dive bomber approach dive and getaway

Completed SBDs and A-24s lined up awaiting delivery at El Segundo. (McDonnell Douglas, Long Beach)

30ft (9m)/second. To allow for this distance the SBD had to be pulled out through an angle, called the bombing angle, before the bomb was released. This angle was found to be not greater than the angle between the flight path of the aircraft, and a line from the pilot's eye to the top of the engine cowling (if no sight was utilized). If this angle was exceeded for any reason the target would move out of sight at the moment of bomb release and the pilot would have great diffi-culty in judging his bombing angle. It was also desirable that this bombing angle should be kept small in order to reduce errors due to variation in the speed of the pull-out or due to the pull-out being crooked. The steeper the dive, the smaller the bombing angle, all other factors being constant.

With the target lined up in the crosshairs of the sight, and with wind de-flection and drift being calculated, the pilot had only to keep his concentration and, with slight alterations of aileron, rudder and tabs, to keep 'on'. The engine was kept revving over just enough to make sure of an instant response when called for.

A common error found early on in the war, was that with the manual 'D' lever for bomb release being operated by the pilot's left hand, the automatic instinct was often for the right hand to react by pulling up on the control stick simultaneously, resulting in a large sighting error. Any jerky move-ments or over-reaction on the controls at this crucial juncture would gravely affect accuracy. The fitting of the electric push button – marked 'B' – atop the stick for bomb release prevented such a combination, although pilots generally also operated the 'D' lever in addition to the button, to ensure that the bomb had left the crutch. In this case the instinctive safety reflex did not matter, as the manual operation was made *after* the bomb had left the aircraft and so did not affect its trajectory.

## Individual Withdrawal

Once the bomb had gone, the priority of each surviving Dauntless pilot was to make his escape through the zone of enemy fire – criss-crossed by thousands of AA shells and flak bursts – and out over the screening vessels, avoiding as many as he could, and then to make an effective rendezvous with his squadron to form up defensively as before. Pre-planning and training for this manoeuvre was no less vital than for the attack sequences, for it was often at this point that losses were taken. The defending Zero fighters would be ineffective once the dive bombers had commenced their attack dives, but once the SBDs were 'down on the deck' and out beyond the flak barrier, they were terribly vulnerable to fighter attack. Their only defence was a hasty concentration of force and mutual support until their own defending fighters could join them, or until the Japanese fighters were diverted to deal with further attacks.

Therefore once the weapon was clear of the aircraft, the pilot would open up the throttle, pull the stick back, retract the dive brakes and '. . . get the hell out of there': with flaps adjusted and the aircraft in a 'clean' aerodynamic trim to gain maximum velocity for the escape run, he would try and pull clear as fast as possible.

All this concentration on the tasks in hand would leave the pilot little or no time to observe the effects of his bombing, unless a direct hit on his target was accompanied by a spectacular explosion to make it obvious. Other than this satisfactory result, the pilot would rely totally on his rear-gunner for observation of the attack and the probable result achieved. Some SBDs carried camera guns to record the whole sequence, and this became quite common as the war moved on; resultant film footage could then be analysed and results recorded more accurately. Otherwise claims and counter-claims, so avidly seized upon by the press and exaggerated, became a matter of honesty or self-aggrandizement and accordingly unreliable.

## Rendezvous

To avoid the worst effects of the defending AA gunnery the Dauntless pilot would adopt a highly evasive flight pattern, weaving and twisting and constantly varying his altitude, speed and course. The leader would adopt a lower throttle setting than normal to enable those individual aircraft and sub-sections following him out to have a sufficient margin of speed to catch up and re-form on him.

Once the pre-arranged rendezvous point was reached, the leader would then form up his flight as before, and the cruising pattern and altitude would then

The single rear machine-gun installation in the early models; this is a mock-up at El Segundo with the gun in the stowed position. (McDonnell Douglas, Long Beach)

be regained as speedily as conditions permitted for the flight back to the home carrier. Damaged or straggling aircraft were of great concern and were protected as best they could without the sacrifice of the whole unit. An excellent system of air-sea rescue was built up by the US fleet and a large number of aircrew were picked up from the sea – if forced to ditch close to the task force, the screening destroyers were most proficient in this chore. Those unfortunates who 'went in' close to the enemy fleet or shore-line were not to be envied, as not all Japanese military personnel observed the niceties of the Geneva Convention.

## Homeward Flight

One nagging worry on the return flight would be fuel. Operations were often carried out at extreme ranges, and even with drop tanks, careful husbanding of aviation gas and good flying was called for. The usual fear was that a flak or splinter might have hit the fuel tanks during the attack, which even if not lethal at the time, could mean an early ditching far from friendly aid and in shark-infested waters.

## Landing

Similar concerns would apply to the landing back aboard the carrier. Here a fine judgement had to be made by both flight personnel and the carrier team, regarding priority of landing. While the strugglers would be given priority as far as possible, be they damaged or low on fuel, in an all-out carrier duel, speed of turn-around to get in another strike before you yourself were hit might be vital, in which case no delay in re-arming and re-fuelling flyable machines could be tolerated. In such instances – or in extreme cases such as at the Battle of the Philippine Sea where night landings were an unavoidable hazard of the battle plan adopted – many aircraft had, necessarily, to make water landings adjacent to friendly warships and take their chances.

For those fortunate enough to make it back to their own carrier, again the worry about whether their landing gear was intact and fully operational, or whether wounded pilots (and sometimes rear-gunners) could actually make a safe landing, was always there. The SBD was tough, rugged and reliable, but sometimes even the trusty old Dauntless would absorb more punishment than it was capable of withstanding, and a rough landing on a carrier was often an unforgiving one.

## De-Briefing

After each mission the aircrew would be interrogated, and they would also have to fill in a confidential action report for analysis. If they were lucky they were then allowed time to rest before the next mission. Sometimes they were not, however, and every available aircrew had to go again. Even when they were not thrown back into the battle immediately, their 'rest' period more than likely coincided with the arrival of a Japanese attack with the ship under full helm, all guns firing and the shock of near-miss explosions and often direct hits also!

# CHAPTER EIGHT

# War: The First Clashes

The fighting war started for the SBD with the Japanese carrier attack on the US Fleet at Pearl Harbor on 7 December 1941. Located at Ewa was the Marine Air Group 21 (MAG-21), Lieutenant Colonel Claude A. Larkins, with two squadrons: VMSB-231 equipped with seven SB2U-3 Vindicators, and VMSB-232 equipped with nineteen SBD-1s and three SBD-2s.

The Pacific Fleet's only two carriers were at sea, and this saved them from sharing the fate of the battleships. The *Lexington*, as well as her own SBD-2s of VS-6 and VB-6, was far from the scene,

undertaking an aircraft delivery of twenty-five aircraft, which included nineteen further Marine SB2U-3 Vindicators of VMSB-231 under Major C. J. Chappell Jnr to Midway Island. The *Enterprise* was returning to Hawaii after conducting a similar replenishment of Marine Grumman F4F-3 Wildcat fighters of VMF211 to Wake Island, and aboard her were the thirty-six SBD-2s of VS-6 and VB-6.

In view of the heightened tension between the USA and Japan, Vice-Admiral William F. 'Bull' Halsey had already approved 'Battle Order No 1'

which informed the crew that 'The *Enterprise* is now operating under war conditions'. The Dauntless aircraft were therefore readied and armed with live 500lb (227kg) bombs for combat even before war had begun. They had already been repainted, the garish peacetime markings being placed with dark blue-grey on the upper fuselage and wings to merge with the sea, and light grey on the under-surfaces to blend into the sky; but they still carried the prominent national markings of the white star in a blue roundel with a startling red 'meatball' in the centre – although this was not long to survive the initial dominance of the Japanese in the skies.[85]

The first mission under these changed circumstances had been mounted by Commander Howard L. 'Brigham' Young, Commander *Enterprise* Air Group (CEAG) with some of the VS-6 Dauntless bombers which led the Marine Wildcats to Wake on 3 December 1941.

As they returned to Hawaii from the west the weather closed in, and this forced the refuelling of the escorting destroyers and meant that the arrival of Task Force 8 was delayed from the 6 to the 7 December. That same bad weather had hidden the final approach of the Japanese Navy Task Force under Vice-Admiral Chuichi Nagumo. Thus it was that early on the 7th both Japanese and American dive bombers began to roar off their respective flight decks and into battle – but *not* against each other's carriers.

The fifty-one Japanese Navy Vals of the first attack wave, led by Lieutenant Commander Kakuichi Takahashi, had as one of their prime targets the air base of Ewa Mooring Mast Field, where lay MAG-21. The Marine SBDs were all caught on the ground where seventeen were destroyed and the remaining five damaged to a varying degree.

The *Enterprise* in the meantime was in a

In the immediate aftermath of the Japanese attack on Pearl Harbor, the few remaining warships left to the US fleet were grouped around their surviving carriers, and these small task groups carried out a series of hit-and-run raids on outlying Japanese outposts, more as a morale booster than anything else. Wake Island, Marcus, the Carolines, Kwajelein and other islands were hit. An SBD-2 ready for take-off from a carrier and awaiting the final 'Go' signal. (Pratt & Whitney Company, via San Diego Aerospace Museum)

position 250 miles (400km) due west of Ewa, and at 0615 the first aircraft off was CEAG himself, carrying as his passenger Lieutenant Commander Bromfield B. Nichol of Halsey's staff, with a report of the Wake Island operation for personal delivery. Young's Dauntless was followed in quick succession by his wingman, Ensign Perry L. Teaf, and then twelve other SBDs from VS-6 and four from VB-6; these were all to conduct a search pattern to the north and the east, covering an area 150 miles (240kg) from the carrier which centred on the Oahu and embraced the islands of Kaula, Niihau and Kauai as well. These searches were uneventful, and the orders were to carry on and land at the Ford Island naval air station on completion of their outward legs.

The various SBDs arrived at different times, but their return to base coincided with the arrival of the first wave of the Japanese air armada and their reception was a hot one, both from the Japanese Zero fighters they ran into, and their own anti-aircraft defence which was literally firing at anything that flew! Not surprisingly confusion was absolute, some refusing to believe it was all for real until it was too late, others understanding at once but being powerless to do more than try to avoid the carnage and land safely.

The first casualty, and perhaps the most poignant, was the SBD of Ensign Manuel Gonzalez, whose despairing last signal, the only clue to his fate, epitomized the American reaction to the Japanese attack: 'This is 6-B-3, an American plane. Do not shoot'. No trace was ever found of 6-B-3 or the two men, shot down by Aichi D3A1 dive bombers into whose post-attack rendezvous area they had blundered. Other SBDs met the same fate or were shot down by their own AA gunners who were understandably trigger happy.

7 December 1941 therefore ended with the destruction of twenty-four SBDs, and severe damage to a further twenty-one, and the loss of five aircrew. In return, one Zero had been destroyed by a Dauntless. This was to be the worst combat ratio that the SBD was ever to endure.

Japanese submarines had been stationed in a crescent to the south of Oahu in order to intercept any American heavy ships that had escaped the air attack.[86] One of them, the I-70, was damaged sufficiently by a near-miss from a VB-6 Dauntless as to be immediately incapable of diving. Lieutenant Dickinson of VS-6, aloft again

These raids continued in varying intensity, and although the effects on the Japanese were minimal they provided the Dauntless aircrews with valuable combat experience to shake down ready for the real battles which were soon to follow. Here, SBD-3s are being readied aboard USS *Yorktown* (CV-5) ready to hit Eniwetok atoll in February 1942; this raid was abandoned, however. (San Diego Aerospace Museum)

in a replacement Dauntless and with a personal score to settle for Bill Miller as well as himself, flew a course which he estimated would 'cut the corner' to reach the best-speed option of his target which was last seen heading north-east.[87] His judgement was rewarded with a sighting from 800ft (245m) of a submarine on the surface fifteen miles (24km) away, some 180 miles (290km) north of Oahu. It took Dickinson a good ten minutes to gain enough altitude to avoid return fire and to be in a position to make a diving attack, but he kept his enemy in sight throughout and, just after 0600, commenced his attack dive from 5,000ft (1,500m).[88] He later recalled:

By the time I was able to pull out of the dive, and turn so as to get my plane's tail out of the way of my eyes it was probably fifteen seconds after the bomb struck; it struck right beside the submarine, amidships.[89]

Dickinson reported a 'probable' hit, but in fact he had killed her, the first Japanese submarine to be sunk in World War II and another 'first' for the SBD. Then on 11 January 1942 the *Saratoga* was torpedoed

by the Japanese submarine I-16 off Johnston Island, south of Hawaii, and badly damaged. Before she sailed home to repair she disembarked Air Group 3; her place was taken by the *Yorktown*.

Between 25 and 27 January 1942, the *Enterprise* and the *Yorktown* carried out 'revenge raids' against the Marshall and Gilbert Islands. At 0443 on 1 February the *Enterprise* made the first two attacks:[90] Commander Howard Young led the strike which included a total of thirty-seven SBDs from VB-6 and VS-6 against Kwajalein, Roi and Tarora in the Marshall Islands.

The SBDs climbed to 14,000ft (4,300m) and headed west, stacked together in stepped-down Vs and the Vs themselves forming other Vs and echelons. The attack was scheduled to hit at 0658 before the enemy was awake, but in order to correctly identify the various targets the Dauntlesses were forced to make a wide circle around the atoll while Young satisfied himself on that score. Thus the dive bombers were met by an alert defence with AA fire and enemy fighters scrambling off the airstrip.

The six SBDs of VS-6, led by Lt Cdr Hal

The SBD-3 had modern combat requirements such as self-sealing fuel tanks, armour protection for the aircrew and an armoured windscreen. They featured the new R-1820-52 Wright Cyclone engine, and could only be distinguished physically by this power-plant's slightly larger ventilation slot to the rear of the cowling. They began to reach the combat fleets in the early spring of 1942, just in time for the major carrier duels that lay ahead. This is the very first production model SBD-3, No 4518, seen at naval air station Anacosta on 28 March 1942. (San Diego Aerospace Museum)

SBD-3 of VS-3 here seen aboard USS *Hornet* (CV-8) in 1942. The tail of one of Lieutenant Colonel James H. Doolittle's modified B-25B Mitchell medium bombers can be seen, ready to be flown off for the famous attack on the Japanese mainland on 18 April 1942. This raid showed the versatility of the aircraft carrier, and it was the *only* way the USAAF could reach the enemy mainland. (San Diego Aerospace Museum)

Hopping, attacked first, adopting a long, flat glide approach to the target; they were followed by six more led by Lt Earl Gallaher and a final six led by Lt Clarence Dickinson. All released at the airfield itself at a height of about 1,000ft (300m) and pulled away, but Hopping's lead aircraft absorbed most of the flak and failed to pull out. The SBD hit the water and sank like a stone, Spike Hopping and his gunner Harold Thomas dying but having made history by dropping the first bomb on Japanese-held territory in World War II.

The rest of his section cratered the airstrip, levelled administration buildings and blew up an ammunition dump with a satisfactory explosion, all with just their wing bombs. Then VS-6 conducted a second, strafing run over Roi hitting a variety of ground targets, two hangars, a fuel depot and an estimated seven aircraft on the airstrip, and three Japanese fighters were claimed shot down in the air-to-air combats; but they did not find anything sufficiently worthy on which to expend their 500lb (257kg) bombs. Interception by defending fighters and fierce AA fire brought down another three SBDs, however.

## Dauntless Men - Lieutenant-Commander Richard H. Best. US Navy.

This photograph was taken on the hangar deck of the *Enterprise* in April, 1941, by Admiral Halsey's flag photographer. 'It was an order', Best told me. 'I had no choice!'

One of the legendary SBD leaders at the Battle of Midway, Richard H. Best had come to the Dauntless only by accident. He told me that he had previously served with the Navy in a fighter squadron between 1935–38. With war obviously imminent he went back to sea again in 1940. 'I had asked for assignment to a torpedo squadron, believing that was where we would win the forthcoming battle. I was not then aware of the shortcomings of our notorious Mark XIII torpedo. In a scramble at the last moment I ended up in dive bombers. The lessons I learned in a fighting squadron were of enormous value in defensive combat.'

Although he considered himself a non-regular officer when the war started on 7 December 1941, Best was instructed not to keep war diaries and not to take pictures in the event of loss of the *Enterprise* and a possible compromise of US operations. 'For some reason, I complied. My recollections are all from memory and not diaries or pictures.' At that time Best was the Executive Officer of Bombing Squadron 6. 'The Commanding Officer, Lieutenant-Commander W. R. Hollingsworth, was a close friend and an admirable officer', he told me, 'When we disagreed it was without animosity and quite rare.'

Lieutenant-Commander Best is sure in his praise of the SBD:

The Dauntless was a charm; rock steady in a vertical dive, completely responsive to the controls (unlike the Curtiss SBC and SB2C) and ready to absorb punishment and still get you home. I was worked over by two Japanese Type 97 fighters over Maloelap on the afternoon of 1 February 1942, and came out of it unconcerned with fifty holes through the tail surfaces and left wing tip (not enough lead), a hole in the gas tank in the root of my right wing (good lead but prob-

ably out of range) and one small calibre that broke apart when it hit the back of my armoured seat. None of our 'planes had the glass chins of the Japanese. They had the manoeuvrability, but at what a cost.

The incident he refers to took place during the first strike made by the *Enterprise*, against Japanese shipping and shore installations at Kwajalein. Best himself led a nine-plane formation which was intercepted by enemy fighters stirred up by the earlier attack. Richard described to me the defensive tactic of the SBD when set upon by Japanese fighters:

Our greatest vulnerability was the inadequate armour protection for the rear seat gunner. At Midway a good number of our torpedo plane losses must have come after the gunner was killed. At that point the dive bomber or torpedo plane is dead unless he is not too badly outnumbered and is able to use effective single plane evasion tactics. It was my observation that as long as the tail gunner was firing, the attacking fighter tended to break off the attack before getting in killing range. For the defending plane a nose down hard turn becoming a vertically banked turn as the fighter came in range caused the fighter to break off early. He is a no deflection target for the gunner and at the same time finds his target a full deflection target. As he gets close if he gives the target the proper lead, he finds himself flying blind and into the cockpit of the bomber at the kill stage. The ones I saw were not Kamikazes.

On 1 February I was in the morning attack against the Japanese warships and transports and in the afternoon attack against the airfield on Maloelap. On 26 February we made one attack against Wake Island and five days later against Marcus Island. We flew air cover on the Doolittle raid on Tokyo. Air cover is day-long CAP (combat air patrol), morning search flights two hundred miles on either bow and evening eighty miles on either quarter. My only engagement on the last mentioned was against a 35 or 40mm bow gun on a Japanese picket boat. My bomb missed and when I twice turned in to attack my fixed 0.50 calibre guns were jammed.

At Midway Best, then a lieutenant, and on his second wartime cruise, led VB-6 and flew with the first division. He recalled, 'My last action was in sinking the *Akagi* on the morning of 4 June 1942, and the *Hiryu* in the afternoon. At no time, except over Maloelap Atoll, was my plane hit by shipborne AA or fighter fire.'

He was left with just five SBDs of his own division when the rest of VB-6 followed McClusky down on the nearest target and these five Best pulled out of the attack and led against *Akagi* which would have otherwise not have been targeted, with who knows what result on the battle as a whole. He instructed the division not to let her escape and led in the attack dive from 15,000ft, scoring a direct hit plumb centre of her flight deck with his 1,000lb bomb.

During the later attack on *Hiryu*, Best's experience again paid great dividends. Again he contributed to her demise by hitting her solidly, the fourth direct hit she had received.

Lieutenant-Commander Best flew both the SBD-2 and SBD-3 from 7 December 1941 until 5 June 1942, after which he was hospitalized and later retired from the Navy on 1 March 1944 as 100 per cent physically disabled. With great modestly today he told me that in his opinion, 'Good luck is always better than any ability.'[251]

In the interim, Young had scouted Kwajalein anchorage where he found some warships and transports which he deemed were far more suitable objects for the heavier bombs. Accordingly VB-6 was instructed to hit these ships forthwith, along with the surviving Dauntlesses of VS-6.

Commander W. R. Holllingsworth led VB-6 in echelon attack with full-blooded 70-degree dives, and claimed three direct hits. The SBDs then returned to the carrier where they were hastily refuelled and re-armed, the Wildcat fighters having discovered forty twin-engined bombers at the airstrip on Taroa; Bill Hollingsworth was instructed to destroy as many of these as he could in this second strike. His initial wave consisted of seven VB-6 and two VS-6 dive bombers, and it was followed by a second wave led by Lieutenant Richard Best with a further nine Dauntlesses.

The first strike hit Taroa in a dive attack and was met with little but light flak, but Best's men found both Japanese fighters and heavier flak awaiting them on their run-in. One enemy fighter was claimed destroyed by Ed Kroeger's gunner Achilles Georgiou, and Perry Teaff was jumped by another but escaped unharmed after a good scrap plane-to-plane; but an enemy Mitsubishi A5M4 nailed Ensign Jack Doherty's mount, the last of the line in, and there were no survivors. Lieutenant Clarence Dickinson identified his target as a liner of the 17,000 ton *Yawata* class, converted to a tender with a seaplane aft.[91]

For the loss of five SBDs with their aircrew, they and the torpedo bombers had only managed to sink one small naval auxiliary craft; they had also caused *some* damage to the cruiser *Katori*, minelayer *Tokiwa*, and four auxiliary and transport ships, none of which were sunk, however. In reply, the Japanese attacked with five Betty bombers and scored fifteen near-misses off the port side of the *Enterprise*. One of the attackers then attempted a suicide dive, having already been damaged by protecting fighters. A sharp turn frustrated this intention, and one crew member, aviation machinist 2nd class, Bruno Peter Gaido, manned the rear guns of the aftermost parked SBD and engaged the oncoming bomber from there. The Betty's right wing-tip cut right through this SBD within a few feet of Gaido who was still blazing away and knocking the rest of the aircraft over to the extreme port after-edge of the flight deck, from which

precarious position he continued to fire the twin .30s into the wreckage of the Betty as it drifted away.

Meanwhile the *Yorktown*'s air group, including VB-5 under Lieutenant Wallace C. Short, Jr, the executive officer, and VS-5 led by Lt Cdr William O. Burch, struck at Jaluit, Mili and Makin islands with a total of thirty-seven aircraft. Worthwhile targets were sparse, VB-5 for example bombing freshwater tanks on Mili in lieu of anything else; and for this, six aircraft were lost.

On 31 January 1942 *Lexington* sailed from Pearl Harbor with TF 11 to cover two important troop convoys from the Panama Canal; then on the 17 February she was instructed to launch air strikes against the Japanese base at Rabaul, New Britain. Located by Japanese reconnaissance aircraft while still 300 miles (480km) ENE of their target, the American warships were subjected to a heavy air attack on 20 February and the American raid was called off. After a brief foray into the Coral Sea between 27 February and 4 March, *Lexington* rendezvoused with the *Yorktown* off the New Hebrides on the 6 March 1942.

In the same period the *Enterprise*, with TF 8, sailed from Pearl Harbor on 14 February 1942, and ten days later launched an air attack at 0500 on the Japanese defences of Wake Island with a force which included twenty-seven Dauntlesses; just one aircraft was lost. At 0650 the eighteen surviving SBDs of VS-6 and the eighteen of VB-6 under Bill Hollingsworth had formed up with the torpedo planes and fighters and headed toward their targets. The VS-6 Dauntlesses gradually moved up to 18,000ft (5,500m) before pushing over in succession to dive down on the ten oil storage tanks that were their prime target. They met no opposition and claimed to have hit and destroyed seven of the tanks. Simultaneously VB-6 made their dives, one section under Lt (jg) A. Smith making a glide attack on small craft off the pier at Peale Island, while Ensign Delbert W. Halsey chased a big Kawanishi flying-boat which left him standing.

Moving swiftly westwards, another raid was launched by the SBDs of the *Enterprise* against Marcus Island, at 0449 on 4 March, with Young leading a force of fourteen VS-6 dive bombers, with eighteen VB-6 aircraft led by Lieutenant Jack Blitch. The assembly of the force in the darkness was now becoming routine and was termed 'the Group Grope.'[92]; moreover heavy cloud

between 4,000 and 8,000ft (1,200 and 2,400m) made their ascent even more hazardous. Nonetheless the strike was despatched, and sighted Marcus at 0630 through a break in the cloud.

The initial dive attack was made from 16,000ft (4,800m) and was completed by 0645; the targets were oil storage tanks and the radio station. Defensive flak was the heaviest yet encountered and several SBDs took hits; this vicious AA fire brought down the VS-6 aircraft of Lieutenant Dale Hilton who survived a water landing and was taken prisoner, along with the rear-seat man Jack Leaming. The remaining aircraft were safely recovered by 0845.

The *Yorktown* sailed from Hawaii with TF 17 on 16 February 1942 to make a similar raid on Eniwetok Atoll in the Caroline Islands; this was abandoned, however, and she was diverted to join the *Lexington*.

To cover the transport of the American division from Brisbane to Noumea Island, New Caledonia, two Task Forces – TF 11 centred on the *Lexington* and TF 17 centred on the *Yorktown* – were concentrated: on 10 March 1942 they attacked Japanese landing forces in Papua, New Guinea. Of a total of seventy-nine SBDs from the carriers, four squadrons took part, flying off at 0749 from a position in the Gulf of Papua and crossing the southern neck of New Guinea, then striking Lae and Salamaua.

In the bay offshore, a large assembly of Japanese shipping was surprised, and attacks commenced at 0930. Confirmed sinkings were only of the armed merchant cruiser *Kongo Maru* and the transports *Yokohama Maru* and *Tenryu Maru* (hit and beached), as well as damage to the cruiser *Yubari*, the minelayer *Tsugaru*, destroyers *Asanagi* and *Yunagi*, a third transport and two auxiliary vessels. In return, one *Lexington* Dauntless failed to return.

Between the 2 and 25 April, the *Hornet* was engaged in the Doolittle raid on Japan, with the *Enterprise* accompanying her as TF 16 for protection. Embarked aboard was VB-3 of *Saratoga*'s air group, taking the place of VS-6 which was training with new consignments of SBDs ashore. Running into a Japanese patrol line on the 18 April, *Enterprise*'s SBDs destroyed two and damaged another pair. The sixteen B-25 Mitchell bombers were launched early because of this, and the two carriers withdrew before the Japanese could react.

# CHAPTER NINE

# Impossible Odds

An A-24 in dive configuration with the flaps 'split', being tested at about 45 degrees, which was the 'norm' for the USAAF who had little or no experience, and hardly any interest in true vertical dive bombing as practised by their Navy and Marine Corps counterparts. Note the early national markings. (US Air Force via Nick Williams)

It has become fashionable for historians to write off the Banshee's combat record and belittle the efforts of their aircrew. Thus one writer was to state that in the defence of the Dutch East Indies '. . . they performed with a spectacular lack of success',[93] and this exact quotation has been used by others.[94] Strangely, only the A-24 is singled out for such criticism.

We have already seen how the 7th Bombardment Group, working in double shifts for twenty-four hours a day, had, within a week, assembled twenty-seven of the A-24s that had lain idly in Brisbane harbour as Americans died in the Philippines. We know, too, how they were found to have been shipped without solenoids and gun-sights, and with insufficient trigger motors, defective rear-gun mounts, worn-out tyres and '. . . mud picked up during the Louisiana manoeuvres the year before still clinging to the undercarriage.'[95] Also how Major Davies had organized scratch training of fresh replacement pilots straight from Stateside training schools, many of whom had neither fired a gun nor sat in a combat plane.

The lack of essential parts was severe.[96] It was not until 1 February 1942 that enough triggers were completed to enable just one of the Group's squadrons, the 91st, to be equipped. But with other improvisations, such as using truck tyres, Australian gun-mounts and hand-triggers for those that had no solenoids, enough Banshees were assembled to make *some* effort, even though they lacked armour plate protection or self-sealing petrol tanks, and their engines were old and tired. Thus with an allowance of six practice bombs each, and their home-made bomb sights, the green flyers were turned into, if not proficient dive bomber pilots, then aircrew that could at least nurse these machines as far as Darwin.

Three Banshees of the 91st Squadron,

led by Captain Edward N. Backus, duly arrived at Darwin via Charlesville, Glencurry and Daly Waters airstrips, on the evening of the 8 February, and next morning were ordered to fly to Penfui, near Koepang,[97] in Dutch Timor, and then on to Java in company with nine P-40s and led by a Dutch LB-30. The three A-24s were soon left behind due to their slow speed and had to make their own way across the Timor Sea in poor weather. This was their good fortune, because the LB-30 failed to find the airfield and turned back to Darwin, while all eight of the P-40s that had managed to sortie, ran out of fuel and crashed. Backus got his three dive bombers safely to Koepang, but then the defending Australians blasted them with AA fire! All three A-24s got down safely, but Backus was hit in the fuel tank and had the stabliser on his right elevator removed, while the other two were also so damaged by the flak that they had to return immediately to Darwin for repairs. The intrepid Backus made repairs and continued on to Pasuruan, Java, alone, the following morning.

On 11 February 1942, Lieutenant Harry L. Galusha took off from Darwin with eleven more A-24s and flew to Koepang, a distance of 530 miles (850km), with the cloud ceiling at times down to 50ft (15m). After an overnight refuelling stop, First Lieutenant J. Summers and Second Lieutenant H. H. Launder took off at daybreak for Den Pesar airfield on Bali, flying directly over two Japanese destroyers on the way, but having no bombs, being unable to do anything about them. Galusha and Second Lieutenants J. P. Larronde, Douglas B. Tubb, Robert F. Hambaugh and Haines left five minutes later for Maingapore, Soemba. The last section, Lieutenant James R. Smith, Second Lieutenants J. W. Ferguson, C. R.

The A-24 Banshee in flight, showing the perforated flaps from underneath. Notice the larger, pneumatic tail wheel, and also the fairing for the carrier tail hook, left in place in case they were required to be converted back to Navy use quickly. (US Air Force via Nick Williams)

Abel and J. B. Criswell, left after another five-minute interval, to join the other two at Bali, similarly being impotent against the enemy ships sighted on the way.

At Maingapore, Haines' aircraft ground-looped on landing and had to be pulled from the mud and patched up before it could follow the rest of the flight later that day. The remaining ten flew on to Pasuruan in north-east Java, arriving at 1500. Summers, Launder and Ferguson then flew into the new airstrip at Modjokerto, where another four days were spent patching up the Banshees and making them fit for combat. On the 16th all flew to Batavia, except for Abel who nosed over on take-off and bent his propeller. This was fixed, but on test flight the wheels stuck in the 'up' position and he had to belly land in the sea off Soerabaya. Larronde was grounded due to engine

trouble. However, both later joined up at Batavia.

On the 18 February the surviving seven Banshees were switched to Malang airfield which had no control tower and no bomb-shackles and adapters; however, used to relying on the resourcefulness of Lieutenant Bill Coleman, the procurement officer, the 91st eventually managed to improvise all three!

The composition of the survivors of the 91st at Malang is given in the table on this page.

Meanwhile of the 27th's other two squadrons, the 16th followed the 91st north twelve days later, on 16 February, with Captain Ronald D. Hubbard leading a total of fifteen dive bombers; but by the time the unit had reached Glencurry, five of these were using oil or had other problems and had to be left behind for further repair

| Aircraft | Pilot | NBR. | Gunner | NBR. |
|---|---|---|---|---|
| 41-15786 | Major E. N. Backus | 0303125 | Pvt F. H. Larronde | 19049952 |
| 41-15757 | Capt H. L. Galusha | C-373895 | T/Sgt H. A. Hartman | 6713737 |
| 41-15796 | 2n Lt H. H. Launder | 0429818 | Pvt W. L. Kidd | 19020343 |
| 41-15810 | 2nd Lt R. Hambaugh | 0421591 | Pvt J. K. Bryning | 6579749 |
| 41-15804 | 2nd Lt J. Ferguson | 0429779 | Pvt D. A. Simpson | 19010446 |
| 41-15760 | 2nd Lt D. B. Tubb | 0411633 | Cpl I. A. Lencicka | 6581779 |
| 41-15800 | 1st Lt J. Summers | 023271 | Pvt D. S. Mackay | 19000309 |

overnight before they eventually joined the rest at Batchelor airfield. Here they were informed that, as the Japanese were investing Koepang, it was too risky for them to leave for Java as planned and they were held back. The next day the Nagumo Task Force made a devastating air attack on Darwin itself, while Koepang was overrun – so the 16th never did get to Java.

The 16th Squadron remained at Batchelor, and over the next few weeks they '. . . bombed up, evacuated, dropped our bombs, bombed up again, flew patrols, wrecked a few ships and generally kept busy.' On the 22 February they were joined by the 17th Squadron led by Major Davies, comprising another fifteen aircraft.[98] Both squadrons remained stuck at Darwin and got no further north.

Meantime the 91st Squadron at Madang was in action: on 19 February, seven A-24s were waiting to have their 660lb (300kg) and 110lb (50kg) bombs hand-loaded, for a chance to attack the Japanese invasion fleet which was reported in Sanur Roads, unloading troops to conquer Bali. The only two Banshees with bombs aboard were ordered to take off and circle to field as a safety measure while the rest took cover. These, crewed by Captain Harry L. Galusha with T/Sgt H. A. Hartmann, and Lieutenant Julius B. Summers with Pvt D. S. Mackay, turned south as told, but then decided between them over their radios, to mount a reconnaissance mission of their own.

They were hidden from detection by the enemy fleet by two layers of stratus clouds at 10,000 and 11,000ft (3,000 and 3,300m) and at Den Psar they sighted a troop transport and a cruiser through gaps in this cloud. Selecting one ship each, both Banshees nosed over from 11,000ft (3,300m) diving down to 3,000ft (900m) before releasing. Surprise was achieved and only light AA fire rose up to meet them, Galusha taking a solitary hit in the fuselage.

Their daring was rewarded with good attacks, and both pilots claimed direct hits on each of the ships with their 110lb (50kg) wing bombs, and near-misses with their 660lb (300kg) main bombs, due to the makeshift sights they employed being off-line. Their observations were later confirmed by a Navy PBY Catalina seaplane which witnessed their assault and which stated that both vessels had been sunk! It was stated that '. . . the near-misses had been perfect shots for success. By

Photograph taken on 3 February 1942, of an Army A-24B being test flown (no rear-seat man). (USAF via National Archives, Washington DC)

hitting in the water the bombs penetrated below the line of armour plate before exploding, therefore having a terrific buckling effect and breaking the bulkheads of the boats.' This was the very first combat dive-bombing attack conducted by the US Army.

Unfortunately, although both attacks were accurate and the freighter *Sagami Maru* (7,189 tons) took a 660lb bomb into her engine room, she was later able to get underway and was escorted to safety by two destroyers. It seemed that the 91st's work was over almost as soon as it had begun, but on the 20 February plans were made for a combined attack on Japanese troops and shore positions at Bali by the seven Banshees, in conjunction with three LB-30s and sixteen P-40s. The dive bombers – the first section consisting of Backus, Ferguson and Launder, a second Galusha, Tubb and Hambaugh, and with Summers bringing up the rear – took off as planned from Singosari, but on arrival over the Badung Strait, between Bali and Nusa Besar, further enemy shipping was sighted. This force was reported by Cpl I. W. Lenicka, one of the A-24 gunners, as comprising two troopships lying close inshore, with one cruiser and three destroyers

steaming down the straits towards them.

The dive bombers tipped over from 12,000ft (3,600m), the leading three Banshees making the light cruiser *Nagara* their target, while the second section took on one of the damaged troopships and the rear aircraft, Lieutenant Summers, selected the other. Defensive AA fire from the *Nagara* was severe and accurate: Second Lieutenant Douglas B. Tubb and his gunner, Pvt D. S. Mackay, had their Banshee hit during the dive, with the result that it continued straight down into the sea with no hope of survivors.

The next A-24 was that of Second Lieutenant Richard H. Launder with his gunner, Cpl I. W. Lenicka: they had pressed home their attack on the *Nagara* to point-blank range and claimed to have scored two direct hits on her. On pull-out they were very low over the water, however – 15 to 20ft (4 to 6m) – and were hit twice as they screamed away over the Tafel Hoek peninsular. The elevator sustained damage from the first hit, and a second shell severed the main oil line to the engine, plastering the windshield and cockpit with oil. They attempted to land at an airfield before realizing it was an enemy one, and finally crash-landed in the sea 8 miles

(13km) up the coast and 150 yards (140m) offshore. Although both men sustained head bruising from the ditching they managed to get ashore, and after three days and two nights in the jungle, rejoined the squadron at Malang.

Major Backus had also dived on the *Nagara* and claimed to have hit her with all three of his bombs, leaving her heavily on fire and dead in the water. A third A-24 was so badly damaged by AA fire that, although it got back to base, it was declared a complete write-off. In all, the 91st claimed to have made ten direct hits, five on the *Nagara* and one each on a destroyer and the two troopships. In the afternoon a reconnaissance aircraft reported that two ships were definitely sunk, and that the cruiser was being towed away by a destroyer, while a damaged destroyer was being towed by a cruiser; later, Brereton claimed that all four damaged ships were subsequently finished off by submarine attack. But yet again, none of these statements bore any resemblance to the truth: they were pure fiction, and again, not one solitary enemy ship was lost in this attack.[99]

For the next three days the surviving aircraft had to endure nine Japanese bombing and three strafing attacks on their field. On the night of 23 February another first was recorded: it being a bright moonlit night, Galusha and Hambaugh took off at 1815 and made a night raid on Bali. The main target was enemy shipping, with Den Pasar airfield as the secondary objective. In fact they sighted no shipping; they did bomb the airfield, however, but without being able to observe the results.

On the 26 February a further mission was preparing to be carried out by the four serviceable Banshees left at Malang; these were now under the command of Galusha who had succeeded Backus as squadron commander. Unfortunately one of the dive bombers' hydraulic system failed and it had to abort the mission; but Galusha led the other two, piloted by Summers and Ferguson, into the air at 1615 that afternoon to attack a Japanese invasion convoy reported heading for Java and sighted north-east of Bawean Island. Galusha had orders to attack the troop transports, but as he later confessed, if there was a Japanese aircraft-carrier about he intended to go for that!

The three Banshees flew right over the mass of enemy shipping seeking suitable targets before finally deciding to go for the transports. They claimed to have hit two or

The classic view of an A-24 Banshee with dive brakes extended. (McDonnell Douglas)

three of the Japanese troopers, and sunk one, and their accompanying fighter escorts also claimed to have seen one 14,000-ton transport that the dive bombers had attacked, sink, while three or four destroyers '. . . believed to be Japanese, were burning'. Unfortunately these reports also appear to be incorrect, and not one of the targets was seriously damaged, let alone sunk in this attack.[100] This marked the last combat mission by the 91st Squadron in the defence of Java.

The 3rd Bomb Group had meanwhile arrived in Australia, under-strength and very short of equipment, and Major Davies went to Townsville to see if some sort of merger could be arranged. As part of that group, the 8th Bombardment Squadron (L) had left Savannah Air Base on 19 January, and on 31 January had boarded the Army transport ship *Ancon* in San Francisco, in which vessel they had arrived at Brisbane on 25 February, setting up their base at the Ascot racecourse before moving to

Charters Towers airfield to carry out training with the A-24s.[101]

On 16 March 1942, the 16th Squadron took over fifteen other Banshees from the 3rd Bombardment Group, which had finally arrived at Townsville from the States. The rest of the 16th and the 17th Squadron also moved to Townsville, and then to Charters Towers on the 24 March where it was announced that the 27th was going into the 3rd. It was recorded that the 3rd Bombardment Group '. . . had no ships, and they were even glad to get our old and rickety A-24s.'[102]

A general reorganization followed, with many of the 27th pilots going into the 3rd Group which also had B-25s and a few A-20s, while Rogers, Ruegg, Oliver G. Dean and the new pilots were sent to the 8th Group to continue to operate the Banshees. On 31 March 1942 the 8th Squadron was ordered north, with Captain Rogers leading with thirteen A-24s; but five of these had to be left at Cooktown,

Overhead view, taken on 3 February 1942, of an Army A-24B being test flown. (USAF via National Archives, Washington DC)

and a wrong report as to the time of sunset at Port Moresby led to the remaining eight arriving after dark and two further aircraft being lost while landing in the blackness due to bomb craters in the runway.

As Captain Rogers reported sick on arrival, Lieutenant Bob Ruegg took over command. An attack against the Japanese forces at Lae was planned for the following day, and at 0600 on 1 April 1942 – an inauspicious date – five A-24s were bombed-up and took off. On arrival over the target – the Lae airfield some 175 miles (282km) north of Port Moresby – the weather was so bad with low cloud that an alternative target had to be sought, and so Salamaua was dive bombed. The five 500lb (227kg) demolition bombs were planted along the runway, and buildings were blown up and set on fire; but unfortunately at this period the Japanese were only using this field as a refuelling base. There was no opposition but it was recorded that '. . . the boys were careless about staying in formation'.[103]

Although the 8th was supposed to return to mainland Australia, General Kenney visited the unit and told them that '. . . we could kill more Japs by staying at Port Moresby – so we stayed'. The men of the squadron told him that they had four aircraft in commission with just seven bombs and two dozen adapters, so if they didn't get some help soon they didn't have much to kill Japs with! They urgently requested plugs and plug pencils; hydraulic fluid; a booster pump; wheel and wing jackets; grease for wheels and guns; tyres both front and tail; batteries and acid; engines, an unlimited supply; patches; cleaning rods and brushes for the .30 and

.50s; twelve crew chiefs and eight armourers; lots of mosquito eradicator and, most sincerely of all, '. . . twelve new Curtiss dive bombers or Brewsters (*urgent*)!' The General promised most of these things, but not the latter.

On 6 April Captain Virgil A. Schwab arrived with six more A-24s from Charters Towers, and after refuelling at Kila airfield, they, together with the first contingent, planned another strike at Lae. The Banshees took off as planned, but the promised fighter cover failed to materialize at 1100 – but alas, the Japanese did, with a heavy air attack on their home field, and so the Banshees moved out over the ocean until the raid was over. They landed and spent the rest of the day moving into the 3-mile (5km) airfield at Kila-Kila.

On 6 April nine Banshees were airborne early, but one had to abort the mission due to engine trouble. The remaining eight dive bombers took off at dawn; they were led by Lieutenant Reugg and piloted by First Lieutenant Schwab and Second Lieutenants Schwartz, Wilkins, Chudoba, Anderson, Kitchens and Emerson, with Sgts Vance, Stevenson, Gaydos, Childs, Stevens, Sam, Kehoe and Lennon as rear seat men. After assembly, approach was made to the target at 13,000ft (3,900): they struck at the Japanese airstrip at Lae and found a great many enemy aircraft lined up on the ground, perfect targets. Five Navy Type 0 Zeroes were spotted in a circle on the airfield being refuelled from a central tanker, and Ruegg chose these as the main target, scoring direct hits which wiped out all five plus the facility. The other seven A-24s planted their seven 500lb (227kg) demolition and fourteen 25lb (11kg) incendiary bombs up and down the other seven parked aircraft with equally satisfactory results: '. . . We left smoke, fire, flying debris and dust pretty well covering everything.' They were credited with destroying twenty enemy fighter aircraft in this attack.

Again, some of the A-24s lost formation and one, Hank Schwartz did not return. Another stray, Lieutenant Chudoba, was immediately set upon by a defending Zero. He sought the protecting gunfire of the rest of the squadron who had reformed, and the pursuing fighter was caught in a cross-fire which sent it into the sea. 'From then on, there were no more loose formations!'[104]

The next strike against Lae was made on 11 April 1942, with the 8th operating nine A-24s. There was considerable cloud but

the Japanese were not caught napping again. As Ruegg commenced his attack dive against a small ship in the harbour, he saw three Zeroes taking off right beneath him, being followed down by Lieutenants Gus Kitchen and 'Long John' Hill. The enemy fighters each attacked a Banshee of the first flight, accomplishing the attack by a wingover from a climb, immediately gaining a position to the rear of the A-24s, even though the latter were in a steep dive, and latched themselves onto the tails of the Banshees, commencing shooting. Ruegg dumped his bombs, closed his flaps and took avoiding action and the Zero was shot down by an escorting Australian P-40 Kittyhawk. The other eight Banshees laid their bombs carefully among the enemy aircraft and AA guns at the airfield, claiming mostly direct hits. Again, two stragglers, Lieutenants Anderson and Dean, drew enemy fighters, but once they had closed up properly they were left alone; Gus Kitchen's aircraft, however, was destroyed by another Zero. The fires the Banshees started burned for several days.

Two days later a big Japanese oil tanker was reported berthed at Lae, and the 8th were sent off pell-mell to sink her. However, on arrival over the roadstead there was no tanker to be seen, so they took their time and selected alternative targets. An anti-aircraft gun opened fire, revealing itself, and Ruegg made that his target, silencing it. The rest of the A-24s then again bombed enemy bomber aircraft on the ground. The same day Lieutenant Hesselbarth arrived from Australia with some fresh A-24s.

A lack of defending fighters meant that the Banshees had to bide their time for a period, and on 17 April Captain C. A. Baumhauer with seventy ground crew and cooks arrived to help the 8th settle in to their new home. Another visitor on the 20th was General G. H. Brett: 'We put the pressure on him for faster dive bombers, but he didn't promise them right away.'[105]

On the 22 April four aircraft, led by Rogers and Hambaugh, sortied but the target was weathered out, and one pilot had to belly-land on return, writing off his machine save for use as spare parts! Three days later they needed them. Japanese air attacks on their airfield were increasingly heavy, and the defending fighters, only five, were unable to halt them. A hunt for a Japanese submarine on the afternoon of 23 April was unrewarded. On the 26th the Japanese Bettys scored a success by

Silhouetted against the Pacific sunset, an A-24 patrols the darkening skies. (McDonnell Douglas, Long Beach)

bombing through heavy cloud, and one stick landed right in the A-24 dispersal area, destroying three bombed-up A-24s, damaging others, although no aircrew were injured.

A squadron of P-39s arrived on the 29th so a mission was planned, but heavy losses wiped out so many of these Airacobras within a short period that it was abandoned. On 1 May, Rogers, Ruegg, Hambaugh, McGillvarvy, Summers and Anderson went to Seven Mile airfield to collect some more A-24s; on the night of the 2nd, Rogers, Ruegg and Anderson were put on alert for night fighting, but it turned out to be just a stray Catalina. Next day the Japanese fleet was reported heading south and every available A-24, nineteen machines, was bombed up and readied to sortie by the 6th. This was the invasion fleet on its way to occupy Port Moresby, and the result was the Battle of the Coral Sea.

Although held on stand-by from the 5–9 May in readiness to strike at the convoy first reported forming up off Misima Island, the 8th was destined to play no part in this fierce battle, an air-raid alert on 7 May sending them out to sea for safety. The Japanese invasion convoy was already turning back from the Jomard Pass through

the Louisiades at 0700, and heading back north to Rabaul. Denied these targets as a consequence of the insufficient fighter protection available and with their airfield beset by low cloud and poor visibility, the Banshees could only sit and listen as the battle developed. The stand-by was finally called off on 9 May; on that morning, ten A-24s were lined up on the runway waiting to go when the Japanese struck again, strafing and destroying another four of them. Lieutenant Heidinger was killed during this raid while sitting in the cockpit of his plane preparing to start the engine.

After this anti-climax, Captain Ruegg's flight took departure back to Australia for a rest. After they had departed, the squadron settled down to a normal routine of working over the remaining A-24s in a effort to get them all into combat condition. Very little actual flying was done in this period save for a few test flights. HQ once or twice requested a mission be mounted, but Captain Rogers refused unless fighter escort could be given. As this was not forthcoming, no such missions took place. Captain Rogers ordered all the remaining five Banshees back to Charters Towers airfield on 14 May 1942. This completed the 8th Squadron's contribu-

tions to the air fighting in New Guinea for the next two months.

On 22 July the A-24s returned to the combat zone with a mission against Buna, but six of the seven Banshees employed were shot down by the defending Japanese fighters. We shall examine these missions later, but this tragedy, according to one source, meant that '. . . they were thereafter withdrawn from front-line service'.[106] Such, however, was far from the case, and even as late as April 1943, Lt General George C. Kenney's 'Allied Air Forces, South-West Pacific' command still included five A-24 Banshee squadrons on its operational combat strength; that was soon to change, however.[107]

Back in the States, plans were still being pushed ahead to mass-produce 1,200 more A-24s at the Douglas Tulsa plant, and at a conference held at El Segundo on 21 May 1942 between Lieutenant Colonel V. R. Haugen and his team for the Army Air Force, and Ed Heinemann and others for Douglas, it was agreed that '. . . every effort should be made to keep the SBD and A-24 type airplanes identical (except for radio) in an effort to expedite production to the utmost'.[108] It was also felt that '. . . a further effort on the part of the Army and Navy will be necessary in order to obtain the best results in the standardization effort.' It was strongly recommended that a procedure should be established whereby the Army and Navy co-ordinated all their respective contemplated changes in order to keep them to a minimum and make them most effective.

On 1 July, Colonel O. R. Cook was writing that:

Of the 1,200 A-24 type airplanes to be manufactured by Douglas Aircraft Company at Tulsa, Oklahoma, the first fifty-five airplanes will be A-24As and the remaining 1,145 will be A-24B airplanes. The difference is that we have changed to R-1820-40 engines for the A-24B airplanes.[109] [He added that,] . . . immediate action must be taken to present these lists to the Bureau of Aeronautics in order that the proper equipment can be furnished by the Bureau for the 1,200 A-24 type airplanes being fabricated at Tulsa, Oklahoma. This is the only possible way these airplanes can remain standardized.

The engines, radios and .50 calibre guns were to be furnished by the Army Air Force.

# CHAPTER TEN

# Shadow Boxing: The Coral Sea

By May 1942 the two prongs of the Japanese assault encompassed both sides of the Solomon Sea: one prong involved the landing of a force on Tulagi Island and an airfield construction team on neighbouring Guadalcanal, both at the south-east tip of the Solomon Islands chain. The other prong was on the southern side of eastern New Guinea, where they intended landing a large force to capture Port Moresby and thus protect their beach-heads at Lae and Salamaua. For this operation, codenamed MO, twelve transport ships with covering warships had sailed from Rabaul on 4 May 1942, to pass through the Louisiades and then turn west into the Coral Sea. As we have seen, this force was turned back when American carrier activity was detected, to await the outcome of the battle. A

At the confused Battle of the Coral Sea, for the first time two fleets clashed and fought for two days without the ships of either side ever sighting one another. It was the first of many carrier-to-carrier exchanges of the Pacific War, and many mistakes were made on both sides. The main lesson was that chance and luck could play as big a part as skill and bravery in deciding the outcome. The power of the dive bomber was demonstrated as decisive in this type of naval action. Here a fully bombed-up SBD-3 taxis forwards, steadied by two deck crew, ready for take-off, while a second revs up aft with chocks still in place. (San Diego Aerospace Museum)

supporting force consisted of the light carrier *Shoho*, four heavy cruisers and one destroyer.

With American Intelligence able to de-code all Japanese signals, the US commanders knew about both operations, but had only limited resources with which to deal with them. They were also made aware of a larger threat looming up in the central Pacific and had to act accordingly. The original plan was for Task Force 17, led by Rear Admiral Jack Fletcher and built around the *Yorktown*, three heavy cruisers and four destroyers, to rendezvous with Task Force 11, under Rear Admiral Aubrey W. Fitch with the *Lexington*, two heavy cruisers and five destroyers, on 1 May, while Task Force 44 – consisting of two heavy cruisers, one light cruiser and two destroyers – was to join TF11 on 4 May. These plans were thrown into disarray by the discovery of the Japanese invasion convoy off Tulagi, and Fletcher sent the *Yorktown* group off alone to strike at these while he refuelled.

The *Yorktown* duly launched her strike at 0730 on 4 May, with heavy clouds shielding her and her movements from the enemy who were thus caught completely by surprise. Both the fifteen VB-5s and the thirteen VS-5 SBD-2s put into the air carried 1,000lb (450kg) GP bombs: their attack broke over Tulagi anchorage at 0920, and they found the transports and auxiliaries busy offloading troops, protected only by the minelayer *Okinoshima*, two destroyers and some minesweepers. Burch's team attacked from 19,000 ft (5,800m), going into their 70-degree dives at 10,000ft (3,000m) and releasing high, at about 2,500ft (800m). They could not fully observe the results of their dives due to fogging of the telescopic sights, but claimed four bomb hits.

VB-5 under Short suffered similar aiming difficulties but claimed two direct hits. Despite the size of the strike, the only

ships actually sunk by the two squadrons were the destroyer *Kikuzuki*, hit by a 500lb (225kg) bomb in her starboard engine room, beached but later lost, and three minesweepers. Damaging hits were made on the *Okinoshima* and the transport *Azumasan Maru*, and VB-5 claimed to have destroyed a Nakajima A6M2-N 'Rufe' seaplane they met on the way in.

A second strike was launched by *Yorktown* and arrived over Tulagi at 1210, with VB-5 mustering fourteen SBDs and VS-5 thirteen; but they found the pickings even leaner as the main group of Japanese ships had up-anchored and left. The Dauntlesses of Short's team managed to sink two small patrol vessels and also scored a hit on the transport *Tama Maru*, so damaging her that she sank two days later. The other SBDs led by Short claimed two hits on a destroyer, and this ship, the *Yuzuki*, was indeed set on fire near Savo Island and her captain and nine of her crew were killed, but she survived. No Dauntlesses were lost, and again, they claimed to have strafed and destroyed another four seaplanes.

Yet a third strike from the *Yorktown*, reaching the area at 1510, damaged another transport, the *Koei Maru*; after which TF 17 recovered her aircraft and moved to the new rendezvous with the *Lexington* on 5 May. Both American carriers refuelled and then began to search for the Port Moresby invasion convoy, but during the next two days no enemy carriers were found other than the *Shoho*.

To the north of the searching American carriers was Vice-Admiral Takagi's carrier strike force hunting for the perpetrator of the Tulagi attack, with the carriers *Shokaku* and *Zuikaku*, two heavy cruisers and six destroyers. At 0730 the Japanese leader received a report of an American carrier and cruiser to the south of him, and launched a full strike against them. Both targeted ships were sunk, but they were in

64

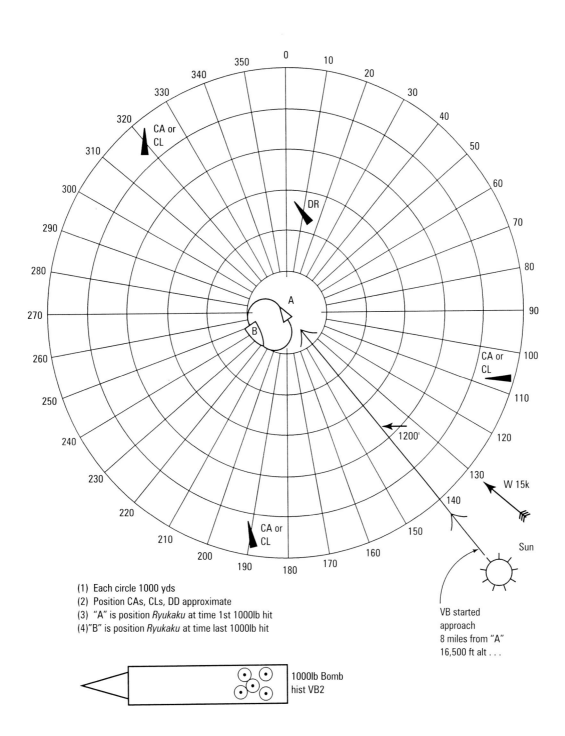

350  0  10
340     20
330      30
320       40
CA or CL
310        50
300         60
DR
290          70
280          80
A
270          90
B
260         100 CA or CL
250         110
240        1200'  120
230        130 W 15k
220      140
210    CA or CL  150  Sun
200 190 180 170 160

VB started
approach
8 miles from "A"
16,500 ft alt . . .

(1) Each circle 1000 yds
(2) Position CAs, CLs, DD approximate
(3) "A" is position *Ryukaku* at time 1st 1000lb hit
(4) "B" is position *Ryukaku* at time last 1000lb hit

1000lb Bomb
hist VB2

The dive bombing attack of VB-2 at the Battle of the Coral Sea.

fact the oil tanker *Neosho* and the destroyer *Sims* of Fletcher's refuelling force.

While wasting their Sunday punch on these two unfortunates, the Japanese missed their best chance of making Fletcher pay for his own poor reconnaissance and getting in the first blow. Instead it was the US carriers that were able to make an historic first assault carrier-to-carrier[110] when, at 0826, *Lexington* began launching her air group, followed at 0930 by *Yorktown*.

The range was 170 miles (270km), and the American aircraft had to climb to 15,000ft (4,600m) as they crossed over the Louisiades group on their way from the Coral Sea northwards.[111] Protected themselves by cloud cover, at 0950 the first American strike found the *Shoho* operating in bright sunshine some 90 miles (150km) to the north and was able to attack in ideal conditions, meeting stiff flak from the escorting heavy cruisers but hardly any aerial opposition. The seventeen Dauntlesses of VS-2 under Lieutenant Commander Weldon H. Hamilton, and led by the Commander Air Group 2, Commander William B. Ault, at once attacked in steep dives, while the eighteen SBDs of VB-2, under Lieutenant Commander Robert Dixon, circled to co-ordinate their attacks with the TBDs.

On the approach at 10,000ft (3,000m) Ault and his two wingmen met heavy fire from the escorting cruisers, and this continued to engage them at high intensity as they carried out their attack dives – in fact it was so accurate that no hits were made at all. Dixon's group then followed him in with a high-speed (180 knots) approach down to final attack commencement height of 12,500ft (3,800m) – but as they did so, the *Shoho* made a violent turn to port to put the dive bombers across wind.

The time was 1105, and defending fighters were making passes as Dixon tipped over in his 70-degree dive: Ensign Leppla's rear seat man, ARM3/c John Liska, nailed two of them, while the pilot flamed a third which had overshot him, an incredible performance in the middle of an attack dive! However, although three direct hits were claimed on the carrier target by Dixon's team, all ten of VS-2's bombs were near-misses. But in evading this attack the Japanese carrier left herself open to VB-2's dive bombers coming in from a different sector. She was immediately thrown into another violent turn, but

Although SBD strikes were usually launched from their carriers as part of comprehensive air groups, along with torpedo bombers and escorting fighters, actual combat practice and the hazards of this type of long-range operation, more often than not meant that the Dauntless was left to fend for itself against clouds of Japanese Zero fighters. In theory this should have led to a very high loss rate, as with the A-24 over Buna, but in actual combat, at the Battle of the Coral Sea, the slow but highly manoeuvrable Dauntless more than held its own, and in fact destroyed more enemy aircraft than the Grumman Wildcat fighters during the course of the battle. It was one occasion when the dive bombers were deliberately employed as aerial defenders of the fleet instead of in their true role. This is the twin .30 calibre machine gun of the rear-seat man as fitted to late production SBD-3s, with a fixed top panel and sliding side panels, some token armour protection. 8 July 1942. (McDonnell Douglas, Long Beach)

it was too late to save her this time.

Hamilton's SBDs carried their dives down to below 2,000ft (600m) and at 1116 the leader himself scored a direct hit which resulted in huge clouds of black smoke that drifted astern in a pall. Four more hits were claimed by his team as they followed him down. The Zeroes and the heavy anti-aircraft fire from the Japanese cruisers knocked down two of the *Lexington*'s SBDs in reply, that of Lieutenant Edward H. Allen, 2-S-10, and of Ensign A. J. Quiqley, 2-S-9; while another from VB-5, flown by Lieutenant J. Win Rowley, ran out of fuel *chasing* a Zero and had to ditch! Otherwise VB-5 was unscathed save for flak damage to six of their machines, while one of their number, 2-S-14, added to the Zero toll when rear gunner ARM2/c F. G. Stanley riddled it on the way out. The irrepressible Leppla even found time to score his fourth victory of the morning when he shot down yet another floatplane on the way back home.

The second strike, the *Yorktown*'s air group, now arrived over the already badly

damaged *Shoho* at 1025, but despite her obvious plight, they all continued to pile in on her, so elated were they at finding an aircraft-carrier to attack; thus the rest of the Japanese warships remained largely unmolested. Hit after hit smashed into her already riven flight deck.

Burch's VS-5 led the procession, the seventeen SBD-3s – each armed with a 1,000lb (450kg) bomb with a 1/100 second delay fuse – making almost unopposed dives in line astern and claiming at least twelve direct hits; they were followed by the eight dive bombers of VB-5 following Short in another devastating attack, one which was described by him as 'like a peace-time training dive'. One pilot, Lieutenant John J. Powers, had pressed in even closer, not releasing until below 800ft (240m) and had been rewarded with a hit; but this was a dangerous procedure which he only got away with because the target was already wide open. By the time the last SBD, flown by Ensign Ben Preston, was on its way down the Japanese carrier was almost obscured by smoke. Indeed one VB-5 pilot, Ensign Tom Brown, could not make out the carrier at all and dive bombed one of the heavy cruisers instead. He was awarded the Navy Cross for sinking this vessel, a completely fictional occurrence!

The *Shoho*'s fate was sealed, for it was estimated that this small carrier was hit by no less than seven torpedoes and thirteen bombs: she was a blazing wreck and was abandoned, sinking at 1035. Her fate was almost identical to that handed out by the Nagumo force to the similarly small and unprotected British aircraft-carrier *Hermes* off Ceylon just a few weeks earlier, and showed up the vulnerability of aircraft-carriers once their own aircraft had left them. Dixon's exultant radio signal at 1136 has since gone down in history: 'Scratch one flat-top!'

Although it has been subsequently claimed that the Port Moresby invasion force turned back because of this sinking, the truth, long known, was that it had already turned around some days before. Nonetheless the annihilation of the *Shoho* was a great occasion and the coming-of-age of the Douglas SBD Dauntless.

Gleeful as the returning aircrews were at this success, they were sobered up when it was revealed that scouting Japanese aircraft had located the two US carriers, but that the two big Japanese carriers themselves remained undetected by Fletcher's searches. Fletcher decided to head west, deeper into the Coral Sea, to strike at the Port Moresby invasion convoy, not aware that they had already temporarily been turned back. Bad weather continued to shield the American ships. At 2200 the two forces were within 100 miles (160km) of each other, but neither dared to risk the uncertainty of a night attack.

Dawn on the 8th saw renewed air searches by both fleets, the *Lexington* sending out eighteen SBDs – fourteen from VS-2 and four from VB-2 – at 0625, to make a 360 degree search pattern from 150 miles (240km) to the south to 200 miles (320km) to the north. This careful reconnaissance was rewarded by a report from a VS-2 aircraft – 2-S-2 flown by Lieutenant (jg) Joseph G. Smith – away to the north-north-western part of the circle, who sighted the main Japanese force at 0820 and signalled 'Two CV, four CA, many DDs': the bearing was 006 degrees true of the American Task Force. Smith's transmissions were almost inaudible, but they were sufficient. Not getting any acknowledgement, he turned back to the carrier, his place on watch being taken by his neighbour, Lieutenant Commander Dixon, his CO. But in the meantime Takagi had also located Fletcher's force, and was already launching his striking force against them. At 0900 and 0908 respectively, both American carriers commenced launching their strike forces.

The *Lexington* flew off nineteen Dauntlesses of VB-2 under Commander Ault, along with three of VS-2's aircraft, all that remained aboard. Inexperience showed again, for they were sent off 35 gallons (160l) short of their precious maximum fuel load. The *Yorktown* got away seven VS-5 dive bombers, with another seventeen Dauntlesses of VB-5 soon after, all armed with 1,000lb (450kg) bombs, and they set off to cover the estimated 175 miles (280km) between them and the two big Japanese carriers. They were homed onto the enemy at 0930 by Dixon who had found the Japanese force again in the murk, he radioing his contact as 'Two CV, two DD bearing 000 degrees, 160 miles'.

As they closed with the enemy ships, the *Lexington* Air Group began to lose cohesion: fighters lost bombers, some turned back, the dive bombers lost the torpedo bombers and started a box search to locate them, and the fuel shortage in the

A trio of SBDs tip over for the aerial camera. The total domination of the Japanese Navy aircraft meant that at this stage of the war anything that flew with even a hint of the Japanese national marking of a red 'meatball' was fired upon regardless. This led to an official order in May 1942, to paint out the red spot in the national markings and enlarge the white star. These aircraft carry only their individual aircraft numbers forward and not the full squadron designation. (San Diego Aerospace Museum)

Dauntlesses started to become a serious problem. Hamilton with VB-2 had reduced height down to 1,000ft (300m) in his search but was unrewarded, and the whole squadron was forced to abort the mission and dump their main bombs in order to be able to get back intact.

It was thus left to the indefatigable *Yorktown's* group yet again to get in the first attack, and at about 1050 they sighted both Japanese carriers operating approximately 8 miles (13km) apart with their respective screening ships. The *Zuikaku* opportunely found low cloud in which to conceal herself just in time, but her sister was not so fortunate. However, the dive bombers had arrived over the target well before the slower Douglas TBD Devastator torpedo bombers, and in order to make a concerted attack, Lieutenant Commander W. O. Burch, Jnr, was obliged to keep his squadron circling for half an hour waiting for them to come up. Thus all surprise was lost and the *Shokaku* was able to launch more defending Zero fighters. Not until 1100 did the VS-5 Dauntless attack go in from 17,000ft (5,000m), and as they opened their dive flaps and commenced their dives, they were hit by the defending

Zero fighters. In the resulting mêlée the dive bombers claimed to have shot down four of the defenders, while all seven Dauntlesses took hits, many in their fuel tanks – fortunately of the self-sealing type – whilst one SBD, flown by Ensign J. H. Jorgenson, was splashed; luckily the crew survived to be rescued.

Meanwhile the aircraft of VB-5 were caught out of position and had to go round once more before following them down, and the torpedo bombers launched at too great a distance to be effective. Moreover the problem with the fogging of the telescopic sight recurred and hampered the VS-5 aircraft, who scored no hits whatsoever. However, the seventeen Dauntlesses of VB-5 made no mistakes even though they were equally beset by Zeros, of which they claimed to have destroyed no less than five! They scored two direct hits, one on the port forward side and one to the starboard side of *Shokaku's* bridge, both of which penetrated her decks, wrecking them and starting huge fires in the aviation fuel below decks. These fires were eventually brought under control and she was able to land her aircraft, but she could not launch fresh ones. The Dauntlesses lost two of VB-5's aircraft in this attack, one of them the brave Short who, true to his ideas, had held his dive down to below 300ft (90m) before releasing, even though his aircraft had been hit and his gunner wounded; he failed to pull out and plunged straight into the sea alongside his victim. He was posthumously awarded the Congressional Medal of Honour. The other VB-5 Dauntless lost was that of Ensign David Chaffee.

Finally, at 1040, the remnants of the *Lexington* strike arrived. This was an inexperienced combat group however, and only eleven torpedo planes launched, and they all missed. Most of the dive bombers had not even found the target, including all eleven of VB-2's Dauntlesses that had turned back; but the four SBDs that did make dives claimed two direct hits, by Ault and Ensign Harry Wood. Another Dauntless, that of Ensign John Wingfield, had its bomb 'hang up'. In fact only one aircraft scored any hit, on the *Shokaku's* after-starboard side of the flight deck; it was not fatal, but it completed the wrecking of her flight deck. Thus as a combat carrier she was out of the fight, although she was not fatally wounded, and once the fires were put out she was detached north ultimately to be repaired in Japan. Forty-six of her aircraft managed to land aboard *Zuikaku* and were saved.

This damage had cost *Lexington* her commander air group, shot down by Zeros during the withdrawal, and two other SBDs, one of them being the gallant young Wingfield who had returned alone to make a second attempt. The other victim was Wood, in 2-S-5, who had to force-land on Tagula Island.

In the interim the Japanese air groups, far more experienced, had got in some heavy blows in reply, the *Lexington* being hit by two torpedoes[112] and two direct-hit bombs, with many near-misses. Internal fires started, heavy explosions ripped her innards apart, and she sank at 2000, helped on her way by an American destroyer torpedo. Down to the sea bottom with her went fourteen SBDs, and only five of her dive bombers survived the battle, having managed to land aboard the *Yorktown*. The *Yorktown* herself fared slightly better, taking a solitary bomb at the base of her island; the subsequent fires were brought under control, and she was able to continue to retrieve and to launch both carriers' aircraft. Fletcher eventually retired from the battlefield to Noumea, and

**Attack Organisation of VB-2 during the Battle of the Coral Sea. 7th May 1942**

| Aircraft | Bu. Number | Pilot | Rear-Seat Man |
|---|---|---|---|
| 1 | 2117 | Lt-Cdr W. L. Hamilton | ACRM G. C. Gardner |
| 17 | 2157 | Ensign C. B. Connally | RM3c R. J. Haas |
| 3 | 2115 | Ensign F. R. McDonald | RM3c C. H. O. Hamilton |
| 4 | 2175 | Lt. R. W. Cousins | ARM1c. J. W. Woods |
| 6 | 2154 | Ensign J. A. Riley | RM3c G. E. Eiswald |
| 7 | 2163 | Lt. W. F. Henry | ARM1c M. Maciolek |
| 8 | 2127 | Lt. (j.g) G. O. Wood | ARM2c C. E. Schindele |
| 9 | 2176 | Ensign J. D. Wakeham | RM3c J. W. Nelson |
| 10 | 2121 | Lt (j.g.) H. B. Bass | ARM2c H. S. Nobis |
| 11 | 2116 | Ensign R. P. Williams | Sea1c C. J. Young |
| 13 | 2188 | Lt J. H. Newell | Sea1c R. C. Hynson |
| 14 | 2113 | Lt. (j.g.) R. B. Buchan | ARM2c F. G. Stanley |
| 18 | 4655 | Ensign R. P. Lecklider | RM3c O. A. Bowling |
| 16 | 2126 | Lt (j.g.) J. G. Sheridan | RM3c L. T. McAdams |
| 5 | 4680 | Lt (j.g.) P. J. Knapp | ARM2c L. A. De Salvo |
| **Torpedo Patrol** | | | |
| 15 | 2186 | Ensign T. J. Ball | RM3c L. T McAdams |
| 2 | 2104 | Ensign J. M. Clarke | ARM3c R. H. Horto |
| **With Group Commander** | | | |
| 12 | 2143 | Ensign A. A. Simmons | ARM3c J. G. Teysha |

**Attack Organisation of VB-2 during the Battle of the Coral Sea 8th May 1942**

| Aircraft | Bu. Number | Pilot | Rear-Seat Man |
|---|---|---|---|
| 3 | 2115 | Lt-Cdr W. L. Hamilton | AGRM G. C. Gardn |
| 2 | 2104 | Ensign C. B. Connally | RM3c R. J. Haas |
| 11 | 2116 | Lt (j.g.) J. G. Sheridan | ARM2c A. S. Margar |
| 7 | 2163 | Lt. W. F. Henry | ARM1c M. Maciole |
| 8 | 2127 | Lt (j.g.) G. O. Wood | ARM2c C. E. Schind |
| 9 | 2176 | Ensign J. D. Wakeham | RM3c J. W. Nelson |
| 12 | 2143 | Lt J. H. Newell | Sealc R. C. Hynson |
| 14 | 2113 | Lt. R. W. Cousins | ARM1c J. W. Wood |
| 18 | 4655 | Ensign R. P. Lecklider | RM3c O. A. Bowlin |
| 10 | 2121 | Lt. (j.g.) H. B. Bass | ARM2c H. S. Nobi |
| 17 | 2157 | Ensign W. C. Edwards Jr. | ARM2c R. H. Horton |

then *Yorktown* was rushed north for repairs at Pearl Harbor.

One unique feature of this battle was the American employment of no fewer than twenty-three Dauntlesses, including eight of the VS-5 led by Lieutenant Roger Woodhull and used as additional protecting fighters, held back to guard the carriers against torpedo bomber attack and termed the 'inner air patrol'. This certainly seems excessively cautious, and incredibly defensive to so (mis-)use aircraft whose

sole reason was to strike the enemy. In a way it was a tribute to the versatility of the Dauntless, more so perhaps a tribute to its manoeuvrability and agility.

However, maintaining their patrol at 2,000ft (600m), Woodhull's SBDs proved powerless to stop the Japanese torpedo bombers which passed overhead some 3,000ft (900m) higher and launched their attacks at 2,000 yards (1,800m) range and at over 180 knots. The Dauntlesses were then pounced upon by the accompanying

Zeros, and two were shot down at once, and two more followed them in short order. One of these sitting ducks, piloted by Lieutenant Stanley Vejtasa, bore a charmed life and claimed to have shot down three Zeros on his own, while another SBD splashed a fourth.

In a similar manner *Lexington's* inner patrol lost three Dauntlesses – 2-S-18 piloted by Lieutenant (jg) R. O. Hale, 2-S-16 piloted by Lieutenant (jg) C. W. Swanson, and 2-B-13 piloted by Ensign R. R. McDonald – which went in while attempting to land on the carrier's canted flight deck. Also, Ensign W. A. Austin's plane was damaged by Zero fire and crashed into the carrier's island while attempting to land. The Dauntlesses claimed to have destroyed eleven of the enemy in return. We have seen how just one *Lexington* aircrew, Ensign J. A. Leppla of VS-2 with rear-seat man John Liska, were credited with shooting down no fewer than four Japanese aircrew already in this battle, and he was to add three more Zeros to this, making a total of seven 'kills', four with the forward guns and three with the flexible .30 cal. weapon. Whether this score line is correct or not, it certainly gave emphasis to the ability of this slow dive bomber to at least hold its own under certain conditions, with the best fighter aircraft and pilots the Japanese could muster.

Lieutenant (jg) William E. Hall in 2-S-8 proved another SFDD ace, shooting down two Kates and then duelling with five Zeros, shooting down two of them before the other three broke off the combat; for this he was awarded the Congressional Medal of Honor. Lieutenant (jg) R. B. Buchanan bagged a Kate as well. In all, thirty-five enemy aircraft were claimed as 'destroyed in combat' by the Dauntless 'fighters' during this battle.

Many of the Dauntless pilots questioned the use of their aircraft in this manner: they considered it a mis-use, and one even went so far as to accuse Admirals Fitch and Fletcher of carrying out '. . . an act that bordered on defensive paranoia. . . '[113] so concerned with the safety of their carriers that they were prepared to throw away a chance of total victory, which might have been possible had the twenty-three SBDs been used in their proper roles to strike at the *Zuikaku*. Whatever the truth, this was the last time the Dauntless was so used, although extreme caution continued to dictate American carrier warfare tactics

The deck park of the *Enterprise* (CV-6) after the Marcus Island raid, 4 March, 1942. (Official US Navy photograph, courtesy National Museum of Naval Aviation, Pensacola).

right through to the Battle of the Philippine Sea more than two years later, and with the odds far more in their favour.

On the tactical side, the loss of the *Lexington* far outweighed the sinking of the little *Shoho*, with the sinking of the *Neosho* and *Sims* further tilting the balance in favour of the Japanese. The damage to *Shokaku* was balanced by that to the *Yorktown*, but the efficiency of the American dockyard negated this, because *Yorktown*

was able to take part in the next carrier battle, while *Shokaku* was not. Moreover, the Port Moresby invasion convoy never did turn back south: instead, an overland campaign was considered safer for the Japanese attack, and this ultimately foundered in the mud and dense jungles of the Owen Stanley mountains. Strategically therefore the Battle of the Coral Sea led to Allied victory in the area.

# CHAPTER ELEVEN

# Showdown: Midway

The main Japanese thrust across the central Pacific, Operation MI, was aimed at the two small islands, Sand and Eastern, that formed the Midway atoll. This lay just across the International Date Line in the central Pacific and was an obvious outpost either to threaten Hawaii with invasion, or to defend it from such a threat. Knowing, from their brilliant Intelligence sources, just what was coming, the US forces were busy cramming into Midway every available aircraft and gun they could muster; however, the defenders would still not have much of a chance should the whole weight of the Imperial Fleet be thrown at it, as seemed likely.[114]

The dockyard at Pearl had managed to get the badly damaged *Yorktown* patched up and fit to take her place in the battle line, with her reconstructed air group. She again formed Task Force 17 under Rear Admiral Fletcher, with two heavy cruisers and six destroyers. Aboard her was VB-3, with eighteen Dauntlesses led by Lieutenant Commander Maxwell Leslie; and VS-5, with nineteen SBDs led by Lieutenant Wallace C. Short, Jr. On the instructions of ComAirPac the *Saratoga* squadron was embarked as the quickest way to replenish the carrier's dive bomber strength in the short time available, while VS-5 was really the old VB-5, redesignated to avoid confusion and made up from a mix of ten veteran survivors from that outfit with an influx of eight relatively new and combat-fresh pilots.

Task Force 16, under Rear Admiral Raymond A. Spruance, comprised the carriers *Enterprise* and *Hornet*, five heavy cruisers, one AA cruiser and nine destroyers. The dive-bombing complement of these two carriers was high, with VB-6 led by Lieutenant Richard H. Best, and VS-6 led by Wilmer E. Gallaher aboard the *Enterprise*, each with nineteen SBD-3s and with the *Hornet's* CAG, Commander Stanhope C. Ring, was VB-8 led by Lieutenant Commander Robert R. Johnson with a mix of nineteen SBD-1s, -2s and -3s, and VS-8 led by Lieutenant Commander Walter F. Rodee, with eighteen SBD-2s and 3s (reduced by a crash on the 29 May to seventeen).

Even with the aircraft on Midway itself, this looked a pitiful force to stand against the main strength of the Japanese Navy, now well on its way towards them, for the enemy had sortied in great strength, fielding no fewer than eleven battleships, six aircraft-carriers, ten heavy and seven light cruisers, fifty-two destroyers and many lesser warships. But although a massive and awe-inspiring force, the Japanese fleet was widely dispersed in small groups separated from each other by hundreds of miles, and therefore unable to provide each other with support. Thus the

## Marine SBD Aircrew for Initial Attack

### First Division

#### Command

| | | | | |
|---|---|---|---|---|
| 1 | Henderson, Lofton R. | Major | Reininger, Lee W. | Pfc |
| 2 | Fleming, Richard E. | Cpt | Card, Eugene T. | Corp |
| 3 | Stamps, Clyde H. | T/Sgt | Thomas, Horace B. | Pfc |

#### 1st Section

| | | | | |
|---|---|---|---|---|
| 4 | Glidden, Elmer G. Jr | Cpt | Johnson, Meade T. | Corp |
| 5 | Gratzek, Thomas J. | 2nd Lt | Recke, Charles W. | Sgt |

#### 2nd Section

| | | | | |
|---|---|---|---|---|
| 6 | Iverson, Daniel Jr. | 1st Lt | Reid, Wallace J. | Pfc |
| 7 | Bear, Robert J. "R" | 2nd Lt | Sidebottom, Truell | Pfc |

#### 3rd Section

| | | | | |
|---|---|---|---|---|
| 8 | DeLalio, Armond H. | Capt | Moore, John A. | Corp |
| 9 | Ward, Maurice A. | 2nd Lt | Radford, Harry M. | Pfc |

#### 4th Section

| | | | | |
|---|---|---|---|---|
| 10 | Tweedy, Albert W. | 2nd Lt | Raymond, Elza L. | Sgt |
| 11 | Hagedorn, Bruno P. | 2nd Lt | Piranaeo, Joseph T. | Pfc |

### Second Division

#### 1st Section

| | | | | |
|---|---|---|---|---|
| 16 | Blain, Richard L. | Cpt | McFeely, Gordon R. | Pfc |
| 17 | Ek, Bruce H. | 2nd Lt | Brown, Raymond R. | Pfc |
| 13 | Rollow, Jesse D. Jr. | 2nd Lt | Ramsey, Reed T. | Pfc |

#### 2nd Section

| | | | | |
|---|---|---|---|---|
| 19 | Moore, Thomas F. Jr. | 2nd Lt | Huber, Charles W. | Pvt |
| 15 | Schlendering, Harold G. | 2nd Lt | Smith, Edward O. | Pfc |

actual Battle of Midway was fought mainly between four Japanese aircraft-carriers and three American aircraft-carriers supplemented by a Marine air group, and became, in effect, a balanced exchange.

Prior to 21 May 1942 – the date which signalled the commencement of the reconnaissance and alert phase of the Battle of Midway – the only aviation unit on Eastern Island was Marine Aircraft Group 22, consisting of Marine scout-bombing Squadron 241 (VMSB-221), VMF-221 and a small HQ and service squadron.[115] The former had twenty-one SB2U-3 Vindicators, seventeen being operational. On 26 May the Navy aircraft transport *Kitty Hawk* arrived with twenty-two officers and thirty-five men for MAG-22, along with nineteen SBD-2 Dauntlesses. Of these reinforcing pilots, on the eve of battle with Japan's finest naval aviators, seventeen were '. . . fresh out of flight school'.[116]

By the start of the Midway battle,[117] the total strength of the VMSB-241 was twenty officers and 201 enlisted men under command of Major Lofton R. Henderson, USMC. It was equipped with nineteen SBD-2 dive bombers and sixteen SB2U-3 dive bombers. As there were only twenty-nine pilots, one pilot from VMF-221 was assigned to fly with VMSB-241; thus eighteen Dauntlesses and twelve Vindicators were scheduled for

employment in the battle.

At about 0525 on 4 June 1942, the commanding officer of the naval air station (CO NAS) on Midway Island received a report from a patrol plane that enemy carriers had been sighted at 0515, bearing 320 degrees, distance 180 miles (290km), course 135 degrees, speed 25 knots. All the Marine Corps aircraft were manned and their engines started. At 0555 the radar reported 'Many bogey aircraft 310 degrees, distance 93 miles (150km), angels 11'. By 0556 all the Marine aircraft were airborne.

Rendezvous was completed at Point Affirm, on bearing 90 degrees, distance 20 miles (32km), at about 0630. By the time the first Japanese bombs started to fall on Eastern Island at 0635, the Marine dive bombers were well on their way to their destiny. The Dauntless force was made up in two divisions of four boxes, as demonstrated in the table below.

At about 0705 the Japanese force, including two aircraft-carriers, was sighted. Major Henderson started a wide let-down circle from 9,000ft (2,700m) with the intent of commencing the final attack, by glide bombing, from an altitude of 4,000ft (1,200m). He radioed to his team: 'Attack two enemy CV on port bow.' Almost as soon as this manoeuvre started, however, while still at 8,000ft (2,400m), the SBDs were hit by defending Zero fighters, and in addition, violent AA fire

was received from all surface vessels within range. Eyewitness to this was Captain Elmer Glidden, leader of the second section, who recalled: 'The first [Zero fighter] attacks were directed at the squadron leader in an attempt to put him out of action. After two passes, one of the enemy put several shots through the plane of Major Henderson, and his plane started to burn.'[118]

Henderson was attacked by several Zeros and his aircraft was soon well ablaze; it was obvious that he was badly injured and out of action, so Captain Elmer Glidden took over and committed the squadron to the attack. The fighter attacks were very heavy, so the Dauntlesses dived to the protection of a heavy cloud layer at 2,000ft (600m) over one of the enemy carriers, and from that point completed the attack, the SBDs releasing at altitudes that varied from 400 to 600ft (120 to 180m). Even at this low altitude the Japanese fighter attacks were persistent throughout, and each Dauntless was engaging and being engaged by one or more Zeros long after their bombs had been dropped. The AA fire over the Japanese ships at this point was reported as being '. . . of tremendous volume'.[119]

The surviving SBDs claimed to have scored two direct hits and two close misses[120] on the target carrier, and this ship was observed to be burning, with a large column of smoke issuing from it, as they withdrew at masthead height. In fact the carrier they had attacked, the *Hiryu*, did not take a single hit, and although there were five near-misses, no damage at all was done to the ship, although the rear-gunners spraying the huge target killed four of the Japanese flak gunners at their posts. The Vindicators followed the Dauntlesses in but fared no better. One thing the surviving Dauntless crew agreed upon unanimously was that 'Glide bombing is more hazardous than dive bombing in the absence of our own protective fighters.'[121]

Henderson had thought everything through in a professional manner, and had even supervised the arming of his squadron: he had had '. . . the fuse vanes of all the bombs carried by his squadron screwed down about seventy turns out of a possible ninety turns, thus regardless of extra hazard, assuring arming of the bombs from a very low release altitude.'[122] Even this care could not prevent heavy losses, and eight of the sixteen SBDs failed to

In a few vital minutes the Dauntless dive bomber virtually won the vital Battle of Midway, destroying three Japanese carriers along with the bulk of their air groups and veteran aircrews. Later in the battle they sank a fourth carrier and a heavy cruiser. This battle was one of the most decisive in naval history. Sequence of Norman Bel-Geddes models of the Battle of Midway showing the SBD sinkings of the Japanese aircraft carriers *Kaga, Akagi* and *Soryu*, 4 June 1942. (US Navy via National Archives, Washington DC)

Sequence of Norman Bel-Geddes models of the Battle of Midway showing the SBD sinkings of the Japanese aircraft carriers *Kaga*, *Akagi* and *Soryu*, 4 June 1942. (US Navy via National Archives, Washington DC)

*(Above)* Sequence of Norman Bel-Geddes models of the Battle of Midway showing the SBD sinkings of the Japanese aircraft carriers *Kaga*, *Akagi* and *Soryu*, 4 June 1942. (US Navy via National Archives, Washington DC)

return to Midway; of those that did, six were shot full of holes. One machine, that of Lieutenant Daniel Iverson, had taken a total of 259 hits but still managed to stagger home, such was the sturdiness of the Douglas dive bomber. Iverson was luckier than most, because a bullet had torn off his throat microphone without even nicking him.[123]

Back at the Marine air group, all serviceable aircraft were placed on the usual alert condition but no further air-raids were received. One false alarm was occasioned by the arrival of twelve SBDs from the *Hornet*, led by Lieutenant Commander R. R. Johnson, who were lost and short of fuel.

At 0430 the *Yorktown* launched ten SBDs which commenced a 180-degree arc search pattern to the north with a leg range of 100 miles (160km) out. At 0534 the *Enterprise* received the first enemy sighting report made by the Midway PBY Catalina flying boat, and as the minutes ticked by this was further amplified by subsequent signals, all of which gave Spruance the information he needed. At first he planned to close the gap between himself and the Nagumo carriers to within 100 miles (160km) in order not to extend his air groups, but this would have resulted in allowing the Japanese an extra three hours warning in which to prepare themselves. Instead it was decided to launch at 200 miles (320km) and to then continue to steam hard so that the returning planes would still be able to make the round trip.

Accordingly, at 0702 an all-out launch was ordered, and the whole of the Task Force 16 striking force was airborne by 0806. From the *Enterprise* was CAG with three machines, VB-6, and VS-6 with thirty-three more. From the *Hornet* came a further thirty-five dive bombers. The *Yorktown* commenced launching at 0845 with seventeen of her dive bombers; she thus lost two hours on the rest of the force, and at the time this looked like a recipe for disaster – however, things turned out rather differently.

This was not the only lack of co-ordination, for many of the air groups lost contact with each other, and instead of combined attacks, each squadron made its own way to the target and, if they were lucky, out again. The *Hornet* dive bombers, as we have seen, never even made contact with the enemy and so played no part in the day's fighting.

The sacrifice of the Devastator squadrons, although heart-breaking, led

They arrived over the Japanese carriers at 1000 hours, just at the same time as the seventeen *Yorktown* Dauntlesses put in an appearance, having been launched at 0806 and been led unerringly by Leslie straight to the target. They attacked without hesitation from 14,500ft (4,400m). Three of the Japanese carriers were visible, the *Kaga*, *Akagi* and *Soryu*, and seen to be careering violently round in circles with their screening ships trying to keep in contact having beaten off the torpedo attacks. The *Hiryu* had got out of station due to the same causes, and was hidden from the sight of the dive bombers, being some distance to the north; she thus escaped the attention of any of the SBDs on this occasion.

In total, forty-six Dauntlesses commenced their attack dives on the three carriers – although of these, four of the VB-3 Dauntless-3s did so without their bombs aboard! It later transpired that due to a mistake by the armourers on the carrier, the wiring on the new electric *arming* switches had been crossed with the *release* circuit wiring, so that when the pilots 'armed' their bombs they in fact dropped them in the sea. This happened to no fewer than four aircrew: Leslie himself, Isaman, Lane and Merrill. Leslie, however, continued with his attack dive regardless, hoping at least to divert some flak from the aircraft of his fourteen colleagues who, forewarned, had armed their weapons manually. Likewise McClusky's dive bombers had been reduced to thirty machines when two of VS-6s machines had had to turn back early on with engine failures; while Ensign Schneider's VB-6 aircraft ran out of fuel and had to ditch in sight of the enemy.

A total of thirty-eight bombs were aimed at the three visible carriers, nine being direct hits. Not all the SBDs chose the carriers as their targets: Lieutenant O. B. Wiseman and Ensign John Butler both attacked a battleship, either the *Haruna* or the *Kirishima*, but failed to score hits; and Ensign Robert M. Elder and Randy Cooner attacked a destroyer of the screen, but again with no success.

The *Akagi* was made the target for twenty of the Dauntless assaults, and was hit twice: one bomb struck the edge of the centre lift, penetrated on down the lift-shaft, and exploded bombs and torpedoes which the deck crews had been in the process of changing around. The second hit detonated on her port quarter aft

*(Right)* Sequence of Norman Bel-Geddes models of the Battle of Midway showing the SBD sinkings of the Japanese aircraft carrier *Kaga*, 4 June 1942. (US Navy via National Archives, Washington DC)

Sequence of Norman Bel-Geddes models of the Battle of Midway showing the SBD sinkings of the Japanese aircraft carriers *Kaga*, *Akagi*, *Soryu* and *Hiryu*, June 1942. (US Navy via National Archives, Washington DC)

directly to the victory of the Dauntless squadrons because all Japanese attention had been brought down to sea-level: both fighters and AA defences were subsequently caught flat-footed by the almost simultaneous appearance overhead of the SBDs. Caught equally off-guard was Nagumo himself, for he was exposed with his carrier decks full of aircraft armed and ready to go: they and their incomparable aircrews, which had run riot throughout the Pacific and Indian Oceans for six stunning months, were now annihilated in almost an instant.

It was pure chance that the dive bomber attack was so concentrated, for the *Enterprise* SBDs had, like the *Hornet's*, completely missed the enemy fleet when they reached the estimated point of contact at 0930. They conducted a search far to the south-west in vain, then turned north. Then at 0955 they had a lucky sighting of the destroyer *Arashi* steaming hard to the north-east after carrying out a depth-charge attack on an American submarine: this led McClusky to follow his hunch and trail her, and she led them straight to Nagumo.

## Dauntless Men: Major Lofton R. Henderson, USMC

Major Lofton R. Henderson was the commanding officer of Marine Dive Bomber Squadron (VMSB–241) and was killed in action during the Battle of Midway, 4 June 1942. For his extraordinary heroism in leading his group of sixteen dive bombers in an attack on the Japanese task force at this battle, he was posthumously awarded the Navy Cross.

Shortly after his death, the famous airstrip on Guadalcanal, hacked out of virgin jungle by the Japanese and captured and used by the US forces, was named in his honour. In August 1945, the destroyer USS *Henderson* (DD-785) was commissioned in his memory and the action in which he gave his life.

Major Henderson was born in Cleveland, Ohio, on 24 May 1903. He graduated from the US Naval Academy in 1926 and was immediately commissioned a second lieutenant in the Marine Corps. Prior to World War II he served in China, Nicaragua, Cuba and Puerto Rico, as well as at various posts and stations in the United States. He saw duty at sea aboard the aircraft-carriers *Langley*, *Ranger* and *Saratoga*.

In 1927 he saw active service with the Asiatic fleet, and in 1928 he served with the Third Marine Brigade in China. In October 1928 he was transferred to the Naval Air Station, Pensacola, Florida, as a student naval aviator. He completed the course of instruction and

was designated a naval aviator in September 1929.

From January 1930 to September 1931, Major Henderson served with the Aviation Squadron attached to the Second Marine Brigade in Nicaragua. In recognition of this service he was commended by the commandant of the Marine Corps and awarded the Nicaraguan Cross of Valour by the President of Nicaragua. From 1931 to 1933 he served as an instructor at the Naval Air Station, Pensacola. Following this, he served with a Navy observation squadron, VO 8–M, at the Marine Corps Base in San Diego until 1937.

As a member of VO 8–M, he shared in the commendation awarded the squadron for its performance of duty at the National

Air Races in Los Angeles in 1936. Further, the squadron was commended for its standing as first among carrier-based squadrons participating in the Herbert Schiff Trophy competition of 1936. His home service also included duty at Quantico, Virginia and Parris Island, South Carolina.

During World War II, Major Henderson was assigned to VMSB–241 of Marine Aircraft Group 22, located on Midway Island. He became squadron commander on 17 April 1942. Early on the morning of 4 June 1942, following a warning from a Navy PBY plane that the enemy fleet had been sighted, Major Henderson led his dive bombers in an attack on the enemy carriers. As his citation later recorded:

With utter disregard for his own personal safety, Major Henderson, with keen judgement and courageous aggressiveness in the face of strong enemy fighter opposition, led his squadron in an attack which contributed materially to the defeat of the enemy.

Eight of the sixteen dive bomber pilots, including Major Henderson, did not survive the brief encounter.

In summing up the deaths of the Marine aviators at Midway 4–6 June, Admiral Nimitz recorded that they had 'written a new and shining page in the annals of the Marine Corps'. (US Marine Corps photo)

amidst the parked bombers there, and their gasoline tanks ignited, which in turn set off their bombs and torpedoes in a chain effect of explosions. Huge fires spread rapidly, and although some were quenched by the indefatigable efforts of her fire-fighting teams, others raged on and gradually spread along her deck, igniting further aircraft and causing widespread devastation to her bridge structure. These fires raged on internally all day, gradually

wiping out engine and boiler rooms and then spreading with renewed fury as magazines blew up. With 221 officers and men killed, the survivors eventually abandoned ship and she was finally sunk by torpedoes from escorting destroyers at 0500 the next morning.

The *Kaga* was taken under attack by nine SBDs, these scoring no fewer than four direct hits on her, despite her barrage and a hard turn to starboard. The first hit

aft, to starboard, again right amidst her parked dive and torpedo bombers, and decimating their irreplaceable aircrew as they sat. The second bomb hit close by the forward lift, blowing all the windows out of her bridge and setting off explosions among the bombs and torpedoes. The third bomb also detonated forward on the flight deck forward, just in front of her bridge among the parked aircraft there, scything down most of those on the bridge and killing her captain among them. The fourth bomb hit in the exact centre of the flight deck and punched down into her hangar deck before exploding and causing huge fires there among her fighter aircraft. Again, despite heroic efforts of her crew, the fires raged out of control with many of the pumps destroyed; by evening there was no hope, and at 1925 the forward gasoline tanks blew up with two enormous detonations and she sank, taking with her all her aircraft and some 800 of her crew.

The *Soryu* was attacked by thirteen SBDs who, without loss to themselves, hit her three times. The Dauntlesses had again caught her with a deckload of aircraft, with other refuelling and re-arming on her hangar decks. The first bomb hit amidships, just forward of her centre aircraft lift, pentrating down to the hangar deck before detonating; the resulting explosion threw her forward lift right up out of its well and against the front of her bridge. The second direct hit was almost in the same position as the first, but to port, among her massed air strike on deck: again, fire-balled with gasoline, bombs and other ammunition, these combusted in one lethal blast.

The third bomb almost struck on the port, but further back close to her after lift, and also drove on down into the hangar deck. Again the explosion chain-reacted through the innards of the vessel, wrecking engines and steering. The first bomb had hit at 1025, and by 1040 she was dead in the water, fiercely ablaze from end to end, with 'abandon ship' being ordered five minutes later. She burnt all day with spasmodic explosions, and at 1915 slid under the waves, her boilers exploding as she went down, taking with her the captain and 717 other members of her crew and aircrews.

The fact that they had failed to stop the SBDs destroying their home carriers gave added spleen to the Japanese defending fighters to make amends on the retiring dive bombers while they could, and eighteen Dauntlesses were lost in this mission. Five of the *Hornet's* VS-8 under Commander Ring made it back to their carrier, whilst the others that had landed at Midway were eventually refuelled there. VB-3 escaped unscathed, but had to witness the dive-bombing of their own carrier by the Japanese Vals, and were forced to land aboard the *Enterprise*, where there was now plenty of space for them.

This event made it clear that there was still at least one Japanese carrier afloat and

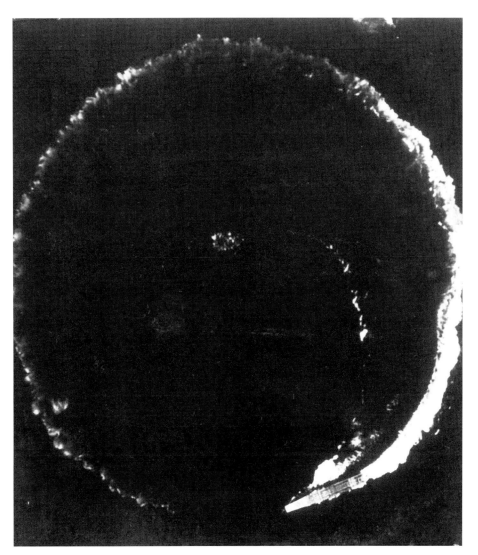

The Japanese Navy aircraft carrier *Hiryu* turns full circle manoeuvring to avoid US Navy Dauntless attacks in the Battle of Midway, 4 June 1942. Although cloud cover protected this vessel during earlier strikes, in this later attack she was hit by four bombs from the SBDs and wrecked. The floating hulk was later sent to the bottom by torpedoes from accompanying Japanese destroyers (National Archives, Washington DC)

indeed these attacks were mounted by the *Hiryu*. Accordingly, a second strike was launched by the Americans to deal with this vessel. Ten SBDs from VS-5 had been launched to conduct a search on a 200 mile (320km) leg to the north-west, and at 1445 hours one of these scouts, piloted by Lieutenant Samuel Adams, located the lone Japanese carrier 110 miles (177km) out, steering north at fifteen knots in company with two battleships, three heavy cruisers and four destroyers.

The *Hiryu* had managed to get in a second strike at the *Yorktown* in the interval, which further damaged her, but now her time had come. A striking force was sent off at 1530 under the command of

Lieutenant W. Earl Gallaher of VS-6 with six aircraft, and VB-6, led by Lieutenant Richard H. Best again, with five. Even this force, with only eleven dive bombers between them, was soon reduced to ten when one aborted, but there were fourteen more Dauntlesses on their way from VB-3, under Lieutenant DeWitt W. Shumway, to make up numbers. It should be noted that only one aircrew on this second strike had *not* flown and survived the morning attacks. The twenty-four Dauntlesses climbed to 13,500ft (4,100m) and headed north, and at 1630 the *Hornet* launched her strike force, Lieutenant Edgar L. Stebbins heading up a sixteen-plane force from VB-8.

**Marine SBD Aircrew for Night Attack**

| Pilot | Rank | Gunner | Rank |
|---|---|---|---|
| Tyler, Marshall A. | Cpt | Underwood, Robert A. | Sgt |
| Vaupell, Robert W. | 2nd Lt | Hickman, Carl T. | Sgt |
| DeLalio, Armond H. | Cpt | Ramsey, Reed T. | Pfc |
| Glidden, Elmer G. Jr | Cpt | Johnson, Arlow A. | Pvt |
| Bear, Robert J. 'R'. | 2nd Lt | Sidebottom, Truell L. | Pfc |
| Iverson, Daniel, Jr | 1st Lt | Reid, Wallace J. | Pfc |

**Marine SBD Aircrew for Attack on Heavy Cruisers**

| Pilot | Rank | Gunner | Rank |
|---|---|---|---|
| Tyler, Marshall A. | Cpt | Underwood, Robert A. | Sgt |
| DeLalio, Armand H. | Cpt | Ramsey, Reed T. | Pfc |
| Vaupell, Robert W. | 2nd Lt | Hickman, Carl T. | Sgt |
| Glidden, Elmer G. Jr | Cpt | Johnson, Arlow A. | Pvt |
| Iverson, Daniel Jr | 1st Lt | Reid, Wallace J. | Pfc |
| Bear, Robert J. 'R' | 2nd Lt | Sidebottom, Truell L. | Pvt |

The fifth major victim of the US Navy SBD Dauntless dive bombing attacks at the Battle of Midway, June 1942, was the Japanese heavy cruiser *Mikuma*, seen here dead in the water and heavily on fire after taking six direct hits. Already an easy target having been damaged through collision with her sister ship, she received heavy damage: her gun turrets are askew fore and aft, her bridge structure and light AA batteries wrecked. She later sank after yet further bomb hits and an internal explosion, going down with very heavy losses among her officers and men. (National Archives, Washington DC)

The *Enterprise* aircraft found their target at 1650 and, incredible as it now seems, totally surprised her, with just six protecting fighters in the air and her aircrews eating dinner! Climbing to 19,000ft (5,800m) the dive bombers circled the *Hiryu*, and Gallaher split his force, with the *Enterprise* aircraft told to plummet down on the carrier while the *Yorktown* flyers were assigned the battleships – although in the event, all found the open flight deck of the Japanese flat-top irresistible, and all but two – Ensigns R. K. Campbell and R. H. Benson, who dive-bombed the *Haruna* with no success – concentrated almost exclusively on her.

The defending Zeros attacked the SBDs during the dive and most bravely pursued them down into their own flak.[124] They shot down Ensign Fred Weber's aircraft and there were no survivors, and this, combined with a hard turn by the *Hiryu*, resulted in initially no hits being made despite the surprise achieved. The Dauntlesses of VB-6, arrowing in behind VS-6, suffered from similar attention, losing the aircraft of Lieutenant O. B. Wiseman and Ensign John Butler; however, they managed to score four direct hits in very quick succession which ripped open the carrier's flight deck, spelling the doom of the vessel. The first hit was directly on the forward lift, and again it was flung up against the ship's bridge, then two more bombs landed amidships, while the last landed forward of the island structure again. As usual, fires broke out and were freely stoked by detonating bombs and torpedoes. Her fate appeared assured, so much so that when the *Hornet's* air group arrived over the force at 1730, Lieutenant Stebbins directed their attacks at the alternative target of the battleship *Haruna*; however, that ship's heavy AA fire was sufficient to put them off aim and again, she emerged completely unscathed from this attack.

Aboard the stricken *Hiryu* there were not many aircraft left aboard to further inflame the blaze, and none of the bombs had penetrated deeply enough initially to affect her engines, so she was still capable of steaming at thirty knots, an incredible achievement. Gradually, however, the fires spread, the engine room staff were trapped and died, and the carrier began to list and sink. Finally she was abandoned and torpedoed by one of her escorts, although she did not sink completely until the following morning. With her went 416 of her crew,

## Attack Organisation of VB-6 during the Battle of Midway.

### 4 June 1942

| Aircraft | Pilot | Rear-Seat Man |
|---|---|---|
| 6-B-1 | Lt. R. H. Best | ACRM (PA) J. F. Murray |
| 6-B-2 | Lt. (j.g.) E. J. Kroeger | RM3c R. W. Halterman |
| 6-B-3 | Ensign F. T. Weber | AOM3c E. L. Hilbert |
| 6-B-5 | Lt. (j.g.) W. E. Roberts | ARM1c W. B. Steinman |
| 6-B-6 | Ensign D. W. Halsey | RM3c J. W. Jenkins |
| 6-B-7 | Lt. J. R. Penland | ARM2c H. F. Heard |
| 6-B-8 | Ensign T. F. Schneider | ARM2c G. L. Holden |
| 6-B-9 | Ensign E. A. Greene | RM3c S. A. Muntean |
| 6-B-11 | Ensign T. W. Ramsay | ARM2c S. L. Duncan |
| 6-B-12 | Ensign L. A. Hopkins | RM3c E. R. Anderson |
| 6-B-13 | Lt (j.g.) J. J. Van Buren | ARM1c H. W. Nelson, Jr. |
| 6-B-14 | Ensign N. F. Vandiver | Sea1c L. E. J. Keaney, Jr. |
| 6-B-15 | Ensign G. H. Goldsmith | ARM3c J. W. Patterson, Jr. |
| 6-B-16 | Lt (j.g.) E. L. Anderson | ARM2c S. J. Mason, Jr. |
| 6-B-18 | Ensign B. S. Varian, Jr. | ARM3c C. R. Young |

## Attack Organisation of VS-6 during the Battle of Midway.

### 4 June 1942

| Aircraft | Pilot | Rear-Seat Man |
|---|---|---|
| 6-S-1 | Lt. W. E. Gallaher | ACRM (AA) R. E. Merritt |
| 6-S-2 | Ensign R. W. Stone | RM1c W. H. Bergin |
| 6-S-3 | Ensign J. Q. Roberts | AOM3c T. R. Swindell |
| 6-S-7 | Lt. (j.g.) N. J. Kleiss | RM3c J. W. Snowden |
| 6-S-18 | Ensign C. E. Dexter | RM3c D. L. Hoff |
| 6-S-10 | Lt. C. E. Dickinson, Jr. | ARM1c J. F. De Luca |
| 6-S-15 | Ensign J. R. McCarthy | RM2c E. E. Howell |
| 6-S-12 | Ensign C. D. Peiffer | RM3c F. C. Jeck |
| 6-S-16 | Lt. (j.g.) J. N. West | RM2c A. R. Stitzelberger |
| 6-S-17 | Ensign V. L. Micheel | RM3c J. D. Dance |
| 6-S-14 | Ensign J. C. Lough | RM2c L. D. Hansen |
| 6-S-4 | Lt. C. R. Ware | ARM1c W. H. Stambaugh |
| 6-S-5 | Ensign F. W. O'Flaherty | AMM1c B. P. Gaido |
| 6-S-6 | Ensign J. A. Shelton | RM3c D. W. Craig |
| ***Photographic Planes with EAGG*** | | |
| 6-S-8 | Ensign W. R. Pittman | ARM2c F. D. Akins |
| 6-S-11 | Ensign R. A. Jaccard | RM3c P. W. Pixley |

## Marine SBD Aircrew for Night Attack

| Pilot | Rank | Gunner | Rank |
|---|---|---|---|
| Tyler, Marshall A | Cpt | Underwood, Robert A. | Sgt. |
| Vaupell, Robert W. | 2nd Lt | Hickman, Carl T. | Sgt. |

and all her surviving aircraft.

Meanwhile at 1700, back at Midway Island, CO NAS received a report of enemy carriers on fire bearing 320 degrees, distance 180 miles, (290km), and asked that VMSB deliver an attack. Major Norris, then CO VSMB, was consulted, and he stated that he and his officers would prefer a night attack since the target would be illuminated by its own flames and since the Zero fighters would not then be active. This was allowed. In an effort to get all possible VMSB arcraft armed and in the air the flight was delayed until 1905, at which time Norris, with five SB2Us and Tyler, with six SBD-2s, took off for the objective. But night was pitch black, the target could not be found, and only the six SBDs returned on schedule at 2200 without having sighted the objective. Norris flew into the water on the return leg, and he and his gunner were lost.

The loss of four carriers was not the end of the Japanese casualties in this battle. The 7th cruiser division, with four heavy cruisers and two destroyers, were *en route* to carry out a bombardment of Midway, but when they were recalled, the threat of an attack by the US submarine *Tambor* caused confusion in the line, and the latter two cruisers collided and both were heavily damaged. They were only some 80 miles (125km) from Midway and clearly the two crippled ships were in grave danger. As they struggled back to the west they were pounded by air strike after air strike which compounded their already extensive damage. Normally tough targets, with high speed and heavy anti-aircraft defences, the two cripples were reduced to easy target practice, the SBDs taking full advantage of their plight.

At about 0525 on 5 June, orders were received from CO NAS to attack two enemy 'battleships', one already crippled, on bearing 268, distance 140 miles (225km); at 0700, Captain Tyler with six Dauntlesses and Captain Fleming with six Vindicators, all carrying 500lb (227kg) bombs, executed this mission (see table). Tracking the *Mogami* by the 50 mile (80km) long oil slick that she trailed behind her, the dive bombers were soon in sight of the enemy squadron. Arriving over the target ships at 0805, they attacked. Captain Marshall Tyler, the third CO of VMSB-241 in little over twenty-four hours, planned for the Dauntlesses to make a dive-bombing attack from 10,000ft (3,000m), while the Vindicators glide-bombed from 4,000ft (1,200m); the SBDs dived in first, and both groups met thick flak. They claimed to have bracketed the heavy cruiser with all six bombs and to have scored one direct hit.

The pilots of VMSB-241 sometimes pushed home their bombing attacks to within 500ft (150m) of their objectives. Several close misses were observed, and they pulled out unscathed, but the Vindicator attack following them in was not so fortunate. Captain Fleming's plane was hit by the very heavy and accurate AA fire and his plane plunged straight into the target. This, and the damage to the cruiser's bows caused by the original collision, made her speed drop to twelve knots, which gave the Navy Dauntlesses their chance to have a go at her in the hours which followed.

At 1543 on 5 June the US carriers launched a strike to search over a 30-mile (48km) sector at extreme range to the north-west, despatching twenty-six SBDs from the *Hornet* and thirty-two from the *Enterprise*. Not surprisingly they found the ocean empty in that direction and were returning to the carriers with their bomb loads when, at 1820, they sighted a solitary Japanese destroyer heading west. This was the *Tanikaze*, which had been despatched to ascertain whether the *Hiryu* was still floating and was returning from this mission.

This one small destroyer showed just what could be done in the face of overwhelming air attack. The *Tanikaze* had already been attacked twice that day, each time by high-flying B-17s, and had dodged all seventy-nine bombs dropped with contemptuous ease. Now she was the subject of the concentrated fury of fifty-eight dive bombers. In theory she should have been totally overwhelmed; in practice her captain, Commander Motomi Katsumi, conned her through this mass assault with skill and aplomb. Her only damage was the result of a near-miss which put a splinter in No 3 gun turret killing six men – but in return her anti-aircraft gunnery brought down Lieutenant Sam Adams's

machine which was lost with both crew members. The SBDs returned to their carriers claiming that the near-miss was a 'possible hit' on a 'light cruiser', both assumptions being false.

The crippled cruisers presented Spruance with a less elusive and agile target, and the American ships moved west overnight and launched eight scouts to locate them, which they did, at 0645. The Americans then sent off three strikes at these vessels on the morning of 7 June: the first wave included twenty-six Dauntlesses led by Commander Stanhope C. Ring from the *Hornet*, sent off at 0800; the second included thirty-one Dauntlesses led by Lieutenant Wallace C. Short from the *Enterprise*, of which five were from VB-5, six from VS-5 and the rest from the *Yorktown* units embarked, and these were despatched at 1045; while the third wave incorporated twenty-four SBDs from the *Hornet*, which were sent off at 1330.

These waves struck the two cruisers at 0945, 1230 and 1445 respectively, their attacks pressed well home against strong flak. Both heavy cruisers were hard hit, the *Mogami* taking two bombs in the first attack, including one direct hit on No 5 turret which cremated its crew. In the second assault she took two more hits which started large fires, while the third attack annihilated the entire ninety-man team of one of her engine rooms, to add to more than two hundred others who died. But she did not sink: she resolutely fought the fires and overcame the damage, and finally managed to win through to Truk anchorage, and she was later fully repaired in Japan.

Her sister ship *Mikuma* was less fortunate. She was hit once in the first attack, although this caused only minor damage, but in the second attack no less than five direct hits were received and fierce fires consumed her innards, wiping out her engine and boiler room complement and bringing her to a halt. These fires reached a magazine at 1058 which exploded, and this blow was terminal. Her captain

ordered the ship to be abandoned, and while this was being done the third wave of dive bombers arrived at 1200 and hit the wallowing wreck two or three more times, causing carnage among those abandoning her. The two escorting destroyers *Arashio* and *Asashio* were both slightly damaged in these attacks, but not seriously, although the loss of life among the *Mikuma* survivors they were rescuing was high. About 650 of her crew were thought to have been killed in total.

For the SBDs this was mere target practice, and the only aircraft lost in these three sorties was to AA fire. A final sortie was made by two SBDs from the *Enterprise*, Lieutenants Edward Kroeger and Cleo Dobson of VB-6, and they photographed the final moments of the doomed cruiser for posterity. The *Yorktown* was finally sunk by the Japanese submarine *I-168*, and with her went a further nine Dauntlesses of VS-5, among others, to swell the total lost in this battle; but this was little enough when compared with the magnitude of their achievement. Their loss was immediately made good, because the *Saratoga* arrived on station with her thirty-four SBDs, ready to take her place in the battle line on 8 June had Yamamoto wished to renew the fight. But he did not.

The Battle of Midway was *the* supreme justification of the dive-bombing ethos and *the* acme of performance for the Douglas SBD Dauntless.

The Marine flyers had also suffered heavily. In total, MAG-22 lost eight Dauntlesses shot down and five severely damaged. It was reported after the battle that 'The SBD-2 airplanes, while being far superior to the SB2U-3 type, are deficient in performance to such a degree as to indicate that their only practical usefulness is for training purposes.'

Whether this judgement was correct or not, the Dauntless would go on to perform other valiant deeds in the hands of both Navy and Marine pilots. Midway was the apex maybe, but there was much yet for the SBDs to do.

# Slugging It Out: Guadalcanal

The Japanese onslaught had been checked at the Coral Sea and given a bloody nose at Midway, but the probes down either side of the Solomon Sea continued, and it was to take a period of fierce eye-to-eye slugging at both tips of these dual tentacles to stem once and for all the hitherto inexorable expansion of the Japanese 'co-prosperity zone'. None of this came easily, however, and those who have written that the sinking of the four carriers of the Nagumo force meant the end of hard fighting could not have been more in error. The scales had tipped back to the point of balance, but it was to take six months' hard fighting before they finally tipped in favour of the

Allies. Many of the successes and the failures during this tough period of the Pacific war centred around the Douglas dive bomber.

In New Guinea it seemed as if the turning back of the Port Moresby invasion fleet had only been a temporary reprieve. In order to attack that port overland the Japanese sent another invasion convoy, Operation 'RI', from Rabaul on 20 July 1942, protected by two light cruisers, a minelayer and three destroyers. The next day their 2,000 troops stormed ashore at both Gona and Buna near Oro Bay.

The 8th Squadron's dive bombers were at once recalled from Australia and thrown in

to try and attack these ships, and on that day Major Rogers led eight A-24s to Port Moresby via Cooktown. They all arrived safely at the Seven-Mile airstrip, whereupon Rogers arranged for a flight of seven Banshees to strike the Japanese landing forces at Buna.[125]

On 22 July the seven A-24s attacked with 500lb (227kg) bombs, and although they were unable to observe the results, their attacks did cause damage. Next day the Banshees were switched to attacking the troops ashore, and eight A-24s dive bombed Japanese positions in the Gona mission compound. All their bombs fell in the target area and a fire was caused in the long shack at the compound which was being used as the enemy HQ. The 8th Squadron conducted another mission on 27 July, when five Banshees dropped 500lb demolition bombs along the Buna road at Serananoi. One of these direct hits caused an abnormally big explosion and an extensive fire when it fell in a large shack alongside the road – this had been suspected of being an arms dump.

These three assaults were splendidly accurate and not at all to the enemy's liking. On the 26th, Japanese reinforcements were despatched from Rabaul in another eight-ship troop convoy. Allied Intelligence soon got word of this sailing when the ships were sighted some 50 miles (80km) north of Buna. Major Rogers was 'eager to contest their right to be there . . .'[126] and a flight of seven Banshees was organized, led by him and with the aircraft of Captain Schwab and Lieutenants Cassels, Hill, Wilkins, Dean and Parker with their respective gunners. The dive bombers were to be given protection by P-40 fighters – but when the Banshees tipped over and went down into their attack dives, these fighters were unable to protect them, and the force was immediately beset by swarms of defending Zeros.

A fierce but one-sided engagement

An SBD-3 airborne. This was the mark that took the brunt of the first three months' fighting in the Solomon Islands, the Mark 4 not joining the front line units until December 1942. Several Navy SBD squadrons disembarked from their carriers at Henderson Field and joined with the Marines in bringing the Japanese plans of further expansion southward and eastward to a decisive and ignominious halt. (McDonnell Douglas, Long Beach)

followed, during which the A-24s of Rogers, Schwab, Cassels, Dean and Parker were massacred. Lieutenant Wilkins completed his dive and claimed a hit on a 6,000-ton troopship, which was thought to have sunk, while the other A-24s damaged a destroyer and several other fighters. They had indeed scored hits on both the transport *Ayastosan Maru* and the destroyer *Uzuki*, although both vessels managed to struggle back safely to Rabaul to repair.

Lieutenant Hill's aircraft was pursued by Zeros, while his gunner, Sgt Sam, fought a lone fight '. . . of unparalleled heroism . . .'[127] he was hit early on in the right hand which was disabled, but he kept firing his .30 cal. gun until its ammunition was totally exhausted. Sam then pulled out his .45 pistol with his left hand and emptied it into a Japanese fighter although hit again and again. Hill managed to land his riddled A-24 at Milne Bay with his seriously wounded gunner still alive, but sadly, Sergeant Sam died a few days later from his wounds. The only other Banshee to get back to base safely was Lieutenant Wilkins; Lieutenants Parker and Dean, and their gunners, survived to be picked up by an Australian army patrol, but then their luck ran out and all were captured soon afterwards by the Japanese.

The remaining A-24s were declared unfit for use, and back at Charters Towers training was concentrated instead on the A-20 medium bomber. However, not even the A-20 would have survived such an onslaught without any fighter protection, but it seems that those who did not understand the dive bomber used this opportunity as an excuse to get rid of it. The direct hits that they had achieved when all other types of Allied bombers had failed to score a solitary one, were conveniently ignored.

A more realistic view of the Air Corps 'anti-dive bomber bias' was given to the author by Richard K. Smith:[128]

If the US had not gotten kicked into the war when it did, and 'Pearl Harbor' had been delayed for a year, the USAAF would have had some time to work up experience with the A-24s it had in hand and were forthcoming, and by the end of 1942 dive bombing would have become familiar. But as it was, I suspect that there was an overwhelming urgency to simply get on with what they were already well familiar (viz: level bombing from higher altitudes).

Meantime the Dauntless focus shifted away to the end of the other arm of the Japanese advance, and here there was *no* doubt or reservation about its efficiency at the job in hand. Like the Army, the Marines had been given little time to train with the new Dauntless, as we have seen at Midway. It had long been the aim of the Corps to build up its dive bomber strength, and when in June 1940 the Congress had authorized 1,167 new aircraft for them, it was planned to re-equip the SBD fully. Amphibious landing exercises conducted in 1941 in the Atlantic, had concluded even then that at least eight dive bomber squadrons were a minimum requirement for such a task. Identifying the need and voting the funds did not, however, provide the planes immediately, although by the time of the Tulagi landings fresh supplies were beginning to reach Marine units.

Since the three attacks by the *Yorktown* Air Group on 4 May, the Japanese had been unmolested at Guadalcanal and Tulagi and able to go about their business as they pleased. Accordingly, Operation 'Watchtower' was mounted to evict them from the seaplane base and garrison they had established at Tulagi Island, and also from the small airstrip that one of their construction battalions had been hewing out of the virgin jungle close to Lunga Point, in the centre of the northern coast of the much larger island of Guadalcanal across the narrow strip of water of the Indispensable Strait from Florida Island.

The First Marine Division was charged with the task, and was to be landed from fifteen attack transports, protected by a cruiser and destroyer escort; heavy cover was also to be given by the full weight of the US fleet, with three carriers: the *Enterprise* with thirty-six Dauntlesses embarked, the *Saratoga* with thirty-seven, and the *Wasp* with thirty in her VS-71 and VS-72 squadrons. It was a clear challenge to the Japanese, and showed the new-found strength of the American Navy. On 7 August the troops went ashore at Tulagi, Gavutu and Guadalcanal, covered by gunfire from the warships and heavy bombing from the SBDs.

The *Wasp* contributed fifteen dive bombers to the destruction of the seaplane base, while from the *Enterprise* Lieutenant Turner F. Caldwell had nine of VS-5's

Dusk at Espiritu Santo, the main supply base from which SBD units formed up, practised and trained and then moved into the combat cauldron of Guadalcanal. Often the Dauntlesses had to be patched together after battleship bombardments or crash landings on the primitive strips, just to keep bombing sorties going against the Japanese troop convoys. (Peter C. Smith)

aircraft airborne armed with 1,000lb (450kg) bombs in the pre-light dawn at 0540. Their targets were AA guns and the radio station on Tulagi's south-western coast. Overall direction at Guadalcanal was by Commander Harold D. Felt, the *Saratoga's* CAG, while Lieutenant Commander Maxwell F. Leslie of the *Enterprise* performed the same function over Tulagi. A second wave went in at 0700, including eighteen SBDs from VB-6 also with 1,000lb bombs.

The first Japanese reaction did not manifest itself until after midday, when strong air attacks from fighter-escorted bombers winged down from Rabaul. First of the Dauntless groups to get involved were eight SBDs of VB-6 led by Lieutenant Carl Horenburger, who were over Tulagi at 8,000ft (2,400m) when they were jumped by two Zeros. Two of the five bombers took machine-gun hits but were not seriously damaged, while the concentrated fire from all the Dauntless gunners despatched one of the Zeros in reply. The eight SBDs of VS-5's second strike were also taken under attack at this time, and they also claimed to have destroyed one Zero for no loss to themselves. All the dive bombers then carried out their attacks without further aerial hindrance. The average Dauntless aircrew flew about seven such missions during 'Watchtower' and enemy strong-points were hit as and when required by the Marines ashore.

Admiral Fletcher however still remained ultra-cautious, and kept his heavy ships some 120 miles (190k) to the north-east of the landings; he then pulled back south-east on the evening of 8 August, leaving them to face Japanese retribution on their own.

Although the incomplete airstrip at Guadalcanal was taken easily, it was not in a fit state to receive aircraft; until it was the Marines had to rely on the carriers, and they had gone. Work was intensified, and by 19 August the airstrip was ready – and not before time, because the Japanese had reacted strongly and were sending in troop convoys and warships to wrest the strip back again. For six months a series of intense sea/air battles took place which saw the end of many a proud ship and many an aircraft; and in this struggle the Dauntless again proved itself supreme.

At the end of June 1942, the forward echelon of Marine Air Group 23, containing VMSB-231 and VMSB-232 and led by Major Richard C. Mangrum, were to have flown into Guadalcanal from a carrier – even before the pilots of the Dauntlesses had been taught how to land on, or take off from a flight deck! It was not until 20 August that twelve SBD-3s of VMSB-232 took off from the escort carrier *Long Island* and landed on the improved airfield (which they quickly named Henderson Field). Like their Army dive-bomber colleagues in Java and New Guinea before them, the Marine flyers soon found that the primitive conditions caused enormous difficulties in just getting their aircraft in operational order. At Henderson in the early days there were no bomb hoists and the 500lb (227kg) weapons had to be hauled to the SBDs and loaded by hand. Their aircraft were still fitted with the hard rubber wheels required for carrier landings, and not the normal pneumatic tyres for ashore use and these hard tyres churned up the coral surface of the airstrip '. . . like a plough sheet.'[129] An attempt by Air South Pacific Command at Noumea to utilize wooden wheels proved no solution to this problem either, and in the end the dive bombers operated from a nearby meadow, known as the 'Cow Pasture', leaving the strip to the fighters. In the interim VMSB-231 continued to train hard at Espiritu Santo in readiness to reinforce their colleagues.

There now began a period of intense activity for the SBDs and a time of ordeal for their air- and groundcrews: just keeping the dive bombers flying was a major achievement, as quite apart from the usual battle damage from enemy fighters, and from the bombing, shelling and AA fire, the hazards of landings, the frequency of the operational flights and the lack of spare parts, all added to the difficulties. However, in spite of everything, a striking force of Dauntlesses was always maintained, and while the Japanese ruled the waters around Guadalcanal by night, the SBDs dictated events up to a 200-mile (320km) range from Henderson Field during daylight. Their main job was hitting the Japanese troop convoys as they came down from Rabaul, and clearing up the remnants from the many naval surface battles that raged up and down 'Iron-bottom Sound'[130] during the night hours. The codename allocated to Guadalcanal had been 'Cactus,' and from this time the Marine and Navy flyers that operated from the death-begirt isle became known as the 'Cactus Air Force'.[131]

The SBDs of VMSB-232 soon established a routine of two-plane patrols up the Solomons' chain every day at dawn and dusk, and these patrols were supplemented by the eyes of the Australian and British civilians who pre-war had run the plantations in the islands; they were known as the 'Coastwatchers'. In lieu of radar, their radioed reports of Japanese shipping, especially bombardment squadrons and the 'Cactus Express'[132] troop runs, and also of Japanese aircraft movements down from Rabaul, often gave the Marine dive bomber crews the essential edge in knowledge of enemy intent. The Dauntlesses also flew frequent anti-ship strikes, land strikes in support of the Marine infantry around the perimeter, anti-submarine patrols and liaison missions.

On 25 August a Japanese convoy with 1,500 reinforcements on their way down from Rabaul was sighted at 0223 by a flying boat. This led to the carrier battle of the Eastern Solomons, which we will describe in detail later; but as part of Operation 'KA' four Japanese destroyers carried out a bombardment of Henderson Field and then joined up with the troop convoy and Tanaka's escorting force, the light cruiser *Jintsu* and three more destroyers.

Lieutenant Colonel Richard H. Mangrum, Captain Daniel Iverson and Lieutenant Larry Baldinus flew the first Dauntless mission in the early hours of that morning, taking off at 0230 to harry the bombarding ships; they were unrewarded, however. Three more SBDs from Flight 300 left at 0400; the patrol was led by Lieutenant Roger Woodhull, VS-5's Exec, but again, it failed to damage the enemy ships, and one aircraft was forced to ditch off Malaita Island through lack of fuel.[133]

The third strike was by the Marine Corps' five Dauntlesses, who arrived over the convoy at 0740; thinking these were friendly aircraft, the Japanese initially held their fire, allowing the SBDs to make unopposed dives. They were led by Mangrum, but infuriatingly his bomb hung up; he was followed in by Second Lieutenants Henry W. Hise, L. E. Thomas and C. B. McAllister who scored three near-misses which exploded hard alongside the target. The fifth dive bomber down, however, piloted by Lieutenant Larry Baldinus, scored a direct hit on the *Jintsu,* his bomb exploding plumb between her two forward gun turrets; as well as destroying her radio office, the resulting fire threatened to engulf her. Her forward magazines were flooded and this saved a worse explosion, but her bulkheads forward had been buckled, and Tanaka was forced to transfer his flag to a destroyer; the damaged cruiser was sent back to Truk under escort. Mangrum himself returned and carried out a solo dive, this time managing to release his bomb at another transport, but again without scoring a hit.

A second part of this attack deployed at 0807: this time it was three Navy Dauntlesses, again led by Lieutenant Turner F. Caldwell, and again one, piloted by Ensign Christian Fink, scored a direct hit, setting the transport *Kinryu Maru* on fire and causing her to be abandoned. At noon the remaining two of the transports turned back. Another striking force of nine SBDs searched for them during the afternoon, but found only one destroyer 150 miles (240km) north-west of Guadalcanal. Six dive bombers attacked and claimed to have scored three near misses, one on the starboard side and two to port, and to have left the destroyer badly injured,[134] but there seems to be no confirmation of this in any Japanese record.

On the 26 August, 390 soldiers from the transports were transferred to four destroyers at the Shortland Islands, and two days later they sailed to join up with four more destroyers with yet more troops embarked from Borneo. Before these two groups could unite they were found, at 1700, by a pair of SBDs, piloted by Ensigns J. T. Barker and Harry Liffner, 125 miles (200km) north-west of Guadalcanal, just to the south-east of Santa Isabel Island. This duo attacked, without result, but their radioed sighting report resulted in the scrambling of a mixed Marine/Navy striking force totalling eleven SBDs.

Flight 600's five Dauntlesses, led by Caldwell, reached the ships soon after 1830 at sunset. The Japanese had reversed course, steering north to evade detection before nightfall, when they would again have turned towards Guadalcanal. They had left it too late however, for it was light enough for the Dauntlesses to make a split attack, with the Navy group coming in from the east and the Marines from the south-west.

Although the Japanese anti-aircraft fire was later described as 'lousy', one of the Marine Corps Dauntlesses, piloted by Second Lieutenant O. Mitchell Jr with gunner Private P. O. Schackman, was shot down. The others pressed home their attacks to within 2,000ft (600m) before releasing. Ensign Harold L. Buell saw his

bomb explode almost amidships: 'She started exploding in her magazines and I saw a heavy red fire burst out of her.'[135] This was the *Asagiri*, and she blew up with the loss of sixty-one of her crew.

Ensign Christian Fink scored a hit with a 1,000lb (450kg) bomb and severely damaged the *Shirakumao* in the engine room, and she had to be towed back. Attacks by Marine pilots set afire the *Yugiri* with a bomb which hit her funnel, and she too had to turn back; they also slightly damaged the *Amagiri*. The other Japanese destroyer flotilla failed to make contact, and joined forces with yet a third destroyer squadron which successfully landed soldiers near Cape Taivu the following night.

Casualties and wear-and-tear had reduced VMSB-232 to nine operational aircraft at this date, plus the ten of Flight 300. Thus every available aircraft had to be flown time and time again, and regular maintenance had to go by the board just to 'keep 'em flyin''. Out at sea the carrier-born Dauntlesses were also further reduced when, at 0746 on 31 August, the submarine *I-26* hit the *Saratoga* with a torpedo amidships, and she had to withdraw from the area to be repaired. Worse was to follow because at 1430 on 1 September another brilliant Japanese torpedo attack by the *I-19* scored three hits on the starboard side of the *Wasp*. The American carrier was engulfed by fires and rent with great explosions, finally being sent to the bottom at 2100 with all but two dozen of her aircraft. These two incidents left only the *Hornet* available to hold the ring and fly in reinforcements to Henderson Field, as the *Enterprise* was repairing her damage received at the Eastern Solomons battle.

Because most of the troop landings were nocturnal affairs, the Japanese having learned to keep out of range of the SBDs during daylight hours, many night sorties were flown, even though none of the aircrew had much practical experience of this type of operation. Known as 'night harassment flights', these excursions were rarely successful but just served to add yet more strain to both friend and foe alike in this grinding conflict. One such night mission, of three hours' endurance, was carried out on the night of the 29/30 August, but no contact was made. A similar sortie was conducted the following night, but this one had more dramatic consequences. The mission was to search

for a destroyer squadron reported earlier by Coastwatchers, and as part of this force Captain Fletcher Brown of VMSB-232 led a two-plane patrol with a Navy SBD piloted by Ensign E. A. Conzett with ARM1/c James H. Cales as his rear-seat man. When Conzett was wounded by an AA shell from the enemy ships, Cales managed to fly the aircraft back to Henderson Field from the rear-seat position, an outstanding achievement. It was a miraculous escape for both men, but showed what could be done by steady nerves, a stout heart and a rugged airplane.[136]

In a similar mission, at 2100 on the night of 1 September, the SBDs were scrambled from Henderson while it was under destroyer bombardment, the Dauntlesses rolling down the bumpy airstrip with 5in (127mm) shells dropping all around them. One section of three Navy planes, piloted by Ensigns J. T. Barker, H. L. Buell and H. C. Manford, was caught by an accurate salvo and Buell's plane was written off in a collision with the airstrip's steamroller: The Dauntless disintegrated, the engine parted company and was mashed into a metal ball, the wheels broke off along with the struts, and the wings outboard of the centre-section panel also went their own ways. Fortunately the 500lb bomb failed to detonate, and both Buell and his rear-seat man, John L. Villarreal, managed to get out, albeit both injured.[137] Under the same deadly hail of shells another SBD, that of Second Lieutenant Thomas F. Moore, was also written off when his engine was knocked out and his Dauntless was taken apart by the trees at the end of the runway. The Dauntless was a tough bird, but there were limits!

The next Japanese move was to try and infiltrate troops ashore by moving them from island to island in small landing barges, which they hoped might escape detection. Fifteen of these were located off San Jorge Island on 4 September and were attacked by a sixteen-plane strike from Henderson. The nine Navy and seven Marine SBDs carried out low-level bombing and strafing attacks throughout the morning, claiming the destruction of several barges along with their soldiers. An identical mission was mounted on 5 September as the Japanese persisted, and again the Dauntlesses claimed to have sunk three landing craft and to have damaged many more, with Japanese casualties estimated to number 700 officers and

**The Personnel of Flight 300, Guadalcanal 24 August – 27 September 1942**

| Pilot | Dates | Rear-seat man | Dates |
|---|---|---|---|
| Lt T. F. Caldwell | 24/8–27/9/42 | ARM 3/c E. K. Baraun | 24/8–21/9/42 |
| Lt R. B. Woodhull | 24/8–17/9/42 | ARM 1/c J. H. Coles | 24/8–27/9/42 |
| Ens. J. T. Barker | 24/8–27/9/42 | ARM 2/c N. A. Fives | 24/8–27/9/42 |
| Ens. W. E. Brown | 24/8–27/9/42 | ARM 1/c A. W. Garlow | 24/8–27/9/42 |
| Ens. H. L. Buell | 24/8–19/9/42 | ACRM W. E. Glidewell | 24/8–27/9/42 |
| Ens. E. R. Conzett | 24/8–27/9/42 | ARM 1/c C. A. Jaeger | 24/8–27/9/42 |
| Ens. W. W. Coolbaugh | 24/8–27/9/42 | ARM 3/c H. L Joselyn | 24/8–27/9/42 |
| Ens. C. Fink | 24/8–27/9/42 | ARM 2/c M. L. Kimberlin | 24/8–27/9/42 |
| Ens. T. T. Guillory | 24/8–19/9/42 | ARM 1/c S. J. Mason, Jr | 24/8–27/9/42 |
| Ens. H. W. Liffner | 24/8–19/9/42 | ARM 3/c E. J. Monahan | 24/8–27/9/42 |
| Ens. H. C. Manford | 24/8–21/9/42 | ARM 3/c J. L. Villareal | 24/9–27/9/42 |

**SBD Units of the Cactus Air Force, Guadalcanal 1942–3**

| Squadron | Commanding Officer | Dates | Killed in action |
|---|---|---|---|
| VMSB-232 | Lt Col R. C. Mangrum | 20/8–2/10/42 | 6 pilots, 3 crewmen |
| Flight 300 | Lt T. F. Caldwell | 24/8–27/9/42 | Nil |
| VMSB-231 | Maj L. R. Smith | 30/8–16/10/42 | 3 pilots, 2 crewmen |
| VS-3 | Lt Cdr L. J. Kirn | 6/9–17/10/42 | 2 pilots |
| VMSB-141 | Maj G. A. Bell | 23/9–19/11/42 | 16 pilots, 14 crewmen |
| VS-71 | Lt Cdr J. Eldridge, Jr. | 28/9–7/11/42 | 4 pilots, 2 crewmen |
| VB-6 | Lt Cdr R. Davis | 14/10–3/11/42 | Nil |
| VMSB-132 | Maj L. B. Robertshaw | 1/11–1943 | 2 pilots, 2 crewmen |
| VMSB-131 | Lt Col P. Moret | 12/11–1943 | Nil |
| VMSB-142 | Maj R. H. Richard | 12/11–1943 | Nil |

men. The Japanese reverted to the 'Cactus Express' again.

The war of attrition between the Dauntlesses and the Japanese destroyers continued unrelentingly. On 30 August, twelve SBDs of VMSB-231 led by Major Leo Smith reached Henderson Field, and on 6 September six SBDs from *Saratoga's* VS-3, with Lieutenant R. M. Milner and Lieutenant (jg) A. S. Frank, flew in from Espiritu Santo. On 10 September a force of two destroyers was reported late in the day. The accompanying light cruiser, the *Yura*, was attacked by two Dauntlesses piloted by Ensigns Barker and Buell, who approached undetected at 14,000ft (4,300m) before making their dives out of the sun, scoring near-misses which left her unimpaired. Salvoes from her main armament followed the two dive bombers out as they withdrew at low level, but they escaped unscathed. Bad weather rendered subsequent SBD sorties ineffective and the Japanese were

able to complete their mission.

The night of 12 September saw the bombardment of the airstrips by the light cruiser *Tenryu* and three destroyers, an attack planned to coincide with Japanese land attack. The front line was only some 2,000 yards (1,800m) from the airfield, and the 5.5in (140mm) shells that fell short of this hit the aircrew dug-outs and trenches where they had taken cover. One direct hit landed on the Marines shelter, and two of the VMSB-232 pilots were killed outright, Lieutenant Lawrence Baldinus and D. V. Rose; two others were badly wounded. Another Marine Dauntless, piloted by Second Lieutenant O. D. Johnson, was lost with its crew when it was ambushed by a Japanese Rufe seaplane fighter while landing with wheels down and rear machine-gun unshipped. The next day the Marines lost yet another SBD when Second Lieutenant Y. W. Kauffman and his rear-seat man, Private B. J. Arnold,

were splashed, while their companion aircraft, piloted by Second Lieutenant A. F. O'Keefe, was also hit and the pilot wounded in the same attack. Some compensation was the arrival at Henderson of the residue of *Saratoga's* VS-3, twelve Dauntlesses led by Lieutenant Commander Louis J. Kirn.

On a mission on 16 September a mixed force of twelve Navy and Marine Dauntlesses, led by Lieutenant Commander Kirn, made a late afternoon strike on a Japanese force coming down The Slot at 140 miles (225km) range. Meeting heavy AA fire, three Navy planes claimed near-misses on a cruiser, while a direct hit and three near-misses were claimed on one of the destroyers. None of these is confirmed in post-war records, however. In reply, the flak nailed the Dauntless of Ensign O. Newton of VS-3, and his rear-seat man, ARM3/c R. S. Thornton. Two days later, Lieutenant L. E. Thomas's aircraft fell victim to 'friendly fire'.

The newly appointed commander of the Cactus Air Force, 57-year-old Marine aviator Brigadier General Roy S. Geiger, arrived on the island on 3 September; on the 22nd he led from the front by commanding a Dauntless strike at Japanese positions at Kamimbo Bay on the north-western tip of the island. More reinforcements from Noumea, New Caledonia, landed the next day, namely five SBDs from Marine squadron VMSB-141, followed by a further twenty-one from the same unit on 5 October. On the 28th, six Navy Dauntlesses also flew in from Espiritu Santo, their arrival making up for the departure of the survivors of Flight 300 to Noumea.

These newcomers were soon in action against Tanaka's flotillas. On 24 September the destroyers *Kawakaze* and *Umikaze* were slightly damaged by the dive bombers from Henderson Field. In reply, VS-71 lost Lieutenant R. H. Perritte's aircraft which failed to return from a sortie on 2 October. The same mission located two Japanese seaplane tenders laden with tanks, heavy artillery and 728 officers and men of the 2nd Infantry Division, with a six-destroyer escort heading down The Slot towards Tassafaronga from Rabaul.

An eight-plane Dauntless strike was made against this force, led by Lieutenant (jg) A. S. Frank of VS-3, but one SBD was forced to abort, and heavy flak negated the dive attacks of the remainder. The

Japanese force continued on to Cape Esperance and commenced unloading. A night strike by four SBDs from each of the four squadrons at Henderson was then instigated, led by Lieutenant Commander John Eldridge of VS-71; only two aircraft reached the target area however, and their attacks, delivered blind, failed.

On 5 October, in co-ordination with the SBDs from the *Hornet*, nine SBDs attacked enemy ships south of the Shortlands Roadstead. Bad weather meant no results for *Hornet* flyers, although both hits and near-misses were claimed on two ships by the Henderson Field flyers. In fact, only near-misses caused some damage to destroyers *Minegumo* and *Murasame*, which had to return to base, but the other four destroyers unloaded at Lunga Point without harm, despite a further night strike during which the Dauntlesses dropped flares for the first time.

Another Japanese force, comprising the light cruiser *Tatsuta* and nine destroyers, was attacked by VMSB-241 north of New Georgia. Lieutenant W. H. Fuller was sure he had scored a direct hit on the cruiser and one of the destroyers was reported as being damaged. However, it has been known for a long time now from Japanese records that in fact *no* damage at all was done in this attack, and that no ships were even damaged.[138]

Between the 9–13 October, the battle of Cape Esperance was fought between two opposing cruiser and destroyer task forces, during which the Japanese heavy cruiser *Furutaka* was sunk. On the morning of 12 October two destroyers turned back to rescue survivors and picked up about 400 men. But they tarried too long in their humanitarian work, and the SBDs caught them north of Russell Island with a series of attacks from a total of seventy aircraft.

First in were sixteen Dauntlesses from VS-71 under Lieutenant Commander John Eldrige, and they reported a succession of hits and near-misses; but in fact only one near-miss was scored, on the *Murakumo*, splinters from which penetrated one of her fuel tanks. A second wave drove in at 0800, with six SBDs from VS-3, VS-71 and VMSB-141 under the command of Lieutenant Commander Louis J. Kirn. These scored at least three close misses, knocking out most of the *Murakumo*'s armament and engines; she was then hit by an aerial torpedo from an accompanying TBM Avenger, which reduced her to a floating wreck. Finally she

had to be scuttled, and the few who survived abandoned ship.

This left the *Natsugumo* crammed with survivors from both the cruiser and her companion, and she tried to escape northwards; but a third strike, again led by Eldrige this time with ten mixed Dauntlesses, found her before sunset. The SBDs claimed one direct hit amidships, and two bombs close alongside which caused her boilers to explode. As the sun went down, so did the *Natsugumo*.

By 13 October the American air strength at Henderson had risen to about ninety aircraft, half of them SBDs – but that strength was soon to be diminished in a dramatic manner. On the night of 13–14 October, the Japanese battleships *Kongo* and *Haruna* bombarded Henderson Field, firing in 913 accurate rounds of 14in (35cm) APHE shell, and destroying forty-eight out of the ninety aircraft; this left only seven SBDs operational, and with little fuel. Casualties among the squadrons' complement included Major Gordon H. Bell, his Exec, Captain R. A. Abbott, and three flying officers from VMSB-141; also Captain E. F. Miller and Second Lieutenants J. A. Blumenstein and H. A. Chaney Jr, all being killed, as was Lieutenant W. P. Kephart of VS-71.

Four Dauntlesses were made serviceable and were sent off to attack the troop convoy sighted the next afternoon, but they failed to score any hits; nor was another night sortie led by Lieutenant Commander L. Kirn any more successful. On a more poignant note, Lieutenant Colonel Mangrum left the island that day; he was the last of the twelve original Marine pilots, half of whom had died. On the battle front, the dive bombers were given *no* time to recoup their losses: orders went out for eight SBDs of VB-6 under Lieutenant Commander Ray Davis – then in reserve at Espiritu Santo with nine spare aircraft after the *Enterprise* had gone to repair at Pearl Harbor – to fly to Guadalcanal immediately, and for nine fighter pilots to take over the rest and join them. But before they could do so the Japanese took a hand once more.

They repeated their bombardments on the night of 14–15 October, with heavy cruisers *Chokai* and *Kinugasa*, and also two destroyers, which shelled Henderson Field continually from 0149 to 0216. Their 752 8in (20cm) and numerous 5in (13cm) shells further reduced the flyable Dauntless total to just four aircraft[139], with

enough fuel for one return mission, and two of these were wrecked trying to launch a night sortie. Under cover of these assaults the Express was confidently run in at the same time. Only one Dauntless finally got airborne, piloted by Marine pilot Lieutenant Robert B. Patterson, and he made an attack on the ships, claiming one hit.

By an incredible feat of improvisation, enough SBDs were patched up and sufficient fuel salvaged from wrecked aircraft to send out another strike at 1000 the following day with twelve machines. These reached the discharging transports at Tassafaronga at around 1000, the SBDs diving from 9,000ft (2,700m) and claiming hits and near-misses. After refuelling, a shuttle of attacks was kept up from Henderson, and at 1140 a second dive bomber assault went in, followed by twenty more aircraft at 1315. Between them, the Dauntlesses hit and damaged the *Azumasan Maru* and the *Sasago Maru*, while the *Kyushu Maru*'s cargo of ammunition exploded – she was beached and subsequently lost. In addition, the destroyer *Samidare* was slightly damaged. The remaining transports were sent back at 2300.

On the night of 15-16 October, the heavy cruisers *Maya* and *Myoko* bombarded Henderson Field, firing 450 and 465 8in (20cm) shells respectively, while three screening destroyers contributed more misery from their 5in (13cm) guns. Thus in two days, twenty-three Dauntlesses had been destroyed and thirteen damaged, and this reduced the operational Dauntlesses to ten machines again. However, seven replacement SBDs were hastily sent up from Efate, arriving at Henderson in the middle of a dive-bombing attack by Japanese Navy Vals. One of these scored a hit on the destroyer transport *McFarland*, killing twenty-seven of her crew and passengers; but the Marine SBDs survived. These continued to attack shore targets, losing one of the VMSB-141 aircraft to flak that day. On the 17th another Dauntless was lost, that of Lieutenant (jg) C. H. Mester of VS-71 who was shot down by Japanese seaplane fighters off Santa Isabel Island; the crew were rescued.

In response to these setbacks the Americans changed their commanders, with Vice Admiral William F. Halsey replacing Vice Admiral Robert L. Ghormley, and the *Enterprise* and the battleship *Indiana* were rushed down from Pearl to replace the damaged *Saratoga* and *North Carolina.*

Events were building up to a climax: the Japanese Army was preparing to make a final assault on Guadalcanal, so more reinforcements were being run in almost nightly. On the 19 October during an Express run, the destroyer *Ayanami* was damaged by SBD attack. Between the 22–27 October the carrier battle of Santa Cruz was fought, resulting in the loss of the *Hornet* and damage to the *Enterprise.* On the disputed island, an all-out Japanese land assault on Henderson Field between 24 and 25 October only just failed to overrun the Marines' defences.

Six VMSB-141 Dauntlesses were airborne early on the 25 October, and one of these sighted the two approaching Japanese attack units heading down The Slot. The largest of these groups consisted of the light cruiser *Yura*, with four destroyers, while another four destroyers were also on their way to attack Tulagi. Over-confidence by the Japanese Army ashore – who were certain they had captured Henderson Field, but in the event had not – led the Japanese Navy to believe they had nothing to fear from the SBDs. They were wrong, and while deep in the Indispensable Strait, the *Yura* group were taken under repeated attack.

Again it was Lieutenant Commander Eldrige who led the first assault with five Dauntlesses just after 1300 that afternoon. His initial diving attack was made, and his 1,000lb (450kg) bomb was released from the unusual height of 3,000ft (900m) – but in spite of this he scored a direct hit, and this was followed by two more near-misses from the four following SBDs. The culmination of the damage and the shock of these three bombs knocked out the *Yura's* engines and she came to a halt.

At 1500 a three-plane attack led by Lieutenant Commander Ray Davis of VB-6 scored a further two close misses on the *Yura*, accelerating her leakages, while Davis himself near-missed the *Akizuki*. The *Yura* was clearly doomed; the *Akizuki* was then near-missed again, but she managed to reach Shortlands for repairs. The Japanese then decided to cut their losses, and once the crew were taken off, the *Yura* was sunk by destroyer torpedoes.

Although the island was still in dispute, the two Navy Dauntless squadrons of the Cactus Air Force, VB-6 and VS-7, were now withdrawn, leaving the Marine squadron, VMSB-141 under Lieutenant

Out in the Pacific the fighting was concentrating around Guadalcanal and the Solomons. The SBD formed the main backbone of the 'Cactus Air Force' which caused the Japanese fleet and troop convoys heavy losses, despite all odds. The extreme youth of the young Navy and Marine flyers of the dive bombers that won this bitter struggle is shown in this photo taken at Henderson Field. (McDonnell Douglas, Long Beach)

W. S. Ashford, to continue to fight, along with new arrivals VMSB-132, led by Major Joseph Sailer. These two dive bomber units were joined by a third on 12 November: this was VMSB-142 led by Major R. H. Richard with ten aircraft, thus giving a total of thirty SBDs. In fact the newcomers soon took losses, and in a mixed night harassment sortie, the three Dauntlesses involved – flown by the indefatigable Eldrige and the Marine pilots Lieutenant Wayne Gentry and Melvin Newman –

failed to return.

The Japanese decided to run in yet more troops under cover of further bombardments, and the Americans threw in all available warships, regardless of the risks, in an effort to thwart them. On 7 November another Express was run, and on the way in they were attacked by seven dive bombers from Henderson Field, led by Major Sailer, who reported hits on a 'cruiser' target. In fact no cruiser was present, but both the destroyers *Naganami* and *Takanami* were damaged in this attack. On the 10–11 November, an Express run destroyer force successfully beat off SBD attacks.

On the night of 12–13 November the Japanese battleships *Hiei* and *Kirishima* bombarded Henderson Field while a further Cactus Express and transport run was taking place. Then the battleships were intercepted by an American cruiser and destroyer force, and in the resulting Battle of Guadalcanal, the *Hiei* took an estimated thirty to eighty shell hits from 8in (20cm), 6in (15cm) and 5in (13cm) guns, some at extremely close range (from 300 to 4,500 yards/ 274 to 4,115m). These hits hacked away great segments of her upper-works and even penetrated her armour decks; her steering gear was severely damaged and her boilers could only operate at reduced capacity. Despite intensive efforts she was little more than a floating wreck as dawn broke.

Dive- and torpedo-bombing attacks against this crippled ship were almost continuous throughout the day, and as fast as the SBDs could be refuelled and re-armed they were sent out in relays. A single aircraft opened the dive bombing at first light, but missed the huge target. Two scouting Dauntlesses followed with the same result, and then the first full strike was made, led by Major Robert H. Richard with five VMSB-142 aircraft.

They only had to fly for a quarter of an hour to find the *Hiei* and commence their dives at 0615, and they claimed one 1,000lb (450kg) bomb on target and one near-miss. At 1120, five more Marine Dauntlesses waded in, claiming three further direct hits. A third sortie was far less successful, however, for only Major Sailer found the target in the dusk and poor weather conditions, and he claimed a near-miss on a destroyer. Of the remaining six Dauntlesses, from both VMSB-132 and VMSB-141, two – piloted by Second-Lieutenants J. Knapp and A. Sandretto of the latter unit – failed to return.

In addition to these blows, the *Hiei* was the target of innumerable Avenger attacks from both Henderson Field and the *Enterprise*, but these were surprisingly inef-fectual against the armour and bulge protection of the thirty-year old vessel – indeed, some torpedoes were seen to run straight and true and then observed to bounce off her sides![140] At 1020 she was hit by two torpedoes right aft which locked her steering gear, so she could only turn in slow

circles. At 1430 another attack developed and two more aerial torpedoes struck the hapless vessel, flooding her engine room. Finally the accumulative damage proved too much for even the tough old *Hiei*: by 1800 she was clearly doomed and her crew abandoned ship, and an hour later she settled and sank off Savo Island with 450 of her complement. Sharing the credit, the Dauntlesses certainly helped accelerate her destruction.

The loss of a battleship did not deter the Japanese from continuing with the all-out effort, and on the night of the 13–14 November the heavy cruisers *Chokai*, *Suzuya* and *Maya* again shelled Henderson Field, dropping 1,370 rounds of 8in (20cm) APHE shells on the American defences, and aided by the 5in (13cm) contribution of two destroyers. Despite the volume of fire delivered on the target they actually achieved little success, and only one Dauntless and seventeen Wildcats were wrecked by their deluge of 8in shells. The bombarding warships then joined forces with a covering group consisting of the heavy cruiser *Kinugasa*, the light cruiser *Isuzu* and two destroyers.

At 0806 on 14 November, five of the Henderson Field Dauntlesses, again led by Sailer, attacked this cruiser squadron, starting fires aboard the *Maya*. Meanwhile at 0850, two scouting Dauntlesses from the *Enterprise* also located this squadron, then south of Rendova Island. They were searching for a reported Japanese carrier group, and sighting warships they reported the cruisers as, 'Two battleships, two cruisers, one possible converted carrier . . .!'[141]

After making their sighting reports and amplification reports, the two VB-10 pilots, Lieutenants Robert D. Gibson and Ensign R. M. Buchanan, made attack dives on the force. Gibson's Dauntless took a 5in (13cm) shell through the fuselage on the way down, but the tough little bomber carried on, and both aircraft dropped their 500lb (227kg) bombs accurately from 2,000ft (600m). The heavy cruiser *Kinugasa* was hit on a forward gun turret and holed by a near miss.[142] Big fires swept her decks and she also began to list as water poured in through the gaps in her side plating.

A second pair of VB-10 SBDs, piloted by Ensigns P. M. Halloran and R. A. Hoogerwerf, attacked at 0836, com-mencing their approach dives out of the sun from 17,500 ft (5,300m) and into their

attack mode at 12,000ft (3,600m). Halloran's aircraft was shot down during the attack and, this crashing Dauntless impacted into the side of the *Maya*, wiping out an AA gun position, two of her search-lights and a torpedo tube, and killing thirty-seven of her crew. Hoogerwerf thought they had scored a hit and a near-miss on their targets.

Soon after, the *Enterprise*'s Dauntlesses arrived to carry on the assault. A seven-teen-plane group – seven from VB-10 led by Lieutenant Commander John A. Thomas, and ten from VS-10, each armed with a 1,000lb (450kg) bomb and led by Lieutenant Commander James R. Lee – after making a fruitless search for the Japanese carrier to the north, finally happened upon the cruiser force just after 1030. While VB-10 went for the damaged heavy cruiser, the VS-10 SBDs selected the light cruiser *Isuzu*.

The first target was *Kinugasa*. Although no direct hits were taken, the near-misses were close enough for the concussion to shake up her engines and boilers badly and to open up her old wounds again. She drifted helplessly until her crew took to the water at 1122, and she sank some 15 miles (24km) west of Rendova Island. The *Chokai* was not hit, but was near-missed and holed, while strafing by the Daunt-lesses caused damage to her upper-works. Several bombs close alongside the light cruiser *Isuzu* shook her up considerably and started numerous leaks, and finally she had to be taken in tow; but she managed to reach the Shortlands anchorage. The destroyer *Michishio* was also crippled by near-misses and she, too, had to drag herself to safety in the Shortlands.

Another bombardment had been sched-uled for that night: the battleship *Kirishima*, three heavy cruisers and one light cruiser and destroyers under Admiral Kondo, was to have conducted another bombardment of Henderson to facilitate the landing of the troops; however this force was ambushed on the night of the 14th/15th by two American battleships and four destroyers, and another titanic battle took place in which the Japanese battleship was so badly damaged she had to be scut-tled.

The Dauntlesses had no chance to help in her destruction, but they had plenty of work to do and concentrated their main efforts on the troop transports. Having badly mauled the cruiser squadron, the SBDs from the *Enterprise* landed at

Henderson Field, and their companions, still scouting for the reported Japanese flat-top, soon turned their attentions to the Cactus Express convoy which was proceeding south with eleven transports, escorted by eleven destroyers and with air cover provided by the small carrier *Hiyo*. This force was located off Santa Isabel Island by two SBDs, piloted by Lieutenant (jg) Martin Carmody and Lieutenant (jg) W. E. Johnson who, after sending their sighting reports, very courageously attacked at 1000 with their 500lb (227kg) bombs. Johnson's aircraft was shot down by defending fighters, but Carmody survived, claiming that one direct hit and one near-miss had been scored on two transports.

This was soon followed by others, as SBD sorties were despatched from Henderson Field all day long. At 1250 this convoy was attacked by nineteen Marine SBDs from both VMSB-132 under Sailer and VMSB-141 under Richard, deep in The Slot; the first wave achieved some hits and close misses on the transport columns, twenty-four SBDs hitting the convoy at 1430. The last section of this strike to attack included *Enterprise* pilot Gibson once more, with Ensign Len Robinson and Marine flyer Sergeant A. C. Beneke, each armed with a 1,000lb bomb, and they survived Zero attacks on their way into the target. They commenced their attack dives from 6,000ft (1,800m) and strafed on their way down, claiming two direct hits which they maintained broke the ship in half.

Four more Dauntlesses attacked at 1530; then three Marine aircraft, led by Ensign John Richley of VS-10; then nine SBDs, seven Marine aircraft and two Navy, Lieutenants James R. Lee and Glen G. Estes. Finally, at 1715, another eight SBDs from the *Enterprise* VS-10, led by Lieutenant Bill Martin, joined in the slaughter when the convoy was still some 60 miles (100km) north-west of Savo Island. Their attacks were followed by a lone effort, Chuck Irvine claiming a direct hit despite a mass of protecting fighters.

Eight dive bombers from the *Enterprise* reached the stricken convoy at 1615, and at 16,000ft (4,900m) they split into two groups: the larger, of five aircraft – piloted by Lieutenants Ralph H. Goddard, B. A. McGraw and J. N. West, Ensigns Daniel H. Frissell, and N. E. Wiggins – attacked from the starboard of the convoy lanes, while three others – Lieutenants (jg) Martin D. Carmody and Edward Edmundson and

For use against enemy battleships and cruisers the SBD relied on heavier and heavier bombs to penetrate their substantial deck armour. Unlike the Japanese Navy's wooden decked carriers, its conventional heavy warships could only be penetrated to their vitals by considerable weight. This is the main bomb on the swing crutch of an SBD-5 pictured on 13 October 1943. With such weapons even battleships like the *Hiei* could be seriously hurt. (McDonnell Douglas, Long Beach)

Ensign Robert Edwards – hit from port. Again the protecting Zero fighters tried to intervene, but Edwards' gunner, ARM2/c W. C. Colley, shot one down, while Edmundson's rear-seat man, ARM2/c R. E. Reames, nailed another. Between them they claimed seven direct hits on various ships.

As they departed, more Dauntlesses appeared over the horizon, flying at a height of 12,000ft (3,700m). These were the seven aircraft from VB-10 at Henderson Field, under Lieutenant Commander J. A. Thomas, who led the first section, and with Lieutenant V. W. Welch (executive officer) heading up the second, and also Lieutenant (jg) R. D. Gibson, Ensigns Jefferson H. Carroum, E. J. Stevens and J. D. Wakeham. Again the SBDs were fiercely attacked by defending Zeros and had to fight their way through to the target ships. Two slashed into Gibson's machine, badly damaging it, and he only escaped destruction by hitting the deck and flying low over the water; but his two companions, Stevens and Thomas, made good attacks, claiming direct hits with 1,000lb (450kg) bombs on an apparently hitherto undamaged *Maru*. Wakeman's aircraft was

another victim of the Zeros, and his wing man, Robinson, only survived by good flying and good fortune, eventually to reach Henderson and count eighty-six holes in his Dauntless.

In the strike the VB-10 planes piloted by Lt Cdr J. A. Thomas, with Lieutenant V. W. Welch, had covering fighters slash into them; these were responsible for downing both Wakeham and Welch's aircraft, while Carroum was hit by flak and crash-landed on the water – he survived, but his rear-seat man, ARM 3/c R. C. Hynson, later died while trying to get back to Guadalcanal. The Dauntlesses of Gibson and Robinson were shot full of holes but made it back to Henderson Field. Then the three SBDs of Lieutenant Stockton B. Strong, Ensigns H. R. Burnett and J. H. Finrow attacked; again, many hits and near-misses were claimed. They were followed down by Lt Cdr J. R. Lee with five more Dauntlesses who claimed to have scored four near-misses, while the other two bombs 'hung up'.

The final sortie came from three Dauntlesses, three Marine aircraft led by Lieutenant (jg) C. G. Estes of VS-10, who left Henderson Field a quarter of an hour behind Thomas. They claimed at least one direct hit after an attack out of the darkening sky.

They indeed left the convoy in a dire way. In the first attack the *Canberra Maru* and *Nagara Maru* were both hit and sunk, while the *Sado Maru* was damaged and had to be sent back. In the second attack the *Brisbane Maru* was set on fire and later went down, and in the third attack the *Arizona Maru* and *Shinanogawa Maru* were both sunk. Finally, in the last attack the *Nako Maru* was set on fire and also later sank. While some destroyers were sent back to pick up the survivors from the water, Tanaka pressed on with the remaining four transports and these beached themselves off Tassafaronga. The *Kinugawa Maru*, *Yamatsuki Maru*, *Hirokawa Maru* and *Yamaura Maru* were then subjected to repeated attacks and were all subsequently destroyed on the 15th.

The Dauntless casualties received in decimating this convoy were not light; one unit, VB-10 under Lieutenant Commander John Thomas, lost three out of seven aircraft to defending fighter attacks, and of the surviving machines, two – those of Lieutenant (jg) Ralph D. Gibson and Ensign Len Robinson were so badly damaged as to be non-operational on return to Henderson. The Marine squadron VMSB-141 was finally relieved on 19 November, having had nineteen pilots and fourteen rear-seat men killed out of the thirty-nine aircrews with which it had commenced the campaign.

The fight was not yet quite over, and Cactus Express runs still featured for the rest of the year in sufficient quantities to keep the Marine Dauntlesses busy. On 24 November the destroyer *Hayashio* was sunk by Dauntless dive bombers when engaged in a supply mission. On 7 December a force of eleven destroyers was intercepted by the SBDs, and although it was claimed that five of them were damaged in the attacks, only the destroyer *Nowaki* took minor damage. But the price paid was a heavy one, because veteran Marine pilot, Major Joseph Sailer of VMSB-132 and his gunner, were killed in this action, falling victim to flak fire. The Marines SBDs struck back again when, on the 16 December, the destroyer *Kagero* was hit.

Between the 15–25 December the Tanaka force conducted six transport escort sorties to Munda, because a new

**Summary of Japanese warships sunk or damaged by SBD attack during the battles for Guadalcanal August 1942-February 1943.**

| Name | Type | Tonnage | Attack Result |
|---|---|---|---|
| *Hiei* | battleship | 36,400 | Assisted sinking |
| *Kinugasa* | heavy cruiser | 10,651 | Sunk |
| *Maya* | heavy cruiser | 14,604 | Damaged |
| *Chokai* | heavy cruiser | 14,604 | Damaged |
| *Yura* | light cruiser | 5,570 | Sunk |
| *Jintsu* | light cruiser | 5,900 | Damaged |
| *Isuzu* | light cruiser | 5,570 | Damaged |
| *Asagiri* | destroyer | 2,389 | Sunk |
| *Murakumo* | destroyer | 2,389 | Sunk |
| *Natsugumo* | destroyer | 2,370 | Sunk |
| *Hayashio* | destroyer | 2,450 | Sunk |
| *Shirakumo* | destroyer | 2,389 | Heavy damage |
| *Yugiri* | destroyer | 2,389 | Heavy damage |
| *Ayanami* | destroyer | 2,389 | Heavy damage |
| *Akizuki* | destroyer | 3,340 | Heavy damage |
| *Naganami* | destroyer | 2,480 | Heavy damage |
| *Takanami* | destroyer | 2,480 | Heavy damage |
| *Michishio* | destroyer | 2,635 | Heavy damage |
| *Ariake* | destroyer | 2,066 | Heavy damage |
| *Maikaze* | destroyer | 2,450 | Heavy damage |
| *Shiranui* | destroyer | 2,450 | Heavy damage |
| *Isokaze* | destroyer | 2,450 | Heavy damage |
| *Amagiri* | destroyer | 2,389 | Light damage |
| *Kawakaze* | destroyer | 1,950 | Light damage |
| *Umikaze* | destroyer | 1,950 | Light damage |
| *Minegumo* | destroyer | 2,330 | Light damage |
| *Murasame* | destroyer | 1,950 | Light damage |
| *Kuroshio* | destroyer | 2,450 | Light damage |
| *Hamakaze* | destroyer | 2,450 | Light damage |

Japanese airfield was to be built there to replace Henderson Field. On the 26th the destroyer *Ariake* was damaged by a near-miss bomb while running supplies to Guadalcanal. Splinters penetrated her thin hull and upperworks, and mowed down those crew members in exposed positions, killing twenty-eight with another forty wounded.

On the night of the 1–2 January the Cactus Express began evacuations of the remaining Japanese troops on Guadalcanal. 'Tenacious' Tanaka had ten destroyers for this mission, but during the first attacks, the SBDs damaged the destroyer *Suzukaze* with a near-miss 1,000lb bomb which disabled one of her engines, reducing her speed to a mere ten knots, so she had to be sent back to Shortlands under the escort of one of her companions. The remainder completed their mission.

On the 14–15 January, nine Japanese

destroyers undertook yet another troop-carrying mission to Guadalcanal, Operation KE, to land 600 troops who were to form a rear-guard while the existing troops were evacuated. Although this was done successfully, the flotilla was caught by a force of fifteen Marine SBD dive bombers on their way back to Rabaul. Their attack slightly damaged the *Arashi*, *Urakaze*, *Tanikaze* and *Hamakaze*, all of which, however, returned safely to Shortlands.

From time to time the Navy Dauntlesses still lent a hand, and one such mission was conducted by the *Saratoga's* air group on 23 January 1943, which operated from Henderson Field on a twenty-four Dauntless strike against the new Japanese airfield being constructed at Vila on Kolombangara Island.

The Marines took losses on 1 February when attacking a twenty-strong destroyer force off the coast of New Georgia. The

Dauntlesses, led by Major Ray L. Vroome of VMSB-234, lost three SBDs in this attack. Outstanding courage was displayed by one rear-seat man, Sergeant Gilbert H. Henze: when his pilot, Lieutenant Abram H. Moss, was wounded by flak, Henze took over the rear-seat control, instructed by Major Vroome who flew alongside. Unfortunately the SBD ran out of fuel and the radio failed, so Henze put the machine into a dive and bailed out; but the stabiliser hit him amputating one leg below the knee. He managed to staunch the flow of blood before he hit the sea and blacked out. Found by natives, he was returned to Tulagi in good condition, although tragically the deeper effects proved long lasting and he died two months after his ordeal.[143]

On 1–2 February another Cactus Express evacuation was run, with one light cruiser and twenty destroyers, from Rabaul to Cape Esperance. At 1820 on the evening of the 1st a strike by seventeen Dauntlesses hit this flotilla at sunset. Despite the advantage of surprise, only one ship was even damaged, the *Makinami*, and despite claims to the contrary, she was not hurt enough to turn back but continued with her mission. In the small hours of the morning, another of these destroyers, the *Makigumo*, struck a mine[144] off Savo Island and was badly damaged. Attempts by her companion, the *Yugumo*, to take her in tow were hampered by attacks from six Dauntlesses on a night harassment sortie, but they failed to hit her. Nonetheless with the coming of daylight her fate was obvious, and after her crew were taken off she was scuttled. Attacks on the rest of the force by Marine SBDs the following day went unrewarded.

On the 4–6 February the light cruiser *Isuzu* and twenty-two destroyers proceeded to Guadalcanal to evacuate the second group of the 17th Army. This force was attacked by a contingent from Henderson Field, which included thirty-three SBDs. Again, estimations of damage, both at the time and since, were exaggerated. The destroyers *Maikaze* and *Shiranui* were badly damaged, the former having to be towed back to the Shortlands anchorage, but the *Kuroshio* and *Hamakaze* received only light damage and were able to continue the operation. In return the Marines lost ten aircraft of all types.

Then on the 7–8 February, the final evacuation was conducted by eighteen Japanese destroyers; in the process *Isokaze* was damaged, losing ten of her crew, while the *Hamakaze* was lightly damaged in attacks through rain squalls by fifteen Marine SBDs from Captain Roscoe M. Nelson's newly arrived VMSB-144. Altogether some 10,695 Japanese soldiers were taken off Guadalcanal by Tanaka without the loss of one man, and it was not until the 9 February 1943 that the American defenders realized they had gone. Finally, the major credit for both the stubborn defence of Henderson Field and its final securing must rest firmly with the Douglas Dauntless dive bomber, whether flown by Navy or Marine aircrew

Not surprisingly, the toll taken from the Dauntless units which served on Guadalcanal was severe, for example the Marine Corps dive bomber squadrons lost no less than four of their commanding officers here.[145] They were:-

| Name | Squadron | Date |
|---|---|---|
| Captain Ruben Iden | VMSB-231 | 20-9-42 |
| Major Gordon A. Bell | VMSB-141 | 14-10-42 |
| Lieutenant Wrotham S. Ashcroft | VMSB-141 | 8-11-42 |
| Major Joseph Sailer Jr. | VMSB-132 | 7-12-42 |
| Major William J. O'Neil | VMSB-233 | 4-9-43 |

# CHAPTER THIRTEEN

# Stand-Off: Eastern Solomons

We have already described how, on 23 August 1942, the Japanese were determined to run through a strong convoy in order to land the 1,500 troops of the Kawaguchi detachment brought in from Borneo to reinforce their hard-pressed garrison on Guadalcanal and to retake Henderson Field. Termed Operation 'KA', this basic objective proved to be the kernel of another of Admiral Isoroku Yamamoto's elaborate and complex schemes to bring the remaining United States naval strength in the south-west Pacific to battle, and to destroy them with cunning and ambush.

To protect the troop convoy, which consisted of three transports and four patrol boats, no less than three forces were involved. Rear Admiral Tanaka's close escort force, and the four heavy cruisers of

Vice Admiral Mikawa which were to bombard Henderson Field at night, we have already dealt with. In addition to these there was also a detached carrier strike force built around the light carrier *Ryujo*, with the heavy cruiser *Tone* and two destroyers, under Rear Admiral Hara; this was placed some 190 miles (300km) to the north-west of Guadalcanal, from where her small air group could both contribute to the attacks on the US airfield and provide air cover for the troop convoy. Most historians have claimed that the presence of the *Ryujo* was placed thus to act as a lure or bait for the American carrier aircraft; however, while this may be the case, her role is not thus defined in the Japanese plans.[146]

To achieve the destruction of the American carriers the veteran Admiral

Nagumo was on hand with his carrier strike force, although this now only consisted of the sister carriers *Shokaku* and *Zuikaku*, escorted by six destroyers. To give them some powerful artillery protection from both air and sea attacks was the vanguard force under Rear Admiral Abe with two fast battleships, three heavy cruisers, a light cruiser and three destroyers. There was a further force, under Vice Admiral Kondo, which comprised the seaplane carrier *Chitose* (whose aircraft were to be used for scouting), five heavy cruisers, one light cruiser and six destroyers.

Nor was this the final count, because Admiral Yamamoto was also out, his flag flying in the giant new battleship *Yamato* (armed with nine 18.1in (45.6cm) guns), the escort carrier *Taiyo* and two destroyers, while further away (and destined not to be in the battle) was a so-called standby force with the light carrier *Junyo*, the battleship *Mutsu* and three more destroyers. Once more, instead of concentrating his carriers and heavy ships, Yamamoto had them strewn all over the area north and east of the Solomon Islands. In all, then, the Japanese sortied out with fifty-eight warships and a total of 177 carrier-based aircraft.

Before the fighting commenced the Americans, although out-numbered in ships – they only had thirty in all – vastly exceeded the Japanese carrier air strength, for the *Enterprise*, *Saratoga* and *Wasp* had a total of 259 aircraft embarked. However, Vice Admiral Frank Jack Fletcher threw

A quartet of SBD-3s airborne. Among the many major naval battles off the Solomons in 1942 were two more carrier duels, of which the first, the Eastern Solomons, was as confused and haphazard as had been the Coral Sea scramble. Although the SBD conducted itself well, the result was more of a victory for the Japanese than the Americans. (San Diego Aerospace Museum)

The twin flexible .30 calibre machine guns mounted on a scarf ring in a SBD-3 at El Segundo, 8 July 1942. The original rear-firing gun had proven itself totally inadequate and many Dauntlesses had to be retro-fitted with the new twin mounting in the field.(McDonnell Douglas)

away this priceless advantage right at the beginning when he sent the *Wasp* with her eighty-three aircraft away to the south to refuel on 23 August. On the first day Fletcher still believed the bulk of the enemy warships continued to be at Truk and that he had ample time. He was very wrong, and this decision reduced the American carrier aircraft to 176 machines, almost identical to the Japanese total. The Americans on the field of battle were thus left Task Force 11, built around *Saratoga*, with two heavy cruisers and five destroyers; and Task Force 16, built around the *Enterprise*, with the one battleship, one heavy cruiser, one light cruiser and six destroyers. The Douglas Dauntless strength on the two American carriers was with VB-5 and VS-5, and VB-3 and VS-3.

At dawn on 23 August the two American carriers were steering NNE some 150 miles (240km) east of Malaita Island, heading up the eastern side of the Solomons chain of islands on a seeming collision course with Yamamoto, and as usual, both sides were flying dawn searches to locate the other. Unbeknown to the Americans, the Japanese had prepared a submarine line across this obvious approach path, while a second group patrolled to the west and a third formed another trip wire to the east of Santa Cruz Island. Not surprisingly then, with so many submarines lurking in the vicinity, the first contacts that the SBDs had in this battle

were with these, and not the Japanese carriers. The first sighting was at 0725 by Lieutenant Turner F. Caldwell and Ensign Harold L. Buell of VS-5, who picked up the small conning tower and upper hull of a submarine running southwards on the surface. They nudged over to make a low-level bombing run, but lookouts

aboard the boat spotted the Dauntless at the same time and she crash-dived. Calwell's single 500lb (227kg) bomb appeared to hit abeam the conning tower on the starboard side, while Buell was unsighted and held his release hoping for a better shot.[147]

In fact this weapon, useful enough for most purposes, was not of much practical good when used against a submarine. Their pressurized hulls were tough, and a direct hit with this size bomb would be required to do any sort of permanent damage to them.[148] While a 1,000lb (450kg) bomb would have been much more effective, scouts rarely carried them on reconnaissance missions where range was important. For purely anti-submarine patrols (ASP) around the Task Forces the Dauntless could carry a single 325lb (147kg) – or later, a 650lb (295kg) – depth-charge which, being designed for the job, was much more potent; but the priority at this time was to find the Japanese carriers before they found you. Nonetheless, in stumbling into such a wasps' nest as Fletcher's ships had done, sighting continued at an abnormally high rate throughout the battle. Good attacks were made, and it was claimed that the SBDs had definitely sunk one submarine and severely damaged two or perhaps three others. As usual the truth is more prosaic,

### Dauntless Men: William I. Martin, USN

Admiral William I. Martin, USN, seen here when he was commander of the US Sixth Fleet in the Mediterranean, 1967–9. One of the many former SBD pilots who went on to achieve Flag Rank in the fighting Navy, having established the power of the dive bomber and the Navy's Air Arm during the dark days of 1942. As a young Dauntless pilot Bill Martin had been blooded at the Battle of Midway. Serving with VS-10 aboard the famous USS *Enterprise* (CV–), Bill fought in the Guadalcanal campaign and the associated sea battles of Santa Cruz and the Eastern Solomons, before taking over as CO of that unit from Commander James R. Lee in February 1943. (Admiral William I. Martin)

Matching the steadily increasing flow of Dauntless dive bombers to equip the fleet in readiness to taking the offensive in the Pacific, a vastly expanded training programme for dive bomber pilots and gunners was put into place. Here, an SBD on the deck of a training carrier gets the take-off signal and revs up down the deck. (McDonnell Douglas, Long Beach)

and this they proceeded to do vigorously until she made a controlled dive and escaped.

A second air search was launched at 1445 that same afternoon, to cover the arc 290 to 354 degrees up The Slot and to the west and north of Malaita Island. Two Dauntlesses of this VS-5 patrol, those of Ensigns C. G. Estes and Elmer Maul, flushed out the *I-121* and attacked her. Like the previous two sightings the surfaced submarine was running south at five or six knots when she was seen at 1530. Yet again, although both pilots attacked immediately, the *I-121* was alert and crash-dived. As the waters closed over her, both aircraft's 500lb bombs detonated in the swirl of her departure, and they obviously were close enough astern to rupture at least one tank because about ninety seconds later oil was visible on the surface.[149] The sea was a flat calm and the oil slick gradually spread, observed by both pilots as they orbited the scene. They could only tarry for a certain time before moving on, but on the basis of that slick they claimed *I-121* as 'probably sunk'. However, she survived intact.

The enemy troop convoy was located at 1000 that day, heading down The Slot, and at 1445 the *Saratoga* launched a force led by Commander Donald Felt; this included thirty-one Dauntlesses to check out the PBY sighting report, which had included a cryptic reference to 'a small carrier' (presumably the *Ryujo*).

The strike duly reached the area of the reported sighting, finding low cloud and bad weather but seeing nothing at all of either the troop convoy or the carrier. After casting about for a while at the extreme limit of their range, and with fuel failing, the whole force landed at Henderson Field to overnight there, and did not land back aboard the *Saratoga* until 1130 on the 24th. Tanaka, realizing he had been seen, had reversed course and this manoeuvre, plus the bad conditions, thwarted Felt.

At 0600 next day, Tanaka and the other Japanese forces turned around again and headed back south; at 0905 they were once more picked up by a PBY from Ndeni Island, and again the *Ryujo* was reported, some 265 miles (426km) from Fletcher's force. At 1128 another report placed her another 35 miles (56km) closer down. At 0630 Fletcher sent out a twenty-three plane search, which included fifteen SBDs, to cover a 200-mile (320km) arc either side

and in fact no Japanese submarine was sunk by the Dauntlesses during this battle, and only one, the *I-121* of the 7th Flotilla, was damaged.

Another attack was carried out by another Dauntless team from VS-5, that of Lieutenant Stockton B. Strong, CO, and Ensign John F. Richley. They were also on the 0645 search patrol covering the 345- to 045-degree arc north-east of Malaita when, at 0805, they also spotted a surfaced submarine. Their sighting was about 80 miles (125km) away from that of

Caldwell's but clearly part of a patrol line. Both SBDs swung into a low-level approach from 1,000ft (300m) altitude, but again, vigilant lookouts saw them coming and the target immediately crash-dived. This time the two 500lb (227kg) bombs were close enough to their submerged target to shake her up severely, and in a flurry of foam and spray she bucked to the surface once more as the two Dauntlesses circled. There was little they could do about it as they had no more big bombs, but they could machine gun her, of 200 degrees, at 250 miles (400km) range from his flagship. Meanwhile the American task force had itself been located by the Japanese, one of the *Chitose's* ubiquitous floatplane scouts sighting them at 1100, and Nagumo knew what he was up against. The Americans thus wasted a whole morning's warning, giving the Japanese ample time to prepare. A second search was readied and took departure at 1315, with another sixteen SBDs, eight of VB-6s Dauntlesses and seven from VS-5, to cover a sector form 290 degrees to due east, as 250 miles (400km) range.

Fletcher still stayed his hand, preferring to wait, putting his faith in his own scouts and waiting for *Saratoga's* strays to be refuelled and armed so that he could launch a full strike. Even a spate of further sightings failed to alter his careful approach, and it was not until 1435 that he despatched the *Saratoga* strike force, with Commander Felt again in command of a mixed group; this included thirteen SBDs from VB-3 under Lieutenant Commander DeWitt W. Shumway, and fifteen from VS-3 under Lieutenant Commander Louis J. Kirn.

Soon after they took their departure at 1440, another enemy carrier sighting was made, putting her 60 miles (100km) north of the first one, by two Avenger TBMs piloted by Lieutenant Commander C. M. Jett and Ensign R. J. Bye. They made a high-level bombing run ten minutes later, but all bombs missed astern of the carrier and failed to score any hits. Interestingly, because this attack was delivered from a high altitude, the Japanese reported it as an attack by B-17s[150] proving that naval aircraft recognition was as poor as the aviators' ship recognition on both sides! Twenty minutes later this same group was located by the SBD team of Lieutenant Strong in S-1 and Ensign John Richey in S-2; they sighted the heavy cruiser *Tone* and the two destroyers at 15 miles (24km) range (reporting them as two cruisers and a destroyer), and shortly after spotted the *Ryujo* too. Accordingly Strong sent off an uncoded report, but then returned to the *Enterprise* to report in person as they received no acknowledgment. At just about the same time, 1510, yet a third team located the *Ryujo*: this was the Dauntless S-18, piloted by Ensign J. H. Jorgenson, and a TBM piloted by Ensign Bingaman. They too sent off unacknowledged sighting reports, and tried to evade the carrier's combat air patrol (CAP) to deliver their own attack, but were spotted and chased

away. They finally returned to the *Enterprise* but had to ditch through lack of fuel; they survived, however.

The bigger picture was slowly emerging, and yet another part of the mosaic fell into place when, also at 1510, the B-13 of VB-3 piloted by Lieutenant J. T. Lowe, and B-5 flown by Ensign Robert D. Gibson, located Admiral Abe's vanguard force.

Felt's striking force had received Jorgenson's contact signal and had altered their direction to match the new co-ordinates, but on arrival at that position had found that she had moved on and was not in sight. Felt had therefore reverted to his original heading again, but it was not until 1606 that they finally homed in on the little *Ryujo*, circling her at 14,000ft (4,300m).

Unknown to Felt as he began to deploy his aircraft for the attack on the little *Ryujo*, much more important targets were in the offing, for while he was casting around for her, not aided in his quest by her convoluted movements, the *Shokaku* and *Zuikaku* had been spotted and reported. This important sighting had been made at

Learning to be a dive bomber pilot, even in such a docile and handy machine like the SBD, could sometimes prove a harrowing experience for new pilots and carrier landings were particularly demanding. Many of the preserved SBDs in museums today were those which crashed into Lake Michigan while attempting this manoeuvre for the first time. Here is shown one very spectacular, and individual, attempt at landing. (McDonnell Douglas, Long Beach)

Japanese Navy view of the SBD! This machine is shown astern of its wingman during a routine training flight in 1942. (McDonnell Douglas, Long Beach)

The launch, the moment of truth as an SBD roars off the flight deck of a carrier on another mission. This 1942 photo shows the national markings being carried on the port wing only of the dive bomber, with the enhanced marking on the fuselage. (McDonnell Douglas, Long Beach)

1545 by VB-6's Lieutenant (jg) S. R. Davis flying B-1, and Ensign R. C. Shaw in B-6. They had flown the 350–260-degree sector of the search and were at an altitude of 1,500ft (450m) when they sighted two of the destroyers screening ahead of the carriers. As they pressed on and flew in over the screen, the two SBDs were rewarded with the sight of the huge yellow wooden deck of the Shokaku, and a little later, some 5 miles (8km) astern of her, the Zuikaku, the most sought-after targets for the whole American Navy!

The two big Japanese carriers had already launched their main strikes against Fletcher's ships, then some 200 miles (320km) distant, but the Shokaku, the closest vessel, was steaming hard at twenty-eight knots, and had a deck-load of aircraft preparing for a second strike, with

eight aircraft amidships and twelve parked on her after-deck.[151] Nor, apparently, had the two Dauntlesses been sighted themselves, and so they were afforded the luxury of a fifteen-minute period of immunity in which they were able to climb unhindered and up-sun to a height of 14,000ft (4,300m). They broadcast their excited sighting reports as they climbed. Both Davis and Shaw then made their approach dives against the Shokaku, which had now sighted them and was putting up a belated AA barrage while turning hard to starboard, totally surprised. This was insufficient to deter either pilot and both made their attacks from 7,000ft (2,100m) releasing their 500lb (227kg) bombs at 2,000ft (600m). Both bombs near-missed astern off the starboard side aft, one detonating close enough for splinters to kill six

of her crew, but her flight deck and her aircraft remained pristine. Both SBDs survived and made further sighting reports, then headed back home. It was 1600.

One mile (1.6km) away to the southwest and a quarter of an hour later, at 1615, Commander Felt, still in ignorance of the presence of the main Japanese carrier force and with his own radio unable to receive messages, was circling the Ryujo group at 14,000ft (4,300m) and allocating targets to his striking force. He split his force, half being assigned the carrier and half the heavy cruiser.

The carrier strike was led by VB-3's Lieutenant Commander Louis J. Kirn with fifteen aircraft, and he took his flight to the north-west. Two more flights, each of three SBDs from VB-3, led by Lieutenant DeWitt W. Shumway, meanwhile climbed to 16,000ft (4,900m) and positioned themselves off the carrier's opposite quarter, thus splitting the defensive fire, while five more Avenger torpedo planes went in at sea level. The remaining seven Dauntlesses, along with five more TBMs, made the *Tone* their objective. Both dive bomber formations began tipping over at 1620, as the *Ryujo* turned her bows into the wind in readiness for a far-too-late launching of her remaining seven Zero fighters. The first ten aircraft released but none hit, only scoring a few near-misses – the little flat-top seemed to bear a charmed life. As the other eleven SBDs pulled out of their dives with the same results, Felt cancelled his original instruction and re-directed the *Tone* strike at the *Ryujo*.

This group comprised seven Dauntlesses from VB-3 led by Lieutenant Harold S. Bottomley, and they had already commenced their approach dives against the heavy cruiser when they got their new instructions; but most were able to abort and re-form. They followed Felt himself down, as the CAG, frustrated at the lack of accuracy of his first waves, had made a single-handed assault. Despite accurate flak fire which hit his aircraft (removing the mast of his already useless radio), and the attentions of defending fighters, Felt's effrontery was rewarded with a direct hit with his 500lb (227Kg) bomb, amidships on the flight deck. He was rewarded with the sight of thick black smoke gushing from the stricken carrier, which was continuing to circle at high speed.

Meanwhile the majority of Bottomley's team had climbed back to 15,000ft (4,600m) and made a classic diverging attack on the carrier, and as befitted veterans of Midway – they made few errors, claiming no less than three hits and four close misses.[152] The *Tone* was reputedly attacked by some dive bombers, but even if this was so, they scored no hits.

The SBDs which attacked last faced the finally alerted fighter defences in full cry and they were roughly handled, but although many were hit – Ensign W. A. Behr, for example, survived the attentions of no less than five Zeros which peppered his aircraft but failed to down him – all got back safely to the Task Force. Lieutenant F. J. Schroeder claimed to have shot down a Japanese Nakajima Kate attack bomber around this time, presumably one of the *Ryujo's* returning Guadalcanal strike.

Once again the Dauntless was able to add to its claim to be a fighter as well as a dive bomber, because no less than three *more* Japanese aircraft were claimed by SBDs that day, all Aichi D3A Vals: this was because, on returning to their home carriers, they found the Japanese air attack in full swing. Unable themselves to land while the attack was in progress, some Dauntlesses took a hand in the defence. Both Lieutenants R. K. Campbell and William E. Henry claimed kills, and they were joined by Lieutenant H. R. Burnett, returning to *Saratoga* from an inner air patrol, who nailed another. However, neither they, the CAP, nor the ship's gunfire were able to save the *Enterprise* from receiving heavy damage from the Japanese dive bombers, and she took three direct hits. She was forced to retire and Fletcher, with only *Saratoga* operational against the two big Japanese carriers, retreated.

When the Japanese air attack had been plotted boring in on the American ships, the carriers hastily scrambled away all available aircraft. From the *Saratoga*, two SBDs, piloted by Lieutenant (jg) R. M. Elder and Ensign R. T. Gordon, along with eight Avenger torpedo bombers, were sent away at 1700, with orders to strike at Abe's Vanguard force, now recognized as containing at least one battleship and five cruisers. The *Enterprise* got away the eleven Dauntlesses, all armed with 1,000lb (450kg) bombs and led by Lieutenant Turner Caldwell, along with seven Avengers, and this force, Flight 300, was off decks by around 1705.

After orbiting the Task Force for a while and seeing their home carrier hit and set on fire, Flight 300 received their mission orders to find and strike at the enemy carrier on its last reported bearing. This of course was the *Ryujo*, which had already been dealt with, although they were not to know that.

The Flight flew north-west following the CAG, Max Leslie's Avenger. Gradually those two hours began to be eaten up with still neither sight nor sign of any enemy ships, let alone carriers. The sun set and the fuel situation was giving grave cause for concern, especially to the shorter-ranged SBDs. They reached the expected point of contact, found only calm empty sea, and pushed on for a further 50 miles (80km), with the same negative result.

The Avenger flight had already jettisoned its torpedoes and headed back to the Task Force, and so, finally, Caldwell was left with no other option but to do likewise.

It was already too late to return to the *Enterprise*, so eleven 1,000lb bombs were dropped into the wide Pacific, engine settings were carefully retuned to lean fuel mix to give every last precious mile of endurance, and course was set for Henderson Field. It was touch and go, but by the aid of a bright moon and a good deal of beginners' luck, all eleven Dauntlesses bumped down safely on Guadalcanal and began their nomadic existence alongside their Marine Corps companions.

The *Saratoga* pair had better fortune, although they also failed to find their allocated targets. At 1740, after a forty minutes' flight, what the two SBDs *did* come across was Vice Admiral Kondo's support force, main body, with the *Chitose*, the five big cruisers screened by the light cruiser *Yura* and her six destroyers. Here was a target of sorts, and climbing to 12,500ft (3,800m), they tipped over into their diving attacks. Somehow they identified the 11,023-ton seaplane carrier, armed with two twin 5in (12.7cm) guns and four catapults, as the 67,123-ton battleship *Musashi*!

The two Dauntlesses faced a heavy flak barrage from the accompanying heavy cruisers as they made their dives out of the setting sun, but this failed to deter them from making good runs, releasing at around 2,000ft (600m). One shell ripped through the flaps of Gordon's aircraft, but both SBDs got away and managed to land back aboard the *Saratoga* that evening.

Both bombs were near-misses close alongside the *Chitose's* port side, the concussion of which stove in her thin plating and caused some flooding in her port engine room, which was put out of action. Bomb splinters scythed inboard and set on fire some of her seaplanes. For a time she looked in big trouble, taking on a 30-degree list, but eventually her crew got the fires under control and the pumps working, and at sixteen knots she made her way slowly back to Truk for temporary repairs.[153]

This attack marked the finale of the battle, named at the time the Battle of Stewart Islands. The sacrifice of the *Ryujo* had been in vain. On the American side only two Dauntlesses had been lost, but on the other hand their bombing accuracy had taken a knock, with only four hits at the most from thirty-six bombs dropped. However, they were to more than make amends in the months that followed.

## CHAPTER FOURTEEN

# Stalemate: Santa Cruz

With the failure of Lieutenant General Harukichi Hyakutake's Eighteenth Army's all-out land effort to wrest back control of Henderson Field from the US Marines between the 23 and 25 October, despite the pulverizing Japanese battleship and cruiser bombardments of the 14 October, Admiral Yamamoto was finally forced to seek a decision at sea once more. On the American side, Vice-Admiral William F. Halsey had now been appointed as ComSoPac and he was determined not to yield an inch of Solomon Islands' territory: the stage was therefore set for the last great carrier battle of 1942.

On 11 October the Japanese fleet had begun moving out of Truk anchorage and heading south, once more divided into complex forces, with the main change that the battleships were sent ahead of the carriers in the hope of luring all American air attacks and leaving the carriers, in the rear, free to strike at their opposite numbers. Thus Admiral Koso Abe led the way with his vanguard force (the battleships *Hiei* and *Kirishima*, three heavy and one light cruisers and eight destroyers) which, after marking and awaiting in vain for a confirmation signal from the troops ashore that they had succeeded, by 25 October 1942 were some 60 miles (100km) south of Admiral Nagumo's carrier strike force (the carriers *Shokaku*, *Zuikaku* and *Zuiho*, one heavy cruiser and eight destroyers).

These carriers were on a course set to pass east of Malaita Island, in the same waters as the previous battle had been fought. To the west of Nagumo was the advance force of Vice Admiral Kondo, with four heavy and one light cruisers and six destroyers, and beyond them the air group force of Rear-Admiral Kakuji Kakuta, with the light carrier *Junyo* and two destroyers. (The light carrier *Hiyo*, which had been part of this force, had to return to Truk with another two destroyers when she had developed engine problems on 22 October.) For additional heavy metal there was Vice Admiral Kurita's close support force, the battleships *Haruna* and *Kongo*, with six destroyers whose mission was to subdue the Henderson-based aircraft. In total, then, the Japanese sortied with four battleships, two large and two light carriers, eight heavy and two light cruisers and thirty destroyers, while twelve submarines again set up advance patrol lines.

Yet again the Americans were fully forewarned, and adopted the same battle tactic as before, with two carrier task groups: Task Force 16 was led by Rear Admiral Thomas C. Kinkaid, with the carrier *Enterprise*, the battleship *South Dakota*, one heavy and one light cruiser, with eight destroyers. They had sailed from Pearl Harbor on the 16 October and had rendezvoused with the other units below the New Hebrides on 23 October. These were Task Force 17, built around the carrier *Hornet* under Rear Admiral George D. Murray, with two heavy cruisers, two light cruisers and six destroyers. A third group, Task Force 64 led by Rear Admiral Willis A. Lee, had the battleship *Washington*, one heavy and two light cruisers and six destroyers. This gave a total of two battleships, two carriers, four

An SBD-4 airborne. Arriving in time to see combat action in the savage fighting off the Solomon Islands, the -4 only differed from the -3 in small ways, such as a 24-volt electrical system rather than the earlier 12-volt to cope with the increasing amount of equipment being crammed into the original design. (McDonnell Douglas, Long Beach)

heavy and five light cruisers and twenty destroyers. In the air, the American carriers' air groups had a total of seventy-two SBDs. Thus in total air strength, as well as in ship strength, the Japanese at 212 far outnumbered the Americans at 159.

The Japanese vanguard force was located by a US Navy Catalina PBY in the afternoon of 23 October, and Yamamoto – who once more directed this battle at long range from aboard his flagship the battle-ship *Yamato* anchored at Truk – ordered his carrier forces to reverse course to the north on the 25th, while his heavy ships continued south-east, therefore widening the gap between them. Thus it was not until the 25th that these same American scout aircraft also located the three Japanese aircraft carriers bringing up the rear. Shore-based air attacks accomplished nothing, while the *Junyo* sent her air striking force against Guadalcanal, bombing shore positions at Lunga Point. Neither of the two opposing *carrier*-based scouting forces had managed to locate the other side's ships.

Even before the battle was joined, the SBDs were taking heavy losses: during the afternoon of the 25th the *Enterprise* had sent out twelve dive bombers to scour an arc 200 miles (320km) deep from west to north, and these were followed an hour later by a full attack strike force including a further twelve Dauntlesses. They flew north to the limit of their range, but found the darkening seas empty. By the time these aircraft had returned to the *Enterprise* the sun had set, and they were obliged to make a night landing – the first that many of the more junior pilots had ever undertaken. Not surprisingly seven aircraft ditched, including three of the SBDs which had run out of fuel; their aircrews were rescued, however.

Early on 26 October, at 0650, a scouting seaplane from the heavy cruiser *Tone* finally sighted the American carriers and they launched their own aircraft in two waves, followed by a third one of twenty-nine aircraft from the *Junyo*, which tried to co-ordinate. Almost at the same time, 0300, another PBY located the Abe force and also the Nagumo force. The latter had turned back south at 1800, but at 0400 the next day had reversed course yet again; however, the sighting report did not reach Kinkaid until 0512. At 0610 he had launched sixteen SBDs carrying 500lb bombs on a scout-and-attack sortie, to cover a 200-mile (320km) arc between 235

While the action in the south Pacific was reaching a crescendo for the SBD, Douglas itself was now swinging into full-scale production to meet the unexpected continuing demand for the Dauntless. When the expected replacement, the Curtiss SB2-C Helldiver, failed to materialize, yet further orders were placed for the good old reliable 'Slow But Deadly'. Here the production line is seen working all night at El Segundo. (McDonnell Douglas, Long Beach)

and 360 degrees true to his north. Another six Dauntlesses took off to carry out anti-submarine patrols around the force. At this time the Americans were steering north-west, and were closing the 220-mile (354km) gap between them and the oncoming enemy.

Two of the *Enterprise*'s sixteen-plane scouting force, Lieutenant V. W. Welch and Lieutenant (jg) B. A. McGraw of VB-10, found the vanguard force at 0617 and made a sighting report, which they repeated a quarter of an hour later; but no Japanese carriers were mentioned. Not until 0650 did two more of the scouting groups SBDs – piloted by Lieutenant Commander James R. Lee, CO of VS-10, and Ensign William E. Johnson – sight

Nagumo's ships. Lee's rear-seat man, Chief I. A. Sanders, sent a sighting report of two carriers and accompanying vessels *three* times before the SBDs were chased away by the Zero CAP, and claimed to have shot down three of them before evading the CAP in thick cloud.

These sighting reports were picked up by a further two Dauntless crews, and they surprised the enemy to make an unopposed, target-of-opportunity dive bombing attack at 0720. This pair of SBDs – piloted by Lieutenant Stockton Birney Strong and Ensign Charles Irvine, with rear-seat men Clarence H. Garlow and Eligie Pearl Williams – left their own sector 100 miles (160km) away on their own initiative, and at 14,000ft (4,300m) unerringly zeroed in

*(Right)* The El Segundo production line busy assembling SBD-4s on 4 February 1943. Visible in the bay to the right are central sections under construction. (McDonnell Douglas)

*(Below)* VB-5 dive bombers from the new *Yorktown* approach much-bombed Wake Island in October 1943. Enemy positions burn as two more fully laden SBDs close in to add their quota to the enemy's discomfiture. The national markings now have the bars added to the roundels to further emphasize the aircraft's identity to trigger-happy ships' gunners. (McDonnell Douglas, Long Beach)

on the Japanese carriers and managed to get up-sun without being observed.

In the words of Irvine they then[154] ' . . . split our wing flaps . . . and pushed over into 80-degree dives, all the time expecting the fleet to start pitching up lead . . .'. To their continued surprise, however, nothing of the sort happened as they continued to bore in until they reached release height: at 1,500ft (450m), both bombs left the crutches as the Dauntlesses hit the deck to escape from the Zeros which were now totally aroused, but far too late to influence events.[155] The rear gunners each claimed to have destroyed a Zero apiece in the stern chase, and took hits in return over a 45-mile (70km) chase before the fighters gave up. Both dive bombers eventually made it back to *Enterprise,* as did all the other search teams.

Their daring had its just reward, for these two SBDs obtained two perfect direct hits aft on the *Zuiho,* one of which decimated her after anti-aircraft positions. The other went right through her flight deck after, and penetrated down into her hangar deck, leaving a 50ft (15m) hole which meant she could then no longer land her aircraft, although she remained manoeuvrable herself. She was thus able to launch all of her striking force, before returning to Truk for temporary repairs. Another of these enterprising scout teams dive bombed the heavy cruiser *Tone* at 0626, but with no hits and no effect on her. The two American carriers then despatched their own striking forces in three groups, totalling seventy-three aircraft. These were not very well co-ordinated and went off in three small waves, the *Hornet* launching twenty-nine aircraft at 0730, the *Enterprise* nineteen at 0800 and the *Hornet* twenty-five more at 0810.

The Japanese first strike evaded the American CAP completely, and at 0910 commenced their dives. The Vals had to face a very heavy barrage, but in ten minutes they had overwhelmed the *Hornet*'s defences, obtaining five bomb and two torpedo hits, while two further aircraft crash-dived into the ship where their payloads detonated, adding to the carnage. With 111 dead and many wounded, she was immobilized. Large fires were finally brought under control and she was taken in tow by the heavy cruiser *Northampton.*

The second main Japanese air strike arrived just after 1000 and this force located the *Enterprise,* which had earlier hidden in a rain squall. A large number of

A SBD-4 with the Hamilton-Standard hydramatic propeller, and with a 1,000lb G.P. bomb in place on the swinging crutch and the yagi radar antenna beneath the wing. (McDonnell Douglas, Long Beach)

aircraft concentrated on her and hit her twice, while also scoring a very near miss with bombs, killing forty-four of her crew and wounding seventy-five more; but no torpedoes hit her. Despite her damage she continued to operate her aircraft. Finally, at 1121, the *Junyo* aircraft arrived and also attacked the *Enterprise* group, but initially managed only one hit and one near-miss on the carrier.

In reply, the *Hornet*'s first strike found the burning *Zuiho* and the *Shokaku* at 0918. Fifteen SBDs from VB-8 and VS-8, led by Lieutenant Commander Gus Widhelm, with six TBF Avengers and eight F4F Wildcat fighters as escorts, arrived over the enemy ships. They were hotly engaged by the CAP as they approached the target at 12,000ft (3,600m), and the Zeros shot down four of the SBDs, including Widheim's machine. He ditched in the water, but both he and his rear-seat man, ARM 1/c George Stokely, survived and were rescued by a seaplane some days later. Another Dauntless staggered back to the *Enterprise* with a wounded pilot, but the other two aircraft were lost with no survivors.

As they tipped over into their attack dives, command of the dive bombers devolved onto Lieutenant James Vose. These eleven SBDs made a well-nigh perfect attack, scoring at least four, and probably six direct hits with their 1,000lb (450kg) bombs on the *Shokaku,* two forward and four in the area of the after lift, confirmed by Japanese photographs taken of the fire fighting. These almost destroyed the ship and she was forced to withdraw from the battle. Many of her aircraft found sanctuary on the *Zuiho.*

Meanwhile the second wave had taken off from the *Enterprise;* this included three SBDs from VB-10 but piloted by VS-10's Lieutenant G. G. Estes, Ensign Henry N. Ervin and Ensign John F. Richey, and they were armed with 1,000lb bombs. These, along with the second *Hornet* strike including seven SBDs, missed the carriers, and as the Japanese had planned, dashed themselves against the heavy flak of the Abe force's big ships. Ervin, Estes and Richey made their dives against the *Kirishima* and claimed to have scored two direct hits, one on 'B' turret and one starboard amidships, plus a near-miss off her

**SBD Versus Japanese Aircraft Carriers 1942**

| Carrier | Tonnage | Date | SBD Hits | Result |
|---|---|---|---|---|
| Akagi | 40,650 | 4-6-42 | 4 | Sunk |
| Kaga | 41,869 | 4-6-42 | 4 | Sunk |
| Soryu | 18,500 | 4-6-42 | 3 | Sunk |
| Hiryu | 19,930 | 4-6-42 | 4 | Sunk |
| Shoho | 13,730 | 7-5-42 | 11 | Sunk |
| Ryujo | 12,531 | 24-8-42 | 4 | Sunk |
| Zuiho | 13,730 | 25-10-42 | 2 | Damaged |
| Shokaku | 29,330 | 25-10-42 | 4/6(?) | Damaged |

starboard bow. However, Japanese records show that only slight damage was recorded on the battleship *Kirishima* in these attacks. All three American aircraft returned to their carrier, again claiming to have shot down at least one Zero fighter on the way.

Then the *Hornet* Dauntlesses arrived overhead at 0915 and began their dives. The SBDs immediately scored two bomb hits on the *Chikuma*, and these pierced her bridge from both port and starboard sides, almost demolishing it and killing most of her bridge personnel. The splinters from three more near-misses very close alongside the same ship perforated her hull and upperworks, and wiped out several AA gunnery crews. Then two more direct hits

were made, one of which plunged through her deck and detonated in one of her engine rooms. The Dauntlesses had seemingly crushed this ship, with 190 officers and men killed and 154 wounded in this devastating assault. But these Japanese heavy cruisers were tough nuts to crack, the SBDs had still failed to sink her, and she crawled back to Truk for repairs. The rest of the American assault kept up the barrage against other targets, but it lacked the concentration of effort shown to the *Chikuma*, only registering near-misses on the heavy cruiser *Tone* and the destroyer *Teruzuki*.

After the two escorting US destroyers failed to sink the wreck of the *Hornet* despite firing 430 5in (12.7cm) shells and

nine 21in (53cm) torpedoes into her, they abandoned the still-floating wreck and she was finally sent to the bottom by Japanese destroyer torpedoes. Not until 1800 did Abe and Kondo give up their hard stern chase and retire to the north, frustrated. Meanwhile the *Junyo* had joined the *Zuikaku* which had retired through the Indispensable Strait.

The Japanese had not lost any ships, but three carriers, a heavy cruiser and one destroyer were damaged, the *Shokaku* and *Chikuma* very badly, while they had lost almost one hundred aircraft, twenty-six to the AA guns of the *South Dakota* alone.[156] The Dauntlesses again performed their fighter role and claimed at least seven of the enemy. The Americans lost seventy-four aircraft of all types and had the *Hornet* and *Porter* sunk, with the *Enterprise, South Dakota, Portland, San Juan, Smith* and *Hughes* all damaged to a varying degree.

The results, like those of the Eastern Solomons, seemed to indicate a tactical Japanese victory, but one which was very hard bought – and the Japanese yet again failed to exploit it to the full. Thus four Japanese carriers had not totally defeated two American carriers, and Guadalcanal would ultimately be lost, as would the Empire.

# CHAPTER FIFTEEN

# Africa to the Arctic

The very first involvement of the American dive bomber in the European theatre of war came with the despatch of Task Force 99 under Rear Admiral R. C. Giffen, to reinforce the British Home Fleet. This force included the *Wasp*, with the thirty-six SB2Us of VS-71 and VS-72, under Lieutenant Commander John Eldridge, among her air group; she reached the British base at Scapa Flow on 3 April – but hardly before she had dropped anchor there she was detached again. In fact the Voughts were not destined to see combat action here, neither on Arctic convoys nor in the Atlantic, due to the need to carry fighter reinforcements to the island of Malta in the central Mediterranean. By April 1942 the RAF defences were at a low ebb and had been almost overwhelmed and, it was essential that more fighters were got through, and not in dribs and drabs, but in bulk.

The *Wasp* was therefore sent over to the Clyde, with her destroyer escort. In order to make room for the British fighters – which, like the Dauntlesses, did not have folding wings, of course – the SB2Us had to be flown to Fleet Air Arm airfields ashore; this was the first such transfer ever made. On 12 and 13 April the *Wasp* then embarked fifty-two Mk 5 B tropicalized Spitfires, and sailed on the 14th to conduct Operation 'Callender'. Forty-eight Spitfires were flown off and reached Malta, only to be bombed to bits within hours. Therefore the operation had to be repeated on 9 May when sixty-three more Spitfires were flown off *Wasp* in Operation 'Bowery'.

Re-embarking her Vindicators off Scapa Flow on 14 May, the *Wasp* then left British waters in a hurry for her fate in the South Pacific.

The invasion of the pro-German Vichy areas of North Africa, Morocco and Algeria – known as Operation 'Torch' – had been decided upon some months before. The American task forces were divided into groups known as the northern, central and southern groups to cover the main assaults on Morocco's Atlantic coast between Safi and Mehedia, the principal opposition being expected at Casablanca where a powerful Vichy naval squadron lay, deeply hostile to the Allied cause. This comprised the brand-new, but incomplete battleship *Jean Bart*, the cruiser *Primauguet*, and six large destroyers. Each American group contained a carrier force and the SBDs were embarked as shown in the table below.

The American Western Naval Task Force, under overall command of Rear Admiral H. K. Hewitt, were at sea and heading east across the Atlantic by the 24–25 October, while the air group sailed from Bermuda on the 26th. These forces concentrated in 40 degrees north, 51 degrees west, and then headed toward their target areas. On the 8 November the landing on French Moroccan soil commenced.

The southern group landed to the north and south of Safi, below Cape Contin, and was quickly successful. The biggest potential threat came from the Vichy air base at Marrakech inland, and here the *Santee*'s air group could easily have been overwhelmed. All four of the *Sangamon* class carriers had been very hastily converted from fast naval oiler hulls in time for this operation, and the organization and training of their equally hastily assembled air groups was very much a last-minute affair. *Santee* had been the last to commission, and her SBDs had only been granted *one day*'s training for flying and bombing practice before the ship sailed for Morocco.

The air group of the USS *Saratoga* was unique in that it was the only one to land its SBDs on the decks of British carriers in World War II. On the first occasion she was operating with HMS *Victorious* off New Caledonia prior to covering the New Georgia landings. Six SBDs landed on the British flight deck on 20 June, the first-ever Dauntlesses on a Royal Navy carrier. The second occasion was in the Indian Ocean, on 29 March 1944, and this time the *Saratoga* SBDs landed aboard HMS *Illustrious* for exercises prior to their joint attack on Japanese oil installations at Sabang and Soerabaja in the Dutch East Indies. Here Lieutenant Commander Vincent L. Hanthorn's dive bombers wiped out vital oil storage tanks with pin-point accuracy. (Imperial War Museum, London)

| Group | Carrier | Type | SBDs & Unit | Commander |
|-------|---------|------|-------------|-----------|
| Northern | *Sangamon* | CVE | 9 SBDs – VGS-26 | Lt Cdr J. S. Tracy |
| | *Chenango* | CVE | Nil | - |
| Central | *Ranger* | CV | 18 SBDs – VS-41 | Lt Cdr L. P. Carver |
| | *Suwanee* | CVE | Nil | - |
| South | *Santee* | CVE | 9 SBDs – VGS-29 | Lt Cdr J. A. Ruddy |

It was therefore hardly surprising that, with less than a dozen fully experienced pilots in her air group, accidents, forced landings, navigation errors and fuelling shortages were responsible for all the heavy losses suffered by VGS-29, four Dauntlesses. Despite this, and the lateness of the landing, Vichy resistance was minimal: one SBD-3 traded fire with a Vichy DB-7, and in the afternoon a striking force of seven Dauntlesses hit Marrakech airfield, destroying seven Vichy bombers on the ground, and damaging four more with no losses of their own. Safi itself was taken by 1430 that afternoon. The French AA fire was responsible for heavy damage to two SBDs on 9 November, one of which, piloted by Lieutenant William Staggs, managed to land back aboard the *Santee* with both crew members wounded. The skipper of VGS-29, Lieutenant Commander Joe Ruddy, proved the airman of the day, flying no less than eight total hours on day one and nine hours on day two, in his role as aerial liaison between the troops on the ground and the ships at sea. Professor Samuel Morison's account records that this earned Ruddy the nickname 'Galloping Ghost of the Moroccan Coast'.[157] He later wrote off his SBD when

The brand-new Vichy French battleship *Jean Bart* alongside in Casablanca harbour November 1942, in the aftermath of the SBD attacks on her. A bomb-hit on her forecastle, just in front of her forward quadruple 15in gun turret, has ripped open her armour-plated hull along the starboard side exposing her innards. (US Navy via National Archives, Washington DC)

attempting to land at the primitive Safi airfield.

The *Santee*'s SBD strike was flown with top cover from the *Suwannee*'s fighters because seven of her own Wildcats had run

out of fuel and crashed earlier. They also dive bombed troop assemblies, breaking up counter-attacks before they began. The Dauntless added to its fighter label yet again here, for Ensign Bruce D. Jacques claimed a Potez 63 of the Vichy GR 1/52 unit from Marrakech, which crossed his nose at point-blank range. Another five Vichy aircraft were destroyed at Chichaoua airfield in a strafing strike by one SBD and four F4Fs.

In the north, the American troops went ashore both sides of Mehdia river after again being delayed. The Vichy defence here rested on the strong position of Port Lyautey, some way up the river itself, which had a battery of 5.5in (140mm) guns. These were not taken in the first assault and proved troublesome for the next two days, French aircraft bombing and strafing the beaches at daylight and tanks moving down from Port Lyautey to contest the advance. Under the command of Lieutenant R. Y. McElroy, a mixed VGS-26 striking force of SBDs and TBFs acting as bombers, struck at the Vichy armoured column, which had lain up, in the excellent cover of a eucalyptus grove. Repeated low-level bombing severely reduced this French force and the survivors withdrew to re-group, thus giving the advancing Americans a welcome breathing space.

Subsequently the *Suwanee* Dauntlesses of Lieutenant Commander Tracy were

The brand-new Vichy French battleship *Jean Bart* alongside in Casablanca harbour in November 1942, following the American landings in Morocco during Operation 'Torch'. A tug is outboard of her, pumping out her flooded compartments, while the damage done by another SBD bomb-hit on her starboard side aft can be clearly seen. (US Navy via National Archives, Washington)

fully employed against these various targets for the next two days, and their precision attacks and quick response times to requests for attacks from the troops ashore did much to turn the tide. Finally the guns were subdued and the airfield seized on the 10 November.

Meanwhile the main Vichy resistance, based on the Kasba fortress, had been by-passed and was still holding out. A frontal assault would have proved costly to both attackers and civilians in the area, so a precision air strike was called for. The SBDs of VGS-26 replied quickly with a highly accurate attack and this finally proved instrumental in bringing about the surrender of this stubborn strongpoint. What had proven a tough fight ended with the Vichy cease-fire at midnight on the 10–11 November.

The action of the main force, of central group, was even fiercer. Here the troops went ashore to the north of Fedala, 15 miles (24km) to the north of Casablanca, although this was again delayed by heavy surf which wrecked many landing craft. At dawn the strong French coastal gun batteries began firing on the straggling groups of American troops along the beach-head, and also engaged the transports offshore and their covering warships. All this gave the Lieutenant Commander Carver's eighteen SBDs adequate employment during the course of the next three days' operations.

The first mission flown by the Dauntlesses was an attack on the submarine base at Casablanca harbour at first light. The Vichy Navy had eleven submarines on hand which could have posed a very serious threat to the massed warships and transports offshore. The *Ranger* strike went off at 0730 but was intercepted by Vichy fighters, and six F4Fs were destroyed. However, so too were seven French fighters, and this enabled the Dauntless strike to get through unharmed. Despite heavy flak from shore- and ship-based AA positions, the Dauntlesses carried out their dives at 0804, and all returned safely to the *Ranger*, claiming many good hits and close misses on the moored submarines. The *Amphitrite*, *Oreade* and *La Psyche* were all destroyed, but others escaped and made attacks on various American warships, including the *Ranger* herself, but all were unsuccessful. One, the *Sidi-Ferruch*, was both bombed and strafed on the surface in this attack, but managed to get clear of the harbour,

Atlantic anti-submarine patrols in 1944, with SBDs aboard a carrier getting ready for take-off and escorting destroyers in station astern. The Dauntless was extensively used in both the Caribbean and off the Eastern Seaboard on both ASW and blockade runner searches. These aircraft carry the Atlantic Fleet colour scheme of dark gull grey and white. (McDonnell Douglas, Long Beach)

while the *La Sibylle* was sunk off Fedala.

All this was good work and well done, but if the Vichy submarine threat was trouble enough, a far worse one developed with the sailing of a powerful surface naval squadron from Casablanca to attack the transports. This consisted of the light cruiser *Primauguet* and six large destroyers under Rear Admiral Gervais de Lafond. There was also the long-range gunfire from the battleship *Jean Bart* in harbour to contend with.

As the French warships sortied out, a hastily prepared SBD strike was sent off to attack them and a near-miss was claimed

on the *Primauguet* and two destroyers. In return, one SBD was shot down with the loss of both aircrew. As fast as they could land and be re-armed, the Dauntlesses were sent off again to bomb and strafe. Then the American heavy ships took over, the battleship *Massachusetts* with four heavy cruisers decimating the French squadron; those that were not sunk by 16in (40cm) and 8in (20cm) salvoes, were wrecked and beached, and the Dauntlesses were called upon to finish them off. In subsequent attacks the SBDs scored hits on the *Primauguet,* and hit the *Albatros* twice, devastating her hull forward of the

The restrictions imposed by the non-folding wings of the SBD are illustrated here by the tight fit and angled sitting position of this SBD of SGS-29 on the elevator of the light carrier *Santee* off Morocco, November, 1942. (McDonnell Douglas via National Museum of Naval Aviation, Pensacola)

Also on this day the French sailors got the single 15in (38cm) turret of their battleship back in action again and she duelled with the heavy cruiser *Augusta*. This brought further American response: nine SBDs of VS-41 – the famous 'High Hats' – squadron took off from the *Ranger* that afternoon, led by Lieutenant Commander Lee Embree, and at 1558 made their dives against the *Jean Bart* once more.

Embree's bomb was a near-miss alongside which hit a small water-carrier, blowing it asunder; then a second 1,000lb bomb hit a warehouse on a nearby pier, while a third struck the battleship on her bows, splitting open her side plating and bulging her decks. A fourth bomb struck the battleship aft, in almost exactly the same position as the previous day's hit, and this caused heavy damage to the ship's superstructure over a distance of some 100ft (30m) above the lower armour deck. The deck was gouged out and a fire started, the smoke infiltrating the central engine room which had to be abandoned. Flooding wrecked the electrical switchboard, and this flooding gradually spread through the after part of the ship, causing her to sink by the stern until she rested on the bottom. Some 4,500 tons of water had entered her, and although this was soon pumped out, that ended the *Jean Bart's* participation in the battle. Her casualties from all this damage were surprisingly light: twenty-two officers and men killed and the same number wounded.

With the calling of the cease-fire the combat action ceased. The cost to the Dauntlesses in this brisk but successful little action were nine machines lost – three from the *Ranger*, two from the *Sangamon* and four from the *Santee* – but only one aircrew, and most of these losses were accidental rather than through enemy action; for example, one VGS-29 Dauntless ran out of fuel and had to ditch, another suffered mechanical failure on 12 November, while several *Santee* machines crashed on take-off due to pilot inexperience.

In August the *Ranger* was loaned to the British Home Fleet, which at that time had no aircraft carrier available to it again. The carrier arrived at Scapa Flow on 11 August 1943, and the first war operation she took part in here was the abortive attempt to attack the German pocket battleship *Lützow*, which sailed from Altenfiord in northern Norway on 23 September, and

bridge and causing 300 casualties. The SBDs also attacked and damaged the *Alcyon*.

There remained the *Jean Bart* which continued to fire long-range shots with her one operational 15in (38cm) turret. The Dauntlesses gave her continual attention from the morning of the 9th onwards, but she proved a tough nut to crack. The first SBD attack on her was delivered at 0813 on the 9th with 1,000lb (450kg) bombs, but the first dive bomber made no hit and no damage was inflicted. Three minutes later a second Dauntless scored a direct hit with her 1,000lb bomb on her quarter-deck aft on the port side catapult jib. This bomb started a fire on the upper deck, and penetrated on down through the ship and out

of the side, causing severe flooding which locked her helm. A third 1,000lb bomb detonated on the quay alongside the battleship shortly afterwards, and blew a large hole in her anti-torpedo bulges on the starboard side.

Almost immediately after these aerial blows, at 0825, the *Jean Bart* took the first of six salvoes of 16in (40cm) shells from the *Massachusetts* offshore; these scored five direct hits on her. Then the Dauntless attacks resumed, with strikes at 1240 and 1247, although no further damage was done by these. With the battleship temporarily silenced, the SBDs turned their attention to land targets, and on the morning of the 10th an attack was made on French AA batteries located at Ainsaba.

reached Narvik the next day. On the 26th she again sailed, passing down the Norwegian coast and on to the Baltic port of Gdynia, to undergo a refit.

Intelligence warning of her movements had been received reporting her steering south off Vestiord, but no action was taken for a while. The RAF were unable to do anything at all, and while consideration was given to sending the *Ranger* out to a position where she could launch her air strike force, this too was dropped as she could not have got into place in time that day. Planning then began for her to attempt to intercept the enemy vessel on the 27th, but this too fell through, and an attempt by land-based aircraft also failed to find her.

The last chance for the *Ranger* to intervene was the 28th, but this also came to nothing. Thanks to dithering and internal rows between the RAF and the Royal Navy as to whether to send out an attack or not, the *Lützow* completed her journey quite inconvenienced by the Allies. Thus the Dauntlesses were denied the chance to add the scalp of a German battleship to those of the Japanese *Hiei* and the Vichy-French *Jean Bart*.

On 2 October 1943, the British Home Fleet under Admiral Sir Bruce Fraser sailed to a position some 140 miles (225km) off the Norwegian port of Bodo to carry out Operation 'Leader', air strikes against German merchant shipping and convoys concentrated there. Covered by two Allied battleships, four cruisers and destroyers, the *Ranger* reached her flying-off position at dawn on the 4th. After a slight delay due to lack of sufficient wind for the 1,000lb (450kg) equipped SBD-5s to get off the deck, the bomb loads on six of them were switched to 500lb (227kg). Eventually a 31-knot wind was obtained and the rest of the force kept their original payloads, and all twenty of VB-4's Dauntlesses, led by Lieutenant Commander G. O. Klinsmann, flew off at 0718. They were accompanied by eight F4F Wildcat fighters. Sixty per cent of the American aircrews that day were flying their first operational sortie, and they made a stunning debut, ' . . . an outstanding success . . .' according to the *British Official History*.[158]

The distance to the target area was 150 miles (240km) but the weather conditions were good, unusual for this part of the Arctic Circle. Adopting a two-plane section organized in five four-aircraft divisions, the SBDs and their escorts made the

An SBD taking off from a carrier with an anxious rear-seat man leaning out of the after end of the 'greenhouse' and the usual hordes of 'goofers' watching from both the deck side and the island. (US Navy via National Archives, Washington, DC)

best part of their outward leg at very low level, under 100ft (30m) in order to avoid radar detection from the German coast-watching stations.

On reaching the target zone off the Myken Lighthouse, the SBDs went up to 1,500ft (450m) detaching one four-plane section which made a separate approach; at 0830, the main force located a convoy of a large merchant ship and a tanker with warship escort heading north at a speed of twelve knots. The first section dived on the merchant ship, and Lieutenant Commander Klinsmann scored a near-miss on the vessel. His wingman, Lieutenant Weeks, scored a direct hit amidships, however, which was enough to finish the job.

Next, the tanker *Schleswig* was taken under attack by the second and third divisions, who scored one direct hit aft with a second very close astern of her. These hits disabled her rudder and she grounded and listed to port in sinking condition.

Meanwhile the detached division had found their own target, the transport *La Plata* to the south of Aamno, and at 0824 two SBDs made a shallow dive run on her, Lieutenant Gordon releasing from as low as 60ft (18m) and being lucky to escape the resulting explosions. Both pilots claimed good results from this attack, one bomb being a very close miss forward which det-

onated in the water below the ship's bows, while the second was a direct hit amidships, which failed to explode on contact but rebounded to detonate in the sea off the ship's port side.

The second pair of Dauntlesses withheld wasting their bombs on the already crippled ship and steered to rejoin the main group off Bodo itself. These aircraft had continued in towards the harbour itself while their colleagues had been disposing of the two convoys, and here they found an abundance of shipping. While the C.O. took his now bombless section around above them to draw the flak, these Dauntlesses made their shallow glide approaches down at a 30-degree angle at just over 200 knots, and made more good strikes.

Two SBDs attacked a large stationary freighter, and one bomb knocked a hole in her starboard side under the water. However, AA fire was intense from this target, and surrounding vessels and the glide approach left the SBDs open to it for longer than a normal diving attack. One aircraft, that of Lt (jg) C. A. Tucker, was hit at a height of only 200ft (60m) and went straight in with no survivors.

Another freighter was hit by the next pair of Dauntlesses, which made a similar approach; they claimed to have hit her forward with one bomb, which set the vessel ablaze, while the other bomb was yet another close miss amidships. The remaining four Dauntlesses attacked a variety of targets, and again paid for their shallow level approach, losing another aircraft, that of Lieutenant (jg) S. R. Davis. His aircraft was hit in the engine and he radioed that he was having to ditch; his comrades watched as he made a water landing, and they saw both the pilot and his rear-seat man, D. M. McCarley, get away in their rubber dinghy safely; but neither survived. Four further SBDs took flak hits, but not serious ones. The rest of the dive bombers formed up and returned to the *Ranger*, not having sighted a single German fighter.

The final tally was the sinking of five steamers totalling 20,753 tons, including a loaded troopship, and the damaging of six others, including a big tanker, and one ferry so badly that it had to beach. Of these, VB-4 was credited with two sunk, one shared with the TBMs and the damage to another two. A British historian wrote that 'The results were a striking vindication of their dive- and low-level bombing techniques'.[159]

This neat little attack did not mark the end of VB-4s contribution to the European

war, because on 14 October she sailed to take part in Operation 'FQ', covering a relief force carrying personnel and stores to Spitzbergen, arriving back again on the 22nd. On this date, however, the *Ranger* and her companions left Scapa and returned home to the United States where she resumed her training duties off the East Coast.

In the Atlantic convoy battle, which continued to rage throughout 1943 and on until the end of the war in Europe in May, 1945, one of the greatest boons to the Allied convoys was the aerial protection provided by the escort carriers of the US and Royal Navies. These closed the 'Air Gap' and brought about a dramatic transformation of the fight against the U-boats. Although the Dauntless played its due part in this struggle, with land-based SBD squadrons conducting many antisubmarine patrols from American and West Indian airstrips to guard the vital oil-tanker convoys coming up from Venezuela, its role aboard the CVEs was very limited; in fact only the *Santee*'s VC-29 ever utilized the Dauntless as a continuing part of her 'hunter-killer' air groups.

Although the *Santee* herself was a very

successful U-boat killer, the credit for most of her kills must be given to the TBM Avenger equipped with 'Fido' homing torpedoes, and not her nine Dauntlesses which she carried until August 1943. After 'Torch', VS-41 flew mainly anti-submarine patrols from the *Ranger* in the western Atlantic.

Shore-based units like, for example, VS-37 with the Atlantic Fleet, flew varying marks of SBD on anti-submarine warfare (ASW) patrols along the East and West Coast convoy routes, and down into the Caribbean Sea; they were armed with a single depth-charge. In these waters the range of the Dauntless was quite sufficient for them to be a reliable and economic proposition in this role. Marine SBD squadrons also served in this capacity; for instance VMSB-333 underwent antisubmarine training at Boca Chica, Florida, before moving to Ewa and then Midway in June, although it reverted to dive bombing on 30 December. VMSB-342 also trained at Boca Chica. Longest-serving of such units was the pre-war Marine VMS-3, based at St Thomas in the Virgin Islands and which served there throughout the war where it flew SBDs on search, convoy escort and patrol duties, until it was disbanded on 20 May 1944. Although it made enemy submarine sightings on three occasions, no successful attacks were made.

It is convenient here to run ahead of our chronology and recount the other occasion in which the Dauntless operated in conjunction with British carrier forces against the common enemy. This time it was far from the bleak Norwegian coast, for these attacks took place in the Indian Ocean.

The *Saratoga*'s CVAG-12, led by Lieutenant Commander Joseph C. Clifton, included the twenty-four SBD-5s of VB-12 under Lieutenant Commander Vincent S. Hathorn, USN; these had grown a little world-weary pounding away with their elderly SBDs at isolated and cut-off islands in the Marshalls Group. After taking part in Eniwetok Atoll operations, the *Saratoga* escorted by the destroyers *Cummings*, *Dunlap* and *Fanning*, was detached from the Pacific Ocean and sent to join the Royal Navy's East Indies fleet, which had at that time been reduced to a single fleet aircraft-carrier, the *Illustrious*; the smaller *Unicorn* and the escort carriers *Begum* and *Shah* were also on station, but they lacked the speed for fleet work.[160]

During the invasion of French Morocco, once the American forces became established ashore Vichy airfields became available to the SBD Dauntless units supporting the ground fighting. Here a Dauntless of VGS-29, with the typical yellow ring highlighting the nationality markings for easy identification by fresh US troops, is seen taking off from Safi in a cloud of dust. (Imperial War Museum, London)

The only carrier offensive conducted by the US Navy in European waters was the attack on German shipping off Bodo, Norway, carried out by the SBD-4s of VB-4 embarked in the *Ranger* (CV-4). The raid was a success and several targets were hit by the Dauntlesses. At this stage of the war the Royal Navy no longer had a proper monoplane dive bomber of its own: the Blackburn Skua had been phased out of service; the Fairey Barracuda was a disaster; and the Curtiss SB2C Helldiver which they had wanted under Lend-Lease, was still not available. After four years of war the Fleet Air Arm was still using antique Fairey Albacore *biplanes,* having rejected the SBD as obsolete! (US National Archives, Washington DC)

After the rendezvous the two carriers exchanged aircraft and also deck landing and signals officers so that aircraft from either ship could operate from each other. Several of VB-12's Dauntlesses landed aboard the *Illustrious* for a unique first-time touchdown. They also conducted the first mission, a search-and-strike patrol hunting for suspected German armed merchant raiders, but they were unrewarded and had to land back aboard in the middle of rain-storm. Then on Thursday 30 March, 1944, while the combined fleet was steering back to its base at Trincomalee in Ceylon (now Sri Lanka), the eighteen SBD-5s of CVAG-12 carried out a co-ordinated dive-bombing attack on a towed target.

Comparison between the Dauntless-5 (which the Royal Navy had contemptuously rejected earlier as being 'obsolete'), and the ungainly and inelegant Fairey Barracuda dive and torpedo aircraft with which the Fleet Air Arm was equipped, was far from complimentary to the British type – 'Jesus, the Limeys'll be building airplanes next!'[161] – and this sad effort was soon to be replaced by the Grumman Avenger. On arrival at China Bay at 0845 on the 31st, four of the SBDs flew ashore to the Fleet Air Arm airfield there further to cement relations and to plan for the future. Further exercises at sea followed and VB-12 successfully 'dive-bombed' the British battle-cruiser *Renown* after evading the CAP to show they were still on the ball.

As Task Group 58.5 the *Saratoga,* with the *Illustrious,* four battleships and battle-cruisers, six cruisers and fourteen destroyers – the first joint-combat mission – launched a strike on the island of Sabang on We Island off the northern tip of Sumatra. Here the Japanese had vital oil-storage tanks, with adjacent tanker terminals, a power station, a radar station, an active fighter airstrip and a base for their submarines which roamed the Indian Ocean in large numbers at this time. The aircraft started to fly off at 0650 on 19 April 1944, with VB-12's targets being the oil-storage tanks. These were hit hard and set on fire, and some Dauntlesses were switched by Clifton to hit the airfield, which had already received attention from the Barracudas. Only a single American fighter was lost in this attack.

The combined fleet's next operation was scheduled for May: this time it was to be the oil refineries at Soerabaja in Java. As a preliminary move the fleet, built around *Illustrious* and *Saratoga,* moved to Exmouth Gulf, a dreary anchorage on the western extremity of Australia. This was to catch the Japanese on the hop by approaching the target zone from the south instead of the west.

Again the plan, known as Operation 'Transom', was for VB-12 to hit the oil refinery at Wonokromo, six miles (10km) south of Soerabaja itself, while the Barracudas went for the Braat Engineering factory. Lieutenant Commander Vincent L. Hathorn's eighteen SBDs were to be covered by the British Corsairs on the way in, which were also to provide flak suppression. The Dauntless attack sequence was an approach at 12,000ft (3,600m), a roll-over onto their backs, and a dive at between 280–300 knots, with bomb release at 4,000ft (1,200m). This all went off according to plan on 17 May 1994, and the cracker plant and storage tanks were again well hit. One British Corsair pilot was later to recall that 'Hathorn, the Dauntless squadron CO, made a classic attack on the oil refinery which severely damaged the three retorts.'[162]

On both occasions the enemy air defences were taken by surprise and the Japanese lost numbers of aircraft on their airfields. Again only one aircraft was lost on the Allied side, and no SBDs.

This marked the end of *Saratoga*'s assignment and she returned home to Puget Sound, while the veterans of VB-12 were dispersed to training units to impart their knowledge to the new generation of Navy flyers. Sadly though, these did not include Dauntless air groups, for now, in the Pacific War, the Helldiver was quickly taking over the proud job that the SBD had done so well for three long years. But the Dauntless was far from finished yet.

Even though the very last of the *Independence* class light carriers, the *San Jacinto,* did not commission until December 1943, she was still carrying the SBD-6 with her VS-51 when she put to sea in 1944. The standard air group provision for these ships when first envisaged had been twelve F4Fs, nine SBDs and nine TBMs, and although a very snug fit below decks, this was achieved.

CHAPTER SIXTEEN

# Target Rabaul

At the beginning of February 1943, with the last troop evacuations completed, Guadalcanal was finally in American hands. This did not end the fighting for the Solomon Islands however, as the Japanese were busy constructing further airfields up the chain with which to block any movement northwards. The Dauntless dive bomber crews, both afloat and ashore, were therefore given no opportunity to rest on their laurels, and their steady toll of Japanese shipping continued to increase as the Americans fought their way island by island up the chain.

Only the *Saratoga* was left of the American carriers from February until August, by which time *Enterprise* had been repaired again and the first of the new *Essex* class ships had arrived; but until then their SBDs were confined to select intrusions from time to time as the situation demanded or allowed. One such occasion was on 23 January 1943, when the *Saratoga*'s twenty-four SBDs were staged from her flight deck to Henderson Field. From here the next day they struck at a new Japanese airfield being constructed at Vila, on the island of Kolombangara; then they were staged back.

The bulk of the dive-bombing therefore fell to the land-based SBDs of the US Marine Corps and Navy of the South Pacific's Solomon Islands organization (ComAirSols), and was concentrated in strike command of that organization. Initially the main brunt was born by VMSB-132, but other Marine and Navy squadrons quickly supplemented the almost daily sorties.

Following the Japanese evacuation of their remaining Guadalcanal garrison, the initiative passed to the Americans. The main Japanese base was Rabaul, at the north-eastern tip of New Britain; this had been set up as a rear staging and supply base for their planned offensive operations, but had become more and more itself a

defensive front-line position. The neutralization of this base, with its many airstrips and fine harbour, became the prime objective for Allied forces, and it was tackled in a pincer movement from both the Solomons chain and northern New Guinea. A succession of blows drove the Japanese further and further back upon Rabaul, and the base was subjected to almost non-stop bombing which further reduced its effectiveness and its usefulness to them.

The New Georgia islands saw the first of these offensives, with Munda airfield as the principal objective, American Marines

going ashore on 21 June 1943 at Segi Point. The Marines then marched north to take Viru harbour and were aided in this by a strike from VMSB-132 on the 15th which Major Roy J. Batteron Jr said '. . . couldn't have been more perfect if planned'.

On 30 June 1943, an Allied landing was made on Rendova Island, and another the next day at Onaiavisi, while on the 5th the main landing went in at Rice anchorage on the southern side of Kula Gulf, New Georgia Island in the Solomons chain, with the vitally important airfield of Munda being captured four days later. This was followed by the occupation of Vella Lavella

With Guadalcanal finally secured in March 1943, the Americans went onto the offensive and slowly, island by island, climbed their way up the Solomons chain towards the main Japanese base of Rabaul. These leapfrogging attacks were later duplicated in the central Pacific, but the Navy and Marine Corps Dauntless aircrews first led the way in this technique, and much hard fighting eventually wore down the Japanese strength after months of attrition. Here, US Navy SBD bombs explode in the Japanese AA gun-pits alongside a Rabaul airfield, 1944. The Dauntless was often used in the flak suppression role because of its accuracy, clearing the way for the glide bombing of Navy and Marine Corps Grumman Avengers. (Author's collection)

A US Navy SBD-5, 159, operating in the Solomon Islands, 1944. Due to the ever-increasing payloads required of the Dauntless – radar, radio, bigger bomb loads – the -5 introduced another engine change, this time the installation of the 1200 hp R-1820-60 Wright Cyclone; but it was hardly enough to compensate for the extra weight, and performance was disappointing to say the least. (US Navy official)

Island in a remorseless roll-up of Japanese forward defences. The other half of the prong was equally relentless along the north-eastern coast of New Guinea, with the fall of both Lae and Salamaua on 11 and 16 September; and the Huon Gulf was cleared by the capture of Finschafen on 20 October 1943. This was followed by the Allied occupation of the Treasury Islands on 27 October as a stepping stone towards the landings on Bougainville Island, and this became a reality on 1 November, with the US Marines hitting the beaches of Empress Augusta Bay and the fall of the strategically vital airfield of Torokina.

These last conquests now brought Rabaul's four airfields – Lakunai, Vunakanau, Tobera and Rapopo – and the Blanche Bay anchorage within range of dive bombers from both newly constructed airstrips and carrier task forces, which roamed the area at will. As well as Rabaul itself, the various Japanese Navy attempts either to reinforce, supply or evacuate their threatened garrisons in the area gave ample opportunity for both the Marine Corps and the Navy Dauntless squadrons to show their power during this period. We cannot hope here to cover in depth *all* the

contributions made by the Dauntless in these advances, but a few examples will give the feel and flavour of it.

This campaign marked the first steps by the American land and air forces to graft a successful close support system to their operations. Primitive by German standards of the time, they were nonetheless a sincere attempt to make it work, and they were rewarded two years later in the Philippines. The term 'close air support' was taken to mean precision dive bombing within 1,000 yards (914m) of the front of Allied ground troops, which in featureless jungle was not an easy task. The risk of hitting one's own forces was always high, but the Marine/Navy Dauntless teams were to became very adept at the task, and incidents of 'friendly fire' deaths, although not always avoided, were few.

The system was set up with eight officers and eight radiomen under Major Wilfred Stiles; these operated as air liaison parties, with four command cars equipped with SCR-193 radios, Aldis lamp, pyrotechnic equipment and Isenburg cloth for signal panels. They were allocated to work with the various land forces as and when required, and called in air strikes against

difficult Japanese defence positions which were holding up the American infantry advances. The first instance of this was on 13 July, when a strike of twelve Dauntlesses was called in to bomb the right flank of the 169th Infantry Division, who marked the target with mortar smoke.[163]

At sea the Japanese reaction was predictable, and reinforcements were rushed in by destroyer and transport, giving the Dauntlesses another chance to have a go at the Cactus Express, a chance they accepted with alacrity. On the morning of 17 July 1943, a strike which included eighteen Marine and eighteen Navy SBDs struck one such convoy off Kahili, and sank the destroyer *Hatsuyuki*, killing eight-two of her crew; they also slightly damaged three more destroyers.

An attempt by the Japanese to reinforce their Bougainville forces was made on 22 July 1943, when the seaplane tender *Nisshin*, escorted by five destroyers, was sent down with 618 Army personnel embarked, along with twenty-two tanks, guns, fuel and ammunition. The Japanese supply force was then sighted and taken under heavy attack by sixteen Marine Corps SBDs and other units which made the 600-mile (965km) round trip to Kahili. They claimed to have sunk the seaplane tender, which was true, and to have probably sunk a light cruiser, which was not. The dive bombers hit this naval squadron off Bougainville, and although all the eighteen torpedoes aimed at her missed, the Dauntlesses claimed no less than seven direct hits on this unarmoured vessel: four on her quarterdeck, one amidships, one behind her bridge, and one on her bow. The Japanese admitted six direct hits, but anyway she broke in half and sank taking with her almost all her crew and passengers.

Ashore at Munda the narrow strips of land on both sides of Baerobo harbour received a pounding, including a contribution from the Marine SBDs which met only light AA resistance. This was followed by a call for help from the ground forces near Munda, and thirty-two Dauntlesses were accordingly despatched, armed with 1,000lb (450kg) 'Daisy Cutters'; these were all dropped on Japanese gun positions at Bible Hill which the Americans were storming. Next day, the 23 July, eighteen SBDs contributed again by getting at least two direct hits on gun emplacements and thickly covered small targets.

On the 24 July, eighteen Dauntlesses from the Russell Islands armed with 'Daisy Cutters' made a good strike on Rekata Bay, which Coastwatchers reported to be '. . . a complete success'. The enemy bivouac and supply area was plastered. Later, the heavily bombed east shore of Baeroko was hit along a narrow 800-yard (730m) stretch by thirty-six SBDs: 'Exact bombing was required, where a miss or a late release would hit a carefully marked area which our troops now occupy.'[164]

The bitter defence of the vital Munda airfield was finally overcome by the Marines with an offensive that began on 25 July 1943, heralded by 104 Dauntless and Avenger aircraft dropping 1,000 bombs between 0702 and 0720. In what was termed '. . . a tremendous climax', no less than fifty-four SBDs were despatched, each dropping a 1,000lb (450kg) bomb in a total area encompassing the three designated targets of less than half a square mile (1.3 sq km). There were no losses, and that same afternoon another strike by thirty-six more Marine Dauntlesses '. . . put the finishing touches', just prior to the occupation of the airfield by friendly forces.

On the afternoon of 31 July an attack was made on Vila by all available bombers, and these included two dozen SBDs which dive bombed four gun positions and ammunition dumps at 1530. Ten bombs hit the target area, nine hit alternative targets, and three missed. Three of the Dauntlesses were hit by return AA fire, and this gave a good indication of the toughness of the SBD. One Marine SBD was hit by a flin (20mm) shell that pierced the wing and exploded inside. This hit 'tore up the frames, but only caused a bulge in the upper surface'.[165]

During August 1943, VMSB-141 and VMSB-234 worked out of Henderson Field, with one mission being conducted by VMSB-132. In all, sixty-one Marine Corps pilots were available for combat during the period, while an average of forty-nine aircraft were available for operations. The month of August, 1943, was characterized by several days of overcast and squally weather and at least five strikes were hampered by these weather fronts, namely low cloud over the target area and squalls.

On 7 August, for example, an attack on Baeroko harbour was forced back by a heavy front over the Russell Islands, and several attacks on Vila, Baeroko and Baanga Island were made under conditions requiring glide bombing in order to get under the low cloud layer. Prevailing winds were from east to south-east, and the month's precipitation at Henderson Field was 1.5in (3.7cm), half the normal. Approximately 10 per cent of the time was good flying weather, 30 per cent average, 30–40 percent below average and 10–20 per cent poor.

A total of seventeen strikes were carried out despite the conditions, one of which was an attack on shipping in Tonelei harbour, near Kahili. All the attacks were successfully executed, with the exception of one on 7 August, which was forced back by bad weather. Munda was attacked twice early in August just prior to its evacuation by the enemy, as we have seen, while Vila was attacked eight times, the shore installations at Rekata Bay once, Baanga Island twice, Karapahtah Island once and the installations at Baeroko harbour once. In these seventeen strikes, 382 SBDs flew a total of 1,162 hours. There was only one day during August that no flight of any kind was made. Miscellaneous missions included test runs, local familiarization hops, ferry trips to the Russells, Munda, and so on, practice dive bombing, administrative and photo flights and artillery spotting for the Command, New Georgia.

In all, some 319,100lb (144,744kg) of bombs were expended during this month, along with 23,945 rounds of ammunition; the breakdown of this was as follows:

| | |
|---|---|
| 1,000lb (450kg) Mk 103 bombs: | 138 |
| 1,000lb Mk 19 bombs: | 138 |
| 500lb (227kg) Mk 103 bombs: | 2 |
| 500lb Mk 19 bombs: | 61 |
| 100lb Mk 19 bombs | 116 |
| .30 cal. rounds: | 16,545 |
| .50 cal. rounds: | 7,400 |

It was the Marine Corps' practice to fly four to six spare aircraft to accompany these missions, to fill in the formation should aircraft be forced to drop out or otherwise, returning after the flight had reached the vicinity of the Russell Islands. The SBDs had fighter cover and were usually accompanied by from twelve to twenty-four Grumman TBF Avenger torpedo bombers operating in a glide-bombing configuration.

Sharing the burden with the US Navy and Marine Corps was an Allied unit, No 27 Squadron, RNZAF. Here the laden SBDs of RNZAF No 25 Squadron are moving down the metal air strip at Bougainville Island in readiness for another sortie against Rabaul, in 1944. (RNZAF official)

The Army Air Force equivalent to the SBD-5 was the A-24B, but by the time it made its debut the USAAF had successfully divested itself of the need to embrace dive bombing and the bulk of these were used as instrument trainers, or else given to the Navy who in turn passed them on to the Marines. This is the front view of the first A-24B at El Segundo on 9 April 1943, with bomb in place. (McDonnell Douglas)

On 1 August, eleven SBDs plus eighteen TBFs made a co-ordinated attack on Japanese ships off Kahili, near Tonelei harbour, the dive bombers carrying 1,000lb (450kg) bombs with ¹/₁₀ sec delay nose and tail fuses. They made their attack from the north-east with the formation approaching from a height of 14,000ft (4,300m), pushing over at 10,000ft (3,000m) from a high-speed approach, and all eleven Dauntlesses releasing their bombs at heights from between 1,500 to 2,000ft (450 to 600m). One ship, described as approximately 100ft (30m) in length, with one gun at bow and one at stern, was hit on the forward port side while under way. Another transport, three times the size, was possibly hit at starboard amidships with another near-miss alongside the stern; this target was seen circling sharply, and lost way after the bombs exploded. Another bomb dropped near a tug, but the results were not observed. Three further near-misses were made on another transport: one bomb fell near the stern, one on the starboard side throwing water over the deck, and the third off her port side. Only light AA was received, and only one aircraft was hit in dive. The smaller transport was sunk, and three more were damaged and beached on Erventa Island; this was confirmed by cameras.

Two strikes were made against Munda. On 1 August, at 0945, the previous pattern repeated itself, with a morning strike against Munda that included eighteen Dauntlesses from VMSB-132 and VT-26.

The first nine SBDs made a high-speed approach from 9,000ft (2,700m), pushed over at 7,000ft (2,100m) in a full flap 70-degree dive. The TBFs then attacked, and were followed by the remaining nine SBDs dropping 1,000lb (450kg) bombs with a ¹/₁₀ sec delay from 2,000 to 2,500ft (600 to 750m). They reported four hits in the ammunition dump area, four at Gurasai, two on a gun position just north of the taxiway, and three more at a gun position just north of the Lambeti Plantation. The AA fire they encountered was much less than in the previous month – only ten bursts of heavy AA fire were observed, and some small, inaccurate light fire.

After a two-day lull in operations, on the 4 August the Marine Corps' SBDs from VMSB-234 sortied at dawn with a strength of twenty-nine dive bombers, all armed with 1,000lb (450kg) 'Daisy Cutter' fragmentation bombs. Two SBDs reached the target too late to attack, and two others failed to release due to faulty mechanisms, but the remaining twenty-five duly decimated Japanese foot soldiers located on the Gurusai Peninsula, north-east of Munda airfield, in order to stop or delay the escape of these defenders fleeing from the 45th Infantry Division which was advancing over Bibolo Hill and the 37th advancing over the airfield. The airfield itself was taken on the 4 August, after hand-to-hand fighting which precluded the Marines taking a further hand in the proceedings.

The Vila area on Kolombangara Island then became the principal target for the Marine Corps flyers for the rest of the month, with eight strikes. On 8 August two attacks were carried out, one in the morning and another in the afternoon. In the first attack twenty 1,000lb (450kg) bombs with ¹/₁₀ sec delay fuses were dropped on and near gun positions. Considerable light and heavy AA was noted, but only one plane was damaged. In the afternoon raid, fifteen 1,000lb (450kg) bombs with ¹/₁₀ sec delay fuses were again dropped on gun positions. Intense light and heavy AA was again experienced between 4,000 to 7,000ft (1,200 to 2,100m) and high bursts at 10,000ft (3,000m) were also observed. However, only one SBD was damaged slightly.

The Dauntless attacks consisted of high-speed approaches at 10,000 to 13,000ft (3,000 to 3,900m), push-overs in full flap, 70-degrees dives at 8,000 to 9,000ft (2,400 to 2,700m), and bomb releases at 1,500 to 2,000ft (450 to 600m). Three other strikes on gun positions and the radio station were carried out in a similar fashion; Webster Cove, Ringi Cove and Nusatuva Island were also attacked three times. On these occasions, part of the formation had their SBDs loaded with 1,000lb (450kg) instantaneous bombs and the rest with one 500lb (227kg) instantaneous and two 100lb (45kg) instantaneous bombs. Moderate to heavy AA fire occurred each time, and a total of nine aircraft were damaged, one Marine pilot receiving slight shrapnel cuts in his leg and one gunner was also wounded in the leg. In summary, the Vila strikes utilized 212 sorties.

There were other targets for the SBDs during August 1943 including strikes against Recast Bay on the north coast of Santa Isabel Island. These took place on 8 August, when twenty-six aircraft attacked shore installations there, with the majority of the SBDs carrying the 1,000lb (450kg) 'Daisy Cutter' extensions, while a few were loaded with one 500lb (227kg) 'Daisy Cutter' bomb and two 1,00lb (45kg) instantaneous bombs. On this occasion the Dauntlesses approached the target at 10,000ft (3,000m) making their push-overs at 8,000ft (2,400m) and releasing at 1,500ft (450m), with pull-outs coming from between 300 and 700ft (90 to 200m). All the SBDs strafed during the dives. AA was practically non-existent, with only two gun positions noted, and the area was well covered with bombs although no specific observations were made. One Dauntless had to make a forced landing in the water due to propeller trouble off south-eastern Santa Isabel, but both the pilot and gunner were rescued by friendly natives and returned to base by the Coastwatchers.

An attack was made on artillery installations located on the southern tip of Baanga Island by seventeen SBDs. The Marine dive bombers took off in the rain with poor visibility and low ceiling, but the flight found a ceiling of 6,000ft (1,800m) near the target and so pushed over from that altitude. Sixteen made good dives and releases, fourteen of which were in the target area and two in the water; one had its bomb 'hang up' Again, most of the aircraft strafed in their dives.

At the request of the ComAir, New Georgia, two SBDs were provided to locate and bomb gun positions on the southern tip of Baanga Island. This was the first time that Allied aircraft had operated directly out of Munda since it had fallen. They were each armed with one 500lb (227kg) bomb with instantaneous fuses, and both dived successfully on the gun positions, but with no clear observation of the result. Three further such attacks were made during the course of the same day against other Japanese gun emplacements.

Another attack was directed at Karapahtah Island, situated in the Lucas Channel between Arundel and Baanga Islands. A force of nineteen Dauntless dive bombers, carrying 1,000lb (450kg) bombs with instantaneous fusing, scored three direct hits on gun positions, while ten more bombs landed outside the target area and three fell in the sea; one SBD's bomb was a dud, and another aircraft failed to release. Again, several of them strafed in the dive. This was not a very satisfactory attack at all.

On 9 August the target was the outer point of Baeroko harbour, New Georgia, and twenty-one SBDs took part, dropping fifteen 1,000lb (450kg) 'Daisy Cutters' in the target area, five outside or in the water and again, one 'hung up'. A great deal of fire and smoke resulted from the strike, but in return, one dive bomber was slightly damaged by AA fire.

The large island of Bougainville was the next Allied objective, and the 1st Marine Division waded ashore at Cape Torokina, in Empress Augusta Bay on 1 November 1943. To cover this latest invasion AirSoPac assembled powerful air forces, and as usual Strike Command under

Lieutenant Colonel David F. O'Neill, USMC, provided the close support with 100 Navy and Marine Corps Dauntlesses based at Munda.

The Navy's VC-40 was a composite squadron with SBDs and TBMs acting as glide bombers. The Marines deployed three dive bomber squadrons: VMSB-144 under Major Frank E. Hollar; VMSB-234 under Major Harold B. Penne, and VMSB-244 under Major Robert J. Johnson. The principal Dauntless strikes made against Japanese airfields and shore installations to soften them up before the landings are listed in the table below.[166]

The actual touch-down at Torokina was preceded by a bombing and strafing strike on the landing beaches to which VMSB-144 contributed eight Dauntlesses, which ComSoPac called ' . . . excellently timed and executed . . .'.

An attempt by a Japanese naval force to intervene that night was defeated by an Allied task force, but an even larger naval squadron was sent from Truk to Simpson harbour, Rabaul, ready to sortie and terminate the American beach-head. This force consisted of seven heavy cruisers, one light cruiser and four destroyers, all under the command of Vice Admiral Takeo Kurita, and it reached Simpson harbour at 0700 on 5 November. Here they were joined by two more light cruisers and seven more destroyers.

Admiral Halsey directed that Task Force 38, with the Saratoga and the light carrier Princeton, under Rear Admiral Frederick C. Sherman, steer to a position some 230 miles (370km) south-east of Rabaul and launch a strike against the

Japanese ships, relying on surprise and good luck to get through. Under low cloud and heavy rainstorms Sherman's force did indeed achieve a surprise approach, even though they were duly sighted by the enemy. Once again poor ship recognition came to the Americans' aid, as neither of the carriers was reported as such. A powerful air-strike force, which included twenty-two SBDs from the Saratoga's CVAG-3 (formed in September 1943, and which included the former VB-3 and VS-3 Dauntlesses), was sent from the two carriers and arrived over the harbour in clear weather catching the Japanese unprepared.

The subsequent attack was one of the most successful of the war: for the loss of ten aircraft, the Atago was damaged by three near-miss bombs, Maya took a direct hit into her engine room, Mogami was seriously damaged, Takao was near-missed and took a heavy list as water poured in, and the Agano and Noshiro were also both hit, as were two destroyers and a minesweeper; thus nine vessels were hit and damaged to a varying degree.

The Japanese squadron had been neutralized, but the Americans were worried enough by it to divert three more carriers – namely the Essex (with CVAG-9), Bunker Hill (with CVAG-17), and Independence (with CVLAG-22) – from the Tarawa and and Makin invasion operations in the Central Pacific, due to take place on 20 November, to repeat the strike at Rabaul. This was made on 11 November, with all five carriers sending in heavy strikes with 183 aircraft; these included the SBD-4s of the Independence's

| Date | SBDs | Target Airfield | Losses |
| --- | --- | --- | --- |
| 18-10-43 | 32 | Kahili | 0 |
| 19-10-43 | 20 | Kara | 0 |
| 20-10-43 | 7 | Kakasa | 0 |
| 22-10-43 | 48 | Kahili | 0 |
| 23-10-43 | 24 | Kara | 1 |
| 23-10-43 | 24 | Kara | 1 |
| 24-10-43 | 47 | Kahili | 0 |
| 25-10-43 | 31 | Ballale | 0 |
| 26-10-43 | 30 | Kara | 0 |
| 26-10-43 | 49 | Kahili | 1 |
| 28-10-43 | 39 | Kara | 0 |
| 28-10-43 | 38 | Ballale | 0 |
| 30-10-43 | 68 | Kara | 0 |
| 31-10-43 | 34 | Kara | 0 |

| Size of bomb (lb) | Normal use (yd) | Closest Possible use (yd) |
|---|---|---|
| | Flat terrain – own troops troops flat on ground | Other terrain – own troops in dug-outs or trenches |
| 100 | 100 | 75 |
| 500 | 500 | 300 |
| 1,000 | 1,000 | 500 |

VB-22, the first light carrier to embark and employ the Dauntless. This attack also saw the debut in combat of the Curtiss SB2C Helldiver, and it marked the approaching demise of the Dauntless as the principal dive bomber for the fleet.

This time the American aircraft met poor weather, and the Japanese defences were ready for them. Despite this the destroyer *Suzunami* was dive bombed by the Dauntlesses and quickly sunk, and the light cruisers *Agano* and *Yubari* were damaged. The destroyer *Naganami* was dive bombed, and a direct hit struck her amidships abaft her bridge; she had to be towed to shallow water. The destroyers *Urakaze* and *Umikaze* were both slightly damaged by near-misses.

Back on Bougainville itself, the work of improving the close support technique was honed and improved upon. Again, air liaison teams were set up more than three months beforehand, with three attached to the 3rd Marine Division and two others to the New Zealand 8th Brigade Group. A lot of thought had gone into how the dive bombers could be employed, and the safety of the friendly forces was naturally a big factor. Coloured smoke rather than white was employed, as white had been confused with artillery or mortars firing. Testing resulted in a table for guidance on the actual deployment of the SBDs' payloads (left).[167]

The Dauntlesses were called in on 13 December to crack Japanese resistance at a position known as 'Hellzapoppin' Ridge', and three SBDs with three Avengers, all that were immediately available on the newly built Torokina airstrip, struck this target. Unfortunately one aircraft missed the target badly, hitting friendly troops 600 yards (550m) away, killing two and wounding six. This was the only such incident on Bougainville, but it led to a vitriolic attack on the whole concept by an already hostile Army Air Force, who still considered such use of aircraft 'subservient'.[168]

Once the Seebee construction battalion had finished the Torokina airstrip on 10 December, the first six Dauntlesses arrived there the same day. But it was not until a

The limited hangar space of the *Independence*-class light carriers made for a tight fit for air groups including the Dauntless. This is the name ship of the class with SBD-4s of VC-22 embarked, April 1943. Among others of the class which flew SBDs was the *San Jacinto*. (US National Archives, Washington DC)

second strip had been built at Piva on 5 January that Rabaul was within land-based SBD attack range. Immediately 150 Dauntlesses and Avengers flew in to Munda to use Piva North as a staging strip for Rabaul attacks; but the first assault was 'weathered out' while a second, mounted on the 7 January 1944, was a washout with no target airfield hit. Not until the 9th did the SBDs get it right, when they overcame strong fighter defence to heavily crater Tobera airfield. These raids then continued on a round-the-clock basis, with the SBDs using their precision to knock out the defending AA positions, while the TBMs and AAF medium bombers blasted the strips themselves.

On the 14 January 1944, the Marine SBDs hit Simpson harbour itself with a thirty-six plane strike and claimed nine hits on seven ships; but no merchant ship was sunk, and the only result was near-miss damage to the destroyer *Matsukaze*. Another such attack was sent in on 17 January, with a total of twenty-nine Dauntlesses included – sixteen from VMSB-341 under Major George J. Waldie Jr, USMC, and thirteen Navy dive bombers. Again, more than seventy Zeros rose to meet them, but they still managed to carry out their dives, claiming fifteen out of eighteen bombs as direct hits, their most successful dive-bombing attack for a year. They actually hit and sank five of the merchant ships they found in the harbour there: the *Hakkai Maru, Kenshin Maru, Kosei Maru, Lyons Maru* and *Tenshin Maru*.

The climax of these operations came on 19 February when a 145-aircraft strike – including SBDs, TBMs, F4Us, F6Fs and Army P-40s – was intercepted by fifty defending Japanese fighters, who lost almost half their number. The following day, most of the survivors were pulled back to Truk, leaving Rabaul's defence to the dwindling number of AA guns.

Not that much was left at Truk for them to defend. On 4 February two reconnaissance PBY Catalinas had overflown the anchorage and photographed the Japanese combined fleet lying at its mooring there. On the 17th, Vice Admiral Marc Mitscher had sortied out from Majuro with Task Force 58 to lead Operation 'Hailstone': under his command were the carriers *Enterprise, Yorktown II, Essex, Intrepid* and *Bunker Hill*, the light carriers *Belleau Wood, Cabot, Monterey* and *Cowpens*, six new battleships, ten cruisers and many destroyers.

However, they found that Admiral Mineichi Koga had pulled back the bulk of his fleet to Palau on 10 February, forewarned by the reconnaissance sortie. The SBDs were left with just three light cruisers and eight destroyers, as their only targets, along with numerous auxiliaries and merchant ships. Nonetheless they set to with a determination to lay the ghost of Truk, the so-called 'Gibraltar of the Pacific'.

After a pre-emptive fighter sweep had decimated the Japanese air defences, the bomber groups were launched at 0700 and hit at 0810. Eleven of *Enterprise*'s VB-10 Dauntlesses, armed with 1,000lb bombs and under the leadership of Lieutenant Commander Richard Poor, led the dive bombing, claiming two hits on a freighter and near-misses on a cruiser and a tanker. A second strike later that day saw the same Dauntless team claiming to have blown out the side of a tanker and hit a small carrier. One of the SBDs, piloted by Ensign Robert Wilson and with rear gunner H. Honea, was jumped by no fewer than four Zeros as he pulled out at low level, but the skill of the pilot, the gunnery of the rear-seat man and the enviable manoeuvrability of the SBD brought them through this hopeless situation safely. With only one bullet hole in their machine, Wilson and Honea shot down one fighter, damaged a second, and then lost the other two in cloud, and still returned safely to their carrier.[169]

As the air assault broke over them, the Japanese ships that were able to get underway did so – but this failed to save them from the mass attacks. The 17th was a repeat of the 16th, with the *Enterprise*, for example, launching three strikes: the first, with twelve of VB-10's Dauntlesses, claimed hits on a tanker and a transport at the Dublon anchorage. The second saw hits on two more freighters; while the final strike, by ten SBDs, hit the oil storage and ammunition dump sites at Dublon Island, devastating them and sending a column of thick black smoke up to 8,000ft (2,400m) as a kind of farewell funeral pyre for Truk.

They also left behind them the almost total devastation of the Imperial Japanese Navy's squadron stationed there. The carrier planes had sunk outright the light cruiser *Naka*, the destroyers *Fumizuki, Oite* and *Tachikaze*, the submarine tenders *Rio de Janeiro Maru* and *Heian Maru*, the armed merchant cruisers *Aikoku Maru* and *Kiyosumi Maru*, six tankers, and seventeen

freighters. American surface forces disposed of the light cruiser *Katori* and the destroyer *Maikaze* which tried to escape the carnage, while American submarines sank the light cruiser *Agano*.

Back on Bougainville the Japanese, whose main forces were concentrated around Buin in the south and had been by-passed, hurled in heavy counter-attacks against the US bridgehead at Torokina. By early February, MAG-24's ten squadrons included two Dauntless units: VMSB-235 under Major Glenn L. Todd, USMC, and VMSB-244 under Major Harry W. Reed, USMC. When the Japanese onslaught commenced on 8 March they were quickly in action, along with the RNZAF Dauntlesses, whose story we will tell later.

The first casualty the Marine SBDs suffered whilst defending the Torokina perimeter was that of Lieutenant W. B. Gilbert of VMSB-244, on an artillery spotting mission over the battlefront. His Dauntless exploded in mid-air, either the victim of enemy AA fire, or, more likely, caught in an artillery duel between the two sides. Spotting was a hazardous job and no sinecure, as many others had found out before and since. Nor was operating from an airstrip under enemy fire, and VMSB-235 had six men wounded in a single day on 18 March, while VMSB-244 took 10 per cent casualties amongst its ground staff at this time.

No fewer than 114 SBDs from both Navy, Marine and RNZAF units were in operation on a daily basis, as the fight hung in the balance; again they were mainly targeting the Japanese artillery positions, especially those on hills 111, 500, 501 and 600. On the 13th the SBDs flew 131 sorties, effectively silencing these batteries for much of the time. But not until 16 March had the crisis passed, and then the Dauntlesses were left free to attack other targets, and thirty-six SBDs staged through Green Islands to hit Kavieng again on that day.

Marine Dauntlesses were also operating from Funafuti Atoll where VMSB-241, under Major Wayne M. Cargill, had arrived with twenty-two SBD-4s on 26 April 1943, and VMSB-151 under Major Maurice W. Fletcher, had moved into Tutuila on 6 June. In preparation for the assaults on the Gilbert Islands, MAG-31 moved into the Samoa area, with VMSB-331 under Major Paul B. Byrum being based at Wallis Island.

# CHAPTER SEVENTEEN

# Diving Kiwis

Despite the proven versatility and re- liability of the Dauntless dive bomber, there were very few occasions when it was employed in a front-line combat role by any of America's allies during World War II. The first such action took place at Bougainville in very dramatic circum- stances, the unit involved being the Royal New Zealand Air Force's sole dive bomber formation, Number 25 Squadron, RNZAF.

How the SBD came to be flown by the Kiwis dates back to a year earlier, to February 1943. Under General Douglas McArthur's original plan, 'Elkton', Rabaul was to be taken in a two-prong attack, and not merely invested. New Zealand, who held mandated territories in the region, was to be fully represented, and a force of fighters and dive bombers was to be built up to enable her to play her full part.

Accordingly, on 21 April 1943, the British Government's purchasing agency, the BAC, placed an official requisition to the USAAF for '. . . the supply of 120 A-24 aircraft, complete and fully equipped, together with appropriate spare engines and engine spares, spare propellers and propeller spares and corresponding pro- vision of spares for all other items of

No 25 Squadron RNZAF was unique in that it was the only SBD dive bomber squadron to operate in the Pacific theatre during World War II that was not operated by American units. It was intended to be one of four New Zealand Dauntless units, but in the event, none of the others were finally formed. No 25 Squadron operated with great success, minimal losses and much distinction on Bougainville and in the attacks on Rabaul in 1944. (Air Commodore T. J. MacLean de Lange)

Squadron Leader T. J. MacLean de Lange, RNZAF, CO of No 25 Squadron (seated) in his SBD mount, 'Howa- Baht-That- Hic!', at Bougainville. (Air Commodore T. J. MacLean de Lange)

equipment . . .'[170] These dive bombers were to be delivered in two batches of sixty aircraft each in the third and fourth quarters of 1943. It was added that 'It is intended to re-transfer the above- mentioned aircraft to the Government of the Dominion of New Zealand.'[171]

Brigadier General Meyers duly passed this on to the United Nations, Branch, Overseas Section, at Dayton, Ohio, stating that 'Under Munitions Assignments Committee (Air) Case No 200, dated 1 February 1943, 120 A-24s were assigned to the New Zealand government, based upon production objectives, and are approved for long-range planning purposes.'[172] W. E. Donnelly of the produc- tion division noted: '120 A-24Bs from

AC-28716 are allocated to New Zealand on block allocations.'[173]

These A-24Bs were being constructed at Tulsa which had concentrated on the Army variant, leaving the Navy SBD to be built at El Segundo. This led to another problem because, as the RNZAF was to operate its dive bombers alongside the SBDs of the US Navy and USMC, they had necessarily to be similarly equipped. Therefore the Tulsa production line was in the ironical position of having to build these two sixty-plane batches as A-24Bs, and then have them flown over to Wright Field for the Air Force Technical Command there to modify them by installing Navy type radio and oxygen equipment. They still considered it possible to meet the deadline, but then other production difficulties hit the Tulsa plant (see Chapter 18), and the chances of New Zealand getting any of her 120 dive bombers looked exceedingly more remote as the months went by.

A solution had to be found in the interim if the RNZAF was to play its part, and the compromise was eventually found. The final solution was to replace No 25 Squadron's existing SBD-3s, which had been taken on loan from the Marine Air Group 14 (which, between April and August 1943 was itself then resting and refitting at Seagrove, Auckland, between combat spells at Guadalcanal), with a further extended loan of twenty-seven SBD-4s from the same source. This would enable the first dive bomber squadrons to continue their advance training in the type, and it would also take them into combat alongside MAG-14 aircraft as a fully compatible unit, until the situation at Tulsa could be resolved.

In fact so good a solution was it, that in the end, the original request was cancelled completely, on 18 January 1944. This led to a final flurry between General Arnold and the technical executive at Wright Field two days later, when the modifications then being undertaken on these aircraft were identified as '. . . not desired when the airplanes revert to the Army Air Forces. It is therefore requested that the modification of the 120 A-24 airplanes for New Zealand be stopped immediately so

The last take-off by the SBDs of No 25 Squadron from Seagrove, New Zealand, prior to deployment in the combat zone. The squadron is seen forming up in two 'Vics' to fly over the airfield in a farewell salute after initial training had been completed. (Air Commodore T. J. MacLean de Lange)

that de-modification and re-modification work will be held to a minimum.' It was thought that these aircraft would '. . . probably be converted to instrument trainers.'[174]

The cancelling of the requisition terminated the RNZAF dive bomber programme almost before it had started. Of the original six dive bomber squadrons planned, only No 25 and No 26 started their training fully, and the latter was finally equipped with the Chance-Vought

F4U Corsair before it commissioned, while No 25 later converted to that aircraft also. Two other planned dive bomber squadrons, Nos 27 and 28, were cancelled outright, while Nos 30 and 31, although still designated 'dive bomber' squadrons, were actually equipped with Grumman TBF Avenger torpedo bombers, which they used as orthodox glide bombers.

However, when the first unit of the planned RNZAF dive bomber force, No 25 Squadron, formed at Seagrove on 31 July 1943, taking over on loan nine SBD-3s, this was all in the future. The intention was that the squadron would transfer to Waipapakauri airfield in late August, when it would fully equip to its operational strength of eighteen machines, and when its servicing unit would also be brought to full strength. The aircraft signed for on loan from MAG-14, were, naturally, combat-weary machines and it took a week to get one aircraft in a flyable state. The Marines helped out with spares by cannibalizing spare parts to refurbish what were still, officially, their aircraft.

Indeed, it was only through the generosity of the Marines that the squadron could even begin to get ready. Master Sergeant W. W. Carmichael, USMC, was attached as an instructor on 5 August when there was an average of three to four flyable aircraft to train on. The original nine Dauntlesses taken over were added to by four more in August and a further five in September, and these

The original mounts of No 25 Squadron, RNZAF, lined up at Seagrove in late 1943, showing their new New Zealand numbers and markings painted over the standard US paint scheme; NZ 5026 (No 26) can be identified. (Air Commodore T. J. MacLean de Lange)

became permanently transferred in October and November.

Most of the pilots who formed the new squadron naturally came from Army co-operation and anti-aircraft units, while rear-seat men were wireless operators/air gunners (WOAGs). The training programme followed the standard format, with lectures covering tactics, bombing and gunnery, signals, intelligence, aircraft and ship recognition. meteorology and such. This was interspersed with a two-stage aerial course, conversion to the SBD and dive-bomber operations. The RNZAF training methods, based as they were on the then current USMC practice, make an interesting comparison with those of the US Navy and USAAF described earlier.

For a dive-bombing attack the method taught was as follows: an approach in three 'Vics' of three aircraft each, at a height of 10,000ft (3,000m). The target was approached from slightly to one side, and when it was abreast the SBD, the wing flaps were split and the aircraft was rolled over into the vertical dive; then the aileron was turned to get on and keep on the target. Although the Dauntlesses longitudinal axis in the dive configuration was vertical, wind, lift and momentum meant that in practice the dive angle was around 70–75 degrees.[175] The rate of descent was kept at around 240–280 knots indicated air speed, with a bomb release at a high height, 2,500ft (750m), with the pull-out following. The spacing between aircraft for this new unit while at Seagrove was 400 yards (366m), but this was gradually tightened up as familiarity and confidence grew, until the American SBD practice of a 'Vic' of three would follow each other in with very close spacing.

The target was initially stationary, a simple painted circle, but later, moving targets were used, and simulated bomb drops gave way to practice and then live bombs. The SBD-3s were also gradually replaced and sent to storage depots at Hobsonville, where twenty-two of them stayed for the rest of the war, before being sold as scrap. They were supplemented by a batch of nine SBD-4s although apart from inspection flights at Rukuhia, these aircraft were not much employed. By the end of the year, at the time the squadron was ready to move to Pallikulo, Espiritu Santo, pilots had averaged between 100 and 200 hours on the Dauntless, with their WOAGs having between 60 and 120

The last take-off of No 25 Squadron from Seagrove, New Zealand, prior to deployment in the combat zone. This was the largest single formation of warplanes to fly over New Zealand up to that time, 1943. (Air Commodore T. J. MacLean de Lange)

## Composition of No 25 Dive Bomber Squadron RNZAF, Piva, Bougainville, 1944

### Motto: 'Kia Kaha', Maori for 'Constant Endeavour'

| Aircraft | Original Nbr | Pilot | Radioman/Rear Gunner |
|---|---|---|---|
| NZ 5057 | 36925 | Sqdn-Ldr T. J. MacLean de Lange | F/O L. T. Sewell |
| NZ 5051 | 36908 | Flt-Lt J. W. Edwards | Flt-Sgt L. A. Hoppe |
| NZ 5049 | 36897 | Flt-Lt R. F. Johnson | Flt-Sgt R. J. Howell |
| NZ 5060 | 28516 | F/O L. A. McLellan-Symonds | Flt-Sgt R. F. Bailey |
| NZ 5046 | 36862 | F/O B. F. Glanville | Flt-Sgt C. R. White |
| NZ 5047 | 36891 | F/O L. H. F. Brown | Flt-Sgt G. D. Ashworth |
| NZ 5048 | 36895 | F/O G. C. Howie | Flt-Sgt J. S. R. Robertson |
| NZ 5064 | 54201 | F/O A. Moore | Flt-Sgt J. K. Munroe |
| NZ 5055 | 36923 | F/O B. N. Graham | Flt-Sgt O. E. Watson |
| NZ 5050 | 36898 | P/O G. H. Cray | Flt-Sgt F. D. Bell |
| NZ 5051 | 36908 | F/O F. G. McKenzie | P/O G. H. French |
| NZ 5054 | 36914 | Flt-Sgt L. H. Jolly | Flt-Sgt T. E. Price |
| NZ 5059 | 36916 | Sgt P. R. B. Symonds | Flt-Sgt B. Boden |
| NZ 5062 | 28536 | Flt-Sgt N. L. Kelly | Flt-Sgt B. E. Cullen |
| NZ 5053 | 36911 | Sgt C. G. W. Kuhn | Flt-Sgt M. Small |
| NZ 5052 | 36910 | Flt-Sgt H. Clark | Flt-Sgt N. G. Silver |
| NZ 5056 | 36924 | Flt-Sgt C. N. O'Neill | Flt-Sgt D. W. Gray |
| * | | Flt-Lt J. R. Penniket | F/O J. H. Brady |
| NZ 5063 | 10849 | Sgt W. O. Nicholson | Flt-Sgt R. W. Cullen |
| NZ 5058 | 36928 | Sgt A. C. L. Forsberg | Flt-Sgt E. G. Leathem |
| NZ 5068 | *35923 | F/O A. W. B. Hayman | Sgt D. H. Wilkie |
| NZ 5066 | *28435 | Flt-Sgt J. C. Evison | Flt-Sgt H. A. Sharp |

* Relief crew or aircraft brought in from Reserve Flight on 12 April.

hours. They marked their departure with a flight of all eighteen SBDs over Auckland on 6 January 1944. Meanwhile the advanced ground party were readying a new batch of SBD-4s for further training and then operational use at Pallikulo and then Bougainville.

On 31 January 1944 the squadron joined the USMC and Navy Dauntlesses with whom they were to work at Espiritu Santo, and continued training with these aircraft. This gave them invaluable insight into American methods, the handling and organizing of large formations of aircraft, and working in tropical conditions, and it was altogether a very valuable exercise. On 11 February, No 25 Squadron were issued with their final mounts, which they were to take into battle: two dozen brand-new SBD-5s.

They were now ready to take their place in the line of battle as part of ComAirSols, alongside Navy and Marine Squadrons VB-305 (later relieved by VC-306) and VC-40, and Marine Squadron VMSB-235 (later relieved by VMSB-241). Thus on the morning of 22 March they took off for Henderson Field, eighteen strong in two nine-plane formations, and made an uneventful journey. On landing at Guadalcanal, one Dauntless – NZ 5055 piloted by F/O B. N. Graham – was written off on landing.

The next hop was made to Piva airstrip and they arrived at noon on 23 March – right in the middle of the major Japanese ground offensive launched to throw the invaders back into the sea. Ironically their despatch thither had been delayed until it had been considered 'safe' for them, but Lieutenant General Kenda's 6th Division had its own timetable and had started a massive assault on the small Allied perimeter area at 0600 on the morning of the 8 March; and although his initial thrust had been beaten off, the battle was still continuing with Japanese heavy artillery hitting the airfield, especially during the night hours, when the first SBDs touched down.

At 0615 the next morning, Squadron Leader MacLean de Lange took off to get the lie of the land and provide the squadron with its first operational sortie, in this case artillery spotting for counter-battery work. Six of these assignments were carried out by the squadron in the course of the following three days. Although enemy air opposition proved to be negligible, AA fire was heavy, especially

## Dauntless Men: Squadron Leader Theo J. MacLean de Lange, RNZAF

The CO of No 25 Squadron RNZAF, Squadron Leader T. J. MacLean de Lange (right), displaying the squadron insignia on his own personal SBD, at Bougainville, 1944. Theo MacLean de Lange was born in Simila, India, on 16 June 1914, and was educated in England, at Exeter Grammar School, and then Truro College in Cornwall between 1924 and 1929. When his family moved to New Zealand he continued his education at Auckland Grammar School, entering Auckland University in 1932 and studying until 1934.

He joined the Royal New Zealand Air Force in 1938 and served until 1966. In 1942 he was at the Staff College, moving to the Central Group HQ Army Corps where he compiled the *Army Co-Operation Manual*, before moving on to the Pacific Ferry Command between 1942–43. They flew the first Lockheed Venturas into New Zealand from Honolulu, and Douglas Dakotas in from San Diego. He was then appointed as commanding officer of RNZAF, Seagrove. Also at Seagrove Theo first met Marjorie, the only lady on the station at that time, and who later became his wife. And here it was that Theo formed and trained the RNZAF's first (and, as it turned out, only) dive bomber squadron, No 25, of which he was appointed CO and which he took to war in the Solomons at Bougainville Island in 1944.

After No 25 Squadron had finished its tour of combat duty, Squadron Leader de Lange,

with a well merited DFC awarded to him, went to the USA where he attended the Command and General Staff College in 1944. He became the Air Representative South-East Asia Command between 1945–6 and, among other things, he organized the evacuation of all New Zealand POWs from Singapore on its liberation.

Post-war he was appointed CO of No 41 Squadron between 1946–8, which took part in the Berlin air lift; he then became the OC of the flying wing, Whennuapai between 1948–9, and then OC Admin. Wing, Whennuapai 1949–50. His next appointment was as the New Zealand representative of the Joint Services Staff Australia, then Deputy DOSD Air Headquarters, between 1952–3. He became the CO of Whennuapai between 1953 and 1957, then CO Lingram from 1957 to 1960. In 1960 he became the director of training at RNZAF HQ, a post he held for two years. During his time in this post Theo introduced the City & Guilds Certificate of Engineering for the airmen, and the University Training Scheme for officers, before moving over to become the Air Member for Personnel between 1962 and 1966, being awarded a well deserved CBE for his services to the RNZAF in 1965. During his time in the service he had represented the RNZAF at cricket, soccer, squash, and in his retirement today his and his wife Marjorie's leisure activities include gardening, sailing and fishing. (RNZAF official)

The continuous shelling, particularly at night, and the noise of the return fire from our own guns prevented adequate sleep and rest. The shelling of the camp area and revetments while warming up and taxiing out for take-off, was another mental hazard.

No 25 Squadron RNZAF SBDs undergoing maintenance on the front-line strip of Torokina on Bougainville Island. Ron A. Sutherland of 25 SU (wearing hat) noted that, 'In general practice the same pilot and gunner/wireless operator flew their own planes. An engine fitter and a rigger took care of the allotted aircraft, an armourer looked after three aircraft and instrument makers had several they were almost always in the same group. This made for a great deal of team spirit. The Minneapolis Moline tractor unit on which we are seated was a great workhorse around the strip.' (Ron A. Sutherland)

from light flak and small arms, for the enemy troops were still dug in within a few hundred yards of where the SBDs were taking off and landing, which for the first few days of operations made both these normally mundane routines as dangerous as the actual dive attacks. As the operations record noted:

This was made very apparent when the first bombing mission was flown later that morning, with No 25 Squadron providing four SBDs which joined twelve more from VB-305 for a dive-bombing attack on Japanese supply dumps at Tavera. Fourteen 1,000lb (450kg) bombs were placed on the target area, and on retiring, a heavy pall of smoke was observed. This was followed up by twelve sorties in co-operation with fourteen SBDs of VB-305 and some Avengers, for an attack on another supply position just east of Kamo Hill. Embarked in the lead American Dauntless was an officer from the Fijian 1st Battalion, who directed the dive bombers against the hidden enemy positions using knowledge learnt on the ground in the front line. A total of twenty-four 1,000lb (450kg) bombs hit the target area and the officer, Lieutenant Viggers, expressed himself satisfied with the results of the strike.

Next day the long-suffering ground echelon responsible for servicing, fuelling and arming the squadron's aircraft and who were under constant artillery fire, had the unique satisfaction of watching the SBDs taking off and then almost immediately depositing those same 1,000lb bombs onto local enemy gun emplacements only 700 yards (640m) from their camp area. These attacks were considered successful '. . . especially on one gun position which was completely destroyed'. This boosted their morale considerably, since they had been on the receiving end for some weeks and even on that particular morning fifty-two shells had landed in the camp area. They felt that they were doing something towards hitting back.

For the first two days the squadron's tasks were artillery spotting and the bombing of targets around the perimeter. Eighteen aircraft and crews were provided out of a maximum of eighteen of each. The above targets consisted in the main of enemy gun positions and troop concentrations. The squadron was credited with two direct hits on gun positions and it was subsequently ascertained that on one of the strikes the Japanese colonel (subsequently posthumously promoted to

Dauntless No 56 of 25 Squadron RNZAF, all bombed up and ready to go at Marsdon, ready for the flight to Bougainville. (Air Commodore T. J. MacLean de Lange)

general) in charge of operations on Bougainville was killed.

Eighteen sorties were conducted on the 25th in conjuction with No 30 Squadron, and the SBDs delivered their 1,000lb bombs from a height of 2,500ft (750m). For their first two days of operations No 25 Squadron had flown fifty-six sorties, and this set the pattern of their work over the next eight weeks. Although a normal tour of duty was six weeks, the situation was such that the squadron just kept going. Morale was high, and there was much pride in the fact that they were now making a meaningful contribution to the war.

From the third day onwards, commencing with a strike on Kavieng, the squadron's task was to provide twelve aircraft and crews daily for major strikes on Rabaul. The targets were mainly gun positions surrounding the aerodromes and supply areas, and the task of the SBDs was to knock out or quieten these in order that the TBFs could have a clear run through to destroy the strips, which were the primary targets. This was accomplished by dive bombing the gun positions which each aircraft was allocated, and strafing further gun positions on the line of retirement.

During the period 15 March to 15 May, the Kiwi SBDs destroyed the following Japanese guns: 5in (127mm) naval DP: four; 4.2in (105mm): four; 3in (77mm): sixteen; auto: twenty-five; light: forty-two. In four instances heavy gun batteries were brought closer together so as to utilize one set of fire-control equipment for two batteries of guns. This indicated that there had been great destruction of fire control equipment such as height finders, long-range telescopes, and speed and angles of course indicators. In addition the entire fire-control system of two batteries of 5in (127mm) naval guns had been destroyed.

For these missions a set pattern soon developed, with the dive bombers and Avengers taking off early in the morning for their four-hour round trip to Rabaul. Depending on the type of target, bomb loads now varied, with the usual single 1,000lb weapon whose fusing was also according to target, with instantaneous, $^{25}/_{1000}$, $^{1}/_{100}$ and $^{1}/_{10}$ sec delay. This weapon's load was sometimes supplemented by wing-carried 100lb (45kg) bombs, always with instantaneous fuses.

The usual cruise formation was a diamond pattern of fours at an altitude of 14,000ft (4,300m), usually with light fighter protection which was rarely

Engine maintenance for a hard-worked SBD of No 25 Squadron RNZAF at Torokina air strip on Bougainville by 25 SU. Ron A. Sutherland records, 'On one occasion one of our neighbouring American mechanics questioned why we had the cowls off our aircraft so often. We explained that we were simply doing routine daily inspection or thirty- or sixty-hour checks. He informed us that the Americans only took their cowls off their SBD's if the pilot had recorded something on the sheet! Perhaps there was something in the old adage that, "She flew in, so she will fly out!". Pluck the wires, kick the tyres, she's right mate.' (Ron A. Sutherland).

required. On approaching the Rabaul shoreline, descent was made and a 'high-speed' approach dive was made down to 9,000ft (2,700m) at 270 knots. Once over the target, the final attack dive was followed by bomb release at 2,000ft (600m) and pull-out at around 1,000ft (300m). Targets were normally the numerous AA guns in a flak-suppression role, which enabled shallow glide bombing to be employed by the following TBMs. When the SBDs were themselves assigned the airfields they, too, glide bombed from 4000ft (1,200m), releasing at 1,500ft (450m) but this was not popular and was considered needlessly risky for dive bombers, although sometimes weather conditions made it unavoidable.

On this first mission, however, the RNZAF Dauntlesses were armed for the first (and last) time with fragmentation cluster bombs designed to decimate the gun crew and other ground personnel. These 'frag' ordnance loads consisted of two 120lb (54kg) fragmentation clusters, fitted to the type 50 wing racks. Some fifty-four Dauntlesses from Bougainville took part, being joined by twelve more from Green Island, along with two dozen TBFs. Heavy cloud over the original target gun positions caused the strike to divert to

an alternative. A total of forty-one bombs were dropped at Raluana, destroying many buildings and starting one large fire and many small ones. Four more buildings along the beach were hit, as was the barge discharging area at Keravia Bay.

Two of No 25 Squadron's SBDs failed to bomb due to 'hang-ups' and these, piloted by Flt-Sgt L. H. Jolly and Sgt P. R. B. Symonds, brought their ordnance back with them: One aircraft returned with both clusters hung up, and one with one cluster only hung up. On landing back at Piva these clusters left the racks, the safety devices of the M110 nose fuses shattered on contact with the metal airstrip, and the resultant explosion set fire to their parent aircraft, NZ 5054 and NZ 5059, destroying them totally. Sgt Symonds and WOAGs Flt-Sgt T. E. Price and B. Boden were all injured in the fires, and only Jolly got out unscathed.

The next day 25 Squadron contributed twelve aircraft to a forty-eight plane mission against gun emplacements in Vunakanau. They met low cloud and some of the pilots could not locate their targets there, and these made alternative attacks at Tobera, reporting at least one direct hit on a gun position. It is noteworthy how, with only a limited number of aircraft, No

No 25 Squadron RNZAF SBDs at Torokina airstrip on Bougainville, with their maintenance team from 25 SU. Ron A. Sutherland commented, 'As you can see we had only three aircraft parked in each revetment dispersal as widely apart as possible.' (Ron A. Sutherland)

25 Squadron's maintenance crews, working under extreme conditions, managed to keep a very high sortie rate throughout this period. To achieve this much-envied serviceability was due to very hard work by No 26 Servicing Unit (SU), some of whom, fortunately, were familiar with the American SBDs in the South Pacific already. In fact during the eight and a half weeks' tour the operational sorties per head was double that carried out by the American SBD squadrons during their six-week tour of duty. This was accredited to:

1. Lack of sufficient aircraft in the area enforced the use of all available, therefore requiring the squadron to provide twelve planes daily.

2. The fact that fighter opposition was practically negligible. Previously the strikes were governed mainly by weather. When the weather between base and target was at all doubtful, strikes were cancelled or returned to base, the reason being that their own fighter cover was unable to keep track of the bombers when flying through clouds and so were unable to provide sufficient protection. With the falling off of fighter opposition weather became a secondary consideration and only a solid front between base and target or over the target area prevented a strike from reaching its primary target.

These missions continued almost daily until the squadron was well overdue for relief, and in the original plan, the second New Zealand Dauntless unit, No 26 Squadron led by Flight Lieutenant P. R. McNab, should have taken over. Already one of their pilots, Flight Lieutenant J. R. Penniket, had been with No 25 Squadron since December to gain combat experience, and other pilots intended for this unit were already undergoing training in the United States attached to a US Navy squadron.

However, on 13 November 1943 the formation of No 26 Squadron was postponed, and this was later cancelled outright. Among the reasons put forward for this astonishing decision were '. . . the decreasing importance of dive bombers in the Pacific area, and that the operation of too many diverse types of aircraft in the RNZAF was undesirable'.[176] To many people these excuses did not ring true then, any more than they do now.

Whatever the motivation back in the higher echelons of power the 17 May 1944 marked the final operational sortie of No 25 Squadron as a dive bomber unit. Six SBDs flew this mission, accompanying twenty-nine American aircraft in a raid on Lakunai airfield, dive bombing oil barges on the Simpson river. On 20 May all members of New Zealand's only dive bomber squadron left on the first stage of their return flight home, with sixteen SBDs taking off from Piva, and landing at Renard's Field, Russell Islands. Here the Dauntlesses were handed back to the Americans, each with about 120 hours' flight time on them, but with the majority of them in such good condition that the American officer who took delivery commented that he was getting back brand-new aircraft. However, it is on record that at least one, namely NZ 5056, was handed back to MAG-24 on 17 April 1944 '. . . extensively damaged by flak'. These aircraft were then re-absorbed by the USMC.

In summary, the squadron was credited with the following:

| | |
|---|---:|
| Confirmed direct hits: | 18 |
| Reported direct hits: | 30 |
| Confirmed damaging hits: | 7 |
| Reported damaging hits: | 6 |
| Hits in area: | 252 |
| Bombs unobserved: | 106 |
| Bombs hung up: | 46 |

In 1,743.25 hours of operational flying time, 258.8 tons of bombs were dropped in thirty major strikes, twelve local major strikes and fourteen local minor strikes. They flew for forty-nine days in the eight weeks and achieved a serviceability rate of 94.4 per cent, and an availability rate of 99.9 per cent. The squadron dropped 498, 800lb (226,256kg) of bombs and fired 108,000 rounds of .50 calibre and 217,000 rounds of .30 calibre ammunition.

# CHAPTER EIGHTEEN

# Central Pacific Offensive

It was in 1944 that the American offensive really began to roll across the Japanese island bases in the central Pacific. But well before then, from the summer of 1943 onwards as their carrier strength began to grow, they had been repeating the pin-prick raids of 1942 but in much greater strength. Their attacks were supplemented by the work of the USMC dive bomber units across the whole of the vast south and central Pacific area.

VMSB-133, commanded by Major Lee A. Christoffersen, arrived at Torokina and conducted dive-bombing missions against targets in Bougainville and New Britain during October and November, 1944. VMSB-142, commanded by Captain Hoyle R. Barr, moved from Fiji to Emirau and attacked the Rabaul area until December. VMSB-235, commanded by Captain Edward C. Willard, had moved up to Bougainville by April 1944, and flew numerous sorties against targets in the Bismarck region. On 24 June it was transferred to Green Island where it continued to pound Rabaul and the surrounding area until 13 September, at which time it returned to the States.

VMSB-236, commanded successively by Major William A. Cloman Jr, Captain Robert L. Knight and finally Major Floyd E. Beard Jr, had flights based at Torokina by 25 January 1944, as well as at Ocean Field on Green Island, and then Munda, before working again from Torokina between August 1944 and January 1945. VMSB-241, commanded by Major James A. Feeley, arrived at Efate on 16 December 1943, but by 7 February it was operating dive-bombing sorties against Rabaul from Piva, returning to Efate in March and then moving on to Emirau to continue the work.

VMSB-243, commanded by Major Thomas J. Ahern, moved over from Efate to Green Island in March 1944, with flights at Efate and ground crews at Emirau, which combined in June, and continued

A pair of SBD–4s head in towards Wake Island for another strike, October, 1943. (McDonnell Douglas Photo)

the routine bombing until December 1944. VMSB-244, commanded successively by Captain Richard Belyea, Major Frank R. Porter Jr and Major John L. Dexter, had units at Efate, Piva and Torokina, but on 13 May 1944, a flight moved to Green Island where they operated until 21 May, before moving to Emirau, and then to Munda; by 18 September, however, they were back on Green Island, flying sorties into New Britain until December.

VMSB-341, commanded by Major James T. McDaniel, Major Walter D. Persons and then Major Christopher F. Irwin, Jr, reached Efate at the end of 1943, with flights based there and at Munda and Bougainville. In April 1944 the squadron moved to Green Island and continued striking at Rabaul until the end of the year.

While this mundane but essential work was being carried out, significant events were taking place in the central Pacific, where Admiral Nimitz had thrust through the Gilbert Islands and the Marshall Islands towards the Marianas: this was a dagger blow to the very heart of the Japanese 'co-prosperity zone'. The Japanese had been hoarding their fleet as

best they could, still awaiting the chance of the 'final battle', but this policy only led them to disaster, because as fast as they were building up replacement carrier crews, they were then squandering them wholesale in ill-conceived operations from land bases, and as a consequence were having to dilute these elite groups more and more with flyers who had less and less training. Conversely the US Fleet was growing at an astounding rate, and the new fleet and light fleet carriers were packed with new types of aircraft and gadgets which would overwhelm the imperial Navy at the battles of the Philippine Sea and Leyte Gulf. Only one of the many aircraft that still flew from these carrier decks had seen combat from the very beginning, and that was the Douglas SBD Dauntless, but her days as the premier dive bomber in the Navy were clearly numbered.

Initially this was far from the case, and when the *Essex* first commissioned her planned dive bomber complement she was fully equipped with the Dauntless, while the intended aircraft, the Curtiss SB2C-1 Helldiver which VB-9 and VS-9 had tested aboard in November 1942, was dumped back ashore. Next in line was her sister ship, the *Yorktown II*, but a period at sea in May with her VB-4 and VS-6 had produced an enormous number of accidents and little else, so her commanding officer, Captain J. J. Clark, also obtained SBDs for his aircrew and took them off to battle. Similarly the first of the light carriers (CVL), the *Independence*, had her dive bomber squadron equipped with the SBD, even though they were a tight fit in her hangars.

Not until VB-17 – embarked aboard the *Bunker Hill* – hit Rabaul on 11 November 1943, did the Helldiver operate successfully in a combat role, and the Dauntless remained the front-line dive bomber on all other carriers until February 1944. From then on, the Navy's production pro-

Seen from below the forward flight deck of the USS *Enterprise*, an SBD leaves the deck while ahead of her in the distance, three earlier departures are heading low for the 'forming up' point, before taking their departure to the target. (US Navy via National Archives, Washington DC)

gramme had a relentless momentum of its own, and with the Curtiss SB2C-1C Helldiver now in full-scale production during 1944, it quickly replaced the SBDs. Even shore-based units like VC-28 which had employed the SBD-5 in the Solomons campaign, returned home and their experienced crews joined new outfits that were forming like VB-7 at Naval Air Station Wildwood, the main Atlantic coast dive bomber training base. In a similar manner, VB-2 which was forming and training at Hilo, Hawaii, received notice, early in 1944, that their SBDs were to be replaced by SB2Cs; the first of these, brought in by VB-8 pilots, arrived on 6 February.[177] They replaced VB-15 aboard the *Hornet II* shortly afterwards.

The SBD-5 was still utilized as the basic trainer for dive bomber training and tactics in January 1944, and also for training in deck landings aboard the *Sable* and *Wolverine* on the Great Lakes, and the ex-British escort carrier *Charger* (CVE-30) out at sea. Moreover after 2,409 Mark 5s, the -6 was now coming in service with the fleet – too late for carrier combat, but well suited for these training and familiarization functions.

Externally identical to the -5, the -6 had a larger engine installed in a last belated effort to improve performance. A standard production-line -5 (Bu Aer number 28830) was taken as a prototype, and with a new engine fitted became the XSBD-6 for flight testing. This power-plant was the 1,350 hp Wright R-1820-66 Cyclone, which had automatic mixture control as standard, and this pushed the top speed up to 262mph (422km/h) – better, it was true than the earlier production models, but still, it should be noted, 3mph (4.8km/h) *slower* than the original XBT-2.

Despite this, the XSBD–6 was accepted by the Navy on 8 February 1944, after they had changed the existing SBD-5 contract to include this prototype and 1,450 production SBD-6s; but in February 1944, 1,000 of these latter were cancelled due to the decision to go ahead with the long-awaited refitting of the fleet's dive bomber groups with the Curtiss SB2-C Helldiver.

Much of the improvement expected of the larger engine was lost through the resultant large load it involved, the maximum weight now being 10,882lb, (4,936kg) against the -5's 10,700lb (4,854kg). The service ceiling was raised to 28,600ft (8,717m). The self-sealing, lined

An A-24 of the 531st Fighter Bomber Squadron over Canton atoll in the central Pacific, taken by the wingman, Frank A. Tinker. (Frank A. Tinker).

fuel tanks were replaced by the non-metallic bladder type. The range of the –6 showed the biggest improvement, to 1,230 miles (1,979km) as a dive bomber or, with the fitting of a pair of 58-gallon (264l) aluminium drop tanks, to 1,340 miles (2,156km) as a scout. They were fitted with ASV radar as standard, like many of the SBD-5s. The cost of the airplane, after four years of continuous production, had fallen from $85,000 per plane, minus equipment, to $29,000; but even so, this cost-effectiveness failed to save the programme, and with early cancellation of the bulk of the final orders, the end was in sight.

Between March and July 1944 El Segundo produced a total of 450, including the prototype, of this final mark of the Dauntless (Bu Aer numbers 35950 and 54601–55049), the final machine rolling out on 22 July 1944 and bringing the production line to an end. One machine, c/n 4561 (serial no 35922) was earmarked as the prototype for the US Army's proposed equivalent, but as this became a non-event, this machine was finally completed as a standard SBD–5.

The SBD-6 was the last mark in a long and distinguished line, but by the time it appeared, it was effectively obsolete for combat duties, and other than coastal ASW patrolling and dive bomber training, its employment was in subsidiary roles such as target towing, instrument training and squadron 'hacks'. One was utilized by Wright, in the spring of 1944, as a test-bed for an experimental fan installation on their new engine, and other sundry duties came their way.

Modified Photo Reconnaissance (P) variants of most of the major marks of the Dauntless were also produced for the US Navy, and these were fitted with cameras and photographic equipment for this increasingly vital function. They were designated as SBD-1P (eight aircraft), SBD-2P (fifteen aircraft), SBD-3P (forty-seven aircraft), and SBD-4P (sixteen aircraft).

Thus by June 1944, the SBD had been replaced by the SB2C-C1, with VB-1 aboard the *Yorktown II*, VB-2 aboard the *Hornet II*, VB-14 aboard *Wasp II* and VB-15 aboard the *Essex*; but it was still serving with VB-10 aboard the *Enterprise*, VB-16 aboard the *Lexington II*, VB-12 aboard the *Saratoga* and VS–41 aboard the *Ranger*, while the *Independence*'s VC-22 saw combat at Marcus, Wake

## Dauntless Men: Colonel Elmer G. Glidden, US Marine Corps

As a young officer in the United States Marine Corps, Elmer G. Glidden fought at the Battle of Midway and was again in the forefront of dive bomber operations in the hell of Guadalcanal with VMSB-231, the 'Ace of Spades' Dauntless squadron that he was eventually to command. For this work the popular press gave him the unasked for title of 'Iron Man', which embarrassed rather than delighted this soft-spoken man from Massachusetts. He won his second Navy Cross on the fever-infested island, and then returned Stateside to build the squadron back up again, a task in which he was so successful that he found himself back in the central Pacific, leading from the front and achieving more than one hundred dive-bombing missions and further accolades.

Elmer Glidden was born at the small hamlet of Hyde Park on 1 December 1915. He gradu-

ated from Mechanic Arts High School in 1934 and then spent four hard-working years at the Rensselaer Polytechnic Institute at Troy, New York. He had an uncle in the Army, and influenced perhaps by this, the young Glidden joined the Marine Corps Reserve in April 1936 at Quantico, Virginia, and he soon became his class platoon leader. He graduated from the institute with a Bachelor of Aeronautical Engineering degree in 1938.

After a year in a dull factory job he went back to the Marines and asked for flight training, fully enlisting in October 1939 and being appointed as an aviation cadet, going to Pensacola, on Florida's Gulf Coast for his aerial instruction at the naval aeronautical station there. He had orginally wanted to be a fighter pilot, but had early on caught the thrill of dive bombing and was trained on the old biplane Curtiss SBC-3 aircraft with fifty practice dives against 50ft (15m) 'bull's eye' targets ashore, and towed spars out to sea until he became highly proficient in this art.

In September 1940, Glidden was appointed Second Lieutenant, USMC, conducting further specialized dive bomber training at Miami to qualify as a naval aviator and was then sent to San Diego where he was appointed to the scouting/dive-bombing squadron as material officer. He was one of the pilots sent to Connecticut to pick up the new Vought SB2U-3 dive bombers from the factory there and fly them back. Thus he became familiar with the Vindicator – or 'Wind Indicator' – as it was nicknamed by the aircrew, one of a batch of fifty-seven especially modified to carry extra fuel to give it the range the Marine Corps required.

It was never a popular mount, however, and after completing training on these in January 1941, they were shipped out to Hawaii on the decks of a carrier in May, and then in December were hustled away to Midway where they won eternal fame and Elmer got his first Navy Cross. MAG-22 was relieved in July and went back to Ewa where they were given the new Dauntless SBD-3s. Converting to these aircraft and breaking in new cadres to replace their heavy losses kept Glidden – now the executive officer of VMSB-231 – very busy; but after all too short a period the 'Ace of Spades' squaron under Major Leo Smith arrived at Guadalcanal on 30 August 1942, and was pitched straight into yet another life or death situation. As Glidden related to this author:

We soon lost our skipper and then the exec. I was third in line, and after the exec went I became squadron CO. We were in bad shape, what with our flying and living conditions, and were ready for relief. Our relief squadron came in and before getting off the ground lost the three senior people during a naval bombardment.[1]

Flying here, Glidden's trademark became his cigars: he was rarely without one, and they became famous. With just four Dauntlesses left on its strength by 16 October 1942, VMSB-231 were evacuated back to the States and Elmer began the long task of rebuilding it from scratch with the new Dash-4 SBDs. They took these aircraft back to Midway in July 1943 and remained there until December, when they became involved in the ongoing task of subduing the Japanese air strength in the Marshalls, working out of Tarawa, and then from Majuro, as part of Marine Air Wing Four.

From January 1944 until August, Glidden clocked up 800 hours of dive bombing in seventy-three more missions: this gave him the legendary total of 100 combat dives, when most of his generation of pilots were working desk jobs Stateside. He eventually made it 104, a record, for which he won the air medal and was presented with the gold star by Brigadier General L. Woods; he was also promoted to Lieutenant Colonel.

He was appointed assistant operations officer, MAW-4 at Kwajalein, at which post he remained for nine months before returning home in May 1945. In July he was working at the Division of Aviation Headquarters in Washington, DC and here he met and ultimately married his wife Phyllis, a 'Boston Belle'. This was followed by two periods of duty at the Amphibious Warfare School at Quantico in 1948 and 1954, during the time of the Korean War where the value of ground-attack had to be re-learnt all over again.

Glidden had not yet hung up his flying boots however, for in July 1957 he became the CO of the Marine Air Division at Memphis, Tennessee, becoming a full colonel in 1948, and returning to El Toro as assistant chief of staff in January 1959. In 1961, Vietnam loomed large, and for a third time dive-bombing was an urgent requirement, this time with the famed Douglas Skyraider, that worthy and equally long-lasting and popular successor to the Dauntless.

Naturally, Elmer got himself back into the action and served as AC/S G-5 and G-3 at the headquarters of MAW–3 in Vietnam itself between September 1964 and July 1965. He told me, perhaps wistfully, that 'I flew only staff missions, non-combat, during Korea and Vietnam. Not much excitement!' This was followed with a year with III/MAF as deputy chief of staff and assistant chief of staff with G-6. HIs final service appointments were chief of staff, COMCABWEST and then as CO of Marine Barracks, Panama. He took his very honourable retirement on 1 January 1970, and lives in Canton, Massachusetts with two Navy Crosses, the Legion of Merit/Combat Distinguishing Device, three Distinguished Flying Crosses and twelve Air Medals. He remained a Dauntless dive bomber man at heart and confessed that 'I will always miss not being on duty in the Corps and being a part of something good.' (US Marine Corps official photograph)

[1] See Peter C. Smith, Into the Assault, London & Washington 1985, Tokyo, 1986, Taipei, 1997, for a full account of Glidden's career

Island and Tarawa before being replaced by the TBM Avenger whose folding wings made them more suitable for the light carriers.

This was not the case, initially, with the Dauntlesses serving with the USMC, and they continued to soldier on throughout 1944, and indeed, right to the end of the Pacific war. Again, as at Rabaul, the SBD was doomed at first to be relegated to the task of back area bomber. On 9 November 1943, Task Force 57 had been set up. However, in readiness for the Gilbert Islands operation, and this consisted of all the shore-based aircraft of the central Pacific force. A major part of that task force was Brigadier General L. G. Merritt's 4th Air Wing, and it contained a total of seventy-two Dauntless dive bombers from VMSB-151, VMSB-241, VMSB-331 and VMSB-341. Even though it was the Marines that stormed ashore at Tarawa, the supporting dive bombing was carried out by the Navy's dive bombers, not the Marines'.

A rehearsal of the amphibious operations at Makin, Operation 'Galvanic', had been held at Kahoolawe Island, with the Navy SBD units operating on air support missions, and this was followed by a critique held at Ford Island with Admirals Radford, Mullinix and Colonel Erickson, USAAF, Commander Support Aircraft, the squadron commanders and air combat intelligence officers. Between 19 and 23 November the dive bombers, predominately Dauntlesses, blasted the enemy defences from seven fleet carriers, five light carriers and three escort carriers.

Now that the US fleet had been built up to a daunting size, the earlier 'hit-and-run' raids of 1942 were repeated, but on a gradually increasing scale across the whole of the central Pacific area. On the 18 March 1944, the Lexington II's SBDs participated in Rear Admiral Lee's bombardment of Mili, the southernmost of the Marshall Island atolls. Then at the end of March the American task forces conducted a whole series of attacks known as Operation 'Desecrate' against the Western Caroline Islands, hitting Palau, Yap, Ulithi and Woleai as related. Again the Dauntless made a significant contribution to this assault, operating from the Enterprise and Lexington II. Thus on 30 March 1944, Palau was the target for two dozen SBDs and a dozen TBFs from the Enterprise, under overall command of Lieutenant Commander William I. Martin, with enemy shipping as their primary target.[178]

The twelve VB-10 Dauntlesses from the *Enterprise* led by Lieutenant Ira Hardman, attacked the elderly torpedo boat *Wakatake*, making their attack dives from 11,000ft (3,300m). One SBD was lost to the little ship's flak gunners early on. In return, one direct 1,000lb (450kg) bomb hit was made on the target's stern '. . . which seemed to lift her out of the water'. Her speed was reduced from twenty-five knots to eight by this blow, making her a sitting duck. A second bomb hit the torpedo boat forward as she slowed down, still turning a tight circle and firing hard with all her guns. A second SBD, piloted by Lieutenant (jg) Charles Pearson, and the last plane in off the stack, was also hit and dived straight in alongside the sinking ship as she herself rolled over and sank. In four further follow-up strikes the SBDs also sank the repair ship *Akashi* in this raid, along with twenty-seven other merchant ships. On 1 April they bombed Woleai airfield with four deliberate strikes which wrecked it and the surrounding facilities totally.

Their next strike was on 22 April in support of McArthur's forces taking Hollandia, the Dauntlesses of *Enterprise* joining with the air groups from the *Lexington II*, *Princeton* and *Langley* in dive bombing the airfields at Hollandia, Cyclops and Sentani. These strikes were hampered by low cloud, which was down to 600–800 ft (180–240m), but through which the SBDs laid their 1,000lb (450kg) bombs in short, sharp diving attacks with hurried pull-outs at low level. Again there was no opposition from the enemy other than AA fire, and the SBDs took no losses. On 21 April the *Yorktown II* had contributed SBD strikes by the reformed VB-5 to the assault on Wakde and Hollandia, and they flew cover for the landings in Humboldt Bay until the 24th. Moving north-eastwards after these strikes, the SBDs next hit Truk once more on 29 April 1944. A nine-Dauntless strike led by Lieutenant Commander Richard Poor was despatched from the *Enterprise*, and a similar-sized one from the *Lexington II* at dawn, the dive bombers of both groups being armed with 1,000lb (450kg) bombs with instantaneous fuses. The approach was made at 10,000ft (3,000m) through patchy cloud down to 5,000ft (1,500m), which often obscured the target and ruled out a conventional dive attack. To combat the conditions, Poor led his unit in a fast,

Young US Marine Corps Dauntless crews from the 'Ace of Spades' squadron based in the Marshall Islands gather round for a Combat Mission Briefing, for a strike against the Japanese airfield located on Taroa Island. The routine hammering at these by-passed atoll bases preoccupied much of their time in 1944. (US Marine Corps)

shallow approach instead, with no flaps utilized, the targets being the AA gun positions on Moen, thus easing the passage of the following Avengers who were also glide bombing, but against the runway itself.[179] Further attacks followed throughout the day. Meanwhile, SBDs from *Yorktown II*'s decks plastered Dublon Island and the airstrip on the tiny islet of Eten next door.

The following day these strikes were repeated, with VB-10 again targeting Moen, this time the seaplane base and military buildings on the southern side of the island, while VB-16 took out what remained at Paran. The *Yorktown II* also launched four out of five planned dive bomber strikes that day, the worsening weather conditions forcing the cancellation of the last. This marked the last outing for VB-5's Dauntlesses, and as one eyewitness observed at the time:

The planes which had wrought so much havoc to Japan's shrinking empire looked old and tired as they rolled up the deck. They were, too. They deserved replacement, as much as the air group deserved its approaching thirty-day leave. The old Douglas Dauntless dive bombers were to be replaced by Helldivers, new SB2Cs, but they would have to be pretty good to be as reliable as the outmoded old SBDs. The last day several of them came back with big chunks shot out of their wings by AA, but they landed without trouble.[180]

Correct though he might have been about *Yorktown II*'s dive bombers – whose VB-5 dive bombers were indeed replaced by the Helldivers of VB-1 on her return to Majuro – Jensen was a bit premature as regards finally writing off the Dauntless, for the SBD had one last kick left in her before she quit the fast carrier war in the central Pacific.

Events were now shaping up to a grand finale, the mother of all carrier battles, because the Japanese, having seen the Americans advance relentlessly over 2,000 miles (3,200km) with little opposition, were determined to present their full fleet in defence of the Marianas. They did not have to wait very long, for in the prelude to the Battle of the Philippine Sea, Task Force 58 sortied out on 11 June 1944 to carry out pre-emptive strikes in readiness for Operation 'Forager', the invasion of Saipan.

The Americans' vast strength included four carrier groups which totalled seven large and eight light carriers, every one of which, other than the *Enterprise*, had been built *since* Pearl Harbor. Most of the VB squadrons embarked flew the SB2C, but two squadrons at least proudly flew the Dauntless, and if Vice Admiral Marc Mitscher could have had his way, many more would still have done so. Thus it was that on Task Group 58 the *Enterprise* fielded VB-10, led by Commander James D. Ramage with twenty-three SBD-5s; while the *Lexington II* had VB-16 with thirty-four SBD-5s, led by Lieutenant Commander Ralph Weymouth, formerly of VB-3.

It is convenient to summarize here the contribution of the land-based Marine Corps units, which continued using the SBD in the central Pacific long after the last one had flown from a CV deck. In readiness for the operation, VMSB-331 had moved up to remote Nukufetau atoll on 15 November with fifteen SBDs, although it was not initially utilized. This led to calls for some escort carriers to be allocated to the Corps so they could operate their SBDs in support of future landings, but this never came to pass with regard to the Marines' operational use of the Dauntless, other than for transportation and the flying off of units, and they continued to be land-based.

The Marine SBDs did finally manage to get into the action however, once the islands had fallen, and VMSB-331, under Major Paul R. Byrum, arrived at Tarawa's patched-up airstrip with six Dauntlesses on 30 November 1943. They were soon in action, when on 21 December five of them made a strike at Japanese transports located at the Jaluit lagoon. They attacked in conjunction with other forces and claimed to have sunk a freighter, but their

direct hits were in fact scored on the already damaged and beached water-carrier, *Goryu Maru*, which they duly finished off. The squadron then returned to Nukufetau atoll.

It was a similar story for the Marshall Island invasion, in that the USMC

Dauntlesses were relegated to a back-seat role; although MAG-13, under Colonel Lawrence Norman, was made into an entire dive bomber group by the incorporation of VMSB-331 and by the arrival of VMSB-231, commanded by major Elmer Glidden from Ewa.

Once again, Navy Dauntlesses and Helldivers were the main force for the 31 January invasion of Kwajalein atoll, Operation 'Flintlock', after flying numerous softening-up missions against Japanese bases all over the Marshalls during the preceding month. On 21 February 1944, the escort carrier *Gambier Bay* arrived off the atoll and Major Glidden's VMSB-331 Dauntlesses flew off her stubby flight deck to land at Majuro airstrip, where they joined VMSB-231, whose forward echelons had arrived on the 3rd. These two squadrons now began a long stint of hammering away at the various island garrisons and airstrips that still lay untouched in the Marshalls but were not considered worthwhile invading; thus Emidj Island and Enybor Island at Jaluit atoll, Wotje Island, Taroa Island at Maloelpa atoll, and Mille Island, became names with which the Marine SBD aircrews were to become grindingly familiar over the next months.

The first mission was flown on 4 March 1944 and was mounted against Jaluit, VMSB-331 staging via Majuro. It met fierce anti-aircraft fire, and almost half the attacking aircraft received damage of one kind or another. So the next day, VMSB-231 – the 'Ace of Spades' squadron – took the strongest of the Japanese AA positions as their dive-bombing targets, and thereafter the two squadrons alternated attacks until gradually the enemy firepower was beaten down.

On 24 March, VMSB-231 with thirteen Dauntlesses blasted the radio station at Wotje, and on the 27th the same unit again hit targets here; Wotje was also dive bombed by SBDs on the 30 March and 14 April. The next mission, conducted on the 4 May, was one with a difference, a weird combination of threat and bribery, with VMSB-231 bombing and strafing ammunition dumps and the coastal gun position at Taroa, while VMSB-331 dropped propaganda leaflets and seventy-two cans of salmon! Presumably it was offering the Japanese a choice: surrender and eat, or resist and die. Not surprisingly perhaps, the Japanese defenders chose the latter option!

Another variation on tactics was tried

On an Hawaiian airfield in 1944, A-24s alternate with P-47 Thunderbolts of Transportation Command while crates of parts are unpacked in the foreground. The Banshee closest the camera is 42-54520 with the Transport Command badge on the engine cowling. (Smithsonian Institution, Washington DC)

on the night of 13–14 May, when night harassment sorties, like those flown at Guadalcanal, were mounted over Jaluit, with the Dauntlesses just stooging around and dropping a bomb every hour. However, this seemed to have a greater negative effect on the Marine aircrews than on the Japanese defenders. After that the routine bombing continued unrelentingly.

The next great jump westwards was the capture of Eniwetok atoll, some 337 miles (542km) north-west from Kwajalein. Here, once again, the Dauntlesses followed up the successful invasion force fairly quickly, one echelon from VMSB-151 – commanded by Major Gordon H. Knott – flying in to Engebi Island from Wallis Island on 29 February 1944 after a 2,000 mile (3,218km) staged flight. Their duties were to fly anti-submarine patrols and air-search sorties in case the enemy reacted against this exposed position – but they never did, other than bombing raids. VMSB-151's offensive dive-bombing missions included sorties against Ujelang atoll to the south-west and two or three longer-range sorties (367 miles/590km) to strike at Ponape in the Caroline Islands, a major Japanese supply base.

The next big push was against the Marianas, Operation 'Forager', and the invasion of Saipan on 15 June 1944. Again the Marine SBDs were allocated a role, albeit their usual one, of follow-up and

### Radio Call Sign Allocations to VII Bomber Command A-24s at Hawaii

#### 26 June 1943[184]

| Serial | Primary | |
|--------|---------|--------|
| Secondary | | |
| 42-6716 | CK26 | ZO56 |
| 42-6725 | K16 | KIK |
| 42-6792 | KT45 | 4EK |
| 42-6803 | KL44 | 4BLA |
| 42-6805 | BG62 | YX38 |
| 42-6812 | CD17 | ZI2 |
| 42-6813 | CG57 | 1A48 |
| 42-6821 | CH5 | ZL9 |
| 42-6822 | BU8 | Y572 |
| 42-6829 | CI2 | Z94 |
| 42-60772 | B39 | Y623 |
| 42-60773 | BF2 | Y623 |
| 42-60796 | B559 | ZD12 |
| 42-60806 | GL9 | Z72 |

consolidation. They formed part of Brigadier General Thomas J. Cushman's Task Force 59.4, which encompassed the USMC dive bomber and fighter bomber force, and included the seventy-two Dauntlesses; but these latter played only an insignificant part in the operation, both here and at Guam which followed.

The following summary gives an outline of the activities of the Marine Corps' SBDs during this rather lean period for action.[181] Fortunately for most of them, a far more interesting and useful period was to come.

VMSB-151, commanded successively by Lieutenant Colonel Gordon H. Knott, Major Randolph C. Berkeley Jr and Major Bruce Prosser, reached Engebi on 29 February 1944, and between 9 and 12 March covered landings at Wotho, Ujae and Lae, as well as joining in the general attacks on Marshall Island group targets until June 1945, when they returned to the States.

VMSB-245, commanded by Major Julian F. Acers and then Major Robert F. Halladay and finally Major John E. Bell, arrived at Majuro on 13 May 1944, transferring to Makin at the end of that month. Between 1 June and 29 October 1944, it was fully engaged in strikes against Japanese-held islands in the Marshall Group. In October it shifted its base to Majuro again, but the work remained similar in routine. By 15 March the squadron had again moved, this time to Ulithi, and it continued operations from here until the end of the war.

VMSB-331, commanded by Major James C. Otis, Major John H. McEniry and finally Major Winston E. Jewson, was at Majuro by 25 February 1944, and after a period of experimenting with Corsairs in the dive-bombing role, reverted to SBDs at the end of the year. It continued its Marshalls' strike role right through to July 1945.

So much for the Marines, but the USAAF was still in the picture at the beginning of the period under review here. General Kenney continued to rail against the Banshee, even though they were being phased out of his command. His constant theme throughout was that the Douglas was too short-ranged, and was '. . . too slow to argue with the Zeros',[182] This latter description could, however, be applied to almost all his bomber aircraft, none of which could outrun a Zeke, but it was only used against the one bomber that hit what it aimed at, the Banshee, and then, when

he had got rid of them, the Dauntless.

It may come as something of a surprise, therefore, to find that, while the Banshee was being reviled and then relegated to a back-area trainer and hack, USAAF units were continuing to use them in combat in the central Pacific, and to use them very successfully as dive bombers with high accuracy and minimum losses, right through into the spring of 1944. Most historians have written off the Banshee as finished in the summer of 1942, but the truth, as is so often the case, is much different. A number of A-24s were shipped out to the Pacific during the summer of 1943 and initially based at Hawaii before moving westward to the islands. Nine A-24As were assembled by the Aircraft Repair Branch there in March 1943, with five more in April. In August 1943, eight A–24Bs were assembled, one in September, thirteen in October, four in November and nine more in December.[183]

The first unit to receive these dive bombers was the 58th Bombardment Squadron (Dive), which was based at Wheeler Field, Hawaii. Its first combat mission was an attack on Japanese positions at Kiska Island, in the occupied Aleutians, which took place on 4 August 1943. This was a success, and the 58th moved down to the Gilbert Islands where it was re-designated the 531st Fighter Bomber Squadron.

Frank A. Tinker told the author:-

I was a pilot of the 531st Fighter-Bomber Squadron during 1943, stationed on the island of Canton in the central Pacific. This is one of the atolls which the U.S. leased from the U.K. as part of the destroyers-for-bases deal in 1940. Nobody lived there, one palm tree, on the Equator, sand beach, so maintenance was difficult. We flew anti-submarine patrols from Canton until the big push across the Pacific began. We nicknamed our A-24s the Douglas Doubtful!

Taken aboard escort carriers used as aircraft transports, capable of launching, but not retrieving the A-24, we went from Hawaii to a point just off Tarawa and Makin. After bombing the enemy, (perhaps the only U.S. Army carrier-launched Army bombing mission other than the Doolittle raid), we landed on a hastily-built airstrip at Makin, while the Marines and Seebees were still clearing the last of the Japanese from palm trees and dugouts. Thereafter we flew sorties against the Marshall Islands, in particular Mili, Maloelap, and Jaluit. This involved long over-

Another view of an Army Air Force field on Oahu, Hawaii in 1944, showing Hangar Number 5 full of A-24s from the 86th Fighter Bomber Squadron, with others parked outside. On the runway are B-24 Liberator heavy bombers. (Smithsonian Institution, Washington DC)

heavy black smoke was reported by the last five dive bombers. The *Maru* put up some AA defence, described as '. . . meagre to moderate', and this was accurate for altitude but trailing all the time. Similar flak was encountered from that part of the island over which they had to fly after pull-out, but only two A-24s sustained damage as a result, and these were small and insignificant shrapnel holes. The final two reported that thick black smoke completely obscured the ship target by the time they had completed their attack.

The A-24s also strafed enemy gun positions and a barracks area in the south-eastern part of the island, with .50– and .30–calibre machine-gun fire as they pulled out. As for aerial resistance, there was none; the three Japanese fighters observed taking off from Mille failed to make contact with the Banshees, although escorting P-39s and F6Fs claimed one of them was shot down, one probably destroyed, and the other damaged.

Next day, 23 December, a daylight dive-bombing attack was made by ten Banshees on another freighter and also on a Japanese escort vessel and ground installations at Mille atoll; they left Makin at 2001.[186] For this attack the dive bombers again carried three 500lb (227kg) GP bombs with $\frac{1}{10}$ sec nose and $\frac{1}{40}$ sec tail fuses. They took a course of 342 degrees true at 12,000ft (3,600m) to the target, lowering down to 10,000ft (3,000m) before commencing their dives. The target area was reached at 2321 and all the aircraft peeled off in order, starting their pull-outs at 1,000ft (300m).

Lieutenant Moralos, piloting No 527, scored one confirmed direct hit on the transport, while Captain Poulot took the PC boat for his target and scored a very near miss on the speeding vessel. The bombs from Major Wigley's Banshee, No 521, and Lieutenant Larsen's, No 468, landed in the water about 400ft (120m) from the freighter. The remaining six A-24s bombed shore installations in the south-eastern portion of Mille Island. There was one hit observed on an automatic weapons position, but no other damage was observed on ground positions. They did, however, hit the freighter that had been bombed the day before, and she was seen with her deck under water and the centre part of her hull badly damaged.

Once more the AA fire was described as 'meagre' on the approach, but after the dives had been completed, fire from auto-

water flights with minimum navigation equipment, and several planes were lost. I was shot down on 23rd December, 1943, and survived, (eighteen of twenty-one US prisoners were beheaded) to be sent to Japan.

The rest of the squadron stayed only a few months' operations after which the A-24s were retired and the crews transitioned into other aircraft.

The oddest thing about our particular use of these dive bombers was that as Army personnel we were catapulted several times off the decks of these 'Jeep' carriers. In the Pacific we started our dives at about 12,000 feet and pulled out just over the water, always with the canopy open (due to condensation etc.). I was shot down by flak, very heavy over these isolated islands, and my gunner was killed. On the whole, the aircraft and engines performed very well under the difficult circumstances. We started service in Hawaii (Wheeler Field) with the early models (1850 hp) and were given newer ones (2000 hp) prior to going into combat. Fat lot of good it did!

As Frank stated, for a considerable period the 531st Fighter-Bomber Squadron, was based on Makin Island, in the Gilbert Group which had been captured on the 23rd November and turned into an air base very quickly. From here the Banshees conducted numerous dive-bombing missions northwards against Mili atoll and other targets.

On 22 December 1943, eleven A-24s of the 531st carried out a dive-bombing attack on a large Japanese transport ship, discovered in Mille Lagoon the day before.[185] Take-off from Makin was at 0040 and each Banshee was loaded with three 500lb (227kg) general purpose bombs, with $\frac{1}{40}$ sec delay tail fuses. They took a route out on 342 degrees true at an altitude of 10,000ft (3,000m) and located the target easily at 0200. On arrival in the attacking position, each aircraft peeled off in order, into the dive attack, pulling out from heights that varied from 1,000 to 1,500ft (300 to 450m). All the bombs were confirmed as hitting within 150ft (45m) of the target except for No 465, whose bombs failed to release and later had to be jettisoned in the ocean.

The bombs from the first six Banshees down started a large fire amidships of the freighter, and a large explosion followed by matic weapons all missed astern of the formation. A novelty reported was that four aerial bombs were dropped on the formation about 10 miles (16km) from the target, after the A-24s had dived and reformed. These aerial bombs exploded from between 1,500 and 2,000ft (450 and 600m) behind, and 1,000ft (300m) above the American formation.

Two Zekes evaded the fighter cover and made passes at the A-24s, just after these aerial bombs were dropped, in some sort of co-ordinated assault. One approached the Banshees from eight o'clock above to within 150ft (45m) of the formation which held steady, the other was attacked by escorting P-39s and was shot down before he could complete his pass. None of the dive bombers was damaged by either flak or fighter attack, and two Zekes were claimed destroyed, with one probably, by the escort.

Christmas Day brought no let-up, and presents were duly delivered to the Japanese defenders of Mille in the form of thirty 500lb (227kg) GP bombs with instantaneous nose fuses and $1/40$ sec delay tail fuses.[187] The Santa Claus substitutes were ten A-24s from the 531st, eleven of which had taken off from Makin at 1905. All eleven routed out, but as they neared the target and the bomb selector switches were thrown, one aircraft suffered exactly the same malfunction that had plagued VB-3 at the Battle of Midway eighteen months before, and all its bombs were released prematurely into the sea. This aircraft turned back, but the remaining ten pressed on to the target.

Again, only sparse and inaccurate AA fire met the incoming dive bombers, which began when they were still one mile (1.6km) out. The A-24s took normal evasive action by weaving and losing altitude before commencing their attack dives, and were not worried by it. Two Banshees sustained small holes in their left wings, but there was no serious damage.

## Aircraft Assignment VII Bomber Command 23 March 1944

| A-24As | A-24Bs |
|--------|--------|
| 42-6716 | 42-54361 |
| 42-6803 | 42-54403 |
| 42-6805 | 42-54404 |
| 42-6812 | 42-54459 |
| 42-6822 | 42-54461 |
| 42-6829 | 42-54464 |
| 42-60772 | 42-54465 |
| 42-60773 | 42-54466 |
| 42-60796 | 42-54468 |

Once the dives were completed, the flak again intensified, with fire coming from batteries on the west shore near the end of the runway.

The target was reached at 2027 and the lagoon was empty of all shipping, nor were there any aircraft observed on the runways. The dive bombers therefore took what was left, ground installations, runways and AA gun positions on Mille Island all being plastered. Seventeen bombs hit on, or near the medium AA site on the southern shore, six of these hitting the shore near the intersection of the east-west runway and the north-south runway. Six further bombs hit the two intersections of these runways, while a large explosion with grey smoke resulted from a hit on an ammunition storage dump in the rear of an AA position, and all firing ceased abruptly after the fifth Banshee had completed its dive. All aircraft returned safely after a round trip of 442 miles (711km).

After a short lull, the assault was resumed on the 29 December 1943, and it continued for the next three months, with the squadron operating at maximum efficiency and with minimum losses. It was clear that the A-24, when used in sufficient numbers and with a fully trained aircrew

## VII Bomber Command A-24 Allocations April 1944

| Unit | In Service | Under Repair | Total |
|------|-----------|-------------|-------|
| 86th combat mapping | 1 | 1 | 2 |
| 17th tow target | 1 | 1 | 2 |
| 45th fighter | 1 | 1 | 2 |
| 46th fighter | 2 | - | 2 |
| 47th fighter | - | 2 | 2 |
| 72nd fighter | - | 1 | 1 |
| 78th fighter | 1 | - | 1 |
| VII BC training unit | - | - | - |
| 42nd bomb | - | - | - |
| 819th bomb | - | - | - |
| 17th AB sqdn. | - | 1 | 1 |
| 28th photo reconn. | 1 | 1 | 2 |
| 420th sub-depot | 1 | - | 1 |
| Total | 8 | 8 | 16 |

and a planned programme, could do the job asked of it. Unfortunately this failed to save its reputation: with the restructuring of the 531st from fighter bomber to fighter squadron, the A-24s were declared surplus to requirements, and General Order 23 of 5 March 1944 resulted in their release from VII Bomber Command. The Banshees thus relegated to back-area work were as shown in the table above:[188]

In the Pacific theatre, retirement from combat duty did not necessarily mean retirement from useful AAF duties, as the list (above) of A-24s, the units and their duties, illustrates[189]; it covers the period 22 April to 26 April 1944.

Only one TRA-24B remained on the strength of the Hawaiian Air Depot during June through to August 1945, however, to represent the Douglas bomber's final AAF connection with the central Pacific.

# CHAPTER NINETEEN

# Tangles at Tulsa

On 3 July 1942, the Acting Director Bombing at HQ Army Air Forces (AFRDB) was in receipt of a report from General Brett on the performance of the A-24s in Australia. From this they extrapolated one paragraph which they forwarded to AFAMC through AFDMR. It read:

> The A-24 has been most unsatisfactory. It was originally designed for carrier operation and, as a result, is not suitable for landing on soft field. The engines do not stand up and its speed, even at full throttle, is too slow.

AFRDB commented that, 'In addition to the foregoing comment, other reports indicate the A-24 is not a suitable dive bomber.' Someone had underlined these words and added a question mark at the end, as well they might. Here was the Air Force, who until 1940 had shown no

The 1,000 hp Wright R–1820-52 engine of an early SBD-3. This replaced the earlier -32, but overall performance improvement was marginal. (McDonnell Douglas)

interest in the dive bomber or dive bombing, and had little or no expertise in the matter other than the self-sacrifice of its pitifully few combat flyers ill-served by home supply, claiming after just eighteen months, that the current dive bomber they had, which was almost identical to the one that was being used so outstandingly by the Navy and Marine Corps, was not a suitable dive bomber!

The Memo continued in the same vein, stating that they were much concerned because:

> . . . it is understood that 1,200 more A-24s are on order. In its present form the A-24 cannot be considered an operational airplane judged by present standards and is definitely not an airplane of the future. It certainly should be possible to use the production capacity, materials, engines, instruments, etc. which are going into the A–24 to build a more suitable airplane. [They added that,] If improvements have been made in the projected A-24 it is requested that this office be notified as to what they are and the performance expected of the later model.[190]

With regard to making better use of material, the fact that it was the engine that was cited as being one of the main reasons for the A–24's under-performance makes it difficult to understand what other use it could be put to. With regard to the problem of the soft field landings, this was nothing new. The pneumatic tail wheel was fitted to all Army models of the SBD-3A which had been diverted, and this had been a standard design feature from the Mark 1 onwards. Although carrier deck landings required a solid rubber rear wheel to help mitigate the effects of tail bounce and missed arrestor wires, the Marine Corps had been replacing these with pneumatic tyres for a considerable time, as we have already noted following Ed Heinemann's visit to Cuba, so it should

not have been a problem.

The response was immediate, AFRGS informing AFDMR on 9 July that:

> In view of the foregoing report regarding the A–24 airplane and other information regarding this type, it is planned that this type airplane will be used as a trainer in the X322.3 OUT Program. The entire Dive Bomber Program is being revised and charts are being prepared showing desired allocation of this type aircraft. In view of the unsatisfactory report on the A–24 airplane, it is contemplated furnishing the A–20 type for the theatre given in Item 1.[191]

In the meantime the contracts were still rolling, despite shortages and conversion problems. In a TWX message on 14 July, Colonel Oliver R. Cook informed the AAF representative at the El Segundo plant that:

> Armament installation and electrical system modification, for the contractor's information and for the purpose of clarifying the status of armament installation shortages on twenty A-24 airplanes destined for 'Sumac' Project 400, the contractor is advised as follows: Ninety (90) A-24 airplanes off subject contract will not be converted from 12 to 24 volt system at the contractor's plant but at Army Modification Center. These 90 airplanes will leave contractor's plant and will be delivered to San Pedro Naval Base for installation of armament . . . Airplanes will then be delivered by Ferry Command to Army Modification Centre for Radio installation and conversion of electrical system from 12 to 24 volt. It is desired that the above 90 A-24 airplanes be first delivered off contract N–91397 . . .[192]
>
> Subsequent crating for export of the 20 for 'Sumac' will be done after leaving Modification Center either at the contractor's plant or at most equitable port of embarkation.

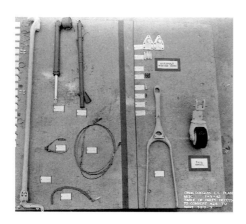

The parts necessary to convert the A-24 into a Navy SBD-3 are displayed at El Segundo on 3 July 1942. It was with the rapid reconversion of Army types – mainly intended as dive-bombing trainers in readiness for the arrival of the Brewster Buccaneer and the Curtiss Shrike – that production was initiated, and the ability to reconvert them back quickly should the Navy require them again was paramount. Parts include the tail wheel, yoke, catapult towing hook, tail hook itself, strut, lever and cable assemblies. (McDonnell Douglas)

General Kenney was keeping up the pressure to get rid of the Banshee from his command and on 12 August 1942 he sent a telegram stating that the A-24 '. . . is not desired as a combat plane in this theatre'.[193] AFADS enquired of AFDMR, 'Can we confine this type of airplane to air-ground support or should we abandon it altogether?' It was a bit late to be discussing this as it was especially for air-ground use that the A-24 had been purchased in the first place, and to abandon it because it would not perform in its mis-use as a strategic bomber was rather perverse. However, these were trying times.

General Arnold in the War Room directed that no more A-24s be sent to Australia. AFDMR responded by stating that General Kenney's message had already been subjected to discussion by that Directorate. Their opinion was firm on the A-24:

It is still the most operational dive bomber the Air Force has. It is an excellent training dive bomber. It has been and can be used with fair chances of success *if properly employed*.[194] The fact must be accepted that dive bombers will not be able to perform their primary function *and* furnish their own complete protection. Where the enemy target is fairly well defended, it will usually be necessary to have

the dive bomber furnished with a fighter escort.[195]

The RAF with their own Wellington and Battle debacles in 1939 and 1940, had already been taught that this lesson did not only apply to dive bombers, and had switched to night bombing, and soon the US Army Air Force was to find out in Europe that even the superlative B-17 and B-29 heavy bombers would have *exactly* the same requirement after suffering even more horrendous losses than the A-24 ever did.

The reply continued: 'The A-24 is not an ideal type bomber but until a better one is put into production the A-24 should be continued in production.' AFADS concurred with this opinion, but added a rider that:

It is believed that an analysis of the entire dive bomber picture will have to be brought up in the Material Planning Council, for every dive bomber in the current RM–80 is reported to be either of dubious value or questionable as to when it can be produced.[196]

This being so, the awarding of Contract W535ac-28716 (8207), preference AA-1, was nonetheless still approved by the Assistant Secretary of War on the same date, 14 August 1942. This contract called for Douglas to supply fifty-five dive-bombers, model A-24A and 1,145 dive bombers, model A-24B, plus spare parts and data for an estimated cost of

$64,086,300 dollars with a fixed fee of £2,563,452, and it superseded the earlier contract letter of 21 May. Approval of this contract was recommended on 27 November 1942, and it was approved on 1 December 1942.[197] Douglas then could have little hint that the AAF was anything other than eager to purchase its product at this date, despite General Kenney's continual sniping and the forthcoming review of policy mooted.

But already straws were in the wind which hinted at further problems which would affect the already complicated supply of a type of aircraft suitable for both the Navy and Army's different operations and expectations. On 3 and 4 November a conference was held at the new Tulsa plant between Douglas representatives and officers from Material Branch. This was followed by a second conference on the 11th of that month. In official jargon these conferences were held to '. . . obtain agreement and co-ordination with Douglas and Bureau of Aeronautics regarding certain changes in subject airplane desired by the Army in order to comply with directives of the Joint Aircraft Committee on standardisation and certain other changes made mandatory due to non-availability of certain items of Navy equipment.'[198]

They tried their utmost to reach a degree of harmony, but early hopes of standardization received a severe knock because the Army requirements differed from the Navy's in many instances. Among those cited were:

Comparison of a Navy SBD-3 and the Army A-2 at the El Segundo plant, to illustrate the differences. The Army machine is only outwardly changed, other than the colour scheme, by the larger pneumatic rear tyre and the lack of tail hook. (McDonnell Douglas)

US Army A-24 in flight, serial number 41-5780. (US National Archives, Washington DC)

1. Deletion of the Mark IV automatic pilot and substitution of the Army-supplied directional gyros and artificial horizons.
2. Provision of all items for carrier operations were to be retained in the airplane, but the Army desired only catapult hooks, hold-back fittings and hoisting slings to be boxed in kits, shipped separately and stored at depots.
3. The fitting of a demand-type oxygen system, furnishing supply sufficient for 3fi hours for each crew member at 15,000ft (4,500m) altitude with the aircraft in 1,000lb (450kg) bomb loaded condition, *instead* of the Navy's rebreather system as fitted.
4. The Army did not want ASB or IFF radar fitted, but provision for it had to continue to be built in should the aircraft revert to naval use.
5. The Navy-type battery was rejected and an F–1 aircraft battery, solenoid switch and battery drain was to be fitted instead.
6. The Army B–16 compass would not fit the provision for the Navy's Mark VIII compass and so the latter had to be fitted instead.
7. A Mark VIII illuminated gun-sight was to be fitted in lieu of the Navy's telescopic sight.
8. The Army required Mark 51 bomb racks instead of the Mark 50 as fitted in aircraft to be built at Tulsa.
9. An Army-type 94-32278 generator relay and control box to be fitted in lieu of the Navy type.
10. In order to have all A–24Bs identical, the sixty of those being produced at El Segundo would be ferried to Tulsa and modified. Army radio would be fitted.

Despite all this, the delivery requirement asked of the brand-new plant and work force at Tulsa for the 1,200 A-24Bs was specified as follows: February 1943, five; March, fifteen; April, thirty; May, forty-five; June, sixty-five; July, ninety-five; August, 120; September to February 1944, 130 per month, with a final March 1944 delivery of forty-five aircraft.[199]

On 1 February 1943, Major John H. Williams sent an inter-office memo to Chief, Production Control Section of Air Material Command in Washington, DC summarizing the reports of visiting officers to the Tulsa plant, one of whom was present on another matter but who was requested to look into the status of the production of the A-24Bs. He reported that '... conditions had not improved since the last visit.' More specifically, he alleged that:

The contractor is apparently more interested in modification than in production, and as this plant will eventually be called upon to build the A-26 airplane, something should be done to impress upon the contractor the importance of manufacture and training of personnel, so

A-24 in flight with modified national markings. (US Air Force via Nick Williams)

When the new plant in Tulsa, Oklahoma, got underway it was quickly geared up to A-24 production to meet expanding Army Air Corps orders. (McDonnell Douglas, Long Beach)

that when the jigs and fixtures are received from Long Beach, there will be trained personnel available . . .'[200]

Events were moving elsewhere too, for on 19 March 1943, Brigadier General K. B. Wolfe called for the convening of the Board at Wright Field, to evaluate the current dive bombers then in production, namely the A-35, A-25 and A-24. 'The Board will make recommendations as to future production of these types and will make recommendations as to the tactical suitability of these types in active theatres. The Board will also make recommendations as to aircraft to be used by dive

bomber groups contemplated in the present program.'[201]

In fact the modifications just about amounted to a different aircraft, and this was finally recognized by all parties, and all attempts at standardization went by the board. On 22 March 1943, Colonel S. R. Brentnall, Chief, Production, Engineering Section, wrote to Douglas at El Segundo, admitting this fact:[202]

It has become increasingly more evident that the large number of changes requested by the Army Air Forces on the A-24B airplanes is resulting in an entirely different airplane than the SBD–5. Further, many of the changes

being made by the Navy to the SBD-5 airplanes are not desired by the Army.

Recently, Material Center Production Engineering representatives visited the contractor's Tulsa plant and it was agreed that the Army A–24B and the Navy SBD-5 airplanes are rapidly becoming two different airplanes, and that the original intent of standardization of the two airplanes should be abandoned.

He therefore requested that changes in procedure should be made which recognized this fact, and that future changes to the SBD-5 should be vetted by the Army Material Center before being implemented at Tulsa. Even this was being overtaken by events, for, with the Dive Bomber Board coming down heavily against the type in total as being unsuitable for employment by the AAF in combat, all production of these types was now considered a liability. Thus the AAF was eager and keen to divest itself of a weapon it had no real experience of, had no great desire to use, and about which they really had only the vaguest knowledge. Production was to cease, but it could not simply be turned off like a tap, because in many plants other than Douglas's Tulsa factory,[203] initial problems had been, or were being overcome, and production lines were finally starting to roll. Donald Douglas of Douglas and Harry Woodhead of Consolidated were duly informed of the bad news by telephone on Wednesday 31 March.[204]

The decision to switch this surplus manufacturing from the Banshee, the Shrike and the Vengeance, into medium bombers like the A-20 or the A-26 was a relief, but it could not be done overnight and the workforce had to be kept in place until such a switch could be introduced. How to effect these changes preoccupied

most of the subsequent discussion on the A-24B from then on. They also had to find a suitable role for dive bombers which, they had now decided, they would not employ to dive bomb.

On 4 May, Colonel Don L. Hutchins at Wright Field, sent an inter-departmental memo to Production Division giving the latest update on Tulsa. 'After considerable difficulty because of engineering changes,' he reported, 'Tulsa is now in a position to produce the A-24B at the rate of two per day.' But there were fifteen items which were still not available in sufficient quantities to ensure a steady increase in this production. He listed some of the more important deficiencies, and went on to state that efforts by the company, the procurement district and the follow-up branch of Production Control Section '. . . have been of little success in obtaining these critical items . . .', due, he felt, '. . . to the low priority group status of this airplane'.[205]

This in itself might not have been important enough to have increased the A-24B's rating, but delay in producing these aircraft would nonetheless have a

### RA-24B Instrument Trainer Allocations
### 1 November 1943

| Delivery Priority | Project | Quantity | Destination |
|---|---|---|---|
| 1 | DOM-676 | 6 | ATC |
| 2 | DOM-672 | 2 | ATC |
| 3 | DOM-673 | 17 | ATC |
| 4 | DOM-674 | 5 | ATC |
| 5 | DOM-675 | 6 | ATC |
| 6 | 92291 | 4 | ATC |

knock-on effect, for B-24 production at Tulsa would not be sufficient to retain all the staff there for long, and unless they could be held by producing A-24s the A-26 production would never get off the ground on time.

There was another adverse report on Tulsa from Colonel Mervin E. Gross, who wrote that it had been noted that Douglas had increased the production of component parts for the A-24 and had recruited a large number of extra employees '. . . in order to build up as large a supply or stockage of component parts as possible so that stocks of component parts on hand could be used as an argument for maintaining the production of A-24s'. It was also reported that this accelerated production was caused '. . . by a rumour reaching the factory that the A-24 would be closed out of production soon'.[206] The workforce was obviously better informed than the unfortunate AAF representative. Colonel Gross added the pertinent fact that:

> In view of the increased interest of certain congressional committees in the production of inoperational war vehicles and the production of others beyond quantity requirements, this should be of interest to the assistant chief of air staff, MM&D, and particularly to Material Command. The A–24 airplane is an inoperational airplane; it has been so declared several months ago.

Colonel S. T. Brentnall, chief of production, duly informed Major Rison of the Bombardment Branch that: 'It is requested that a letter be prepared to Douglas Aircraft Company informing them that there will not be any additional orders for A-24 series airplanes, and that production of the A-24 at Tulsa will cease on completion of the present contract.'[207]

On 18 August, General Arnold

Back at El Segundo, the plant was able to concentrate on the SBD, much-needed by the Navy to replace losses and fill the decks of the expanding carrier fleet. Here wing panels for the SBD move along the lines on 19 November 1943. (McDonnell Douglas, Long Beach)

informed the technical executive, Material Command, that certain aircraft were to be reclassified into the 'restricted' status; these were all dive bombers, the A-24 (all series); A-25 (all series), and the A-34 (the Brewster Bermuda) (all series): 'This recommendation is made in view of current plans by Allocations Division to utilize the greater part of production of the above listed aircraft for training purposes. It is understood that TO 01-1-81 states that the A-24 is already classified as "Restricted".'[208]

Finding suitable employment was next addressed. Arnold informing the technical executive on 24 August 1943, that:

A large number of A–24B airplanes to be delivered from production have not as yet been assigned. It is believed that these airplanes will make satisfactory advanced instrument trainers, and it is requested that immediate action be taken to mock-up A–24B number 42–54455 in accordance with the following requirements:

(A)    Removal of all armament.

(B)    Install SCR 269F with facilities for tuning and electrical controls in both cockpits.

(C)    Install BC–453A component in SCR–274–N.

(D)    Install full panel of flight instruments in rear cockpit.

(E)    Install tachometer and manifold pressure gauge in rear cockpit.

(F)    Install propeller control and throttle in rear cockpit, if not already installed.

(G)    Install trim tab controls in rear cockpit.

(H)    Install satisfactory adjustable hood in rear cockpit.

(I)    Remove gunner's seat and replace with pilot's seat.

As agreed, this airplane will be delivered to Tulsa by Major Garrett who will furnish any additional information required.[209]

All this was confirmed two days later in a letter from Colonel T. A. Sims, deputy chief of staff, to Production Division, Material Command, adding that, 'The decision to modify additional A-24B airplanes as instrument trainers will be based on the success of the modifications outlined . . .'.[210]

The question of reclassification re-emerged briefly. On 28 August 1943, the technical executive recommended to the assistant chief of the air staff that: '. . . no action be taken to classify A-24B

## Additional Instrument Trainer Allocations, December, 1943

| Delivery Priority | Project | Quantity | Destination |
|---|---|---|---|
| 7 | DOM-679 | 4 | 2nd AF |
| 8 | DOM-680 | 6 | 3rd AF |
| 9 | DOM-681 | 5 | 1st AF |

and A–25A airplanes as "restricted", in view of the fact that various quantities of these airplanes are being allocated to beneficiary governments. It is believed that if these airplanes as a whole were classified as "restricted", it would put them in an unfavourable light . . .'. They therefore recommended that only those allocated to the AAF be so reclassified.

On 30 September, Colonel Sims instructed Production Division, Wright Field, that as these aircraft had been declared non-operational, it was advised that they should be delivered. '. . . without turrets (sic), guns and armour . . .'.[211] This action was because they were to be utilized '. . . for administrative purposes only'. The rider was added that 'These instructions do not[212] apply to airplanes allocated to foreign governments.

The approval for the conversion of further instrument trainers was given on 25 October 1943, the technical executive being advised that: '. . . necessary action be taken to ensure that all A-24B-type airplanes to be used as instrument trainers be modified in accordance with mock-up airplane 42-54455, if subject mock-up is approved. Verbal information from Captain Mount, Aircraft Modification Branch, to Captain Nelson, this office, indicated that subject mock-up had been verbally approved by all concerned.'[213]

Even with this programme, it was clear that far too many A-24Bs were on order ever to be justified, and steps were taken to cancel a large quantity of them. Colonel O. R. Cook of Material Command telephoned Ted Conant of Douglas in Santa Monica on 29 October and broke the news to him.[214]

'This will probably hit you hard, but we are going to have to cancel the last 635 A-24s'; Cook added that Douglas had advised that cancellations were best done by shop orders, and that, '. . . we thought 635 would be the least we would require.' Conant took it reasonably well, asking how

many shop orders that would take out. 'Five,' replied Cook. He added, '. . . I just wanted to let you know what I was doing – this thing is so bad from both our standpoints, that whatever hardships are encountered on account of it will probably be justified, because I've been informed that your own people down there at Tulsa that is the workmen, wonder why they are building an airplane that isn't wanted.'

Conant replied frankly: 'They do, particularly because there has been this talk about making trainers out of them.'

After further discussion Cook admitted that, '. . . If that is done, they're going to have lifetime spares for the airplane, and probably many of the parts can be used for the SBDs at El Segundo,' and he asked if that would help with the labour situation there; the situation on the SBDs was not critical, however. 'We are building SBDs for, I believe, two reasons: one is until something else takes its place like the SB2C; the other is to keep it going until we get the SB2D out.[215] There is no other dive bomber that has proved itself yet, so they don't dare drop this one until they get a proven article.'

Accordingly, on 29 October 1943 a letter was sent out confirming that 625 A-24Bs would be cancelled, with the last production aircraft leaving Tulsa in December 1943.[216] This was approved the next day by General Meyers.

The instrument trainer modification programme was then set rolling in earnest, with forty RA-24Bs being allocated under AC-32123 to various commands[217] (see table).

In addition to the modifications carried out on the mock-up, a few extra changes were made to these aircraft: the gun tunnel into the baggage compartment was made accessible from the rear cockpit; the flight instruments in the front cockpit were rearranged by mounting the altimeter under the air speed and rate-of-climb directional gyro; fluorescent lighting type C-5 was added to the rear cockpit; an electrical motor and relay were installed; as was an external power receptacle, a SCR-269 radio compass; the SCR-274-N command set was re-worked with a control box for the BC-453-A receiver installed in the rear cockpit; a T-17 microphone was installed in both front and rear cockpits; and an RC-43-B marker beacon receiver was installed.

To compensate for these additions the following were removed completely: all armour plate, bullet-proof glass, guns and attachments, bomb racks and controls, ammunition boxes, gun- and bomb-sights and parts; chemical tank fittings; bomb displacing gear; pyrotechnics; gun ejection and feed chutes; pilot's head-rest; gun synchronizer and impulse generator and destructor grenades. The Navy tachometer on the front instrument panel was replaced by an Air Force type E–13 model. The final instrument panel looked like this:

A: airspeed indicator, type F-2;
B: directional gyro type AN-5735-1;
C: rate-of-climb type C-2;
D: bank and turn, type A-11;
E: altimeter, type C-14;
F: clock AN-5741-1;
G: compass, type B-16;
H: Gyro AN–5736-1;
I: manifold pressure gauge, type D-10;
J: tachometer, type E-13;
K: tachometer generator AN–5531-1.

On 2 November 1943, Lieutenant Colonel Walter W. Wise, chief, Accessories Section, Maintenance Division, informed the commanding general, Material Command at Wright Field, that a further fifty-five A-24s had been allocated to them, and were to be designated as utility airplanes.[218] As such it was considered '. . . essential that these airplanes be equipped with cockpit heating.'

It was found that more A-24s were now required than at first thought, and on 3 November, the cancellation of 635 A-24Bs was reduced to a total of 585 instead, and a revised delivery schedule was requested (and confirmed the next day) of one hundred machines in November and December and a final twenty-eight in January 1944.[219] Once again, Colonel Cook picked up the telephone, this time to speak to Colonel Frank W. Cawthon, Midwestern District procurement officer at Wichita.[220]

Colonel Cook said that he had told the Douglas people that '. . . we would stop with the 615th A-24 on that contract,' and confirmed that '. . . that means the cancellation of 585, in order to synchronize with

## Breakdown of the 953 RA-24 Airplanes Accepted by the Air Corps

| Contract | Model | Manufacturer | Number |
|---|---|---|---|
| N-77114 | RA-24 | Douglas, El Segundo | 78 |
| N-91397 | RA-24 | Douglas, El Segundo | 90 |
| N-91397 | RA-24A | Douglas, El Segundo | 170 |
| AC-28716 | RA-24B | Douglas, Tulsa | 615 |

the shop order that they are working on now.'

On the same day Colonel Cook also had a telephone conversation with General Meyers on the same subject. He had to explain to Meyers that, '. . . in cutting back these A-24s we have some modification work that has to be done . . .'[221] 'Why are we modifying A-24s', rejoined Meyers. 'Because,' replied Cook, 'We got orders from your outfit to modify them.' He explained, 'We're modifying 180 of them for trainers as I recall it, and about sixty for radar.' 'I'll surely look that up,' was Meyers' reply. The actual new cancellation figure was again confirmed to Douglas at Tulsa, in a teletype from Captain John A. Carr, contracting officer, sent on 16 November.[222]

Meanwhile, it was found that an additional fifteen instrument trainers were now required, to bring the total modified to fifty-five, and this was duly authorized. The allocation for the extra aircraft was as follows (see table):

There remained a few further points to be cleared up before Tulsa's agony was finally over. On 20 January 1944, Arnold telegraphed Material Command in respect of the 120 A-24Bs which were being modified for the RNZAF. As this order had been cancelled effective from 18 January 1944, and as the work on them included Navy type radio and oxygen equipment which was not desired when the aircraft reverted to the AAF, it was therefore requested that all such modification on these aircraft be stopped immediately '. . . so that de-modification and re-modification work will be held to a minimum'.[223] He added, '. . . decisions as to the disposition of these airplanes have not been made, however

Commitments Division, . . . have indicated that they will probably be converted to instrument trainers.'

There still remained those sixty RA-24Bs left over from the suspended El Segundo Navy contract NXS-6970 that the Army had purchased from the Navy. Colonel T. A. Sims wrote to Production Division on this matter on 9 March 1944: 'Due to changed requirements, all of the above airplanes were delivered to the Navy Department.'[224] In view of that, it was directed that these aircraft were cancelled from the 'H' Program, Acceleration.

The final summary of the Army Air Force's involvement with the A–24 was contained in a report prepared by the Resources Control Section, Material Command, Wright Field, and dated 30 June 1944[225] (see table):

An illuminating snippet on the behind-the-scenes work that was put in by the A-24 far from the combat zone, was given by Barton N. Hahn. He recalled:

During 1943 and 1944 I was a civilian pilot with the Third Ferrying Group, Air Transport Command, Romulus Army Air Field, Michigan. In addition to ferrying airplanes, I was also an instrument flight instructor. In about mid-1944 an A-24 was dropped off at the field[226] with no further orders for use or disposal.

Since no one in the Transition Department was qualified on the airplane, I proceeded to read the manuals and then checked myself out. It had marvellous flight characteristics so I then began giving instrument instruction in the plane. Sometime later, another new A-24 showed up and I also used it for instruction.[227]

# CHAPTER TWENTY

# Show Time! The Philippine Sea

We left the great assembly of warships that was Task Force 58 steaming out from their anchorages to take the fight to the enemy in the Mariana Islands (see Chapter 18). In particular the dive bomber complements Task Group 58.3 on the carriers *Enterprise* and *Lexington II*, VB-10 and VB–16 respectively, were waiting to write the Dauntless's final page in the great carrier duels of the Pacific War.

For the third and last time, the carrier aviation strength of the Japanese fleet had been built up sufficiently to man the air groups on the remaining carriers. There were three heavy carriers remaining, the *Shokaku* and *Zuikaku* having been joined by the new *Taiho*; these formed the 'A' Force, with two heavy and one light cruisers and seven destroyers. Supplementing these were six light carriers, and of these three, the *Hiyo*, *Junyo* and *Ryuho*, formed the 'B' Force, while the other three, the *Chiyoda*, *Chitose* and *Zuiho*, formed the mobile force vanguard.

In support was an oiling force of five tankers and five destroyers in two groups, while twenty-four submarines were deployed in a scouting line ahead in the usual manner. Nine carriers was indeed a formidable power, but they would be up against an American fleet composed of *fifteen* carriers, seven heavy and eight light, organized in four task groups.

In ships, then, the Japanese were outnumbered almost two-to-one, but in aircraft the ratio was even more marked: in fighters the Americans would field 475 against 225; in torpedo bombers, 190 against half that number, 81; while in dive bombers 174 Helldivers and 59 Dauntlesses, 233 in total, faced 126 Vals and Judys. Nor was that the end of the Japanese inferiority, because in airborne and surface radar they were totally outclassed, while in experience and training the Japanese flyers were but half-trained youths against, in the main,

An SBD-5 belly-lands aboard the USS *Yorktown* (CV-10) after attacking Truk in the Carolinas, 22 February 1944. (San Diego Aerospace Museum)

experienced veterans – even the most junior American Navy pilot had two or three times the number of flying hours under his belt of his Japanese opposite number.

The Japanese were not fools, of course, and acceptance of these kinds of odds was only made after careful deliberation. Ozawa's aviators were not to be alone in the 'decisive battle': even before they became involved and delivered the key strikes from the sky so the battleships could then follow up and complete the rout, the American carriers and battleships would, in theory, have been heavily attacked by more than 500 shore-based aircraft held under the command of Vice Admiral Kakuji Kakuta's Base Air Force, with its headquarters on Tinian. In fact the Japanese land-based aircraft, sent out from Guam, Rota and Yap airfields, contributed nothing to the battle. Much of this impotence was caused by the pre-emptive strikes that the fast carriers themselves launched against these airfields, and the staging posts on Iwo Jima and Chichi Jima, between the 15 and the 19 June.

With the plotting of the first incoming

Japanese aircraft, at 1005 on the 19th, all the SBDs were scrambled off the flight decks of both *Enterprise* and *Lexington II*, and sent to a safe waiting position on the eastern – the disengaged – side of the fleet. Here they remained for an hour, circling impotently and watching the slaughter. Admiral Reeves thought they could be better employed than this by making a search-and-attack sortie along '…meridian line 260 degrees true…', and suggested as much at 1003 in a signal to Mitscher. At 1010 however, these aircraft were ordered to strike at Guam instead.

This switch was not really thought out, because all the Dauntlesses were bombed up with 1,000lb (450kg) AP and 500lb (227kg) GP ordnance for use against the enemy fleet; nonetheless it was duly complied with. The SBDs from *Lexington II* took Orote Filed at Guam as their target and discovered between twenty and thirty Japanese aircraft on the ground there. Joined by the SBDs from *Enterprise*, they made their attacks at 1300, through heavy flak, losing one of their number; but their weapons drilled holes in the coral rather than devastated the enemy planes.

Similar dive bombing was also carried out against Agana airstrip. But the 19th was the day of the Hellcats, and the Dauntless pilots had to wait for the 20 June to make a more meaningful contribution and leave *their* trademark on the wooden decks of imperial aircraft carriers for the last time.

It wasn't until late on that second day of the battle that Spruance finally obtained detailed information as to the exact whereabouts of his enemy, and while Ozawa was refuelling from his supporting tankers in readiness to strike again with his remaining 120 aircraft on the 20 June, Marc Mitscher ordered the very risky long-range strike against Ozawa's force. The 216 American aircraft took off in the full knowledge that not only would they have to attack at extreme range and therefore might not

US Navy SBD-5, operating in the Solomon Islands, 1944. Note the Yagi radar antenna below the port wing and the new smooth cowling. (US Navy official)

have sufficient fuel to return, but that even if they made it, it would involve a night deck landing, which some had never done before, and which those that had were not keen to repeat. Nonetheless, go they did.

The Dauntless had the shortest range of all the American aircraft in that historic launch, and was thus the limiting factor. The first reports placed the Japanese carriers some 200 miles away, but this was later found to be in error and the true distance from Task Force 58 was 275 miles (442km). The SBDs launched at 1624[228] as part of a large strike that included eighty-five Hellcat fighters, fifty-four Avengers – only twenty-one of which carried their proper armament of torpedoes, the rest carrying four 500lb (227kg) bombs – and fifty-one Helldivers. One of the VB–16 Dauntlesses, that of Lieutenant Jack Wright, accompanied Ramage's aviators, having had to make an emergency landing aboard the *Enterprise* the day before with an oil leak. He had volunteered to go on the mission with them and then land back on the *Lexington II* afterwards.

Both the Dauntless squadrons were very experienced, having almost reached the end of their normal combat tour times.[229] They launched into a clear blue sky and climbed initially at 100ft (30m) per minute, to about 10,000ft (3,000m) at 140

knots. Because of the distances involved it had already been decided to adopt a 'running rendezvous' for the initial form-up, that is to say instead of circling over the carriers in the usual way, the aircraft gained their cruising altitude slowly in task group formations to save precious fuel.

The strike took departure at 1645, but a second strike, already up on the decks and being prepared to follow them, was cancelled due to the lateness of the hour; they were disarmed and defuelled, and struck back down again.

The original course set was of 279 degrees, but at 1715, Lieutenant Commander Weymouth, leading VB–16, took in a signal from one of the Avenger scouts giving a corrected enemy position which placed Ozawa's flat-tops a further 60 miles (100km) out, and course was therefore adjusted to 284 degrees. In the interim, one VB-16 had to abort the mission due to a malfunction in its fuel supply. Half the 1,000lb (450kg) bombs carried were AP, and half GP.

Ramage had already decided that his squadron would use manual lean fuel control for the mission, on a setting of 1,750rpm, and stay at a low altitude in order to avoid usage of the high blower. With 252 gallons (1,146l) of fuel in their tanks and 50 to 75 nautical miles less

combat range than the other American aircraft, it was essential for the SBDs to eke out every precious pint of avgas. Eventually he had to abandon this plan due to the presence of enemy fighters, and VB-10 finally climbed to 15,000ft (4,500m). Another precaution taken, the result of long experience, was gradually to move what fuel remained from tank to tank to even out its distribution; this would give the Dauntlesses greater balance and aid the dive attack, but another factor was the knowledge that any tank that was completely drained would build up residual vapour and therefore be more vulnerable to a lethal explosion if hit.

American signals had already been intercepted by the Japanese heavy cruiser *Atago*, which relayed them on to Ozawa's flagship, and by 1615, he was well aware of what was coming. He abandoned what was left of his refuelling programme, increased speed to 24 knots and proceeded to put more miles between himself and the US aircraft. The Japanese fleet was formed into three groups, each with carriers and protecting warships. At 1754 the whole force went to action stations and some seventy-five fighters were scrambled away to intercept the four groups of incoming attackers.

The first Japanese ships actually sighted by the Americans, at 1825, were of course the big tankers of one of the oiling forces and their guarding destroyers. These were easy and tempting targets, being well within range, proceeding at a relatively slow speed and steering a straight and steady course of 270 degrees. One Helldiver commander decided to hit this target [230] but the Dauntlesses pressed on looking for carriers. They were now at 16,000ft (4,900m) and at a range of about 40 miles (65km), they were duly rewarded at 1830.

The first carrier force taken under assault, between 1810 and 1930 according to Japanese records, was 'A' Force. As with Midway, there is considerable confusion in all accounts about which aircraft attacked which ships. Lieutenant Commander J. S. Arnold's report has it that VB-10 joined his attack on the *Zuikaku*, on the other hand Lieutenant Commander Ramage's account is in absolutely no doubt that it was 'B' Force that he attacked.

Most reports mention the fact that there were *three* carriers, but widely separated, and that these were in an *echelon* formation from north-east to south-west – most probably the *Junyo, Hiyo* and *Ryuho*. The *Zuikaku* was all on her own, the only carrier surviving with the more north-westerly of the three Japanese groups, her two companions having been sunk the previous day by submarines, as recorded. The other three-carrier group was the *Chiyoda, Chitose* and *Zuiho*, which were with the main force to the south-east. Some eyewitness accounts, Lieutenant Commander Ramage's among them, definitely identified a '*Zuiho*' class carrier which would appear to indicate that it was this group that VB-10 actually attacked. All reports are confused by the fact that the American airmen were recording their targets as vessels of a completely mythical '*Hayataka*' class ship, of which there never was, or ever would be, such a carrier, or indeed *any* type of warship, in the IJN.

As they lowered down to 12,000ft (3,600m) in preparation for the actual attack, VB-10 split into its two divisions in order to divide their payloads equally between two of the enemy carriers. At this point the SBDs were met by what remained of *Zuikaku*'s fighter defenders, eight Zeros, and she apparently launched nine more, but they were all ineffectual. All the warships opened a fierce fire with their weapons, ranging from full 8in (20cm) gun salvoes from the heavy cruisers, down to 1in (25mm) and ½in (13mm) light flak. The resulting pyrotechnics was a multi-hued display of firepower as the Japanese used different colour-bursting charges to help determine range, height and accuracy calculations. The American airmen therefore had to penetrate a screen of shell bursts, not only of the normal black, white and yellow, but of reds and pinks of more exotic varieties, to make their dives.

Ramage himself selected the rear ship of the three-carrier column, splitting his flaps at 10,000ft (3,000m) and targeting what he called a '*Zuiho* class' carrier for his division's objective, attacking from downwind from east to west in a standard 70-degree dive, and opening fire with his forward machine guns at 8,000ft (2,400m) to help line up the target in the gathering gloom. He lined up on the ship's forward lift and released at low level, 1,800ft (550m), so determined was he to make sure he scored a hit. A Zero had followed him down, but overshot as he pulled out at 300ft (90m), and the Dauntless was also rocked by the detonation of his own bomb.

In fact he had missed, as the Japanese ship had made a hard starboard turn; the second man down, Lieutenant (jg) De Temple, was able to confirm that Ramage's bomb had detonated close to the carrier's stern, while his own 1,000lb (450kg) bomb had similarly exploded hard in the ship's creamy wake. Next man in was Lieutenant (jg) Hubbard, and his bomb was also a near-miss, off the carrier's port beam; while his wingman, Lieutenant Schaeffer, suffered the frustration of having his bomb hang up on release.

So far the carrier had been very fortunate, and this continued, with Lieutenant Fife placing his bomb just off the starboard quarter of the still-swinging vessel. The concussion from this series of near-misses close astern shook the ship's steering and rudder considerably, but did not affect her speed. Finally, one 1,000lb (450kg) bomb did just about hit her, that aimed by Lieutenant (jg) Albert A. Schaal, and again it was the after-part of the carrier that took the blow. Schaal claimed that his bomb had clipped the port after-edge of the flight deck, had then pushed on through the overhang and again spent its force in the water astern. All this division were heavily engaged by all ships of the Japanese force as they made their exits out over the screen.

The second division of VB-10, led by Lieutenant Lou Bangs, had taken the next carrier in line as their target, a ship they described as a '*Hayataka*' class carrier; the six Dauntlesses therefore steered to the north and then pushed over. However, due to a misunderstanding, only the first section – Lieutenants Bangs, Lieutenant (jg) C. H. Mester and Lieutenant Lewis – attacked the chosen target, which was the leading Japanese ship, while Lieutenant (jg) H. F. Grubiss, Lieutenant (jg) C. Bolton and Lieutenant (jg) Jack Wright of VB-16, hit the second, or middle carrier in the line instead.

Making a fast approach down to 9,000ft (2,740m) and firing their nose guns as they made their final attack dives on the most northerly carrier, all three SBDs of Bangs' section released their 1,000lb (450kg) bombs at about 2,000ft (600m). The first bomb was claimed by Bangs to have been a direct hit on the rear of the carrier's flight deck, and the resulting explosion was said to have blown several planes spotted there over the side. Mester's bomb went to the left of this one, also aft. Finally Lieutenant Lewis claimed his bomb to have been a direct hit just behind the ship's small island superstructure. These three direct hits left the target ablaze as the Dauntlesses made their way out across the enemy fleet to the rendezvous point. They were again intercepted by Zeros waiting for just such an opportunity, and Mester's mount took hits from both cannon and machine gun fire at this stage; however, it survived all. Lewis had taken a different exit route and also got out unscathed.

Almost at the same time the final three SBDs were pulling out after delivering

SBD-6 no 54605. (San Diego Aerospace Museum)

their bombs against the second ship in the line, which Grubiss reported as an 'unidentified light carrier'. They met very little anti-aircraft fire as they strafed this ship's flight deck on the way down and made their releases. Of the three 1,000lb (450kg) bombs, the first was claimed by Grubiss to have been a very close miss astern, Wright's missile also went into the sea off the carrier's port side aft, and the fate of the last bomb, aimed by Lieutenant Bolton, was unobserved by his rear-seat man. At 400ft (120m) they recovered from the dives and headed out to the rendezvous point, unhindered by enemy fighter aircraft.

The Japanese 'B' Force was sighted by VB-16 at 1845, and they estimated that it contained two 'Hayataka' class carriers, one light carrier, two *Kongo* class battleships, two to four heavy cruisers of the *Tone* and *Mogami* classes, and four to six light cruisers and destroyers. They could also make out a second group ('A' Force) 12 miles (19km) further northward, with a third group beyond them (the vanguard force). Despite this somewhat erroneous assessment, there was no doubt that they had found a juicy enough target. Seeing that everybody's favourite target, the 'Shokaku' class carrier (the *Zuikaku*) in the middle group, was already under attack by American forces – including, Weymouth reported at the time, the *Enterprise* dive bombers – he decided to hit the nearest group.

VB-16 therefore passed north of 'B' Force, the protecting Hellcats skirmishing with eight Zeros that tried to intervene in the process, but only one of the SBDs took damaging hits, the aircraft of Lieutenant (jg) W. L. Adams, in the rudder and right-hand fuel tank. Weymouth then turned to make his strike against '. . . the southern Hayataka . . .' at 1904. Most of the SBDs apparently concentrated their attacks on the *Junyo*, while others went for the *Hiyo*, and they claimed seven 1,000lb (450kg) bomb hits on the former and two on the latter, for the loss of one Dauntless.

Boring down through the flak, Weymouth attacked along his target's flight deck out of the setting sun, finally releasing at 1,500ft (450m) and pulling out at 800ft (240m). His 1,000lb (450kg) bomb was claimed to have hit by his rear gunner, who saw black smoke erupting from alongside the ship's island structure. Five direct hits were claimed, with four near-misses and one unobserved – and more was to

come. Both the last two aircraft in the attack, flown by Lieutenant Adams and Ensign Moyers, also claimed to have hit this target, rear-seat man Kelly stating that one bomb went down through the exact centre of the flight deck, and noting Moyers' missile hitting soon afterwards.

Lieutenant (jg) George Glacken was 'wooded' by the preceding section and could not complete his initial dive, so he switched targets to the next carrier in line, which was then commencing a hard-right turn. Unable to get a clear shot at her either, he saw his bomb miss. He was joined in this attack by Lieutenant Cleland and Ensign Caffey, the last two VB-16 Dauntlesses down off the stack. However, they were given the benefit of the enemy flak gunners' undivided attention, and Cleland's mount took three direct hits. Notwithstanding this he rolled with the punches and completed a low-level attack, and was certain that his bomb had punched into the carrier's deck planking dead centre and towards the stern.

The very last Dauntless dive bomber to dive on a Japanese carrier was that piloted by Ensign J. F. Caffey, but the result of his strike was not seen. Meanwhile the Zeros had again closed in, although Cleland's gunner, Hisler, claimed to have shot one into the sea and later to have engaged a Val dive bomber, acting in a defensive role over her parent ship as the SBD had done many times before.

From the enormous number of direct hits that were recorded as 'certains' in the various combat logs, the enemy casualties were incredibly light. The Japanese records state that the *Junyo* was hit by two bombs which both detonated close to her bridge, and that there were six very near misses scored; this made operating her aircraft very difficult, although her engines remained undamaged. The *Hiyo* was not apparently hit by any bomb in this attack, and suffered only slight damage. She did finally succumb to two aerial torpedo hits by the Avengers and blew up and sank at 2032 that same evening.

As for the other Japanese carriers, the *Zuikaku* of 'A' Force took heavy punishment. Direct hits were scored as well as five very near misses, themselves described as 'damaging' in this well delivered attack. These caused dangerous hangar deck fires in the ship's aviation gas stores and she was left on fire from end-to-end. It looked like a repeat of the Midway result for the SBDs, and at one time the Japanese captain ordered to 'abandon ship'. The very experienced and well trained damage control parties did not panic, however, and reported at this time that they were making progress in fighting the blazes. The order was therefore cancelled, and the ship was ultimately saved; she eventually got back to Kure naval base on 23 June, and was dry-docked on 14 July until 2 August for repairs. Considering the number of hits

Head-on view of the SBD-6 on 11 April 1944, displaying the 1,350 hp Wright R-1820-66 engine and the two wing-mounted aluminium 56 gallon (255l) drop tanks. (McDonnell Douglas)

and close misses, this was a remarkable achievement on the part of the Japanese dockyards, and she was ready for action again by 10 August.

The *Chiyoda* was hit by two 500lb (227kg) bombs aft, credited to the *Wasp's* air group which destroyed or damaged several planes parked there, and these hits and the splinters from the many near-misses killed and wounded fifty of her crew; but the *Chitose* and *Zuiho* were not attacked at all.

As the SBDs of VB-16 withdrew, they were again subjected to Zero attacks by eight aircraft and these were pressed home. Lieutenant Kirkpatrick had his rudder, fuselage, wings and cockpit all hit, but somehow survived it all, but Lieutenant (jg) Jay Shields' aircraft was not so lucky, and his SBD was lost with both the pilot and rear-seat man, Leo LeMay. In reply, VB-16 gunners claimed two Zeros destroyed and others damaged. Finally the Dauntless survivors started their with-drawal at 1918 on a course of 100 degrees. In all, nine Dauntlesses made the rendezvous and were then joined by five more which had avoided crossing the heavy flak zone over the enemy fleet, at the cost of using up precious extra fuel.

It was a similar story with VB-10. Ramage survived a full 8in (20cm) salvo from all the eight guns of a *Tone* class heavy cruiser at a quarter-mile (402m) range by diving down to 30ft (9m) and making a 45-degree right turn. Once he had safely cleared the outer ships of the Japanese destroyer screen he made a gentle turn to the left at a height of 1,000ft (300m) and from 1930 collected first six, then another three. As he headed back into the darkness to find his carrier at 150 knots, other formations joined up the with SBDs, which had their running lights on, and then left them behind.

If the outward flight had been a slow affair, the return was pedestrian. The average height was kept to 1,000ft (300m) to conserve fuel, with again lean throttle settings. VB-10's overall flight time turned out to be 5.8 hours. Those with action damage were in dire straits very soon, and faced a lonely death out in the vast expanse of the dark Pacific Ocean.

Ramage's VB-10s had been highly drilled in night operations by their previous air group commander, Commander Roscoe Newman, so the night held fewer fears for them than many of their colleagues. Like the equally experienced VB-16, their SBDs had their engine exhaust ports fitted with flame dampers for night operations – but *any* light would have been welcomed on that lonely voyage back into blackness. This was reflected in the chatter that broke out among other air groups as they winged their way home through the blackness with falling fuel gauges. Ramage's disciplined unit main-tained a dignified silence in the midst of this babble, and then at around 2030 Cawley managed to pick up the ZB/YE homing signals from the *Enterprise* by radar at 90 miles (145km) range. All around them other aircraft were running out of fuel and going down into the sea, but VB-10 remained intact, and at 2120 locked into Task Force 58 some 30 miles (50km) away.

Admiral Mitscher had ordered every carrier group to make maximum illumi-nation to guide aircraft home, but for some this proved more of a hazard than a help. Ramage recorded that with all ships, including destroyers, lit up like Christmas trees, and with some cruisers firing star shell bursts as well, the problem was not so much finding the fleet, but identifying an aircraft carrier amidst the myriad of lights. While it was not surprising that many aircraft landed on the wrong carrier – it had, after all, been so ordered by the C–in–C – others inadvertently made persistently desperate attempts to touch down on other types of warship, even destroyers! Some air group leaders decided to land their whole squadrons on the water *en masse*; others, like Ramage, made every attempt to get their SBDs down on a carrier deck, come what might.

By 2140 VB-10 was over their home base intact, but a bad deck crash, Lieutenant Harrison of VB-16, caused them to be waved away and Ramage ordered them to land on any deck they could find. Most were down to their last thimbleful of gas. Ramage himself and another VB-10 pilot, Lieutenant Commander Don Lewis, both eventually got down on the *Yorktown II*. They found that, up to that time, only two of her VB-1's fifteen SB2Cs had got back – but this was typical, and all save one VB-10 Dauntless made it home: besides the pair on *Yorktown II*, two got aboard the *Enterprise*, five aboard the *Wasp II*, and one on the *Bunker Hill*. Only the aircraft of Lou Bangs had been forced to ditch, although one of the survivors went into a barrier and became a write-off. Bangs and his rear-seat man were rescued by destroyer.

Of the VB-16 Dauntlesses, one had been lost over the target, Shields, while two more had run out of fuel and gone into the sea, but their crews were saved. Weymouth and five more finally got down on the *Lexington II*, while six more ended up aboard the *Enterprise*, including Jack Wright who had apparently grown attached to her. Thus out of twenty-six SBDs, one was lost to enemy action, three to ditching and one to a crash-landing, a ratio which compared very favourably with the thirty-nine Helldivers lost out of the fifty-one launched.

Most aviators were disappointed when the final results of the battle were totalled up. As usual, many more carriers were claimed sunk than the one that actually went down, and although the two sub-marine successes made the score line respectable, some of the veteran Dauntless pilots considered that the American strike force, as a whole, ought to have done much better.

So the Japanese fleet lived to fight another day; but their nemesis was not very long in coming, because in October Leyte Gulf brought about the almost total anni-hilation of their now useless carrier fleet, and many of their proud battleships and cruisers also. Sadly the Dauntless was not there to see it happen or to take part. But in four years of air/sea warfare the SBD had left an indelible mark, one that would never be equalled, let alone bettered. Those who say the Pacific War was won by the Dauntless dive bomber exaggerate – but only a little!

# Swan Song: The Philippines

After their experience of close air support at Guadalcanal and at Bougainville, it seemed natural to assume that, when a similar requirement was thought necessary for the invasion and expected hard land campaign to regain the Philippine Islands, the expertise of the Marine Corps flyers would automatically be called upon.[231] A negative factor however was the attitude of some of the ground troop commanders themselves. Incidences such as the accidental bombing of friendly troops, and the slowness of response to calls for air support during which time the situation on the ground had changed, caused some to reject the whole concept as unnecessary, unhelpful, positively dangerous or impracticable.

Thankfully the example of both naval and Marine Corps close support operations, in comparison to that offered by the Army Air Force, had been so obviously superior in previous campaigns that many of the important ground troop commanders were won over.[232] A great help was the attitude of Admiral William F. Halsey, who neatly hoisted Kenney with his own petard. The AAF anti-close air support stance meant that it could not comply with the requests of its own ground troops, and Halsey wrote to General Douglas McArthur calling to his attention the fact that he had an under-used Marine air group which, '. . . when Kenney was not keeping it idle, he was assigning it to missions far below its capacity.'[233]

Whatever the means, the net result was that on the island of Luzon the aviators of the United States Marine Corps aviators in their Douglas SBD Dauntless dive bombers '. . . set out to perform a distinct mission and they trained for just that speciality: the assistance of ground troops in advancing against the enemy.'[234] The unit selected for the task was MAG–24 commanded by Colonel Lyle H. Meyer, which on 10 October 1944 was based at

Bougainville. The four squadrons of this group were soon reinforced by the addition of MAG-32 with three more. This unit had been scattered all over the Pacific – Ewa, Green Island, Munda and Emirau – but was brought together as quickly as possible. On that very day they received the information that they had been given the mission of providing the Army troops in the Philippines with all the close air support they required, and that this task was to be carried out to the exclusion of all others.[235]

This greatly simplified their task, and they could concentrate their training and tactics solely to this one end. The Marine Corps also found it easier than the Army or Navy to adapt their flying and dive bombing to give the infantry what they required, for most flying officers in the USMC air squadrons had served as company officers themselves and knew the problems that ground troops faced. The first task was to co-ordinate all known data, and this was done by the air group operations officer, Lieutenant Colonel Keith B. McCutcheon. This information was found to be both scanty, and in some cases conflicting, but it was studied and worked upon and gradually assembled into a practical doctrine which was then organized into no less than forty detailed lectures which were delivered as part and parcel of an intensive course to all 500 officers and radio operators of the seven dive bomber squadrons involved.

These lectures were delivered by specialists drafted into MAG-24 from all over the Pacific; also Marine officers who had served with Navy air liaison parties (ALP) during the Gilbert and Marshall campaigns were brought in, Captains S. Ford, F. R. B. Godolphin, F. McCarthy, S. H. McAloney and J. Pratt; and intelligence officers attached to Admiral Kinkaid's Seventh Fleet, who were to land and give sea support to the invasion, and infantry

The SBD came into its own once more in the Philippine campaign and, at a time when it had been replaced aboard the fleet carriers off Okinawa and Japan, gained a new lease of life as a close support aircraft par excellence. Nicknamed by the press the 'Diving Devildogs', the Marine Corps brought the US Army its first truly dedicated close air support squadrons with the First Marine Air Wing, and quickly demonstrated an impressive performance. Here a Marine SBD takes off on another mission from a Luzon airstrip with a range of light bombs. (McDonnell Douglas, Long Beach)

and artillery officers from both the Americal Division and the 37th Division. In cases where the squadrons had not reached Bougainville, selected pupils were put through the course, then returned to their units as local lecturers to pass on the word.

One of the most revolutionary principles adopted by the Marines was the whole-hearted acceptance of the place of the aircrew in the scheme of things. The one which they applied universally was that their close-support missions were to be seen '. . . only as an additional weapon, to be employed at the discretion of the ground commander'. This was in many ways radical thinking, for hitherto both Army and Navy air commanders had been extremely loath to place themselves so totally in the hands of the troops on the ground. But this sea change was seen as

An SBD of MAG-1 squadron VMSB-301 banks over paddy fields – typical of the terrain in the Philippines – towards the distant jungle-clad mountain strongholds of the retreating Japanese Army. Enemy positions are still smouldering from earlier strikes, to which the SBD is to contribute its own 500lb GP payload. (McDonnell Douglas, Long Beach)

essential both to win, and retain, the trust of the PBI, and to ensure maximum efficiency. The core principles similarly accepted and adopted without reservation were that: 'Close support should be immediately available and should be carried out deliberately, accurately and in co-ordination with the other assigned units, namely artillery, tanks or infantry.' In other words, the Marine Dauntless aircrews had, in 1944, turned themselves into what the German Luftwaffe's Stuka crews had been since 1939: 'flying artillery'.

It was not only lectures that occupied the time of the Marine aviators during their training period on Bougainville of course: practical work was carried out as well, and this training also involved the ground troops who were to be the main beneficiaries of the end result, the 37th Infantry Division. Simulated infantry assaults on Japanese strong-points were conducted in conjunction with trainee ALP teams practising their radio codes and procedures, and Dauntlesses carrying out dive-bombing attacks with both practice and dummy bombs. Such exercises not

only turned theory into practice (and sometimes modified it), but gave both participating parties mutual esteem and confidence prior to the real thing; it helped to ease fears and doubts on both sides, and proved invaluable.

In order to guarantee an instant response time, the ALP organization had obviously had to command a high degree of communication availability and flexibility in order to cope with a fast-moving situation on the ground. The plan adopted was for the marines to provide their own

ALPs and to keep these as light and mobile as possible in order to keep up with tank columns and such. The ground team had to be as mobile and available as the air team, keeping at the front-line ground commander's shoulder at all times, and not letting itself become bogged down in the rear echelons and left behind. Speed and precision applied to the men manning the radio-equipped jeeps just as much as it did to those flying the SBDs just above their heads.

The SBDs attached to the Marine close support squadrons were equipped with four very-high-frequency (VHF) channels and two medium-high-frequency (MHF) radio channels, so they could switch to the latter when, as frequently happened during the Luzon campaign, the VHF channels became totally clogged with traffic.

Final preparations began on 7 November, when Colonel Clayton C. Jerome was appointed both as the CO of MAG–32, but also as overall commander of both groups of seven Marine SBD squadrons (see table).

When the invasion convoy arrived at Leyte on 3 January 1945, the Marines found that their own meticulous preparations had not been matched by others and that none of the fifty-two airfields there had been allocated to them! Colonel Jerome, having survived the kamikaze attack on the battleship *New Mexico* in which he was taking passage, got ashore on 11 January; he picked up Lt Col McCutcheon – equally lucky when another had crashed the battleship *Mississippi* in which he was embarked – and set off on a hunt for a suitable site. Eventually they selected a rice paddy field near Mangaldan, south of Lingayen Gulf, and here the base airstrip for the Marine air groups, Dagupan or MDagupan, was established, with the HQ set up in a wrecked school.

**USMC SBD Squadrons giving close air support on Luzon, 1945**

| Squadron | Commanding Officer | Group | Date arrived Luzon |
|---|---|---|---|
| VMSB-133 | Major Lee A. Christoffersen | MAG-24 | Lingayen 24-1-45 Mindanao 21-4-45 |
| VMSB-142 | Captain Hoyle R. Barr | MAG-32 | 24-1-45 |
| VMSB-236 | Major Fred J. Frazer | MAG-24 | 27-1-45 |
| VMSB-241 | Major Jack L. Brushert | MAG-24 | 25-1-45 Luzon – Mindanao 10-4-45 |
| VMSB-243 | Major Joseph W. Kean Jr | MAG-32 | 27-1-45 |
| VMSB-244 | Major James W. Poindexter | MAG-32 | 27-1-45 |
| VMSB-341 | Major Christoper F. Irwin Jr | MAG-24 | 26-1-45 |

For the ground-attack role which was becoming increasingly important in the Pacific war, experiments were made with a wide variety of payloads. Here a selection of light bombs is shown mounted under the wings and fuselage on racks instead of on the customary swing cradle. Philippines, 1944. (McDonnell Douglas, Long Beach)

The strip was ready to receive aircraft by 25 January, and the SBDs began to stage into it in sections via Owi, Peleliu and Leyte. The Dauntlesses to arrive were the forty-six SBDs of VMSB-133 and VMSB-241, and they were quickly followed by the other five squadrons until, by the last day of the month, there were 174 Dauntlesses ready for action[236], manned by 472 officers and 3,047 men.

The first missions were flown on 27 January, but these were not close support sorties as so carefully planned and practised, but conventional pre-arranged sorties laid down the evening before that had been rubber-stamped all the way up the line through Division, Corps, Army and AAF 308th Bomb Wing before any action could be taken. It was clear that there was still a lack of conviction that a small ALP team in a jeep could be trusted to bring down dive bombers' payloads accurately enough to avoid hitting American troops.

So for the first week the SBDs flew their missions working to the old, discarded book rather than their new one. Dive-bombing strikes were made against Japanese-occupied Clarke Field Air Center and San Fernando. A total of 255 sorties were made by the five operational squadrons during this period and they delivered 104 tons of bombs on target, for the loss of one VMSB-133 Dauntless and its crew, Lieutenant Gordon R. Lewis and Corporal Samuel P. Melish, to AA fire.

MDagupan needed a breakthrough, and a visionary ground commander to enable it finally to break with the old tradition and prove what it was capable of. The hour produced the man in the form of Major General Verne D. Mudge of the 1st Cavalry Division. This fast-moving and hard-hitting unit had been assigned the crucial task of blasting a quick passage through the Japanese to relieve Manila itself with the minimum possible delay.

Spearheading the Army's audacious thrust was the 37th Infantry Division's 1st Brigade commanded by Brigadier General William C. Chase, and Marine Captain Samuel Holt McAlone's ALP jeep with its radio-operator driver was assigned to him. Another ALP jeep team under Marine Captain Francis Godolphin, with driver radioman Staff Sergeant A. A. Byers, was given a similar role with Hugh H. T. Hoffman's 2nd Brigade.

The order given to the Dauntless air groups was simple and to the point: they were to act as a permanent and mobile flank guard over the division, on hand at a moment's notice to break up the slightest hint of counter-attack by the Japanese defences. To achieve this, a patrol of at least nine Dauntlesses would have to be maintained continually during the hours of daylight. This meant a constant turn-around of SBDs, with each active patrol being backed up by another en route, one returning, one refuelling and re-arming, and others on immediate standby to take their turn or be thrown in as additional fire-power if serious combat developed.

The 1st Cavalry jumped off from Guimba at 0001 on 1 February. By daybreak the first nine SBDs were already overhead, and from then on they kept up their vigil and the tanks roared southwards. Any potential strongpoint, road blocks or massing of Japanese troops was reported via the ALP and General Chase could make an immediate decision to pull down an air strike upon it or not.

The first challenge was met at Santa Maria on day two of the run, when the 2nd Squadron, 8th Cavalry, ran into a dug-in Japanese battalion holding the high ground. So close were the two sides that the nine SBDs made their runs without dropping any bombs, but the diversion this caused was sufficient to enable the Americans to rush the enemy strongpoint and put them to flight. Also on the 2nd a heavy strike was put in by VMSB-133, VMSB-142 and VMSB-241 against San Isidro, saturating a designated area 200 by 300 yards (183 by 274m) and allowing Chase's men to pass through without delay.

Close air support, which became the principal role of the SBD in the hands of the USMC in the Philippines in 1945, had been refined in the Soviet campaign by the Junkers Ju 87 *Stukas* of the Luftwaffe. Among the innovations they introduced, and which were copied by the Western powers some years later, were machine-gun pods for strafing ground troop formations. Here the Douglas DGP-1 (Douglas Gun Package-1) variant of this idea is being hand-loaded to its underwing fixture at El Segundo for experimental purposes. (McDonnell Douglas, Long Beach)

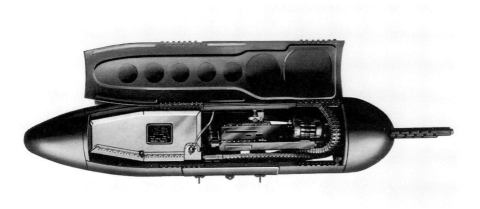

The 0.50 calibre gun package developed by Douglas at El Segundo is shown with access doors open to show the general internal arrangement. (McDonnell Douglas, Long Beach)

Scouting was also a part of the SBDs' duty, and they were able to report which roads seemed clearer or free from obstructions, and as in the case of the Novaliches Bridge on the 3rd, their early reports enabled the ground troops to prevent it being blown up and thus allowed the columns to continue their breakneck pace. Only one Dauntless was lost in this epic operation, a VMSB-241 machine that was forced to crash-land at the Marikina river. Although the SBD came down between the lines, the aircrew, Lieutenant Kerwin W. Jacobs and Corporal Samuel Scheinfield, were plucked to safety by American troops.

Manila was reached in sixty-six hours and the Santo Tomas hostages freed, and at least one Army unit and its senior officers had been converted to the Dauntlesses effectiveness. The SBD might be obsolete, rejected by the AAF and passed over now by the USN, but it did the job, and Major General Mudge was fulsome in its praise.

The fight for Manila then developed into a tough and dour house-to-house slugging match. After their initial confusion and disarray the Japanese Army pulled itself together and began a stubborn resistance in the city itself and with a large force well entrenched in the Shimbu line of fortifications. Here was no quick and glamorous dash, but hard pounding and a steady crumbling away at a skilled and well protected and fanatical enemy. Here again the smashing power of the dive bomber, coupled with its accuracy, brought the Dauntless to the fore.

Again they won converts to their methods by example. During February,

pin-point targeting of Japanese rocket batteries and machine-gun nests had relieved General Mudge's 1st Cavalry from a serious situation around the Balera plant by the Marikina river. One attack by seven Marine SBDs, co-ordinated by Major Benjamin B. Manchester III from the air, on a reverse-slope enemy position just in front of the American troops, resulted in the complete destruction of eight machine-gun and fifteen mortar nests, along with three hundred of the enemy.

This impressive piece of dive bombing was witnessed by Major General Edwin D. Patrick, who commanded the 6th Infantry Division. Up until then he had not been a fan of close air support, insisting on a 1,000 yard (914m) safety margin for his men, but after witnessing what the Marines were

capable of he became a convert and an admirer. So converted was he that, on 24 February, he used the ALP team Marine Captain James L. McConaughy Jr and the Dauntlesses of VMSB-236, under Major Frederick J. Frazer, to break enemy resistance in advance of his regiment's first attacks.

The dive bombers worked their strikes in until they were bombing under 500 yards (457m) from the American forward positions in nine-plane sections. The attacking SBD squadrons frequently 'rang the changes', some simulating bombing while the infantry advanced, others actually bombing when the Japanese rumbled that tactic and inflicting casualties that way. Flight commanders would also take turns in the ALP and visit the troops in the forward positions to evaluate the enemy strongpoints from the soldiers' viewpoint.

Previous to this, on 7 February 1945, it was Major Manchester who had again co-ordinated the biggest Dauntless strike ever made in the Philippines campaign. This was made against oil dumps, AA positions and other enemy concentrations in the Marikina river bend, which were pulverized by an eighty-one SBD strike, with eighteen Dauntlesses each from VMSB-142, VMSB-243, VMSB-244, VMSB-341 and nine from VMSB-241.

Other Army commanders took more convincing, as Colonel James E. Rees of the 1st Infantry, who had already lost men to a careless AAF strike earlier in the campaign; he had to be shown that the Dauntless dive bombing was a very

An SBD (46-B) complete with the MG pack ready for testing. (Douglas Aircraft via National Museum of Naval Aviation, Pensacola)

different proposition to that. For a start just a single SBD hit the enemy troops 200 yards (183m) away with one wing bomb. This was smack on target, so the Colonel gave permission for a repeat performance, and this second strike delivered the other 100lb (45kg) bomb, plus the 500lb (227kg) belly bomb, with equal precision. After that he nodded through the remaining eight SBDs and these laid down twenty-seven bombs on the enemy, the worst of which was still only 30 yards (27m) off target. The Marine flyers had won another convert.

The Marines had been instrumental in introducing napalm to close support, but in the Philippines the AAF kept most of the available stocks of this very effective anti-bunker weapon to themselves, and only allocated 583 gallons (2,650l) to the Marines out of 6,555 tons available; thus only limited use could be made of it by the SBDs.

While MAG-24 was continuing to impress more and more Army commanders, MAG-32's squadrons began to arrive on Luzon; but their stay was destined to be brief because another front was opening with the American landings at Zamboanga on the island of Mindanao in the southern Philippines, which took place on 10 March.

Meanwhile the Dauntlesses of all the squadrons continued to be called upon, and a total of ten Army divisions at Luzon utilized their skills to a varying degree. The SBDs also gave ground support to Filipino guerrilla units working in the jungle-clad mountains of northern Luzon, flying a total of 186 missions; with no heavy weapons of their own, the Dauntless strikes were a welcome addition to the guerillas' power, and indeed, just about the only way to bring heavy ordnance to the enemy in their vicinity.

Heavy strikes using 500lb (227kg) bombs were made at the Japanese positions atop the Bacsil ridge defending San Fernando, and even individual houses were taken out under the direction of the ALP teams under Marine Lieutenant Sydney Taylor. Particularly effective was an eighteen SBD strike mounted by VMSB-142 against defence works on Reservoir Hill during the final phase of the battle, where bombs were placed within 100 yards (91m) of the guerrilla forward positions. Although the hill was taken, it was later lost again, but the Marine flyers merely repeated their performance.

By 24 March space was ready at Moret Field, Zamboanga, and demand was high enough to move four squadrons over from Luzon. Two squadrons from MAG-24 – VMSB-236 and VMSB-341 – were transferred to MAG-32, while VMSB–244 was moved the other way. Two of MAG–32's squadrons flew in on the 24th, followed by the other two on the 25th and 26th respectively. By the latter date a total of 151 Dauntless dive bombers were on hand and ready to operate from the very primitive airstrip.

From their new base the SBDs were tasked to strike out in all directions and to provide precision bombing support for a wide variety of lesser invasions and landings. The first of these was the occupation of the principal islands of the Sulu group, linking the Philippines to Borneo. On 9 April, the 41st Division waded ashore on Jolo Island, supported by forty-four Marine Dauntlesses. The main Japanese defensive positions on Jolo were centred around the caves, ravines and jungle-clad slopes at Mount Daho, and manned by elite imperial Japanese Marines with batteries of flin (20mm) guns and machine guns. On 22 April a precision strike was made by thirty-three SBDs – given the fond, if derogatory nickname of 'eggbeaters' by their Marine flyers – comprising nine dive bombers each from VMSB-142 and VMSB-243 and fifteen from VMSB-341. The resultant bombing was outstanding, and a body count of Japanese corpses afterwards totalled 400 before they gave up, half of them at least to air strikes which hit where artillery could not reach.

Over on Mindanao Island proper the SBDs were also the vital element in easing the path of X Corps in its advance from the landing beaches at Moro Gulf east, and north to Malaybalay and Davao Gulf. The Dauntlesses flew from both Moret and Titcomb airstrips, with VMSB-241 alone making 250 strikes in 1,336 sorties. One of the most notable of these close support missions was in support of the 24th Division's assault on Japanese positions along the Molita river early in May.

As well as the seven front-line SBD squadrons, combat missions were also flown by Marine Dauntlesses belonging to MAG-24's Staff flight and MAG-32's Service Squadron, which together chalked up eighty-eight missions to add to the total of 8,842 SBD sorties. These averaged out at 16 sorties per day, and over 19,000lb (8620kg) of bombs were placed on target during this time. Serviceability of the squadrons' aircraft was excellent, with more than 150 of the 180 SBDs being available for operations at any one time.

The three MAG-24s left behind after the re-organization spent the rest of March 1945 in mounting nine SBD strikes with either 500lb (227kg) or 1,000lb (450kg) bombs against a variety of targets as the army closed in on the last pockets of Japanese resistance. On 7 April an urgent request to support 6th Army's 25th and 37th Divisions at Balete Pass was received, and despite the fact that MAG-24 was under orders to leave for Mindanao and that the tropical rain was almost non-stop, nine SBDs hit with 1,000lb (450kg) bomb strikes there on the 10th of the month. Over the next four days they flew a further 221 sorties in this area.

On 14 April their time at Mangaldan terminated, as the strip was almost awash, and the three squadrons flew out to Malabang on Mindanao via Clarke Field. It began operating from there on 22 April.

By July it was almost all over in the Philippines, and for the Douglas SBD Dauntless in USMC service, the end came quickly. One squadron, VMSB-244, had already ditched its SBDs for Curtiss Helldivers (actually A-24 Shrikes, the AAF version) at the end of May. The other two MAG-24 squadrons, VMSB-133 and VMSB-241, were just disbanded on 16 July. The 'Slow But Deadly' survived for just a few weeks more with MAG-32, but their combat missions ceased on 1 August 1945, and their cadres began preparing to return home.

Except for odd 'hacks' and the odd shore-based flight, plus the occasional experimental test-bed such as the SBD–6 airframe utilized by the Wright Aeronautical Company in April 1944 to evaluate a special fan installation, the SBD passed out of both the USMC and the war in the Pacific it had done so much to win, with no sighs, and hardly a ripple.

# CHAPTER TWENTY-TWO

# Dauntless: C'est Magnifique!

The very last Dauntless dive bomber, BuAer 55049, the 5,936[th] of its long and illustrious line, had rolled out of the factory door at the El Segundo plant on 21 July 1944. The US Navy had ceased to fly the SBD in combat on 6 July 1944; the USMC stopped using them operationally on 1 August 1945. A total of 115 SBD pilots had been killed in action, fifty-six of them from the USS *Enterprise*. Each loss was a tragedy, but in the overall scheme of World War II aircraft casualties, this was a tiny total considering the devastation they caused the enemy in reply. That should have been the end of the story, but it was far from it. The service that had been the most disdainful of the Douglas dive bomber, the Army Air force, continued to use the aircraft, albeit in a completely different role than the one for which it had been designed and built, not just for a short period at the end of World War II, but for many, many years after it.

The RA-24s continued to be widely employed as various forms of training aircraft, and when the Army Air Force became the United States Air Force and gained its independence, the faithful old Douglas was still to be found on their lists, being retitled in June 1948 as the F-24 in a general redesignation of types by the new authority. As such they remained in service until 1950. One pair were modified for experiments in radio control, and serial no 48-044 as it now was, had the necessary equipment installed and became QF-24A-DE. Its controlling aircraft was its stablemate, serial no 48-045, which was redesignated as DF-24B-DT.

However, it was not just as a radio trainer that the SBD continued to fly. The combat days of the Dauntless were not yet over, and those distinctive perforated dive flaps continued to be split and that stubby nose rolled over into the vertical dive position for a 70-degree bombing run against a frightened foe. If the SBD no longer flew for her country of origin, she continued to make her mark as a fully air-worthy battle machine with the Navy and Air Force of France, Chile and Mexico. Other nations flirted with the idea of utilizing the Dauntless, among them China and Great Britain.

The Chinese government requisition C-6016 (V), class 01-A, was detailed in a memorandum dated 31 March 1943 to Major C. W. Newhall, Jr, of Material Command from Lieutenant H. C. Lynch, USNR, secretary to the Munitions Assignments Committee (Air).[237] It indicated that the Board had allocated thirty A–24s '. . . complete with necessary airframe, engine and propeller spares and propeller spare parts including radio, armament, oxygen equipment, tools and the necessary drawings, manuals, spare parts lists for the operation and maintenance of these airplanes, all in accordance with US Army Air Forces practice.'[238] These were to be delivered to China in three batches of ten aircraft each, in April, May and June.

All this was confirmed as contract AC-28716 on block allocations.[239] Under project 96091R (for Republic of China), codenamed 'Iron', two of the allocated aircraft (Bu-Nbr- 42-54290 and 42-54291) had been transferred to the Sacramento air depot to be prepared for export shipment on 23 May. However, almost as soon as this order was placed, it was cancelled again, as a communication dated 12 June 1943 confirmed.[240] No reason for the Chinese change of heart was indicated and these two aircraft, and others, were later converted to target towers.

SBD-5 number JS997 in RAF markings, known to the British as the Dauntless-I. It was flight-tested in 1944 for both the Royal Navy and the Royal Air Force, but rejected by both at this late stage of the war. (Imperial War Museum, London)

Commandante Mailfert, serving at the *Front Atlantique*, at the end of 1944 with the *Vendee* dive bomber unit of the French Air Force. Markings are brooms (for reconnaissance 'sweeps') and bombs for dive-bombing sorties. (Musée de l'Air, Paris)

The French again used dive bombers in direct support of their ground troops during the liberation of the German-occupied ports on the Channel coast in 1944–5. This poor quality (but very rare) photograph shows an A-24 with Allied 'invasion stripes' markings of the *Vendee* unit preparing to take off from Merignac airfield to attack fortifications on the Gironde river in February 1945. (Musée de l'Air, Paris)

It may seem strange that the third major naval air power, that of the Royal Navy's Fleet Air Arm, should have failed to use the Dauntless dive bomber in combat. The history of this must briefly be told.

With the phasing out of the Blackburn Skua the FAA was left with no modern dive bombers, having rejected the Vought Vindicators that they had purchased (and renamed Chesapeake) because they could not operate from escort carriers (although they could have operated perfectly well from fleet carriers). With the Albacore hardly suitable for modern combat and the Barracuda delayed for various reasons, there was a serious gap for the Royal Navy, who believed in dive bombing, unlike the RAF who scorned it despite its proven accuracy.

The Ministry of Aircraft Production had been set up under Lord Beaverbrook to acquire urgently needed aircraft from the USA and, following a visit to the Douglas plant by Dr Lombard, it was suggested in January 1941, that '. . . 165 plus Douglas SBDs be offered to the British'. Deliveries would have been made in October/November of that year. This offer was rejected as the SBD was considered obsolete; instead, orders were placed for the Brewster Buccaneer (known as the Bermuda in the UK) and the Vultee Vengeance, but both were to be for the RAF and not for the Navy!

The lack of dive bombers got worse as the year wore on and, on 30 September 1941, Lieutenant Commander Smeeton informed Mr C. R. Fairey of the British Air Commission, that:

'In connection with your need for a type of aircraft for ship work for which, for lack of any other available machine, you were considering the Bermuda, the following may be of interest. I believe that I have previously called your attention to the Douglas SBD-3, but do not know if it is a suitable type. I have ascertained that it will be possible to acquire 200 of these aircraft, subject to early decision, under the following delivery schedule:

    1941 December – 18
    1942 January – 46
    1942 February – 53
    1942 March – 58
    1942 April – 25

with the additional possibility of a further 100.

Air Commodore Jones has fairly complete technical knowledge of these aircraft, and is ascertaining whether they are, or can be, fitted with folding wings, self-sealing tanks and (British) armament. Admist all the possibilities we have explored, this is the only one that I have so far found that promises reasonably firm deliveries. The supply, subject of course to (US) Army or Navy releases will be limited to the above as I gather that the type is to be replaced as from February next with the new type SB2D'[241]

It was the early decision that proved the problem. On 2 October Lieutenant Commander Smeeton was memoing Fairey that:

'I have not managed to get a decision out of the 5th S.L. (Fifth Sea Lord; Rear Admiral A. L. St G Lyster, also chief of the Naval Air Services, April 1941–July 1942) Unfortunately he is going away for about ten days and I have to go with him. I hope by the time we return he will have decided one way or the other; meanwhile I hope you will be able to retain the option for the FAA'[242]

But already, across the Atlantic, things had changed. Lieutenant Miller advised Fairey on 9 October that:

'I regret to say that serious doubt has now been thrown on the possibility of obtaining these aricraft on the dates previously expected. I have spoken to Mr T P Wright, as has Mr Musson, and he himself was under the impression when he first gave me the information over the telephone, and which I included in my memorandum to Commander Smeeton, that these deliveries would be possible this year owing to an increase of ouptut.

Dr Lombard is expected to return today,

and it is to be hoped that the situation will be cleared up, although the indications are that deliveries are for 1942–43, and not for 1941–42. At the same time, in view of the increased deliveries, there might be a case for applying for some of these aircraft by diversion from US contracts.'[243]

Colonel W. D. S. Sanday also drew Smeeton's attention to the earlier offer made to MAP which had fallen through, and Smeeton duly advised Mr Fairey. Fairey thanked him and wrote on the Memo:

'Thank you! The same old story we have heard before, and doubtless will hear again.'[244]

In any case Pearl Harbor a few week later would have immediately negated any agreements to send SBDs to Britain – Uncle Sam's priorities were suddenly very different. And so the chance presented in January 1941, had passed due to procrastination on both sides and prejudice against the type, even for naval use, on the part of the RAF.

It was not until February 1944, that the SBD again featured in British official thinking, a note on the current orders for the Fleet Air Arm of that date confirming that nine Dauntless dive bombers were due for delivery, but, as the memo makes crystal clear, '*for Training only*'.[245]

Very late in the day, following the outstanding success of the SBD in US Navy service, this batch of nine SBD-5s was delivered to Britain under requisition number N–1004, contract NOa(S)269, for evaluation purposes by the Royal Navy's Fleet Air Arm. Four of the batch were later passed on to the RAF for their own trials. They were designated by the British as the Dauntless–DB Mk.1, and although never employed operationally, they were given British serials (see table, right).

Needless to say, they were spurned by both parties.

The tests were conducted in Britain as comparisons between the SBD-5, the Vultee Vengeance and the Curtiss SB2C Helldiver. The Navy test pilot, Captain Eric Brown, did state that he thought the Dauntless was '. . . certainly one of the most effective . . .' of the many dive bomber types he had flown, and he also conceded that it was accurate; but overall, he was far from impressed: 'To me, the SBD-5 Dauntless looked exactly what it was: a decidedly pre-war aeroplane of obsolescent design . . .'.[246]

A more grateful recipient of Lend-Lease was Mexico. At almost the same date that China cancelled her order, the Material Branch received requisition RFDA M-45 dated 23 May 1943 from Lieutenant Colonel H. A. Mayforth, ADC, for the government of Mexico, for an identical number of A-24Bs and spares. According to the block allocations dated 12 May, they were to be allocated in batches of five in each of the months from June through to November. In fact of the thirty machines which were transferred to Mexico, fifteen were A-24B-1-DTs, ten were A-24B-10-DTs and five A-24B-15-DTs.

The transfer was codenamed 'Wasp', and the procedure was for pilots of Air Transport Command to collect the aircraft from the Douglas plant at El Segundo and fly them down to the air depot at San Antonio, Texas; from here, delivery flights were made into Mexico. Of these dive bombers, two dozen of them were squadron-based with *Fuerza Aerea Mexicana* in the Mexico City area for, it is said, political reasons. One detachment of four A-24Bs was based at Ensenada, just south of Tijuna on the Pacific coast. There were also claims that A-25s were used by Mexico for ASW patrols in the Caribbean and the Gulf of Mexico at the beginning of 1944.

After the war was over, those A-24Bs that were left were distributed to various squadrons in different areas of the country, together with North American T-6

| Bu Aer Serial | R N Serial | Delivered to | Fate |
|---|---|---|---|
| 36022 | JS 997 | Royal Navy | Rejected |
| 36023 | JS 998 | Royal Navy | To RAF, rejected |
| 36456 | JS 999 | Royal Navy | Rejected |
| 54191 | JT 923 | Royal Navy | To RAF, rejected |
| 54192 | JT 924 | Royal Navy | Rejected |
| 54193 | JT 925 | Royal Navy | To RAF, rejected |
| 54194 | JT 926 | Royal Navy | To RAF, rejected |
| 54195 | JT 927 | Royal Navy | Rejected |
| 54196 | JT 928 | Royal Navy | Rejected |

Texans re-armed as tactical ground-attack aircraft to form composite Army co-operation squadrons, and several of these served on border patrol duties. One unit equipped with the A-24 in 1946 was the *Escuadron Aereo de Pelea* 200, based at Pie de la Cuesta. Natural wastage took its toll until by June 1957, only five remained airworthy. Four of these were rebuilt, while the fifth was cannibalized for spare parts to keep them flying for a while longer; they were replaced by T-28s in 1959.

Chile was the second South American state to receive the A-24 under Lend-Lease at around the same time as Mexico. Between June and August 1943, twelve A-24B-1-DTs, codenamed 'Lion', were also flown from El Segundo by Air Transport Command pilots down to the air depot at San Antonio, Texas, and from

### A-24s transferred to Chile under Lend-Lease

| FAC Serial | BuAer Serial | Delivered |
|---|---|---|
| 1 | 42-54309 | 6-Jun-43 |
| 2 | 42-54313 | 10-Jun-43 |
| 3 | 42-54343 | 2-Jul-43 |
| 4 | 42-54344 | 2-Jul-43 |
| 5 | 42-54345 | 2-Jul-43 |
| 6 | 42-54346 | 2-Jul-43 |
| 7 | 42-54347 | 3-Jul-43 |
| 8 | 42-54389 | 30-Jul-43 |
| 9 | 42-54390 | 23-Jul-43 |
| 10 | 42-54391 | 30-Jul-43 |
| 11 | 42-54392 | 23-Jul-43 |
| 12 | 42-54393 | 30-Jul-43 |

### A-24s Transferred to Mexico under Lend-Lease

| FAM Serial | Bu Aer Serial | Delivered |
|---|---|---|
| 1 | 42-54316 | 14-Jun-43 |
| 2 | 42-54317 | 13-Jun-43 |
| 3 | 42-54318 | 14-Jun-43 |
| 4 | 42-54319 | 19-Jun-43 |
| 5 | 42-54320 | 20-Jun-43 |
| 6 | 42-54338 | 7-Jul-43 |
| 7 | 42-54339 | 2-Jul-43 |
| 8 | 42-54340 | 5-Jul-43 |
| 9 | 42-54341 | 2-Jul-43 |
| 10 | 42-54342 | 2-Jul-43 |
| 11 | 42-54384 | 5-Aug-43 |
| 12 | 42-54385 | 5-Aug-43 |
| 13 | 42-54386 | 5-Aug-43 |
| 14 | 42-54387 | 5-Aug-43 |
| 15 | 42-54388 | 5-Aug-43 |
| 16 | 42-54489 | 3-Sep-43 |
| 17 | 42-54490 | 13-Sep-43 |
| 18 | 42-54491 | 3-Sep-43 |
| 19 | 42-54492 | 3-Sep-43 |
| 20 | 42-54493 | 3-Sep-43 |
| 21 | 42-54576 | 18-Oct-43 |
| 22 | 42-54578 | 18-Oct-43 |
| 23 | 42-54573 | 21-Oct-43 |
| 24 | 42-54579 | 21-Oct-43 |
| 25 | 42-54581 | 21-Oct-43 |
| 26 | 42-54682 | 13-Nov-43 |
| 27 | 42-54680 | 15-Nov-43 |
| 28 | 42-54681 | 15-Nov-43 |
| 29 | 42-54683 | 15-Nov-43 |
| 30 | 42-54679 | 29-Nov-43 |

| Aircraft | Unit | Pilot | Radio/Gunner | Date of Loss |
|---|---|---|---|---|
| 176 | 4B | Goffeny | Chauvin | 1-1-45 |
| - | 4B | Gerold | Guenanen | 18-2-45 |
| 54599 | 3B | Abrall | Hague | 22-3-45 |
| 54577 | 3B | Bonnefoy | Bataille | 16-4-45 |
| 54576 | 3B | Auradou | Lebrun | 3-5-45 |

here they were delivered to the *Fuerza Aerea de Chile*, along with three spare engines and two spare propellers, where they were formed into the *Grupo 4*, based at Los Cerrillos, close to Santiago.

They gave good service both during and immediately after the war, and ten of them were still surviving in 1947; but of these only six were serviceable because of natural wastage and lack of spare parts.

Most spectacular of these episodes was the work done by the Dauntless in the European war and afterwards, back in the Pacific area yet again, over the South China Sea. This was accomplished by both SBDs and A-24s of the French Navy and Air Force.

As early as 1943, the revitalized French Navy Air Service, the *Aéronavale*, had again requested a delivery of Douglas SBD-5 Dauntless dive bombers as part of their rebuilding programme. It will be recalled that they had originally requested 174 in June 1940, just before the Armistice had been signed. However, it was not until the autumn of 1944 that delivery was finally taken of thirty-nine of these aircraft, at Agadir, Morocco. These aircraft were immediately formed into two Air *Flottilles* – 3B (*Lieutenant de Vaisseau* Ortolan), and 4B (*Lieutenant de Vaisseau* Behic) under the overall command of *Capitaine de*

French Army A-24s parked at Cognac with assorted ex-Allied and German aircraft during the winter of 1944–5. (Musée de la Marine, Paris)

*Frégate* Francis Laine, French Navy – and commenced training.[247]

This working up was necessarily brief, because shortly afterwards, with a total of thirty-two aircraft, they flew north to Cognac in France. Here they formed part of the French Atlantic Air Forces, formed in August 1944, and initiated by the French underground forces (FFI). They were assigned to the American First Tactical Air Force (P) as GAN2, and were under the aerial control of Captain O'Byrne. Their maintenance teams flew up in US Army Dakotas via Foggia, Italy and joined them there on 22 November 1944.

Both units undertook numerous combat missions against pockets of German troops and fortresses holding out on the Atlantic coast, as the French forces gradually pushed the German forces back through Cazaux and Bordeaux, up both sides of the Gironde estuary, through Royan and across to the Isle d'Oleron, a drive which finished in April 1945.

The naval Dauntlesses therefore saw considerable employment from Vallierres. The first dive-bombing sortie was conducted on 9 December when they hit German gun batteries at Verdon. On the 18 December 1944 they again mounted vertical attacks, their targets being gun batteries, entrenched German positions, and coastal shipping carrying the defending Germans their supplies and ammunition.

The enemy flak defences were described as ferocious ('*féroce*'), and indeed the flak arm of the Luftwaffe had always been one of the German strengths. In this case the SBDs were going down against *Fla Abt* 999, commanded by *Hauptmann* Nolle which defended the Gironde estuary with thirty-three heavy 3in (75mm) guns and 103 lighter pieces, mainly the famous and deadly quadruple flin (20mm) mountings. In addition the Germans were masters at concealing vital targets with camouflage.

All this made for difficult missions,

particularly with ageing aircraft, but the French Navy pilots performed exceptionally well. The vital road at Fontbedeau, on the way to Royan, was subjected to a precision attack in September 1944. In this mission Lieutenante Ortolan flew with Admiral Lemonnier as rear-seat man and an interested observer. Further attacks followed, against Le Verden, La Coubre, the Grave bridge on the 9 December (which was the debut of both the Navy units also being incorporated as part of the 1st Tactical Air Force), La Pallice and at the Ile d'Oleron.

In total they flew twenty-four combat missions, making 1,500 dive-bombing sorties in the period December 1944 to May 1945, flying a total of 1,426 combat hours and dropping some 500 tons of bombs. They also conducted sixty-two single plane sorties. Despite this they lost only five aircraft, listed in the table (left):

### First Batch of A-24s Delivered to French Air Force

| Bu Aer Nbr | Delivered to Embarkation Port |
|---|---|
| 42-54494 | 7-Sep-43 |
| 42-54496 | 10-Sep-43 |
| 42-54497 | 13-Sep-43 |
| 42-54498 | 13-Sep-43 |
| 42-54499 | 13-Sep-43 |
| 42-54500 | 9-Sep-43 |
| 42-54501 | 9-Sep-43 |
| 42-54502 | 16-Sep-43 |
| 42-54503 | 16-Sep-43 |
| 42-54504 | 8-Sep-43 |
| 42-54505 | 16-Sep-43 |
| 42-54506 | 13-Sep-43 |
| 42-54507 | 14-Sep-43 |
| 42-54508 | 13-Sep-43 |
| 42-54509 | 14-Sep-43 |
| 42-54510 | 14-Sep-43 |
| 42-54511 | 13-Sep-43 |
| 42-54512 | 14-Sep-43 |
| 42-54513 | 9-Sep-43 |
| 42-54516 | 16-Sep-43 |
| 42-54517 | 18-Sep-43 |
| 42-54515 | 14-Sep-43 |
| 42-54518 | 16-Sep-43 |
| 42-54514 | 28-Sep-43 |
| 42-54494 | 6-Sep-43 |
| 42-54501 | 6-Sep-43 |

The aircraft of Lieutenant Bonnefoy was shot down on the 16 April over Sainte Palais by one of the new air-ground AA rockets that the Germans had recently introduced to the field of battle. In addition to these combat losses, one 3B-SBD nosed into a bomb crater at Cognac, and two further SBDs suffered accidental damage in this same period although the machines were not write-offs. The potential for such accidents to any of the group's twenty-five machines was high due to the condition of the airfield from which they operated, which had been devastated by the retreating German forces and left a shambles.

In the same manner as the SBDs, a delivery of fifty A-24Bs, in two batches, was received by the French Air Force, *L'Armée de L'Air*, in Morocco under the auspices of the Free French. The aircraft were flown by Air Transport Command from El Segundo to Newark, New Jersey, under project 90303F (for France) code-named 'Pike', and there loaded for sea transportation to Morocco.

Initially they were allocated to fighter units as fast liaison aircraft at Meknes airfield, because it had originally been intended to equip the new dive bomber units with the more advanced Vultee A-35 Vengeance, also acquired at this time. However, due to bad engine problems with the Vultees, it was decided to transfer a second batch of twenty-five of the latest of the A-24s to France.

The French had requested one hundred more A-24s in February 1944, but the United States authorities replied that they would supply one hundred more A-35s instead. This raised a 'strong protest' by the French headquarters, which was conveyed via the French purchasing mission chief in Washington DC:

> We ask you to strongly intervene to obtain a second batch of A-24s. The US are proposing delivery of A-35s and refuse to supply A-24s. Give advice that the two questions are not bound. 1: A-35s were ordered to be used as dive bombers, Allied Commands have unilaterally decided that such planes will not be used above European battlefields, so we have used this aircraft as a gunner trainer. But A-35s proved unsatisfactory because of their extravagant oil consumption. Further, they cannot be used for pilot training since they are too heavy and not equipped with rear seat pilot controls. And they cannot be used by 'police' units because of the unreliability of their engines. 2: Against this the A-24 revealed itself as a makeshift training machine. And its proven reliability permits it to be used in 'police and security' escadrilles, which have to fly their missions over desert and the sea.
>
> We ask you to insist, and obtain US agreement to deliver, a second 100 A-24s, or at least the maximum number of these machines possible.[248]

Under project number 90318F, again codenamed 'Pike', these machines were delivered by the 5th Fighter Group to the CO Atlantic Overseas Aircraft Supply Centre, at Municipal Airport, Newark, New Jersey once more, for shipment across the Atlantic.

The demands of the war saw them moved up from a secondary to a front-line role and some were moved from Morocco to Algerian airfields.

They were formed into two dive bomber units, the GBI/17 *Picardie* and the GBI/18, each of two *escadrilles* of ten aircraft each. After training, *Picardie*'s dive bombers were initially moved across North Africa, via Libyan airfields, to Syria, being based at Rayack and operating in the pacification duties that followed the overthrow of the Vichy government. The remaining twenty-five continued to be retained at Meknes, and were employed at the training school as advance trainers.

Jean Cuny summarized it in this way:

### Second Batch of A-24s Delivered to French Air Force

| Bu Aer Nbr | Delivered to Embarkation Port |
|---|---|
| 42-54741 | 3-Dec-43 |
| 42-54742 | 4-Dec-43 |
| 42-54743 | 6-Dec-43 |
| 42-54744 | 6-Dec-43 |
| 42-54745 | 13-Dec-43 |
| 42-54746 | 11-Dec-43 |
| 42-54747 | 7-Dec-43 |
| 42-54748 | 13-Dec-43 |
| 42-54749 | 13-Dec-43 |
| 42-54750 | 13-Dec-43 |
| 42-54751 | 7-Dec-43 |
| 42-54752 | 7-Dec-43 |
| 42-54753 | 13-Dec-43 |
| 42-54754 | 13-Dec-43 |
| 42-54755 | 13-Dec-43 |
| 42-54756 | 13-Dec-43 |
| 42-54757 | 13-Dec-43 |
| 42-54758 | 13-Dec-43 |
| 42-54759 | 13-Dec-43 |
| 42-54760 | 13-Dec-43 |
| 42-54761 | 13-Dec-43 |
| 42-54762 | 13-Dec-43 |
| 42-54763 | 13-Dec-43 |
| 42-54764 | 15-Dec-43 |
| 42-54765 | 11-Dec-43 |

*Aéronavale* SBD of Flottille 3F in December, 1944 in front of two devastated hangars at Cognac. Note the new moon and star symbol on the tail adopted by this unit during its North African service. (Admiral F. Laine)

### Dauntless Men: Admiral Francis Laine, French Navy.

Francis Laine was born at the naval port of Brest on the Atlantic coast of France on 16 October 1909. He entered the French Naval College as a young officer cadet on 1 October 1926. By the time World War II commenced, Francis had been appointed as Liaison Officer to the *Direction Technique et Industrielle du Ministere de l'Air*. The young officer had no interest in a desk job at such a momentous time, and set about rectifying the situation at once. He told the author that, 'Thanks to some good comrades there I was named as Commander of the dive bomber squadron in the last days of 1939. My new command was AB-4, which was to be formed from scratch and eventually equipped with twelve Loire-Nieuport LN-411 single-seat, single-engined dive bombers.'

In the confused fighting during the German *Blitzkrieg* of France, Laine's dive bomber unit had little chance to do to the Germans what they were doing to the French. In the thick of the fighting with brand-new aircraft and crew not fully trained in the new technique AB-4 was thrown in to try and stem the deluge, and was decimated. Only eight Loires remained intact and airworthy when, on 24 June 1940, Laine was ordered to fly the survivors to a French North African base while there was still some chance of saving them. Here the remaining six LN-411s which survived the flight to safety, were joined by twelve brand-new Loires handed over by the Army Air Force but, in September 1940, all of these aircraft were ordered by the new pro-German Vichy Government to be placed in storage as the unit was to be converted to American-supplied Glen Martin 167F medium bombers for future operations. *Escadrille 7B* was Laine's next command and was based at Tafaruoi, near

Oran, but only began re-equipping in September.

Francis Laine soon found himself back in action, this time against his former allies, when his unit was one of several that took part in the two-day concentrated bombing of Gibraltar on 24 and 25 September, organised by the *Etat Major l'Armee de l'Air*, in North Africa and using all the Army and Navy bombers based in Morocco and Algeria, some one hundred bombers. Laine told the author that for his part, his unit was engaged in two sorties, 'At 1230 on the 24th and at 1400 on the 25th we flew four and six aircraft respectively on these missions, the objective being the harbour itself, the warships therein and the arsenal of the fortress. On both missions we dropped 225kg armour-piercing bombs.'

But he admitted that the results of altitude bombing against warships at Gibraltar were 'mediocre.'

Francis Laine continued to serve with the Navy air arm, returning once more to dive bombers as Commander of the *Groupement Aeronavale 2*, formed at Algiers on 1 March, 1944 with thirty-seven Douglas SBD Dauntless aircraft. These he led into battle during 1944–45, finally able to hit back at the true enemy of his country, and making

numerous precision attacks on German targets in the fortresses they had established along the French Biscay coast.

Admiral Laine's post-war career was a distinguished one and included commanding the great naval base of Mers-el-Kebir, near Oran; and becoming Superintendant of the French Submarine Force where, as a Vice-Admiral he commanded the seagoing submarines and aircraft of the Navy. He later became Prefect of the Maritime Area of Toulon and his career was crowned by appointments as Commander-in-Chief Mediterranean and as Commander of *l'Escadre de l'Atlantique*. On his well-earned retirement he lives with homes at Kersaint and in Paris, from where he told me the full and detailed story of his two dive-bomber episodes.

This photograph, taken on 15 April 1945, shows a French SBD returning to Cognac after an observation mission over the German occupied sectors of Royal, the Minister of Marine M Jacqurinot and the pilot, *Capitaine de Fregate* Laine, Commander of the *Aéronavale* Group. (Admiral Francis Laine)

---

You can conclude that the batch of A–24s (and SBDs) which were then in use, both with the French Air Force and the French Navy, gave complete satisfaction for operational training for pilots who were later to become fighter-bomber pilots flying both P–39s and P–40s.

The Syrian A–24s had to return to North Africa after only a few months, and one French pilot with this unit commented:

During long flights over the sea and western desert, during our travels from Morocco to Damascus and then from Damascus back to Meknes again, and later, from Morocco to the South of France, we were very glad not to be flying the unreliable Vengeance.[249]

The next development was in the spring of 1944, with the idea of using an air support unit to work with the *Alpine Maquis* (Resistance) (*Vercors*) by flying in arms and equipment from North African bases

and making pin-point drops to them. The aircraft selected for these night-time operations was the A-24, and Colonel Morlaix with the two A-24 *escadrilles* in Syria and Morocco began training for it under *Groupement Patrie*. These aircraft were formed into GCB 1/18 *Vendee*, under the old commander of CB 1/17,[250] *Commandant* Lapios; but the concept never proved viable and was not implemented.

Following the fast-moving flow of the

SBD-5 number 167 of the Navy's 4FB Flottille, airborne in 1945. (Musée de l'Air, Paris)

Allied columns, the A-24s were soon moved up to Bourges, in central France. Here they conducted missions against concentrations of German troops cut off in the advance, and also worked with the local *Maquis* in other combat missions, as they had been trained to do.

Following these operations, *Vendee* moved north to be based at Vannes to work on the Saintonge front where it had a strength of sixteen aircraft. From this base it conducted continued dive-bombing missions, the first being mounted by four A-24s against German fortress troops at Lorient. Despite the difficulties of supply, they continued striking with increased power as they drove the Germans northwards. On 1 November 1944, GCB 1/18 attacked the bridge at Belz with several dive-bombing sorties; but it cost them the loss of the leader of the 1st *Escadrille*, *Capitaine* Boucherie, to flak.

Although the Luftwaffe had few fighters for their aerial defence, they did have some, and they also had an abundance of fierce and accurate flak – so these targets were no pushovers. There were also losses in flying accidents and altogether, in addition to Boucherie's aircraft, *Vendee* lost one A-24 at Poitiers on the 31st, another at Vannes on the 24th, a third at Villacoublay on the 29th, a fourth at Pathenay on 17 November, and a fifth over the same area of Vannes-Meucon on 27 January 1945. However, it was more the wearing out of

aircraft through continual action and wear-and-tear that led to half the unit finally being withdrawn from the Bretagne to the Italian frontier area. Here, at the beginning of February 1945, many of its pilots were concentrated in the first *Escadrille* which continued fighting hard.

Their targets were many and varied and

had reached right down to the Spanish border, across to the Alpine Front along the Italian frontier, with many strikes against pockets of German resistance. These six A-24s took part in repeated attacks at Royan and Grave in April, and the final operational Douglas was *Commandant* Laurent's aircraft (Bu Aer Number 42-541651) on 18 April, from Veredon. Again, despite the intensity of the operations they lost only a total of five aircraft in all this period, effectively disproving the strongly voiced opinion of the RAF who had claimed in 1942 that the Dauntless just could not operate over Europe!

In contrast to the dire prophecies of RAF and USAAF pundits, the French pilots found the A–24 ideal for European conditions. One pilot recalled how 'The A-24 was far more manoeuvrable an aircraft, so we were all able to dive closer and to 'pin-point' our heavily defended targets far more accurately.[251]

At the end of the war, the position of the A-24s was that there were five operational aircraft on the strength of 1/18, plus one inoperational, but four of the flyable dive bombers were detached at Vannes. There was also one operational A-24 remaining with 2/18.

In the immediate post-war period the twenty-five flyable A-24s which had

A Douglas SBD returns to the deck of a carrier after another mission, hook down ready to engage the arrestor wire. (ECP Armées, Paris)

remained concentrated back at the Meknes fighter school, *École de Chasse*, in Morocco continued to serve out their remaining time as advanced training aircraft, until later replaced by Morane 472s. The famous agility of the Douglas dive bomber remained with them, for the school's instructors used its versatility to conduct numerous formation aerobatic displays which became well known before the A-24 was finally stood down in 1953. A-24s also served with the Air Gunnery training establishment at Cazaux and with the *Gendarmerie* in Morocco on desert air patrol duties.

Once the war had ended, employment for both carrier and Dauntless was to be found aplenty in French Indo-China colonies, where, after liberation from the Japanese occupiers, Communist uprisings were initiated.[252] Because of this unrest the French SBDs did finally get back to combat duties in Eastern waters, their old home ground, this time aboard the escort carrier *Dixmude*, formerly the Royal Navy *Biter* which had been transferred to France on 9 April 1945. She was far from suitable, but she was a carrier, more or less, and could be utilized as an aircraft transport. *Flotille* 3FB (re-numbered as 3F), began embarking their nine SBDs aboard her shortly afterwards, together with ex-British Seafire naval fighters. Some of the Dauntlesses, having hitherto operated exclusively from land bases, had found non-folding wings meant a very tight fit in the small hangars of the *Dixmude*. Nonetheless, limited flying operations from her tiny deck proved feasible with the SBDs massive and effective wing flaps helping get them into the air.

The French Indo-China war had commenced on 9 December 1946, and by then the *Dixmude*, with her dive bombers embarked, had already sailed for that theatre of war, conveying them to the northern part of Vietnam during February 1947. Soon the nine SBD-5s of 3F were urgently in demand for use against the growing menace of the Communist columns. Because of the limited space aboard the small carrier, coupled with the lack of powerful catapults for launching the aircraft on this type of ship, plus the fact that her maximum speed of 16.5 knots was too slow to permit the SBD to unstick from her deck very easily, 3F operated mainly from shore airfields at Tonkin during the next three years.

The *Dixmude* herself returned to Toulon on 14 April for a refit and to embark the remainder of the dive bombers. On 20 September 1947 she again sailed for Indo-China with *Flotille* 4F (ex–4FB), commanded by *Lieutenant de Vaisseau* Mellet, embarked, and reached Indo-China on 20 October. Three of the Dauntlesses were also sent to Tonkin, the other six left for Cochin China. At the end of November, 1947, they took part in the first battles in Central Anam and afterwards participated in the battle of Tan Son Nhut, during the Plain of Jars campaign.

Both Dauntless squadrons kept up a series of counter-insurgency air strikes and attacks in the Red River area, but they were already ageing and this period of intensive combat duty wore them out completely. They flew their last combat sorties on 26 and 29 March 1948. By July 1949 they had been retired from service and were replaced by fresh purchases of American dive bombers. Meanwhile a larger and more modern vessel, the light carrier *Arromanches* (the ex-Royal Navy *Colossus*), had been obtained for the *Aéronavale*.

On 29 November 1948, the *Arro-*

*manches* duly arrived off Cap Saint-Jacques and disembarked, among other aircraft, ten further SBD-5s of *Flotille* 4F, now commanded by *Lieutenant de Vaisseau* Rollin, to join *Flotille* 3F. Their operational debut was 11 December, 1948, but the co-operation of the *Aéronavale* with the troops on the ground was very difficult due to the unsuccessful understanding of how best to employ such tactics against a guerrilla army.

Operating from a mobile base, the few SBDs of *Flotille* 4F were employed mainly in the Tonkin region, suffering from many breakdowns as the age of the dive bombers crept up on them, the use of such old aircraft making normal operational hazards yet more dangerous for their aircrews.

Eventually, after flying fifty-six combat missions during which they clocked up three hundred hours of combat flying time, these hardy old Dauntlesses finally returned to France again aboard the *Arromanches* on 5 January 1949. The only major loss in all this time had been the death in a flying accident of *Lieutenant de Vaisseau* Rollin himself.

Back in France, *Escadrille* 54S, based at Hyères on the Côte d'Azur on the Mediterranean coast, had employed the SBD in a training role after being set up in October 1946. Its main function was to train aircrew in carrier operations prior to their embarkation. Between 1946 and 1949 the Dauntless was employed there in this role, before being replaced by Helldivers in 1950.[253]

This marked the absolute end to Ed Heinemann's very special dive bomber as a front-line fighting aircraft, ten years after it had been designed.

# CHAPTER TWENTY-THREE

# Final Days and Survivors

Modified for radio-controlled experiments, 48-044 became QF-24A-DE. (Smithsonian Institution, Washington DC)

The controlling aircraft for the radio-controlled aircraft was her sister, 48-045, which was re-designated DF-24B-DT. (Smithsonian Institution)

With the early phasing out of the SBD from the inventory of the US Navy, and the ultimate similar early shedding of most of the A-24s post-war, only foreign Naval Forces continued to fly the Douglas dive bomber, and by the early 1950s these had all gone also. But in the wholesale sale and scrapping of so many aircraft, a few were purchased by private owners and companies and thus enjoyed a far longer active life than would have been expected. There were not many of these, and over the intervening fifty years, accident, neglect, sale and age has taken a steady toll of even these stalwarts. Mr Ed Maloney, founder of the original 'Planes of Fame' air museum can be credited with saving many of those airframes and whole aircraft that somehow survived half a century of neglect. More

recently Mr Charles Nicols has kept up that tradition of preservation and salvation.

An ex-Mexican Air Force A-24B-DE (serial number 42–54682, c/n 17521) was for many years part of the Tallmantz Aviation Collection at Santa Ana, California. It was auctioned off in 1967 and purchased by Scotty McGregor for $5,000 dollars. It lay at San Fernando for many years and gradually deteriorated before being sold to the Admiral Nimitz Centre at Fredericksburg, Texas in 1972. This group had it transported to a trade school at Waco, Texas, where it was restored as an SBD-3. This aircraft had a metal scoop riveted onto its engine cowl while with the Mexican Military which aided the transformation. However, in 1994 the Admiral Nimitz Museum sold this machine on to Mr Kermit Weeks, a noted collector: it was restored as an SBD-5, under a team headed by Ralph Royce, and was due to be unveiled in 1997 at his Lone Star Flight Museum, Galveston, Texas, with the current serial number of N74133.

A second A-24 was obtained from Mexico and acquired by 'Planes of Fame' then at Buena Park, California. In 1971 it went to the Confederate Air Force and was restored by them to full flying condition. Currently it is undergoing another restoration with the Dixie Wing, headed up by Mike Conley Jr, at Riverdale, Georgia.

Previous to that, in 1965, the CAF had previously purchased an A-24B from Aero Flite, at Kent, Washington, but it was lost in a flying accident *en route* to Texas. The hulk was last seen on a dump at Harlingen.

The 'Planes of Frame' subsequently acquired another Dauntless SBD-5 (serial number 28536, c/n 3883) in 1958 which had been returned to USMC at Russell Field in the south Pacific on 10 April 1944 and had subsequently been used as a wind machine (minus its wings) at the MGM studios at Culver City. This aircraft had been accepted on 16 June 1943 and was sent to Hawaii on 17 October, and thence to Espiritu Santo and No 25 Squadron,

**Former SBD/A-24s used as MGM 'Wind-Machines'**

| No. | Type | Bu. No. | Current Owner |
| --- | --- | --- | --- |
| 2478 | SBD-4 | 10518 | Yankee Air Corps |
| 3883 | SBD-5 | 28536 | Air Museum, Chino |
| 17482 | A-24B | 42-54643 | Lone Star Flight Museum |
| 17493 | A-24B | 42-54654 | MAPS Air Museum |
| ? | A-24B | ? | MAPS Air Museum |
| ? | A-24B | 42-5493 | Kevin R. Smith |

An A-24 that lingered for a long while was this machine, serial NL 49449H of the Lammont du Pont Aeronautical Collection. (Nick Williams)

An ex-Mexican Air Force A-24B on exhibition with the Tallmantz Collection post-war. (AAHS via National Museum of Naval Aviation, Pensacola)

RNZAF, becoming the mount of Flight Sgt N. L. Kelly and Flt Sgt B. E. Cullen, as related earlier. After thirty-two combat missions she was returned to USMC and sent to San Diego in June 1944. She subsequently served with the USN carrying the serial number A-29.

One of half-dozen of the same type, also *sans* their wings, was rescued from the storage yard of Metro-Goldwyn-Mayer when it was sold off to realty developers. They had all been utilized as wind machines, being fitted with four-bladed props. Most of these passed into private hands, with one at least going to Chino, and the Maloney 'Planes of Fame' collection, to await the discovery of a suitable supply of wings to enable it to be fully restored. Maloney obtained one wing for it from the east coast of the USA and the other from Alaska, and restoration began in 1982. This SBD first flew on 8 July 1987. With Alan Wojiack at the controls it was registered as N670AM and, painted with an 'oily' appearance, it featured in the shooting of the television series *War and Remembrance*, along with the Confederate Air Force Dauntless. In the autumn of 1987 John Maloney flew it from the deck of the training carrier *Lexington* off the coast of Florida in authentic paint scheme.

Another film studio was found to be the repository for yet another A-24, without its wings, which survived a fire in 1959 at the old Fox Studio on Sunset Boulevard, and

was bought by a San Fernando Valley man; this also finally ended up with Ed Maloney.

The only known surviving SBD-1 is that aircraft which was retrieved some time ago from Lake Michigan after fifty years on the bottom. She was working out of NAS Glenview. On 21 November 1942, this machine, piloted by Ensign Herbert Walton McMinn, with a yellow painted centre wing section and No 15 painted on the wing, was observed by a civilian to make a forced landing in the lake. The Dauntless settled in position 42 degrees 01 minutes 13 seconds north, 087 degrees, 32 minutes, 26 seconds, west and quickly sank in a depth of 50ft (15m) of water. There was apparently time for the pilot to get clear, but unfortunately he was drowned. The machine settled intact and upright on the lake bottom, only the port wing tip and outer leading edge being bent. When discovered fifty years later the rudder and elevators and tail cone, along with the starboard aileron, were all that was missing. The landing gear was retracted and the radio access door was closed. The aircraft's two nose guns and single rear gun were intact, and no human remains were found, but the bomb sight was intact and later a fully loaded flare pistol was found in the cockpit.

After retrieval from the lake it became the property of the naval air museum at Pensacola, and in April 1994 it was transferred on loan from there to the USS

*Alabama* Battleship Memorial Park, arriving on an eighteen-wheel truck still covered in mud and barnacles. In 1996 it was transferred back to Pensacola for full restoration for a project.

Another Dauntless has one of the best pedigrees of all. She originally flew from the *Ranger* during the 'Torch' landings, and took part in the bombing of the Vichy battleship, *Jean Bart*, being the machine which scored the direct hit on that ship's bows which so damaged her, as already related. She continued to serve on anti-blockade running patrols in the Caribbean before also being relegated to a training role. She too was based at Glenview, naval air station, near Chicago, from where she was flown out over Lake Michigan for practice carrier landings on the paddle-wheel training carriers, *Sable* and *Wolverine*.

On 19 September 1943 an SBD-4 being flown by reserve Ensign E. F. Anderson was trying to make a deck landing on the latter ship, when she ran out of fuel: when Anderson switched to his reserve tank he found it was empty, and was forced to ditch in the lake. Although the pilot was saved, the SBD went to the bottom where she remained for half a century until 're-covered.' And there was a happy ending, for after serving in combat which ended up at the naval air museum at Pensacola, Florida, she is currently on loan to the Kalamazoo Aviation 'Zoo' in Michigan where a team of volunteers is busy restoring her to her original condition.

The search for surviving SBDs, not unnaturally, also led back to the Pacific islands and atolls where numerous wrecks lay hidden. The lagoon at Kwajalein in the Marshall Islands, for example, has thirty-plus SBDs sitting sedately on its seabed while the south Pacific also holds its share. One of 25 Squadron's mounts, Paddy O'Neill's NZ5066, found its way to the USA, while another, NZ5037, which went missing in on a training flight in the New Hebrides, was recovered from its jungle resting place by the New Zealand Army and is now the centre-piece of an exhibition at the Air Force Museum at Wigram, Christchurch.

But Lake Michigan is far easier to survey and access, and abounds with wrecks, some of them of famous aircraft. One Dauntless in particular that the NMNA would love to raise and restore is an SBD-2, BuAer Nbr. 2117. This aircraft was originally part of *Lexington*'s VB-2 (as 2-B-1).

# National Museum of Naval Aviation, Pensacola – Underwater Salvage Operations of Wrecks, and Salvaged SBDs

| Type | Bu number | Accession number (denotes NMNA Ownership) | Status of SBD | Current Location (As at 1 May 1997) | Date of Recovery | Latitude |
|------|-----------|-------------------------------------------|---------------|-------------------------------------|------------------|----------|
| SBD-1 | 1612 | 994.005.001 | storage | NMNA, outside Hangar 3221 | 27/04/94 | |
| SBD-2 | 2106 | 994.005.001 | under restoration | NMNA, Hangar 3221 | 13/01/94 | 41-58.2N |
| SBD-2 | 2111 | | not raised | Lake Michigan | – | 42-05.15N |
| SBD-2 | 2117 | | not raised | Lake Michigan | – | 41-53.4N |
| SBD-3 | 54507 | | not raised | off San Diego | – | – |
| SBD-3 | 6508 | 990.535.001 | dispay | NMNA, CV Hangar Display | | |
| SBD-3 | 6583 | 991.258.001 | display | NMNA West Wing, suspended | | |
| SBD-3 | 6624 | 993.527.001 | under restoration | Kalamazoo Aviation History Museum | 27/10/93 | 41.54.9N |
| SBD-3 | 6660 | | not raised | Lake Michigan | – | 41.54.5N |
| SBD-3 | 6639 | | not raised | Lake Michigan | – | 42-08.1N |
| SBD-3 | 6626 | 994.093.001 | storage | NMNA, outside Hangar 3221 | 28/06/94 | 42-09-10N |
| SBD-3 | 6672 | | not raised | Lake Michigan | – | 42-07N |
| SBD-3 | 6694 | 994.110.001 | under restoration | USS Lexington Museum on the Bay | 18/07/94 | 42-01-20N |
| SBD-4 | 6833 | 991.230.002 | display | NMNA Underwater Diorama | | |
| SBD-4 | 6841 | | not raised | Lake Michigan | – | 41-53.8N |
| SBD-4 | 6915 | | not raised | Lake Michigan | – | 41-55N |
| SBD-4 | 6900 | 993.502.001 | under restoration | San Diego Aerospace Museum | 07/10/93 | |
| SBD-4 | 6932 | | not raised | Lake Michigan | – | 42-05.15N |
| SBD-4 | 6976 | | not raised | Lake Michigan | – | 42-05.15N |
| SBD-4 | 10515 | | not raised | Lake Michigan | – | 42-08.9N |
| SBD-4 | 10541 | | not raised | Lake Michigan | – | 41-49.5N |
| SBD-4 | 10575 | 991.230.001 | under restoration | Low Pass Restoration Georgia | | 41-48.3N |
| SBD-4 | 10694 | | storage | Courtesy Aircraft, Rockford, Illinois | | 42-15.75N |
| SBD-4 | 10715 | | under restoration | Museum of Flying, Santa Monica | 01/01/84 | 41-57.2N |
| SBD-5 | 36173 | | on display | Patriots Park Naval & Maritime Museum | | 1987 |
| SBD-5 | 36175 | 994.137.001 | storage | NMNA, outside Hangar 3221 | 07/09/94 | 42-00-20N |
| SBD-5 | 36176 | 995.220.001 | under restoration | Bob Pond, Minnesota | 16/08/95 | 41-50-10N |
| SBD-5 | 36177 | 995.377.001 | storage | NMNA, outside Hanger 3221 | 04/12/95 | 42-07-00N |
| SBD-5 | 36569 | | not raised | Lake Michigan | – | 42-19.5N |

| Longitude | Depth (feet) | Original Crash Date |
|---|---|---|
| 087-13.8W | 138 | 11/06/43 |
| 087-27.9W | 126 | 13/04/43 |
| 087-28.5W | 48 | 03/06/43 |
| – | 3,800 | 04/07/45 |
|  |  | 23/11/43 |
|  |  | 30/11/43 |
| 087-14W | 120 | 29/09/43 |
| 087-26.7W | 55 | 03/01/44 |
| 087-32W | 90 | 22/10/43 |
| 087-09-45W | 245 |  |
| 087-07W | 240 | 04/11/43 |
| 087-12-05W | 188 | 28/07/43 |
|  |  | 24/08/44 |
| 087-33.7W | 32 | 18/08/44 |
| 087-21.1W | 84 | 14/04/44 |
|  | 250 | 03/09/43 |
| 087-27.9W | 126 | 13/04/43 |
| 087-27.9W | 126 | 13/04/43 |
| 087-25.5W | 174 | 08/08/44 |
| 087-33.8W | 30 | 29/09/44 |
| 087-16W | 70 | 14/09/44 |
| 087-04.5W | 318 |  |
| 087-24.2W | 75 | 03/09/44 |
| 41-49.2N | 087-20.6W | 05/03/44 |
| 087-17-32W | 177 |  |
| 087-22-00W | 70 |  |
| 087-03.9W | 252 | 19/01/44 |
| 087-00.5W | 372 | 28/12/44 |

She was flown in the Coral Sea battle on 7 May 1942, by Lieutenant-Commander W.L. Hamilton (who shot down a Zero fighter with her). The next day she was flown on anti-torpedo combat air patrol by Lieutenant (j.g.) R.B. Buchan and again her rear-gunner shot down an enemy torpedo bomber. Subsequently she was landed aboard the *Yorktown* when 'Lady Lex' was sunk on 8 May 1942. Her career ended on 3 June 1943 when she crashed in Lake Michigan and she sits in forty-eight feet of water, but partly covered by debris.

The weirdness of restoration economics means that even aircraft hauled out of the Great Lakes are cheaper to restore if exported all the way to Russia for the work to be done on them, as is the intention with Bruce Lockwood's SBD-4 (BuAer Nbr. 10715), which is a Lake Michigan survivor but with wings salvaged from Guadalcanal!

Another survivor was an SBD-4 (serial number Bu No 10715, c/n 2765), delivered from the Douglas plant at El Segundo on 31 March 1945 (although the US card on that aircraft gave the acceptance date as 25 February 1943). After spending most of its brief active service career at Jacksonville, Florida, this Dauntless had been struck from the USN inventory on 31 October 1943.

A Douglas A-24, serial number NL 9449H, was for some years held by the Lammot du Pont Aeronautical Collection (see photo). A Mr Billy Marsh of Arizona was flying a late model SBD-6 (serial number N 4488N) in 1954. The Bradley Air Museum was listed as having a Dauntless fuselage in 1975. In 1993 an SBD-5 joined the USS *Yorktown* exhibit at Patriots' Point Maritime Museum, Charleston, South Carolina, after being restored by a group of enthusiasts in Atlanta.

Sightings continually occur, and in 1990 it was reported that an A-24 was photographed in an otherwise abandoned Mexican Air Force airfield. Perhaps the most well known survivors were the two A-24s used by the City of Portland and Multnomah County, Oregon, as insect spraying aircraft. These machines were operated by Aero Flite, Inc, an organization operating out of Troutdale, Oregon, airfield. One was an A-24A–DE (serial number 42-60817) with a civilian registration of N9142H. In 1965 the US Navy re-acquired this machine, under the terms of the original conditional sales contract, and it ended up at the Naval Aviation Museum, at Pensacola, Florida, restored as an SBD-3. It is now back in Oregon.

The other was an A-24B-10-DT (serial Number 42-54582), which served as a crop-spraying aircraft for fifteen years, from 1956 to 1971, flown and maintained by Nick Fletcher, under registration N–4488N (see photo). In 1971 it was purchased by three veteran pilots, the Pacific Aeronautical Corporation, and they lovingly restored it as a fully flying SBD-5, using original Bureau of Aeronautics paint and markings for the early 1943 period. It was flown at exhibitions and meetings by Mr J. H. Tillman, of Athena, Oregon, and his son, Barrett Tillman, who was inspired to write his own account of the SBD aircraft in the 1970s. In the spring of 1974 this plane was, in turn, acquired by Mr Douglas Champlin of Oklahoma, with the serial number N 17421; it was then the only privately owned Dauntless. In March 1975 it was presented to the Marine Corps Museum, at Quantico, Virginia.

Another Dauntless which found a watery grave was found off San Diego in mid-1981, when the Sub Oceans Division of the Lockheed Corporation located it some 3,800ft (1,158m) down about 17 miles (27km) off Point Loma. The pilot of the submersible took photographs and notified the then executive director of the San Diego Aero-Space Museum, Edwin D. McKellar, Jr. They reported that the SBD was in remarkable condition and had only suffered minimal damage from a water landing. More importantly, little or no corrosion had taken place in the intervening decades, other than moderate amounts of marine growth on the outer surfaces. The aircraft's 'greenhouse' was completely intact and the propeller was not damaged at all, while the fabric control surfaces were in near-perfect shape.

Mr McKellar had discussions with Vice Admirals Baggett and Schoultz as well as Captain Ranson, COMSUBDEV-GRUONE (Commander, Submarine Development Group One). This resulted in the basic agreement that in principle the raising of this aircraft would serve both as an excellent test-bed for training in undersea retrieval operations, in corrosion control training and in the overall examination of a plane that had been immersed in salt water for thirty-seven years. This particular aircraft, BuAer No 54507, had been assigned to Carrier Aircraft Service

N-4488N crop spraying. (City of Portland and Multnomah County, via Nick Williams)

Unit (CASU) 42 at North Island and struck from the Douglas records on 4 July 1945 when she had ditched off Point Loma. There were no human remains in the cockpit.

The DSV (Deep Submersible Vessel) from COMSUBDEVGRUONE made subsequent dives on the plane during training missions and took additional photographs of the aircraft, which was resting squarely on its belly on the sea-bed. The aircraft's hoisting cable was intact, and this meant that it could be reached easily for cable attachment by the DSV and, in turn, attachment could be made to the hoisting cable of an appropriate amphibian vessel. Mr McKellar therefore wrote to Vice Admiral Ernest R. Seymour, commander, Naval Air Systems Command, in Washington, DC, with copies to Vice Admirals Wesley L. McDonald, Lee Baggett Jr, Robert F. Schoultz and B. M. Kauderer, and Rear Admiral Byron B. Newall asking them to consider the raising of the aircraft and its subsequent long-time loan to the Aero-Space Museum.

Instead yet another survivor from the depths of Lake Michigan, an SBD-4 completed on 30 November 1942 (BuAer number 06900, present serial number B-3) was obtained and is currently undergoing restoration work in the basement of the museum. She was originally accepted by NAS Roosevelt Park for the Carrier Qualification Unit but was transferred to NAS Norfolk, Virginia on 13 January 1942. On 24 December 1942 she was allocated to VB-16 at Glenview, then joined VB–42 aboard the *Ranger* on 22 March 1943 for a period of sea-going duty, until the 26 June 1943. The *Ranger* had just completed an overhaul in the Norfolk Navy yard, after the North African landings, and had then transported Army P-40s to North Africa. She was then employed patrolling and training pilots along the New England coast, steaming between Norfolk and Halifax, Nova Scotia. The SBD–4 was then transferred back to Glenview once more where she spent her final days.

This machine was lost on 3 September 1943, ditched during carrier qualification training operations. Flown by Ensign Stanley Wilbur Bolton, it approached the training carrier *Sable* with its wheels down, instead of with the undercarriage lowered for the deck landing. Ensign Bolton was given the 'wave-off' to go round and try again, but the engine failed to respond and the pilot made a forced landing in the water. He escaped, but 06900 settled in 250ft (76m) of water. When found half a century later, the Dauntless was intact save for the fact that the canopy was missing, and the left wing flap was damaged and the aileron was missing. She was painted two-tone blue/grey, and carried the identification number 'B3' on the side

of her fuselage. The aircraft was recovered on 9 October 1993 and was moved to NMNA on 18 October.

Another survivor is an SBD-4 which was delivered from the Douglas plant at El Segundo on 31 March 1943 (although the US card on that aircraft gave the acceptance date as 25 February 1943). After spending most of its brief active service career at Jacksonville, Florida, this Dauntless had been stricken from the USN inventory on 31 October 1943.

Another Lake Michigan survivor resides aboard the USS *Yorktown* at Patriots' Point, Mount Pleasant, South Carolina, as part of the Midway exhibit. This SBD-5 was restored by Mike Rettke, having been raised in 1987 after forty-four years' immersion. The fund raising was shared by Patriots' Point, the *Yorktown* CV-10 Association and the family of Ensign Samuel J. Underhill, USNR, a pilot killed during the Battle of the Coral Sea flying an SBD in fighter defence of the first *Yorktown* (CV-5). It was handed over to the museum in 1992.

On 24 July 1943, SBD 06694 crashed during aircraft carrier qualification trials and the pilot, Major Edward Harold Drake, USMC, survived the accident but with multiple contusions of the head and face. Salvaged, like so many others, from Lake Michigan, she was lent from the Naval Aviation Museum to the USS *Lexington* Museum on the Bay at Corpus Christi, Texas. Here, as Barbara Cooper explained to me, new wings were found for her in July 1996, and the restoration work continues in the unique atmosphere of the actual hangar deck of the preserved aircraft carrier so that visitors can follow the progress of the task. Many of the parts have been cleaned and polished as time and funding have permitted, and the plane and all of these parts are on display.

The fact that not more of the restored SBD/A–24s are currently flying is due to as prosaic a problem as lack of suitable tyres for them! Colonel Thomas B. Barnes of the Confederate Air Force's Dixie Wing told me:

Our aircraft is about 75 per cent complete and could be flying within six months, except for lack of tyres. Several of us have been searching for tyres for more than a year without success. This includes talking with Dunlop in England and many other producers/dealers in the US and Europe, to include a Russian tyre dealer in Cyprus. We have been working with the Lone

Star Museum in Galveston, Texas, on this problem for several months. The SBDs use a 30 x 7.7 size tyre, with an 8– or 10–ply rating, single bead. The tyre goes on a drop-centre rim made of magnesium. A 30 x 7.7 tyre with a 12–ply rating or higher is too stiff to get over the drop-centre rim without risk of cracking it. We are also investigating using a split-rim wheel from another type of aircraft to accept a higher ply rating tyre, and then modifying the axle and brake system to fit the SBD. The Lone Star Museum is taking the lead in this effort.

The tyre problem is confirmed by Kevin R. Smith, who is also seeking suitable ones. Kevin bought up almost all of the parts that were auctioned off by the widow of Harry S. Doan after he died in a plane crash in 1990. This amounted to wreckage from three different SBD-2s, some of them being just tail sections, and a hunk of fuselage with some broken wings, which Mr Doan had hoped to put together to make one complete aircraft. Kevin Smith has the same plan, but he also has the hulk of one of the former MGM-A-24s to help matters along. He told me: 'I'm going to combine all of these planes, plus parts from several others, to make one plane. I'm going to call this plane an SBD-5/A-24B and I will use the Army serial number for its records.' One of the additional parts Kevin is hoping to get are the wings from the SBD–5 that the US Naval Aviation Museum is using for parts (Bu No 36175).

Greg Morris of Kansas currently owns SBD-4 BU No 10828, recovered from the south Pacific; this is in storage and may be sold. Another former RNZAF Dauntless got out of Espiritu Santo has not been restored but the hulk is used as part of a jungle diorama at the RNZAF museum at Wigram AFB near Christchurch, now known as Air Force World. Another Lake Michigan salvage, an SBD-3 (Bu No 10694) is owned by Courtesy Aircraft at Rockford Illinois and is currently up for sale.

Things in the aviation museum and preservation world change daily; while some museums fail and close or sell off stock, new museums open and acquire 'new' SBDs or A-24s, which they restore according to their own needs. Others change hands with bewildering frequency. All that can be done in any reference book is to present to the reader a 'snapshot' of the situation as it is at the time of publication. Included in the following pages therefore, are the 'known', still preserved and viewable SBD/A-24 aircraft and their locations, along with sample photography of them down the years.

| Type | Number | Serial | c/n | Civil Reg. | Status | Location | To Represent |
|---|---|---|---|---|---|---|---|
| SBD-1 | - | 1612 | 565 | - | Under Restoration | USS *Alabama* Battleship Memorial Park, Mobile, Al. | SBD-1 |
| SBD-2 | - | 2106 | - | - | Under Restoration | National Museum of Naval Aviation, Pensacola, Fl. | SBD-2 |
| SBD-3 | 06624 | 10715 | 2765 | - | Under Restoration | Kalamazoo Aviation History Museum, Kalamazoo, Mi | SBD-3 |
| SBD-3 | 06626 | - | - | - | Under Restoration | National Museum of Naval Aviation, Pensacola, Fl. | SBD-3 |
| SBD-3 | 06583 | - | - | - | Under Restoration | National Museum of Naval Aviation, Pensacola, Fl. | SBD-3 |
| SBD-3 | 06508 | - | 1245 | - | In Store | National Museum of Naval Aviation, Pensacola, Fl. | SBD-5 |
| SBD-3 | 06694 | - | 1509 | - | Static Display | USS *Lexington* Museum on the Bay, Corpus Christi, Tx. | SBD-3 |
| SBD-3 | 10694 | - | - | - | In Storage | Courtesy Aircraft, Rockford, Ill. | SBD-3 |
| SBD-4 | 06900 | - | 1775 | - | Under Restoration | San Diego Aerospace Museum, San Diego, Ca. | SBD-4 |
| SBD-4 | 06833 | - | 1708 | - | Under Restoration | National Museum of Naval Aviation, Pensacola, Fl. | SBD-4 |
| SBD-4 | - | 10518 | 2478 | N4864J | Under Restoration | Yankee Air Corps, Chino, Cal. | SBD-4 |
| SBD-4 | - | DER2 | - | N4522 | Static Display | San Diego Aerospace Museum, San Diego, Cal. | 3/4 Scale Model |
| SBD-4 | - | - | 10715 | - | Under Restoration | Museum of Flying, Santa Monica, Ca | SBD-4 |
| SBD-4 | 10828 | - | 2468 | NZ5024 | In Storage | Greg Morris, Kansas | SBD-4 |
| SBD-4 | 6953 | - | 1858 | NZ5037 | On Display Not restored | RNZAF Museum, Wigram AFB, New Zealand | SBD-4 |
| SBD-4 | 10575 | - | 2565 | - | Under Restoration | USAF Museum, Wright-Patterson AFB, Dayton, Oh | A-24B |
| SBD-5 | - | 36173 | 04812 | - | Static Display | USS *Yorktown*, Patriots' Point, Charlestone, S.C. | SBD-5 |
| SBD-5 | - | 36175 | - | - | Used for spare parts | Wings only to Kevin R. Smith, Fredericksburg, Va. | SBD-5 |
| SBD-5 | | 36176 | - | - | Under Restoration | Planes of Fame Air Museum, Eden Prairie, Mn. | |
| SBD-5 | - | 36177 | - | - | Static Display | National Museum of Naval Aviation, Pensacola, Fl. | SBD-5 |
| SBD-5 | - | 28536 | 3883 | N670AM | Flying | Planes of Fame Museum, Chino, Cal. | SBD-5 |
| SBD-6 | 06119 | 54605 | - | N54605 | Static Display | National Air and Space Museum, Washington D.C. | SBD-6 |
| A-24A | 06583 | 42-60817 | 2350 | N9142H | Static Display | Erickson Air Crane, Medford, Oregon. | SBD-3 |
| A-24B | - | 42-54643 | 17482 | N51382 | Under Restoration | Fantasy of Flight, Polk City, Fl. | SBD-3 |
| A-24B | - | 42-54593 | 17432 | - | Under Restoration | Kevin R. Smith, Fredericksburg, Va. | SBD-5 |
| A-24B | - | 42-54682 | 17521 | NR93RVV | Static Display | Lone Star Flight Museum, Galveston, Tx. | SBD-5 |
| A-24B | - | 42-54582 | 17421 | N17421 | Static Display | USMC Air/Land Museum, Quantico, Vg. | SBD-5 |
| A-24B | - | 42-54654 | 17493 | - | Under Restoration | Military Aircraft Restoration Corp., Long Beach, Cal. | |
| A-24B | 6040 | 42-54532 | 6046 | N54532 | Under Restoration | Confederate Air Force, Dixie Wing, Midland, Tx. | SBD-5 |
| A-24B | - | 42-54812 | 17651 | N46472 | Scrapheap | Confederate Air Force, Harlingen, Tx. | A-24B |
| A-24B | - | 42-54654 | 17493 | - | Under Restoration | MAPS Air Museum, North Canton, Ohio | SBD-3 |

## SAN DIEGO AEROSPACE MUSEUM

Displayed as: Under restoration    Current Serial: 06900
Original:        SBD-4               Original Serial: 06900
c/n: 1775

*Brief History*
Delivered 30 November 1942; ex- NAS Norfolk, January–December 1942; VB-16 Glenview until March 1943; VB-42 aboard *Ranger* (CV4) 22 March 1943 to 26 June 1943. Glenview, operating from the training carrier *Sable*, ditched Lake Michigan. Recovered 9 October 1993. On fifteen-year loan from NMNA Pensacola to San Diego Aerospace Museum; airframe received 24 February 1994. (Peter C. Smith)

## LONE STAR FLIGHT MUSEUM

Displayed as: SBD-5          Current Serial: N93RW
Original:        A-24B-DE     Original Serial: 42-546829
c/n: 17521

*Brief History*
Ex-Mexican Air Force. Sold surplus to Compania Mexicana Aerophoto, Mexico City, without engine in 1963, ex-Rosen-Novak Auto Co, Omaha, Nebraska; Movieland Museum. In 1964 to the Tallmantz Aviation/ Movieland of the air group, Orange County, California and displayed as an SBD-5, ex Admiral Nimitz Centre. Ex-N74133 From 1966 to 1968 acquired by Rosen-Novak Auto Company, Omaha, Nebraska, but stayed as a static SBD-5 display in Orange County, California. Auctioned off during the Tallmantz auctions in 1968 and bought by Scotty McGregor for $5,000. Sat at San Fernando until in 1972 it was sold again to the Admiral Nimitz Centre of Fredericksburg, Texas. Transported to Waco for restoration and configured as an SBD-3. Carried number MB-21. Exhibited from 1990, then sold to Mr Kermit Weeks on 2 September 1994. Again restored as an SBD-5 in full USN colours and was due to unveil in 1997. Could fly in 1997 if suitable set of tyres is located. (Kevin R. Smith)

## ERICKSON AIR CRANE CO.

Displayed as: SBD-3          Current Serial: N5254L
Original:        A-24A         Original Serial: 42-60817
c/n: 2350

*Brief History*
The City of Portland and Multnomah County, Oregon, operated a pair of A-24s for many years as spray planes to combat mosquitoes. Both aircraft were based at the Troutdale, Orgeon, airport, where they were maintained by E. H. Fletcher of Aero Flite, Inc. In 1965 the US Navy acquired Portland's A-24A as it had been sold under a conditional sales contract when released by the Government. It was disassembled and sent to the USMC Museum at Quantico, then transferred to the National Museum of Naval Aviation at Pensacola, Florida, in 1986 where it received a 1941-42 colour scheme and markings (S2-S-12, and Bu No. 6583). Hung for many years (as shown in this picture) in National Museum of Naval Aviation. Traded to Roy Stafford at Black Shadow Aviation, Jacksonville, Florida, in 1993. Sold to Erickson Air Crane. Restored airworthy. Flying, equipped with an R-1820-60 engine and fitted with truck tyres. Painted up like an SBD-3. (Kevin R. Smith)

## National Museum of Naval Aviation

Displayed as: SBD-2        Current Serial: Still carries Commander's Red Stripe.

Original:    SBD-2        Original Serial:  Bu. No. 02106.
c/n:

### Brief History

Was in the Pearl Harbor attack in December 1941, and also served at the Battle of Midway in June 1942. Later used as a training aircraft and lost from the *Wolverine* in Lake Michigan. Recovered in very good condition on 13 January 1994, and static display 1993–96. Currently under restoration at the National Museum of Naval Aviation. (Peter C. Smith)

## National Museum of Naval Aviation

Displayed as: SBD-3        Current Serial:
Original:     SBD-3        Original Serial:  Bu. No. 06508
c/n: 1245

### Brief History

Served with MAG-11 at Guadalcanal and saw combat. Later transferred to VB-10 and served aboard the USS *Enterprise* (CV-10). Later used as training machine and crashed off the *Wolverine* into Lake Michigan. Recovered on 23 October 1990 for the National Museum of Naval Aviation and restored to static display by Low Pass Inc. (Peter C. Smith)

## National Museum of Naval Aviation

Displayed as: SBD-3        Current Serial:
Original:     SBD-3        Original Serial:  Bu. No. 06583
c/n:

### Brief History

Ditched in Lake Michigan off the carrier *Wolverine*; recovered and restored to static display by Black Shadow Aviation, Jacksonville, Florida. Now hanging from the ceiling at National Museum of Naval Aviation. (Peter C. Smith)

## NATIONAL MUSEUM OF NAVAL AVIATION

Displayed as: SBD-4.          Current Serial: B8
Original:        SBD-4          Original Serial: Bu. No. 06833
c/n: 1708

*Brief History*
Ditched in Lake Michigan and recovered in 1991. Not restored, but put
on display at National Museum of Naval Aviation as part of the diorama
of the sunken aircraft found on the lake bottom. (Kevin R. Smith)

## NATIONAL MUSEUM OF NAVAL AVIATION

Displayed as:                 Current Serial: B-22
Original:        SBD-5         Original Serial: Bu. No. 36175

*Brief History*
Recovered from Lake Michigan on 7 September 1994. Fuselage damaged,
but the original inflatable raft is still in its locker. Being stripped for spare
parts, some of which may go to help restore other wrecks. (Peter C. Smith)

## NATIONAL MUSEUM OF NAVAL AVIATION

Displayed as:                 Current Serial: B-24
Original:        SBD-3         Original Serial: Bu. No. 06626

*Brief History*
Recovered from Lake Michigan on 28 June 1994. Fuselage largely intact,
but currently stored outside along with 36175, 36177 and 2106. (Peter
C. Smith)

## NATIONAL MUSEUM OF NAVAL AVIATION

Displayed as:                     Current Serial:  B-23
Original:      SBD-5        Original Serial:  Bu. No. 36177

### Brief History
Recovered from Lake Michigan on 4 December 1995. Fuselage largely intact, but currently stored outside along with 36175, 06626 and 2106. (Peter C. Smith)

## FANTASY OF FLIGHT

Displayed as: SBD-3         Current Serial:  N-51382
Original:      A-24B        Original Serial:  42-54643
c/n: 17482

### Brief History
Ex-RA-24B assigned to Ferry Command, Lockheed Dallas Mod Centre, Dallas, Texas. Disposed of 7 March 1947 to Reconstruction Finance Corporation and acquired by MGM studios as a wind machine minus wings and tail assembly. Acquired by Mr John McGregor of Los Angeles in May, 1970, and subsequently sold to the Admiral Nimitz Center for the New England Air Museum, Windsor Locks, Connecticut, 1972–74. Sold to Connecticut Aeronautical Historical Association, Inc. 4 December 1974. Acquired by Bruce Roberts, New London, Pennsylvania. Restored as SBD-5 for Bradley Field Museum, Hebron, Conn. with wings from SBD recovered from Lake Michigan. Sold to Kermit Weeks 1987. Currently an 'Undergoing Restoration' project at Akron Canton airport. (Kevin R. Smith)

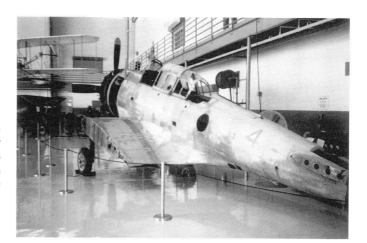

## SMITHSONIAN INSTITUTION

Displayed as: SBD-6         Current Serial:  VS-51/54605/109
Original:      SBD-6        Original Serial:  Bu Nbr 54605
c/n: 6119

### Brief History
Ex-HQ & HQ SQDN Oklahoma City ASC. The NASM's SBD-6, Bu Aer No. 54605, was the last of its type in active service with the Navy, and was the sixth and last modification of the SBD series. It was accepted by the Navy on 30 March 1944 and delivered on 7 April, 1944. Its entire service life of four years was spent with the flight test at Patuxent River Naval Air Station, Maryland. In May 1948 it was put in storage at Weeksville, North Carolina. Saved by US Government in 1961. In 1970 it was restored as static display and put on exhibition, at Marine Corps Air Station Quantico, then transferred to Smithsonian Institute in 1975, hanging from Museum ceiling, in the colours and markings of SBD number 109 of VS-51 which served on the USS *San Jacinto* (CVL-30). (Kevin R. Smith)

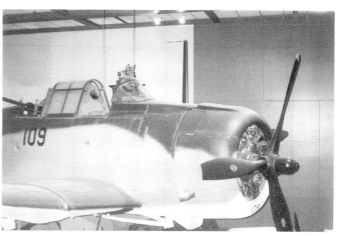

## UNITED STATES MARINE CORPS AIR/GROUND MUSEUM

Displayed as: SBD-5          Current Serial:  SBD-5/USMC/S6
Original:       A-24B-DE      Original Serial:  42-54582
c/n: 17421

### Brief History
Delivered to the US Army on 16 October, 1943. Sold Army surplus post-war to Marsh Aviation, Litchfield, Arizona in 1954. From 1960 to 1970 crop spraying airworthy aircraft, Aero Flight, Troutdale. Restored by the Pacific Aeronautical Corporation, Lake Oswego, Oregon; then rebuilt by the Tillman's in 1971–72 as an SBD-5. Regd. N-4488N then, re-certified as N-17421.

Flown by J. H. Tillman of Athena, Oregon, until obtained by Douglas Champlin of Oklahoma in the spring of 1974. Acquired for display at the Marine Corps Air-Ground Museum at Quantico in March, 1975, and restored to represent a SBD-5 in USMC Markings for static display. (USMC History & Museum Division, Quantico)

## USS LEXINGTON MUSEUM ON THE BAY

Displayed as: SBD-3          Current Serial:
Original:       SBD-3         Original Serial:  06694
c/n: 1509

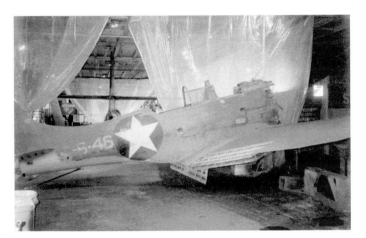

### Brief History
Served with MAG-11 at Guadalcanal and saw combat. Later used as training machine and ditched in Lake Michigan on 24 July 1943. Impacted near vertically in a cartwheel, left wing first, with landing gear down and locked. Left wing badly damaged, right wing crushed and buckled, flaps and dive brakes undamaged. Fuselage generally excellent condition. Recovered on 20 July 1993 and on loan from USN was acquired by Naval Aviation Museum, Pensacola and, from 30 August 1994, on long loan to the USS Lexington on the Bay Museum. New wings made by Marlatt Fabricators, old ones traded to Mr Kevin Smith in exchange for a set of wheels. (USS *Lexington* Museum on the Bay)

## KALAMAZOO AVIATION HISTORY MUSEUM

Displayed as: SBD-3          Current Serial:  06624
                             Markings:       41-S-13
Original:       SBD-3         Original Serial:
c/n: 2765

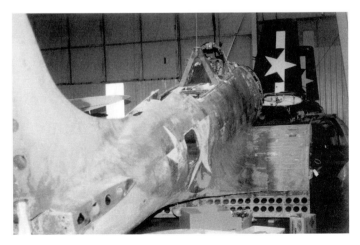

Brief History
1 September 1942, NAS Roosevelt Base, Long Beach, then Norfolk Virginia with VS-41 ('Top Hat' Squadron), replacing SB2U. Embarked USS *Ranger* (CV-4) September 1942 until 23 November, 1942, including Morocco operations. 15 December to VC-29 embarked USS *Santee*, A/S patrols and blockade runner interceptions Caribbean and Recife, Brazil. 30 March 1943, Norfolk A&R and pool. 10 August 1943 Carrier Qualification Training Unit at Naval Reserve Air Base Glenview NAS; *Wolverine* (IX-64) deck landing training. 19 September 1943, piloted by Ensign E. F. Anderson, USNR, as 'Baker 10', ran out of fuel at the ramp and crashed into Lake Michigan, pilot rescued. In fact the recovered airplane was found to still have 40 gal of fuel in left main tank. Raised in 1993 and to Naval Aviation Museum, Pensacola. Currently on loan from the National Museum of Naval Aviation and under active restoration by a team under Richard Bauer. (Kalamazoo Aviation History Museum)

## USS ALABAMA BATTLESHIP MEMORIAL PARK

Displayed as: SBD-1        Current Serial: 15
Original:     SBD-1         Original Serial: Bu. No. 1612
c/n: 565

### Brief History

The only surviving SBD-1. The fuel gauge states BT-1 as it is that old!
Crashed on a training flight into Lake Michigan on 21 November, 1942.
Salvaged and loaned from the National Museum of Naval Aviation,
Pensacola to USS *Alabama* Battleship Memorial Park in 1994, at the
request of the Executive Director, Frank G. Dengler. Currently in USMC
paint scheme, restoration was commenced, but now transferred back to
the National Museum of Naval Aviation in Pensacola for complete
restoration and use in an upcoming project. Currently stored outside
along with 36175, 06626 and 36177. (Peter C. Smith)

## THE CONFEDERATE AIR FORCE DIXIE WING

Displayed as: SBD-5        Current Serial: N-54532
Original:     A-24B         Original Serial: Bu No: 42-54532
c/n: 6046

### Brief History

Ex-export to Mexican Air Force. To Compania Mexicana Aerophoto,
Mexico City in 1947. Between 1960 and 1963 at the Tallmantz
Collection, Orange County, California, and in 1964 sold to the Air
Museum, Ontario, California. Between 1965 and 1967 owned by Robert
L. Griffin, Confederate Air Force, San Antonio, Texas. The Confederate
Air Force, Harlingen, Midland Airfield, Texas from 1970 to 1972. Ex-
Planes of Fame Museum at Buena Park, Cal, in 1971. For many years
this was the only flying A-24, (as an SBD-3, 54532/2-B-4/B14) but was
grounded in 1989 and has not flown since that time. Currently being
restored as an SBD-5 in complete USN colour scheme. Is about 75 per
cent complete (in 1997) and could be flying but for lack of suitable tyres. Due to this problem Colonel Tom Barnes says he is doubtful whether she
will be flying before 1998. (Colonel Tom Barnes, Confederate Air Force)

## THE AIR MUSEUM 'PLANES OF FAME'

Displayed as: SBD-5        Current Serial: N670AM
Original: SBD-5            Original Serial: Bu Nbr. 28536
c/n: 3883

### Brief History

Ex-NZ5062 (New Zealand AF) returned to USMC at Russell Island,
South Pacific on 10 May 1944. Sold as surplus post-war. One of six used
as wind machines at MGM Studios, Culver City, between 1955 and 1968,
without wings which were lost. Then acquired by Ed Maloney the Air
Museum. Chino, from 1968 to 1987. Pair of wings obtained from
Guadalcanal and restored between 1987–96 at the Planes of Fame, first
flying 8 July 1987. Still flying. ('Planes of Fame', Chino)

## THE AIR MUSEUM 'PLANES OF FAME'

| Current | | Current Serial: | |
|---|---|---|---|
| Original: | A-24B | Original Serial: | |
| c/n: | | | |

### Brief History
Another of the ex-MGM 'Wind Machines' with wings and tail cut off.
Cockpit fully restored for a movie set. (Kevin R. Smith)

## YANKEE AIR CORPS

| Displayed as: | SBD-4 | Current Serial: | N4864J |
|---|---|---|---|
| Original: | | Original Serial: | Bu No. 10518 |
| c/n: | 2478 | | |

### Brief History
Sold as surplus at end of World War II. Used by Warner Brothers film studio, Toluca Lake, California, as wind machine, without wings which were subsequently lost. Went to Ed Maloney at the Air Museum, Claremont, California, in 1964, then to the Admiral Nimitz Museum, Fredericksburg, Texas. On loan to Bruce Roberts, New London, Pennsylvania. Then to Bradley Air Museum, Windsor Locks, Connecticut in 1975. Sold to Charles F. Nichols at the Yankee Air Corps, Chino, California. Restored by them to flying status, but never actually flown, using wings found on Guadalcanal Island by the Yankee Air Corps, and used on this and other restoration projects. (Kevin R. Smith)

## PATRIOT'S POINT & MARITIME MUSEUM, USS YORKTOWN EXHIBIT

| Displayed as: | SBD-5 | Current Serial: | 36173/14 |
|---|---|---|---|
| Original: | SBD-5 | Original Serial: | 36173 |
| c/n: | 4812 | | |

### Brief History
Ditched Lake Michigan off the training carrier *Sable* (IX-81) 5 March 1944. Retrieved from Lake Michigan in 1988 and restored by Low Pass Inc., Griffin, Georgia. Restored and transferred to Patriots Point Museum, 1988. Restored and placed on display aboard the *Yorktown* since 1993. (Dr Steve Ewing, Patriot's Point Museum)

## MAPS Air Museum

Displayed as: A-24B          Current Serial:
Original:     A-24B          Original Serial: 42-54654
c/n: 17493

### Brief History
RA-24B ex-San Antonio ASC, Kelly and Love Fields. Disposed of 23 May 1945 to Reconstruction Finance Corporation. Acquired by MGM minus wings and tail assembly cut down for use as a wind machine. Purchased May 1970 by Mr John McGregor. Sold to Admiral Nimitz Center 5 July 1972. Later the deteriorating hulk sold to Mr David C. Tallichet, Jr. of Yesterdays Air Force, Chino. Obtained by MAPS and now under restoration to flying status as an SBD-5 for MARC 91. Located at Akron Canton airport. (Kevin R. Smith)

## KEVIN R. SMITH, DAUNTLESS AVIATION

Displayed as:              SBD-5          Current Serial:
Original:     A-24B, RA-24b Original Serial: 42-54593
c/n: 17432

### Brief History
Sold surplus post-war, one of the MGM wind machines used without their wings and with tails cut off. To Admiral Nimitz Museum, Fredericksburg, Texas, then Trade School, Waco, Texas. In 1975 Nick Pocock, China Springs, Texas. Bought (fuselage only) by Kevin R. Smith in 1991. Currently being restored by Kevin Smith as SBD-5 in full USN colour scheme, from parts of four machines, SBDs and A-24s, including an ex-Santa Anna machine. (Kevin R. Smith)

## MUSEUM OF FLYING

Displayed as: SBD-4         Current Serial:
Original:     SBD-4         Original Serial: Bu. No. 10715

### Brief History
Ditched in Lake Michigan from training carrier *Sable* (IX- 81) on 2 September 1944. Found and recovered from Lake Michigan by Ed Marshall in 1981. The US Navy took it away after legal action. It changed hands to Mr Charles F. Nicols, Yankee Air Corps, Chino, California in 1986, then to Mr David C. Tallichet at the Military Aircraft Restoration Corporation, Chino, before going to the Museum of Flying in 1991. She is scheduled to be shipped to Russia or Poland to be restored to full flying condition using wings found on Guadalcanal by Yankee Air Force. (Kevin R. Smith)

## GREG MORRIS

Displayed as: SBD-4          Current Serial: ex-NZ5021.
Original:       SBD-4         Original Serial: Bu. No. 10508
                                                     (or 10828)
c/n: 2468

*Brief History*
Ex-USMC, then RNZAF, saw combat in the Solomons. Recovered from
a South Pacific island by Ross Jowitt of Auckland, New Zealand. Sold as
Trade-a-Plane. Not Restored. Presently in storage and may be sold.
(Kevin R. Smith)

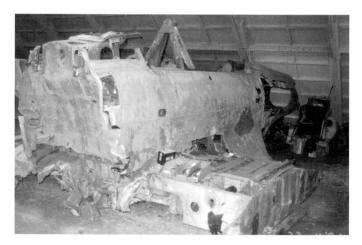

## ROYAL NEW ZEALAND AIR FORCE MUSEUM

Displayed as: SBD-4          Current Serial: NZ5037
Original:       SBD-4         Original Serial: Bu. No. 06953
c/n: 1858

*Brief History*
Ex-USMC, ex-RNZAF, crashed at Espiritu Santo, Vanuatu, South
Pacific. Recovered between 12–22 October 1987 by RNZAF C-130. Not
restored and now displayed as jungle recovery diorama from 1995.
(RNZAF Museum, Christchurch)

## UNITED STATES AIR FORCE MUSEUM

Displayed as: A-24B          CurrentSerial:
Original:       SBD-4         Original Serial: Bu. No. 10575
c/n: 2565

*Brief History*
A twist on the theme of A-24s being converted to SBDs, this is an SBD
which ditched in Lake Michigan from Chicago naval air base on 14
September 1944. She was recovered from Lake Michigan in 1991 by
Naval National Museum of Naval Aviation, and transferred to USAF
Museum in 1994 to be converted to an A-24 as a static display by Black
Shadow Aviation, Jacksonville, Florida, and still, currently, isunder
restoration. (Kevin R. Smith)

## PLANES OF FAME AIR MUSEUM

Displayed as:
Original:      SBD-5

Current Serial:
Original Serial:  36176

Brief History
Recovered from Lake Michigan and on loan from US Navy, with restoration started by Bob Pond of Minnesota. (Kevin R. Smith)

# Assignment and Delivery Schedule – A-24B Aircraft Contract 28716

| Blk | Pr'ty | Quan. | Project | Destination | Authority | Co. Serial | AD Serial | Date |
|---|---|---|---|---|---|---|---|---|
| 1 | 1A | 1 | None | M.C. to remain at Contractor's Plant | OTT-33-20866 8-5-43 | 17124 | 54285 | 22-May-43 |
| 1 | 1B | 3 | None | Eglin Field for Opr. Tests. Permanently assigned to Proving Ground Command | OTT-33-20866 8-5-43 | 17126 | 54287 | 21-May-43 |
|  |  |  |  |  |  | 17127 | 54288 | 22-May-43 |
|  |  |  |  |  |  | 17128 | 54289 | 21-May-43 |
| 1 | 1C | 1 | None | M.C. Wright Field | OTT-33-2-0866 8-5-43 | 17125 | 54286 | 4-May-43 |
| 1 | 1D | 1 | None | 3rd Air Force Flt. Dlvy. 3rd Tow Target Sqdn. Camp Davies, N.C. | OTT-33-30866 8-5-43 | 17135 | 54296 | 28-May-43 |
| 1 | 1E | 2 | Iron 96091R | Sacramento Air Depot for preparation to export | OTT-33-20866 8-5-43 | 17129 | 54290 | 23-May-43 |
|  |  |  |  |  |  | 17130 | 54291 | 23-May-43 |
| 1 | 1F | 5 | None | 84th Bomb Group, Drew Field, Tampa, Florida | OTT-33-20866 8-5-43 | 17131 | 54292 | 23-May-43 |
|  |  |  |  |  |  | 17132 | 54293 | 23-May-43 |
|  |  |  |  |  |  | 17133 | 54294 | 10-Jun-43 |
|  |  |  |  |  |  | 17134 | 54295 | 25-May-43 |
| 1 | 1G | 5 | None | 48th Bomb Group, Key Field, Meridian, Miss. | OTT-33-20866 8-5-43 | 17136 | 54297 | 26-May-43 |
|  |  |  |  |  |  | 17137 | 54298 | 26-May-43 |
|  |  |  |  |  |  | 17138 | 54299 | 26-May-43 |
|  |  |  |  |  |  | 17139 | 54300 | 28-May-43 |
|  |  |  |  |  |  | 17140 | 54301 | 28-May-43 |
| 1 | 1H | 5 | None | 312th Bomb Group, Rice, Calif. | OTT-T-21602 15-5-43 | 17141 | 54302 | 28-May-43 |
|  |  |  |  |  |  | 17142 | 54303 | 27-May-43 |
|  |  |  |  |  |  | 17143 | 54304 | 29-May-43 |
|  |  |  |  |  |  | 17144 | 54305 | 4-Jun-43 |
|  |  |  |  |  |  | 17145 | 54306 | 31-May-43 |
| 1 | 1I | 5 | None | 84th Bomb Group, Drew Field, Tampa, Florida | OTT-T-3321692 15-5-43 | 17146 | 54307 | 31-May-43 |
|  |  |  |  |  |  | 17147 | 54308 | 30-May-43 |
|  |  |  |  |  |  | 17160 | 54321 | 20-Jun-43 |
|  |  |  |  |  |  | 17149 | 54310 | 3-Jun-43 |
|  |  |  |  |  |  | 17150 | 54311 | 4-Jun-43 |
| 1 | 1J | 5 | None | 48th Bomb Group, Key Field, Meridian, Miss. | OTT-T-32-21602 15-5-43 | 17151 | 54312 | 3-Jun-43 |
|  |  |  |  |  |  | 17153 | 54314 | 5-Jun-43 |
|  |  |  |  |  |  | 17154 | 54315 | 5-Jun-43 |
|  |  |  |  |  |  | 17161 | 54322 | 20-Jun-43 |
|  |  |  |  |  |  | 17162 | 54323 | 26-Jun-43 |
| A | June | 5 | Wasp | Flt. Delv. By Air Transport Command to San Antonio, Texas for June delv. to Wasp | OTT-T33-222393 24-5-43 | 17163 | 54324 | 26-Jun-43 |
|  |  |  |  |  |  | 17155 | 54316 | 14-Jun-43 |
|  |  |  |  |  |  | 17156 | 54317 | 13-Jun-43 |
|  |  |  |  |  |  | 17157 | 54318 | 14-Jun-43 |
|  |  |  |  |  |  | 17158 | 54319 | 19-Jun-43 |
| B | June | 2 | Lion | Flyaway by Air Transport Command to San Antonio Air Depot, Texas for June delv. to Lion | OTT-T-33-22393 | 17159 | 54320 | 20-Jun-43 |
|  |  |  |  |  |  | 17148 | 54309 | 6-Jun-43 |
|  |  |  |  |  |  | 17152 | 54313 | 10-Jun-43 |

| Blk | Pr'ty | Quan. | Project | Destination | Authority | Co. Serial | AD Serial | Date |
|---|---|---|---|---|---|---|---|---|
| 1 | 1L | 2 | None | 84th Bomb Group, Drew Field, Tampa, Fla. | OTT-T-33-21692 15-5-43 | 17164 | 54325 | 26-Jun-43 |
| | | | | | | 17165 | 54326 | 24-Jun-43 |
| 1 | 1-O | 1 | 96143 | Sacramento Air Depot for prep. to export. Via Atlanta Mod. Centre, Ga for Tow Target Reel Installation | OTT-T-33-24071 11-6-43 & OTT-T-33-27940 17-7-43 | 17301 | 54462 | 28-Aug-43 |
| | | | | | | 17302 | 54463 | 30-Aug-43 |
| | | | | | | 17303 | 54464 | 21-Aug-43 |
| | | | | | | 17304 | 54465 | 24-Aug-43 |
| | | | | | | 17305 | 54466 | 27-Aug-43 |
| | | | | | | 17306 | 54467 | 23-Aug-43 |
| | | | | | | 17307 | 544608 | 24-Aug-43 |
| | | | | | | 17308 | 54469 | 28-Aug-43 |
| | | | | | | 17309 | 54470 | 28-Aug-43 |
| | | | | | | 17310 | 54471 | 28-Aug-43 |
| 1 | 1-N | 11 | | 84th Bomb Group Drew Field, Tampa, Fla. | OTT-T-24071 11-6-43 | 17166 | 54327 | 24-Jun-43 |
| | | | | | | 17167 | 54328 | 28-Jun-43 |
| | | | | | | 17168 | 54329 | 29-Jun-43 |
| | | | | | | 17169 | 54330 | 28-Jun-43 |
| | | | | | | 17170 | 54331 | 28-Jun-43 |
| | | | | | | 17171 | 54332 | 1-Jul-43 |
| | | | | | | 17172 | 54333 | 8-Jul-43 |
| | | | | | | 17173 | 54334 | 28-Jun-43 |
| | | | | | | 17174 | 54335 | 29-Jun-43 |
| | | | | | | 17175 | 54336 | 28-Jun-43 |
| | | | | | | 17176 | 54337 | 1-Jul-43 |
| C | July | 5 | Wasp | Flyaway by Air Trans. Command to San Antonio Air Depot, Texas for July delivery to Wasp | OTT-T-33-24071 11-6-43 & OTT-T-33-27940 17-7-43 | 17177 | 54338 | 7-Jul-43 |
| | | | | | | 17178 | 54339 | 2-Jul-43 |
| | | | | | | 17179 | 54340 | 5-Jul-43 |
| | | | | | | 17180 | 54341 | 2-Jul-43 |
| | | | | | | 17181 | 54342 | 2-Jul-43 |
| D | July | 5 | Lion | Flyaway by Air Trans. Command to San Antonio, Texas for July delv. to Lion | OTT-T-33-24071 11-6-43 | 17182 | 54343 | 2-Jul-43 |
| | | | | | | 17183 | 54344 | 2-Jul-43 |
| | | | | | | 17184 | 54345 | 2-Jul-43 |
| | | | | | | 17185 | 54346 | 2-Jul-43 |
| | | | | | | 17186 | 54347 | 3-Jul-43 |
| 1 | 1-O | | 96142R | Sacramento Air Depot for prep. for export | OTT-T-33-24071 11-6-43 | 17187 | 54348 | 3-Jul-43 |
| 1 | 1-P | 5 | | 48th Bomb Group, Key Field, Mississippi | OTT-T-33-24071 11-6-43 | 17188 | 54349 | 3-Jul-43 |
| | | | | | | 17189 | 54350 | 6-Jul-43 |
| | | | | | | 17190 | 54351 | 6-Jul-43 |
| | | | | | | 17191 | 54352 | 6-Jul-43 |
| | | | | | | 17192 | 54353 | 3-Jul-43 |
| 1 | 1-Q | 5 | | Air Force School of Applied Tactics for Delivery to 667th Bomb Squadron, Alachua, Fla | OTT-T-33 24071 11-6-43 | 17193 | 54354 | 14-Jul-43 |
| | | | | | | 17194 | 54355 | 6-Jul-43 |
| | | | | | | 17195 | 54356 | 15-Jul-43 |
| | | | | | | 17196 | 54357 | 18-Jul-43 |
| | | | | | | 17197 | 54358 | 23-Jul-43 |
| 1 | 1-R | 3 | 96194R | Sacramento ASC for preparation for export shipment | OTT-33-26180 5-7-43 | 17198 | 54359 | 20-Jul-43 |
| | | | | | | 17199 | 54360 | 21-Jul-43 |
| | | | | | | 17200 | 54361 | 7-Aug-443 |
| 1 | 1-S | 5 | | AAF School of Applied Tactics, Alachua, Fla. for 667th Dive Bomber Squadron | OTT-33-26180 5-7-443 | 17201 | 54362 | 7-Aug-43 |
| | | | | | | 17202 | 54363 | 20-Jul-43 |
| | | | | | | 17203 | 54364 | 20-Jul-43 |
| | | | | | | 17204 | 54365 | 7-Aug-43 |
| | | | | | | 17205 | 54366 | 7-Aug-43 |
| 1 | 1-T | 22 | | Third Air Force Station as directed by Commanding General, Third Air Force | | 17206 | 54367 | 7-Aug-43 |
| | | | | | | 17207 | 54368 | 20-Jul-43 |
| | | | | | | 17209 | 54370 | 7-Aug-43 |
| | | | | | | 17210 | 54371 | 20-Jul-43 |
| | | | | | | 17212 | 54375 | 7-Aug-43 |
| | | | | | | 17213 | 54374 | 7-Aug-43 |

| Blk | Pr'ty | Quan. | Project | Destination | Authority | Co. Serial | AD Serial | Date |
|---|---|---|---|---|---|---|---|---|
| | | | | | | 17214 | 54375 | 7-Aug-43 |
| | | | | | | 17215 | 54376 | 7-Aug-43 |
| | | | | | | 17216 | 54377 | 7-Aug-43 |
| | | | | | | 17217 | 54378 | 7-Aug-43 |
| | | | | | | 17218 | 54379 | 7-Aug-43 |
| | | | | | | 17219 | 54380 | 7-Aug-43 |
| | | | | | | 17220 | 54381 | 20-Jul-43 |
| | | | | | | 17221 | 54382 | 7-Aug-43 |
| | | | | | | 17233 | 54394 | 9-Aug-43 |
| | | | | | | 17234 | 54395 | 9-Aug-43 |
| | | | | | | 17235 | 54396 | 9-Aug-43 |
| | | | | | | 17237 | 54398 | 9-Aug-43 |
| | | | | | | 17237 | 54398 | 9-Aug-43 |
| | | | | | | 17238 | 54399 | 9-Aug-43 |
| | | | | | | 17239 | 54400 | 9-Aug-43 |
| | | | | | | 17240 | 54401 | 9-Aug-43 |
| 1 | 1-U | 3 | 96195R | Sacramento ASC for preparation for export shipment | OTT-33-26180 5-7-43 | 17241 | 54402 | 7-Aug-43 |
| | | | | | | 17242 | 54403 | 7-Aug-43 |
| | | | | | | 17243 | 54404 | 7-Aug-43 |
| 1 | 1-V | 5 | | AAF School of Applied Tactics, Alachua, Fla. for 667th Dive Bomber Squadron | OTT-33-26180 5-7-43 | 17244 | 54405 | 13-Aug-43 |
| | | | | | | 17245 | 54406 | 9-Aug-43 |
| | | | | | | 17246 | 54407 | 13-Aug-43 |
| | | | | | | 17247 | 54408 | 9-Aug-43 |
| 1 | 1-W | 22 | | Third Air Force Stations as directed by Commanding General, Third Air Force, 22nd Bomb Training Wing, Drew Field, Tampa, Fla. OTT-33-26180 5-7-43 3rd AF 3 AFE 616 5-7-43 | | 17248 | 54409 | 10-Aug-43 |
| | | | | | | 17249 | 54410 | 20-Aug-43 |
| | | | | | | 17250 | 54411 | 20-Aug-43 |
| | | | | | | 17251 | 54412 | 10-Aug-43 |
| | | | | | | 17252 | 54413 | 10-Aug-43 |
| | | | | | | 17253 | 54414 | 10-Aug-43 |
| | | | | | | 17254 | 54415 | 10-Aug-43 |
| | | | | | | 17255 | 54416 | 10-Aug-43 |
| | | | | | | 17256 | 54417 | 12-Aug-43 |
| | | | | | | 17257 | 54418 | 12-Aug-43 |
| | | | | | | 17258 | 54419 | 10-Aug-43 |
| | | | | | | 17259 | 54420 | 10-Aug-43 |
| | | | | | | 17260 | 54421 | 20-Aug-43 |
| | | | | | | 17261 | 54422 | 12-Aug-43 |
| | | | | | | 17262 | 54423 | 10-Aug-43 |
| | | | | | | 17263 | 54424 | 12-Aug-43 |
| | | | | | | 17270 | 54431 | 13-Aug-43 |
| | | | | | | 17271 | 54432 | 13-Aug-43 |
| | | | | | | 17272 | 54433 | 13-Aug-43 |
| | | | | | | 17273 | 54434 | 16-Aug-43 |
| | | | | | | 17274 | 54435 | 17-Aug-43 |
| | | | | | | 17275 | 54436 | 13-Aug-43 |
| | | | | | | 17276 | 54437 | 23-Aug-43 |
| 1 | 1-X | 3 | | N.Y. Air Serv. Port Area Cmd, Newark Airport, N.J. | OTT-33-26180 5-7-43 OTT-T-33-28051 17-7-43 OTT-T-33-28143 19-7-43 | 17208 | 54369 | 19-Aug-43 |
| | | | | | | 17211 | 54372 | 23-Jul-43 |
| | | | | | | 17222 | 54383 | 23-Jul-43 |
| 1 | 1-Y | 14 | | AAF School of Applied Tactics, Orlando, Fla. | OTT-T-33 28428 20-7-43 | 17277 | 54438 | 17-Aug-43 |
| | | | | | | 17278 | 54439 | 17-Aug-43 |
| | | | | | | 17279 | 54440 | 21-Aug-43 |
| | | | | | | 17280 | 54441 | 17-Aug-43 |
| | | | | | | 17281 | 54442 | 16-Aug-43 |
| | | | | | | 17282 | 54443 | 17-Aug-43 |
| | | | | | | 17283 | 54444 | 16-Aug-43 |
| | | | | | | 17284 | 54445 | 17-Aug-43 |
| | | | | | | 17285 | 54446 | 13-Aug-43 |

| Blk | Pr'ty Quan. | Project | Destination | Authority | Co. Serial | AD Serial | Date |
|---|---|---|---|---|---|---|---|
| | | | | | 17286 | 54447 | 17-Aug-43 |
| | | | | | 17287 | 54448 | 16-Aug-43 |
| | | | | | 17288 | 54449 | 17-Aug-43 |
| | | | | | 17289 | 54450 | 16-Aug-43 |
| | | | | | 17290 | 54451 | 23-Aug-43 |
| 1 | 1-Z 6 | | To Commanding Gen. AAF for Flt. Del. to 3rd Staff Sqd., Sherman Field, Kan, for use of the AAF Cmd. Sec & Gen. Staff | OTT-33-30630 6-8-43 | 17264 | 54423 | 12-Aug-43 |
| | | | | | 17265 | 54426 | 12-Aug-43 |
| | | | | | 17266 | 54427 | 12-Aug-43 |
| | | | | | 17267 | 54428 | 12-Aug-43 |
| | | | | | 17268 | 54429 | 12-Aug-43 |
| | | | | | 17269 | 54430 | 12-Aug-43 |
| 1 | 1-ZA 3 | | M.C. Flt. Delv. to Romulus Air Field, Mich. 1-9-43 | OTT-33-30887 9-8-43 | 17291 | 54452 | 16-Aug-43 |
| | | | | | 17292 | 54453 | 17-Aug-43 |
| | | | | | 17293 | 54454 | 24-Aug-43 |
| 1 | 1-ZB 2 | | Flt. Del. to 1st A.F. HQ & HQ. Sqdn. 1st Fighter Command, Mitchell Field, N.Y. | OTT-33-31529 21-8-43 | 17295 | 54456 | 17-Aug-43 |
| | | | | | 17296 | 54457 | 19-Aug-43 |
| 1 | 1-ZC 1 | | To Material Command, Bolling Field, D.C. | OTT-33-31653 13-8-43 | 17294 | 54455 | 17-Aug-43 |
| 1 | 1-ZD 4 | | Sacramento ASC, McClellan Field, Calif. 10-9-43 | OTT-33-31765 14-8-43 | 17297 | 54458 | 20-Aug-43 |
| | | | | | 17298 | 54459 | 21-Aug-43 |
| | | | | | 17299 | 54460 | 20-Aug-43 |
| | | | | | 17300 | 54461 | 21-Aug-43 |
| E | Aug. 5 | Wasp | San Antonio Air Depot | T-=3893 30-7-43. OTT:MKA:ES:33 No. 01-A-44-51 24-7-43 | 17223 | 54384 | 5-Aug-43 |
| | | | | | 17224 | 54385 | 5-Aug-43 |
| | | | | | 17225 | 54386 | 5-Aug-43 |
| | | | | | 17226 | 54387 | 5-Aug-43 |
| | | | | | 17227 | 54388 | 5-Aug-43 |
| F | Aug/ 5 | Lion | Flyaway ATC to San Antonio ASC to Lion | T-3893 30-7-43 AAF MC Ltr. MKA:ES:33 52551 24-7-43 | 17228 | 54389 | 30-Jul-43 |
| | | | | | 17229 | 54290 | 23-Jul-43 |
| | | | | | 17230 | 54391 | 30-Jul-43 |
| | | | | | 17231 | 54392 | 23-Jul-43 |
| | | | | | 17232 | 54393 | 30-Jul-43 |
| G | Sept. 5 | Wasp | Flyaway by ATC to San Antonio ASC for delivery to Wasp | OTT-33-32517 23-8-43 | 17328 | 54489 | 3-Sep-43 |
| | | | | | 17329 | 54490 | 13-Sep-43 |
| | | | | | 17330 | 54491 | 3-Sep-43 |
| | | | | | 17331 | 54492 | 3-Sep-43 |
| | | | | | 17332 | 54493 | 3-Sep-43 |
| 2 | 2-A 1 | Base | To Tulsa Mod. Center for mock-up | OTT-T-33-79699 23-9-43 | 17408 | 54569 | 26-Oct-43 |
| 2 | 2-B 19 | Base | Del. by Mat. Cmd. to Douglas Mod. B. Tulsa. Del. by ATC upon request of AMB PES. | OTT-T-33-79699 OTT-T-33 12077 | 17605 | 54766 | 29-Nov-43 |
| | | | | | 17606 | 54767 | 29-Nov-43 |
| | | | | | 17607 | 54768 | 29-Nov-43 |
| | | | | | 17608 | 54769 | 29-Nov-43 |
| | | | | | 17609 | 54770 | 29-Nov-43 |
| | | | | | 17610 | 54771 | 29-Nov-43 |
| | | | | | 17611 | 54772 | 29-Nov-43 |
| | | | | | 17612 | 54773 | 29-Nov-43 |
| | | | | | 17613 | 54774 | 29-Nov-43 |
| | | | | | 17614 | 54775 | 29-Nov-43 |
| | | | | | 17615 | 54776 | 29-Nov-43 |
| | | | | | 17616 | 54777 | 29-Nov-43 |
| | | | | | 17617 | 54778 | 29-Nov-43 |
| | | | | | 17618 | 54779 | 29-Nov-43 |
| | | | | | 17619 | 54780 | 29-Nov-43 |
| | | | | | 17620 | 54781 | 30-Nov-43 |
| | | | | | 17621 | 54782 | 30-Nov-43 |
| | | | | | 17622 | 54783 | 30-Nov-43 |
| | | | | | 17623 | 54784 | 30-Nov-43 |
| 3 | 3-A 6 | | Training Cmd. AAF Pilot Sch. Lockbourne, Ohio | OTT-33-31799 14-8-43 | 17312 | 54473 | 30-Aug-43 |
| | | | | | 17313 | 54474 | 30-Aug-43 |

| Blk | Pr'ty | Quan. | Project | Destination | Authority | Co. Serial | AD Serial | Date |
|---|---|---|---|---|---|---|---|---|
| 3 | | | | | | 17314 | 54475 | 30-Aug-43 |
| | | | | | | 17315 | 54476 | 28-Aug-43 |
| | | | | | | 17316 | 54477 | 30-Aug-43 |
| | | | | | | 17317 | 54478 | 27-Aug-43 |
| 3 | 3-B | 1 | | Hq & Hqs. Sqd. Sta. Nbr 1, Naval Air Station, Atlantic City, N.C. | OTT-33-32223 19-8-43 | 17311 | 54472 | 27-Aug-43 |
| 3 | 3-C | 8 | | 3rd Air Force Flt. Dlvy. 3rd Tow Target Sqd. Camp Davis, N.C. | OTT-33-32223 19-8-43 | 17320 | 54481 | 30-Aug-43 |
| | | | | | | 17321 | 54482 | 3-Sep-43 |
| | | | | | | 17322 | 54483 | 3-Sep-43 |
| | | | | | | 17323 | 54484 | 2-Sep-43 |
| | | | | | | 17324 | 54485 | 3-Sep-43 |
| | | | | | | 17325 | 54486 | 30-Aug-43 |
| | | | | | | 17326 | 54487 | 31-Aug-43 |
| | | | | | | 17327 | 54488 | 2-Sep-43 |
| 3 | 3-D | 15 | 96236R | Del. to 58th Sub Depot, Long Beach, Calif. for export | OTT-T-33-35894 29-9-43 | 17358 | 54519 | 17-Sep-43 |
| | | | | | | 17359 | 54520 | 18-Sep-43 |
| | | | | | | 17360 | 54521 | 17-Sep-43 |
| | | | | | | 17361 | 54522 | 18-Sep-43 |
| | | | | | | 17362 | 54523 | 16-Sep-43 |
| | | | | | | 17364 | 54525 | 18-Sep-43 |
| | | | | | | 17365 | 54526 | 18-Sep-43 |
| | | | | | | 17366 | 54527 | 16-Sep-43 |
| | | | | | | 17368 | 54529 | 18-Sep-43 |
| | | | | | | 17369 | 54530 | 18-Sep-43 |
| | | | | | | 17370 | 54531 | 18-Sep-43 |
| | | | | | | 17371 | 54532 | 17-Sep-43 |
| | | | | | | 17374 | 54535 | 16-Sep-43 |
| | | | | | | 17375 | 54536 | 18-Sep-43 |
| | | | | | | 17381 | 54542 | 18-Sep-43 |
| 3 | 3-E | 2 | | Assigned to AAF Servicing Dept. for use of Com. General, Gen Orana of 6th Service Com. Flt del, to Chicago Municipal airport, Illinois | OTT-33-32498 23-8-43 OTT-33-32912 28-8-43 | 17318 | 54479 | 3-Sep-43 |
| | | | | | | 17319 | 54480 | 1-Sep-43 |
| 3 | 3-F | 3 | | 1st Air Force for del. to 2nd Tow Target Sqd., Bradley Field, Windsor Locks, Conn. | OTT-33-34171 4-9-43 | 17377 | 54538 | 23-Sep-43 |
| | | | | | | 17383 | 54544 | 23-Sep-43 |
| | | | | | | 17394 | 54555 | 25-Sep-43 |
| G-A | Sept. | 25 | 90303F Pike | Del. to Newark Port of Embarkation, New Jersey | OTT-33-34171 4-9-43 | 17334 | 54494 | 7-Sep-43 |
| | | | | | | 17335 | 54496 | 10-Sep-43 |
| | | | | | | 17336 | 54497 | 13-Sep-43 |
| | | | | | | 17337 | 54498 | 13-Sep-43 |
| | | | | | | 17338 | 54499 | 13-Sep-43 |
| | | | | | | 17339 | 54500 | 9-Sep-43 |
| | | | | | | 17341 | 54502 | 16-Sep-43 |
| | | | | | | 17342 | 54503 | 16-Sep-43 |
| | | | | | | 17343 | 54504 | 8-Sep-43 |
| | | | | | | 17344 | 54505 | 16-Sep-43 |
| | | | | | | 17345 | 54506 | 13-Sep-43 |
| | | | | | | 17346 | 54507 | 14-Sep-43 |
| | | | | | | 17347 | 54508 | 13-Sep-43 |
| | | | | | | 17348 | 54509 | 14-Sep-43 |
| | | | | | | 17349 | 54510 | 14-Sep-43 |
| | | | | | | 17350 | 54511 | 13-Sep-43 |
| | | | | | | 17351 | 54512 | 14-Sep-43 |
| | | | | | | 17352 | 54513 | 9-Sep-43 |
| | | | | | | 17354 | 54515 | 14-Sep-43 |
| | | | | | | 17355 | 54516 | 16-Sep-43 |
| | | | | | | 17356 | 54517 | 18-Sep-43 |
| | | | | | | 17357 | 54518 | 18-Sep-43 |
| | | | | | | 17353 | 54514 | 28-Sep-43 |
| | | | | | | 17333 | 54494 | 6-Sep-43 |
| | | | | | | 17340 | 54501 | 6-Sep-43 |

| Blk | Pr'ty | Quan. | Project | Destination | Authority | Co. Serial | AD Serial | Date |
|---|---|---|---|---|---|---|---|---|
| 4 | 4-A | 15 | Base | Del. by Mat. Cmd. to Douglas Mod. B., Tulsa | OTT-T-33 3254 30-8-43 OTT-T-33-12077 24-11-43 | 17624 | 54785 | 30-Nov-43 |
| | | | | | | 17625 | 54786 | 30-Nov-43 |
| | | | | | | 17626 | 54787 | 30-Nov-43 |
| | | | | | | 17627 | 54788 | 30-Nov-43 |
| | | | | | | 17628 | 54789 | 30-Nov-43 |
| | | | | | | 17629 | 54790 | 30-Nov-43 |
| | | | | | | 17630 | 54791 | 30-Nov-43 |
| | | | | | | 17631 | 54792 | 30-Nov-43 |
| | | | | | | 17632 | 54793 | 30-Nov-43 |
| | | | | | | 17633 | 54794 | 30-Nov-43 |
| | | | | | | 17634 | 54795 | 30-Nov-43 |
| | | | | | | 17635 | 54796 | 30-Nov-43 |
| | | | | | | 17634 | 54797 | 30-Nov-43 |
| | | | | | | 17637 | 54798 | 30-Nov-43 |
| | | | | | | 17638 | 54799 | 30-Nov-43 |
| 5 | 5-A | 6 | DOM-673 | 1st A.F., for del. to 2nd Tow Target Sq., Bradley Field, Windsor Locks, Conn. | OTT-33-34171 4-9-43 | 17378 | 54539 | 27-Sep-43 |
| | | | | | | 17387 | 54548 | 27-Sep-43 |
| | | | | | | 17391 | 54552 | 24-Sep-43 |
| | | | | | | 17392 | 54553 | 24-Sep-43 |
| | | | | | | 17395 | 54556 | 24-Sep-43 |
| | | | | | | 17397 | 54558 | 27-Sep-43 |
| 5 | 5-B | 2 | DOM-671 | Camp Young, Calf. Del. to Warner Robins ASC for Tow Reel install. | OTT-33-34171 4-9-43 | 17379 | 54540 | 24-Sep-43 |
| | | | | | | 17386 | 54547 | 24-Sep-43 |
| 5 | 5-C | 1 | | ASC 368th Sub Depot, Army Air Base, Richmond, Va. | OTT-33-34171 4-9-43 | 17380 | 54541 | 24-Aug-43 |
| 5 | 5-D | 3 | | To Bolling Field, D.C. to be assigned | OTT-33-34171 4-9-43 | 17363 | 54524 | 27-Sep-43 |
| | | | | | | 17376 | 54537 | 27-Sep-43 |
| | | | | | | 17384 | 54545 | 28-Sep-43 |
| 5 | 5-E | 2 | DOM-672 | ATC to Mod. Center to be mod. into instrument Trainer | OTT-33-34171 4-9-43 | 17555 | 54716 | 17-Nov-43 |
| | | | | | | 17556 | 54717 | 17-Nov-43 |
| 5 | 5-F | 1 | DOM-673 | ATC to Mod. Center to be mod. into instrument Trainer | OTT-33-34535 8-9-43 | 17557 | 54718 | 17-Nov-43 |
| H | Oct. | 5 | Wasp | Flyaway by ATC to San Antonio, ASC. | OTT-I-33-35576 17-9-43 | 17415 | 54576 | 18-Oct-43 |
| | | | | | | 17417 | 54578 | 18-Oct-43 |
| | | | | | | 17412 | 54573 | 21-Oct-43 |
| | | | | | | 17418 | 54579 | 21-Oct-43 |
| | | | | | | 17420 | 54581 | 21-Oct-43 |
| H-A | Oct. Pike 25 | | 90316-F | Flyaway to Port of Embarkation for 709-AIR-11-NAFUS-16 | OTT-I-33-35576 17-9-43 | 17367 | 54528 | 2-Oct-43 |
| | | | | | | 17372 | 54533 | 2-Oct-43 |
| | | | | | | 17373 | 54534 | 28-Sep-43 |
| | | | | | | 17382 | 54543 | 2-Oct-43 |
| | | | | | | 17385 | 54546 | 8-Oct-43 |
| | | | | | | 17388 | 54549 | 2-Oct-43 |
| | | | | | | 17389 | 54550 | 4-Oct-43 |
| | | | | | | 17390 | 54551 | 10-Apr-43 |
| | | | | | | 17393 | 54554 | 11-Oct-43 |
| | | | | | | 17396 | 54557 | 30-Sep-43 |
| | | | | | | 17398 | 54559 | 1-Oct-43 |
| | | | | | | 17399 | 54560 | 2-Oct-43 |
| | | | | | | 17400 | 54561 | 2-Oct-43 |
| | | | | | | 17401 | 54562 | 8-Oct-43 |
| | | | | | | 17402 | 54563 | 8-Oct-43 |
| | | | | | | 17403 | 54564 | 30-Sep-43 |
| | | | | | | 17404 | 54565 | 11-Oct-43 |
| | | | | | | 17405 | 54566 | 11-Oct-43 |
| | | | | | | 17406 | 54567 | 9-Oct-43 |
| | | | | | | 17407 | 44568 | 11-Oct-43 |
| | | | | | | 17410 | 54571 | 11-Oct-43 |
| | | | | | | 17411 | 54572 | 11—Oct-43 |
| | | | | | | 17413 | 54574 | 11-Oct-43 |

| Blk | Pr'ty | Quan. | Project | Destination | Authority | Co. Serial | AD Serial | Date |
|---|---|---|---|---|---|---|---|---|
| 6 | 6-A | 15 | Bass | Del. by Mat. Cmd. to Douglas Mod. B., Tulsa | OTT-T-33-34535 8-9-43 OTT-T-33-12077 24-11-43 | 17414 | 54575 | 11-Oct-43 |
| | | | | | | 17419 | 54580 | 11-Oct-43 |
| | | | | | | 17639 | 54800 | 30-Nov-43 |
| | | | | | | 17640 | 54801 | 30-Nov-43 |
| | | | | | | 17641 | 54802 | 30-Nov-43 |
| | | | | | | 17642 | 54803 | 30-Nov-43 |
| | | | | | | 17643 | 54804 | 30-Nov-43 |
| | | | | | | 17644 | 54805 | 30-Nov-43 |
| | | | | | | 17645 | 54806 | 30-Nov-43 |
| | | | | | | 17647 | 54808 | 3-Dec-43 |
| | | | | | | 17649 | 54810 | 3-Dec-43 |
| | | | | | | 17650 | 54811 | 3-Dec-43 |
| | | | | | | 17651 | 54812 | 3-Dec-43 |
| | | | | | | 17646 | 54807 | 22-Dec-43 |
| | | | | | | 17648 | 54809 | 18-Dec-43 |
| | | | | | | 17652 | 54813 | 18-Dec-43 |
| | | | | | | 17653 | 54814 | 18-Dec-43 |
| 7 | 7-A | 16 | DOM-673 | Del. by ATC to Mod. Center to be modified into instrument Trainers | OTT-T-33-34535 8-9-43 AFMMD-4E1-10-2003 28-10-43 | 17558 | 54719 | 17-Nov-43 |
| | | | | | | 17559 | 54720 | 17-Nov-43 |
| | | | | | | 17560 | 54721 | 17-Nov-43 |
| | | | | | | 17561 | 54722 | 17-Nov-43 |
| | | | | | | 17562 | 54723 | 17-Nov-43 |
| | | | | | | 17565 | 54726 | 17-Nov-43 |
| | | | | | | 17567 | 54728 | 17-Nov-43 |
| | | | | | | 17568 | 54729 | 17-Nov-43 |
| | | | | | | 17564 | 54730 | 17-Nov-43 |
| | | | | | | 17572 | 54733 | 17-Nov-43 |
| | | | | | | 17575 | 54736 | 17-Nov-43 |
| | | | | | | 17576 | 54737 | 17-Nov-43 |
| | | | | | | 17577 | 54738 | 17-Nov-43 |
| | | | | | | 17506 | 54667 | 20-Nov-43 |
| | | | | | | 17507 | 54668 | 20-Nov-43 |
| 7 | 7-B | 5 | DOM-674 | Del. by ATC to Mod. Center to be mod. into instrument Trainers | OTT-T-33-34535 8-9-43 AFMMD-4E1-10-2003 28-10-43 | 17508 | 54669 | 20-Nov-43 |
| | | | | | | 17509 | 54670 | 20-Nov-43 |
| | | | | | | 17510 | 54671 | 20-Nov-43 |
| | | | | | | 17512 | 54673 | 20-Nov-43 |
| | | | | | | 17513 | 54674 | 20-Nov-43 |
| 7 | 7-C | 1 | | To Flt. Control Cmd, to be del to Hq & Hq Sqdn. Off. of Flying Safety, Winston, Salem, N.C. | OTT-T-33-87703 7-10-43 | 17514 | 54675 | 20-Nov-43 |
| | | | | | | 17436 | 54597 | 8-Oct-43 |
| | | 3 | | Ditto to Cmd. Office of Flying Safety, Fort George Wright, Washington. | Ditto | 17442 | 54603 | 11-Oct-43 |
| | | | | | | 17443 | 54604 | 11-Oct-43 |
| | | | | | | 17446 | 54607 | 11-Oct-43 |
| | | 1 | | Ditto to Comd. Office of Flying Safety, Peterson Field, Colorado Springs, Co. | Ditto | 17468 | 54629 | 14-Oct-43 |
| | | 4 | | Ditto to Comd. Office of Flying Safety, Oakland Municipal. Airport, Calf. | Ditto | 17421 | 54583 | 16-Oct-43 |
| | | | | | | 17428 | 54589 | 16-Oct-43 |
| | | | | | | 17429 | 54590 | 18-Oct-43 |
| | | 2 | | Ditto to Comd. Office of Flying Safety, Mitchell Field, Long Island, N.Y. | Ditto | 17409 | 54570 | 21-Oct-43 |
| | | | | | | 17416 | 54577 | 21-Oct-43 |
| | | 1 | | Ditto to Comd. Office of Flying Safety, Drew Field, Tampaa, Fla. | Ditto | 17422 | 54583 | 21-Oct-43 |
| | | 8 | | Ditto to Hq. & Hq. Sqdn Office Flying Safety, Winson, Salem. | Ditto | 17425 | 54586 | 21-Oct-43 |
| 7 | | | | | | 17423 | 54584 | 21-Oct-43 |
| | | | | | | 17426 | 54587 | 21-Oct-43 |
| | | | | | | 17427 | 54588 | 21-Oct-43 |
| | | | | | | 17430 | 54591 | 21-Oct-43 |
| | | | | | | 17431 | 54592 | 21-Oct-43 |
| | | | | | | 17432 | 54593 | 21-Oct-43 |
| | | | | | | 17433 | 54594 | 21-Oct-43 |
| | | | | | | 17424 | 54585 | 22-Oct-43 |

| Blk | Pr'ty | Quan. | Project | Destination | Authority | Co. Serial | AD Serial | Date |
|---|---|---|---|---|---|---|---|---|
| 7 | 7-D | 1 | | To ASC 96th Service Group, Oscoda, Mich. | OTT-T-33-34535 8-9-43 | 17452 | 54613 | 15-Oct-43 |
| 7 | 7-E | 4 | | To Hq. & Hq. Sqdn. Oklahoma City, ASC | OTT-T-33-35068 13-9-43 | 17438 | 54599 | 15-Oct-43 |
| | | | | | | 17444 | 54605 | 15-Oct-43 |
| | | | | | | 17447 | 54608 | 15-Oct-43 |
| | | | | | | 17449 | 54610 | 15-Oct-43 |
| 7 | 7-F | 1 | | To ASC for distribution to Mobile ASC, Brockley Field. | OTT-T-33-35068 13-9-43 | 17439 | 54600 | 18-Oct-43 |
| | | 1 | | Ditto to Hdq. ASC Paterson Field, Dayton, Ohio | Ditto | 17445 | 54606 | 16-Oct-43 |
| | | 1 | | Ditto to Hill Field, Ogden, Salt Lake City Utah | Ditto | 17448 | 54609 | 18-Oct-43 |
| | | 1 | | Ditto to Fairfield ASC, Paterson Field. | Ditto | 17450 | 54611 | 16-Oct-43 |
| | | 1 | | Ditto to Oklahoma City, ASC, Tinker Field. | Ditto | 17455 | 54616 | 18-Oct-43 |
| | | 1 | | Ditto to Rome ASC, Rome Army Air Field | Ditto | 17457 | 54618 | 18-Oct-43 |
| | | 1 | | Ditto to Sacramento ASC, McClellan Field | Ditto | 17458 | 54619 | 18-Oct-43 |
| | | 1 | | Ditto to Warner Robins ASC, Robins Field | Ditto | 17462 | 54623 | 18-Oct-43 |
| | | 1 | | Ditto to San Antonio ASC, Kelly Field | Ditto | 17469 | 54625 | 18-Oct-43 |
| | | 1 | | Ditto to San Bernardino ASC, San Bernardino Field | Ditto | 17466 | 54627 | 18-Oct-43 |
| | | 1 | | Ditto to Spokane ASC, Spokane Army Air Field | Ditto | 17467 | 54628 | 19-Oct-43 |
| | | 1 | | Ditto to Middletown ASC, Olmsted Field | Ditto | 17472 | 54633 | 16-Oct-43 |
| | | 1 | | Ditto Hq. ASC Paterson Field | Ditto | 17476 | 54637 | 18-Oct-43 |
| 8 | 8-A | 15 | Bass | Del. by Mat. Cmd. to Douglas Mod. B. Tulsa | OTT-T-33-35068 13-9-43 OTT-T-33-12077 24-11-43 | 17654 | 54815 | 3-Dec-43 |
| | | | | | | 17655 | 54816 | 3-Dec-43 |
| | | | | | 17658 | 54819 | 14-Dec-43 | |
| | | | | | | 17660 | 54821 | 14-Dec-43 |
| | | | | | | 17663 | 54824 | 14-Dec-43 |
| | | | | | | 17665 | 54826 | 14-Dec-43 |
| | | | | | | 17656 | 54817 | 18-Dec-43 |
| | | | | | | 17657 | 54818 | 24-Dec-43 |
| | | | | | | 17659 | 54820 | 22-Dec-43 |
| | | | | | | 17661 | 54822 | 18-Dec-43 |
| | | | | | | 17662 | 54823 | 18-Dec-43 |
| | | | | | | 17664 | 54825 | 18-Dec-43 |
| | | | | | | 17666 | 54827 | 18-Dec-43 |
| | | | | | | 17667 | 54828 | 20-Dec-43 |
| | | | | | | 17668 | 54829 | 20-Dec-43 |
| 9 | 9-A | 2 | | To ASC for distribution to San Bernardino ASC, San Bernardino Army Airforce Field | OTT-T-33-35068 13-9-43 | 17456 | 54617 | 19-Oct-43 |
| | | | | | | 17489 | 54650 | 23-Oct-43 |
| | | 2 | | Ditto to Middletown ASC, Olmsted Field | Ditto | 17440 | 54601 | 19-Oct-43 |
| | | | | | | 17465 | 54626 | 22-Oct-43 |
| | | 2 | | Ditto to Mobile ASC, Brookley Field | Ditto | 17454 | 54615 | 19-Oct-43 |
| | | | | | | 17480 | 54641 | 23-Oct-43 |
| | | 2 | | Ditto to Fairfield ASC, Paterson Field | Ditto | 17434 | 54595 | 19-Oct-43 |
| | | | | | | 17463 | 54624 | 22-Oct-43 |
| | | 2 | | Ditto to Ogden ASC, Hill Field, Utah | Ditto | 17461 | 54622 | 19-Oct-43 |
| | | | | | | 17481 | 54642 | 22-Oct-43 |
| | | 1 | | Ditto to Oklahoma City ASC, Tinker Field | Ditto | 17469 | 54630 | 19-Oct-43 |
| | | 2 | | Ditto to San Antonio ASC, Kelly Field | Ditto | 17479 | 54640 | 19-Oct-43 |
| | | 2 | | Ditto to Spokane ASC, Spokane Army Air Field | Ditto | 17471 | 54632 | 23-Oct-43 |
| | | | | | | 17451 | 54612 | 21-Oct-43 |
| | | 2 | | Ditto to Warner Robins ASC, Robins Field | Ditto | 17501 | 54662 | 23-Oct-43 |
| | | | | | | 17460 | 54621 | 21-Oct-43 |
| | | 2 | | Ditto to Rome ASC, Rome Army Air Field, Rome, N.Y. | Ditto | 17497 | 54658 | 25-Oct-43 |
| | | | | | | 17473 | 54634 | 19-Oct-43 |
| 10 | 10-A | 1 | Bass | Ditto to Hdq. ASC, Paterson Field, Ohio | Ditto | 17484 | 54645 | 22-Oct-43 |
| | | | | | | 17459 | 54620 | 26-Oct-43 |
| | | 15 | Bass | Del. by Matl. Comd. to Douglas Mod. B. Tulsa | OTT-T-33-35068 13-9-43 OTT-T-33-12077 24-11-43 | 17670 | 54831 | 14-Dec-43 |
| | | | | | | 17671 | 54832 | 14-Dec-43 |
| | | | | | | 17669 | 54830 | 23-Dec-43 |
| | | | | | | 17672 | 54833 | 22-Dec-43 |
| | | | | | | 17673 | 54834 | 22-Dec-43 |

| Blk | Pr'ty Quan. | Project | Destination | Authority | Co. Serial | AD Serial | Date |
|---|---|---|---|---|---|---|---|
| | | | | | 17674 | 54835 | 20-Dec-43 |
| | | | | | 17675 | 54836 | 23-Dec-43 |
| | | | | | 17676 | 54837 | 30-Dec-43 |
| | | | | | 17677 | 54838 | 23-Dec-43 |
| | | | | | 17678 | 54839 | 22-Dec-43 |
| | | | | | 17679 | 54840 | 24-Dec-43 |
| | | | | | 17680 | 54841 | 22-Dec-43 |
| | | | | | 17681 | 54842 | 22-Dec-43 |
| | | | | | 17682 | 54843 | 29-Dec-43 |
| | | | | | 17683 | 54844 | 22-Dec-43 |
| 11 | 11-A 1 | | To ASC for distribution to Hqs. ASC, Paterson Field. | OTT-T-33-35068 13-9-43 OTT-T-33-12077 24-11-43 | 17487 | 54648 | 25-Oct-43 |
| | 2 | | Ditto to Mobile ASC, Brookley Field | Ditto | 17478 | 54630 | 26-Oct-43 |
| | | | | | 17502 | 54663 | 28-Oct-43 |
| | 1 | | Ditto to Fairfield ASC, Paterson Field | Ditto | 17490 | 54651 | 25-Oct-43 |
| | 1 | | Ditto to Ogden ASC, Hill Field, Utah | Ditto | 17492 | 54653 | 26-Oct-43 |
| | 2 | | Ditto to Middletown ASC, Olmsted Field | Ditto | 17500 | 54661 | 29-Oct-43 |
| | | | | | 17511 | 54672 | 29-Oct-43 |
| | 2 | | Ditto to San Bernardino ASC, San Bernardino Army Air Field | Ditto | 17474 | 54635 | 26-Oct-43 |
| | | | | | 17495 | 54656 | 30-Oct-43 |
| | 1 | | Ditto to Rome ASC, Rome Army Air Field | Ditto | 17494 | 54655 | 26-Oct-43 |
| | 2 | | Ditto to San Antonio ASC, Kelly Field | Ditto | 17499 | 54660 | 26-Oct-43 |
| | | | | | 17503 | 54664 | 28-Oct-43 |
| | 1 | | Ditto to Warner Robins ASC, Robins Field | Ditto | 17515 | 54676 | 28-Oct-43 |
| | 2 | | Ditto to Spokane ASC, Spokane Army Air Field | Ditto | 17488 | 54649 | 28-Oct-43 |
| | | | | | 17504 | 54665 | 1-Nov-43 |
| 12 | 12-A 10 | Bass | To Mod. Center | OTT-T-33-35068 13-9-43 OTT-T-33-12077 24-11-43 | 17684 | 54845 | 30-Dec-43 |
| | | | | | 17685 | 54846 | 20-Dec-43 |
| | | | | | 17686 | 54847 | 22-Dec-43 |
| | | | | | 17687 | 54848 | 23-Dec-43 |
| | | | | | 17688 | 54849 | 30-Dec-43 |
| | | | | | 17689 | 54850 | 22-Dec-43 |
| | | | | | 17690 | 54851 | 29-Dec-43 |
| | | | | | 17691 | 54852 | 23-Dec-43 |
| | | | | | 17692 | 54853 | 28-Dec-43 |
| | | | | | 17693 | 54854 | 29-Dec-43 |
| 13 | 13-A 1 | | To ATC for distribution to Warner Robins ASC | OTT-T-33-35068 13-9-43 OTT-T-33-12077 24-11-43 | 17505 | 54666 | 1-Nov-43 |
| | 1 | | Ditto to Mobile ATC | Ditto | 17517 | 54678 | 1-Nov-43 |
| | 1 | | Ditto for San Antonio ASC | Ditto | 17493 | 54654 | 13-Nov-43 |
| 13 | 13-B 1 | | To Hdq. Weather Wing for Assign. to RCO Weather Region at McClellan Field, Calif. | OTT-33084592 2-10-43 | 17496 | 54657 | 13-Nov-43 |
| 13 | 13-C 6 | DOM-67 | Del by ATC to Mod. Centre, to be mod. into instrument Trainers, thence to 2nd AF, for use of 90th Fighter Wing, TU Mod. C.OTT-T-33-87365 10-7-43 AFMMD-4E1 10-2003 28-10-43 | | 17563 | 54724 | 23-Nov-43 |
| | | | | | 17516 | 54677 | 20-Nov-43 |
| | | | | | 17571 | 54732 | 20-Nov-43 |
| | | | | | 17573 | 54734 | 20-Nov-43 |
| | | | | | 17574 | 54735 | 20-Nov-43 |
| | | | | | 17578 | 54739 | 20-Nov-43 |
| 13 17-Nov-43 | 13-D 6 | DOM-676 | To be del. by ATC to Mod. Cntr., to be mod. into instrument Trainers, thence to AAF instructors School, Bryan, Texas.OTT-T-33-90584 14-10-43 AFMMD-4E1 10-2003 10-28-43 TU Mod. C | | 17544 | 54710 | 17-Nov-43 |
| | | | | | 17550 | 54711 | 17-Nov-43 |
| | | | | | 17551 | 54712 | 17-Nov-43 |
| | | | | | 17552 | 54713 | 17-Nov-43 |
| | | | | | 17553 | 54714 | 17-Nov-43 |
| | | | | | 17554 | 54715 | 17-Nov-43 |
| 13 | 13-E 1 | | To MC to be flt. del. by ATC to Mod. Centre at Continental Denver, Colorado | OTT-T-33-92638 18-10-43 | 17435 | 54596 | 22-Oct-43 |
| | 1 | | Ditto at United Cheyenne, Wyoming | Ditto | 17437 | 54598 | 25-Oct-43 |
| | 1 | | Ditto at Martin Omaha, Nebraska | Ditto | 17453 | 54614 | 23-Oct-43 |
| | 1 | | Dittto at North American Fairfax, Kansas City, Kan. | Ditto | 17475 | 54636 | 23-Oct-43 |
| | 1 | | Ditto at Chicago & Southern, Memphis, Tennessee | Ditto | 17477 | 54638 | 25-Oct-43 |
| | 1 | | Ditto at Lockheed Dallas, Texas | Ditto | 17482 | 54643 | 23-Oct-43 |

| Blk | Prty | Quan. | Project | Destination | Authority | Co. Serial | AD Serial | Date |
|---|---|---|---|---|---|---|---|---|
| | | 1 | | Ditto at Consolidated Vultee, Louisville, Kentucky | Ditto | 17483 | 54644 | 23-Oct-43 |
| | | 1 | | Ditto at Northwest St. Paul, Minnesota | Ditto | 17485 | 54645 | 23-Oct-43 |
| | | 1 | | Ditto at Douglas Tulsa, Oklahoma | Ditto | 17486 | 54647 | 26-Oct-43 |
| | | 1 | | Ditto at Douglas Oklahoma City, Ok. | Ditto | 17470 | 54631 | 23-Oct-43 |
| 13 | 13-F | 4 | 92291 To be del. by ATC to Mod. Centre as directed by Aircraft Mod. Branch PES, WF to be mod. as instrument Trainers. Tu Mod. COTT-T-33-92638 18-10-43 AFMMD-4E1-10-2003 | | | 17569 | 54725 | 23-Nov-43 |
| | | | | | | 17566 | 54727 | 23-Nov-43 |
| | | | | | | 17570 | 54731 | 23-Nov-43 |
| | | | | | | 17579 | 54740 | 27-Nov-43 |
| 13 | 13-G | 1 | | To TCC for 362nd Base Hqs. & Air Base Sqn. Stout Field, Indianapolis, Indiana | OTT-T-33-93348 19-10-43 | 17498 | 54659 | 27-Nov-43 |
| | J | 5 | Wasp Nov. | Flyaway by ATC to San Antonio ASC for delivery to Wasp | OTT-T-33-93131 19-10-43 | 17521 | 54682 | 13-Nov-43 |
| | | | | | | 17519 | 54680 | 13-Nov-43 |
| | | | | | | 17520 | 54681 | 15-Nov-43 |
| | | | | | | 17522 | 54683 | 15-Nov-43 |
| | | | | | | 17518 | 54679 | 15-Nov-43 |
| 13 | 13-H | 1 | 90317-R Pike | To MC for del. to Birmingham Mod. Cntr. Municipal Airport, Birmingham, Alabama. | OTT-T-33-94807 22-10-43 | 17491 | 54652 | 29-Nov-43 |
| JA | | 25 | | Port of Embarkation for 709-AIR-11-NAFUS-16 | OTT-T-33-94807 22-10-43 | 17523 | 54684 | 28-Oct-43 |
| | | | | | | 17524 | 54685 | 17-Nov-43 |
| | | | | | | 17526 | 54687 | 17-Nov-43 |
| | | | | | | 17527 | 54688 | 17-Nov-43 |
| | | | | | | 17528 | 54689 | 17-Nov-43 |
| | | | | | | 17532 | 54693 | 17-Nov-43 |
| | | | | | | 17533 | 54694 | 17-Nov-43 |
| | | | | | | 17539 | 54700 | 17-Nov-43 |
| | | | | | | 17540 | 54701 | 18-Jan-43 |
| | | | | | | 17542 | 54703 | 18-Nov-43 |
| | | | | | | 17543 | 54704 | 18-Nov-43 |
| | | | | | | 17525 | 54686 | 18-Nov-43 |
| | | | | | | 17530 | 54691 | 18-Nov-43 |
| | | | | | | 17534 | 54695 | 18-Nov-43 |
| | | | | | | 17535 | 54696 | 18-Nov-43 |
| | | | | | | 17538 | 54699 | 18-Nov-43 |
| | | | | | | 17541 | 54702 | 18-Nov-43 |
| | | | | | | 17529 | 54690 | 10-Nov-43 |
| | | | | | | 17531 | 54692 | 19-Nov-43 |
| | | | | | | 17545 | 54706 | 19-Nov-43 |
| | | | | | | 17546 | 54707 | 19-Nov-43 |
| | | | | | | 17544 | 54705 | 19-Nov-43 |
| | | | | | | 17548 | 54709 | 20-Nov-43 |
| | | | | | | 17436 | 54697 | 22-Nov-43 |
| | | | | | | 17537 | 54698 | 22-Nov-43 |
| 13 | 13-J | 4 | DOM-679 | To AAF to be del. to Mod. Cntr to be mod into instrument Trainers thence to 2nd AF. | OTT-T-33-12676 25-11-43 | 17724 | 54885 | 29-Dec-43 |
| | | | | | | 17725 | 54886 | 29-Dec-43 |
| | | | | | | 17726 | 54887 | 29-Dec-43 |
| | | | | | | 17729 | 54888 | 29-Dec-43 |
| 13 | 13-K | 4 | DOM-680 | To AAF to be del. to Mod. Cntr to be mod. into instrument Trainers thence to 3rd AF. | OTT-T-33-12676 25-11-43 | 17728 | 54889 | 30-Dec-43 |
| | | | | | | 17729 | 54890 | 30-Dec-43 |
| | | | | | | 17730 | 54891 | 30-Dec-43 |
| | | | | | | 17731 | 54892 | 30-Dec-43 |
| 15 | 15-A | 2 | DOM-680 | To AAF to be del. to Mod. Cntr. to be mod. into instrument Trainers thence to 3rd AF. | OTT-T-33-12676 25-11-43 | 17732 | 54893 | 30-Dec-43 |
| | | | | | | 17733 | 54894 | 30-Dec-43 |
| 15 | 15-B | 5 | DOM-681 | To AAF to be del. to Mod. Cntr. to be mod into instrument Trainers thence to 1st AF | OTT-T-33-12676 25-11-43 | 17734 | 54895 | 30-Dec-43 |
| | | | | | | 17735 | 54896 | 30-Dec-43 |
| | | | | | | 17736 | 54897 | 30-Dec-43 |
| | | | | | | 17737 | 54898 | 30-Dec-43 |
| | | | | | | 17738 | 54899 | 30-Dec-43 |
| K | Dec. | 25 | 90318-F Pike | Del. by 5th FG to C.O. Atlantic Overseas ASC, Municipal Airport, Newark, New Jersey | OTT-T-33-16285.2-12-43 | 17580 | 54741 | 3-Dec-43 |
| | | | | | | 17581 | 54742 | 4-Dec-43 |
| | | | | | | 17582 | 54743 | 6-Dec-43 |

| Blk | Pr'ty | Quan. | Project | Destination | Authority | Co. Serial | AD Serial | Date |
|---|---|---|---|---|---|---|---|---|
|  |  |  |  |  |  | 17583 | 54744 | 6-Dec-43 |
|  |  |  |  |  |  | 17584 | 54745 | 13-Dec-43 |
|  |  |  |  |  |  | 17585 | 54746 | 11-Dec-43 |
|  |  |  |  |  |  | 17586 | 54747 | 7-Dec-43 |
|  |  |  |  |  |  | 17587 | 54748 | 13-Dec-43 |
|  |  |  |  |  |  | 17588 | 54749 | 13-Dec-43 |
|  |  |  |  |  |  | 17589 | 54750 | 13-Dec-43 |
|  |  |  |  |  |  | 17590 | 54751 | 7-Dec-43 |
|  |  |  |  |  |  | 17591 | 54752 | 7-Dec-43 |
|  |  |  |  |  |  | 17592 | 54753 | 13-Dec-43 |
|  |  |  |  |  |  | 17593 | 54754 | 13-Dec-43 |
|  |  |  |  |  |  | 17594 | 54755 | 13-Dec-43 |
|  |  |  |  |  |  | 17595 | 54756 | 13-Dec-43 |
|  |  |  |  |  |  | 17596 | 54757 | 13-Dec-43 |
|  |  |  |  |  |  | 17597 | 54758 | 13-Dec-43 |
|  |  |  |  |  |  | 17598 | 54759 | 13-Dec-43 |
|  |  |  |  |  |  | 17599 | 54760 | 13-Dec-43 |
|  |  |  |  |  |  | 17600 | 54761 | 13-Dec-43 |
|  |  |  |  |  |  | 17601 | 54762 | 13-Dec-43 |
|  |  |  |  |  |  | 17602 | 54763 | 13-Dec-43 |
|  |  |  |  |  |  | 17603 | 54764 | 15-Dec-43 |
|  |  |  |  |  |  | 17604 | 54765 | 11-Dec-43 |
| 14 | 14-A | 10 | Bass | to Mod. Centre | OTT-T-33-12077 24-11-43 | 17694 | 54855 | 28-Dec-43 |
|  |  |  |  |  |  | 17695 | 54856 | 23-Dec-43 |
|  |  |  |  |  |  | 17696 | 54857 | 28-Dec-43 |
|  |  |  |  |  |  | 17697 | 54858 | 20-Dec-43 |
|  |  |  |  |  |  | 17698 | 54859 | 28-Dec-43 |
|  |  |  |  |  |  | 17699 | 54860 | 20-Dec-43 |
|  |  |  |  |  |  | 17700 | 54861 | 23-Dec-43 |
|  |  |  |  |  |  | 17701 | 54862 | 24-Dec-43 |
|  |  |  |  |  |  | 17702 | 54863 | 28-Dec-43 |
|  |  |  |  |  |  | 17703 | 54864 | 10-Dec-43 |
| 15 | 15-C | 1 |  | Crashed ι.p. Del. to OCAD for salvage. | OTT-T-33-20675 13-12-43 | 17547 | 54708 | 10-Dec-43 |
| 16 | 16-A | 20 | Bass | To Mod. Center. | OTT-T-33-20675 13-12-43 | 17704 | 54865 | 28-Dec-43 |
|  |  |  |  |  |  | 17705 | 54866 | 29-Dec-43 |
|  |  |  |  |  |  | 17706 | 54867 | 29-Dec-43 |
|  |  |  |  |  |  | 17707 | 54868 | 29-Dec-43 |
|  |  |  |  |  |  | 17708 | 54869 | 30-Dec-43 |
|  |  |  |  |  |  | 17709 | 54870 | 29-Dec-43 |
|  |  |  |  |  |  | 17710 | 54871 | 28-Dec-43 |
|  |  |  |  |  |  | 17711 | 54872 | 24-Dec-43 |
|  |  |  |  |  |  | 17712 | 54873 | 29-Dec-43 |
|  |  |  |  |  |  | 17713 | 54874 | 30-Dec-43 |
|  |  |  |  |  |  | 17714 | 54875 | 29-Dec-43 |
|  |  |  |  |  |  | 17715 | 54876 | 29-Dec-43 |
|  |  |  |  |  |  | 17716 | 54877 | 29-Dec-43 |
|  |  |  |  |  |  | 17717 | 54878 | 28-Dec-43 |
|  |  |  |  |  |  | 17718 | 54879 | 29-Dec-43 |
|  |  |  |  |  |  | 17719 | 54880 | 24-Dec-43 |
|  |  |  |  |  |  | 17720 | 54881 | 29-Dec-43 |
|  |  |  |  |  |  | 17721 | 54882 | 24-Dec-43 |
|  |  |  |  |  |  | 17722 | 54883 | 28-Dec-43 |
|  |  |  |  |  |  | 17723 | 54884 | 28-Dec-43 |

# Notes

1    Scout Bomber, Douglas

2    Second Lieutenant W. H. Brown, RFC, RAF, on 14 March 1918. See *Impact-the dive bomber pilots speak* by Peter C. Smith, London and Annapolis 1981. Also AIR 1/1797.

3    Tests at the Orfordness testing grounds in May 1918, utilizing the Sopwith Camel aircraft. See *Dive Bomber!* by Peter C. Smith, London and Annapolis 1982.

4    See *Wings Over the Border*, by Stacy C. Hinkle, El Paso 1970.

5    See letter from Admiral F. D. Wagner to Lieutenant Commander H. M. Dater USNR (Op-501-D) dated 30 December 1948.

6    See *Dive Bombers: the pre-war Years* Washington DC 1949.

7    SAP = semi-armour piercing.

8    See Turnbull, Capt. A. D. & Lord, Lt Cdr C. L. *The History of United States Naval Aviation*, Yale, 1949.

9    See Leighton, Lt Cdr B. G. 'The relation between air and surface activities in the Navy', lecture, Naval War College, 23 March, 1928.

10   Leighton, *op cit.*

11   Richard K. Smith, letter to the author, 13 February 1988.

12   'Maximum weight on take-off' based on Sir George Cayley's definition of the basic problem of making any machine fly: '. . . to make a surface support a given weight by the application of power to the resistance of air.' For a scholarly dissertation on this, see 'The Weight Envelope: An Airplane's Fourth Dimension. Aviation's Bottom Line' by Richard K. Smith, in *Aerospace Historian*, March 1986.

13   See Martin BM notes in 'Navy, Bureau of Aeronautics, 1925–1942', in US National Archive Group 72, Washington DC.

14   See 'Diving Tests on Martin XT5M airplane', William H. McAvoy, 3 April, 1930. Also 'Report of acceptance trials of Model BM-1 airplane', 21 September 1931.

15   See 'Low height bombing from Scouts', 18 May 1918, AIR1/1200/04632, and 'Bombing from Sopwith Camel using Aldis sight', 27 May 1918, AIR1/1200/04633.

16   See 'Bombing, dangerous incidents to and methods of minimising', report 5 December 1929.

17   See 'Bomb displacing gear', report 12 February 1931, and 'Bomb displacing gear for 1,000lb bomb', report 15 January 1932.

18   See 'Report on dive bombing', RAE South Farnborough, October 1940 (AIR 14/181/IIH/241/3/406), and report 'Notes on Dive Bombing and the German JU 88 Bombing Aircraft', Air Ministry, February 1941 (AIR 14/181/IIH/241/3/406).

19   For example Rear Admiral Paul A. Holmberg, who spent the latter part of the war as a Navy test pilot at the Air Test Centre, Maryland, told the author (letter, 27 March 1977) that: 'There were no automatic pull-out devices in the US Navy. I tested an experimental model installed in a Dauntless at the Test Centre, Patuxent River, in 1944. It worked all right as I recall, but since the aviators in the fleet were not interested in having them in their dive bombers they were not adopted for operational use.'

20   See 'Helldivers, techniques of dive-bombing conceived for United States naval use', J. L. H. Peck, *Scientific-America*, CLXIII, October 1940.

21   See 'Experiments and production aircraft procurement for fiscal years 1934, 1935 and 1936', dated 19 January 1934. 'VB airplanes – request for informal quotations, dated 15 March 1934. 'VSB and VB airplanes – proposals' dated 25 April 1934.

22   See also 'The Navy's new Brewster dive bomber, SB2A-1' *Popular Science*, CXXXIX, September 1941.

23   See 'Contact 7648-model XSBC-2 airplane', dated 26 June 1935. Also 'Naval Aircraft Design in the mid-1930s', *Technology and Culture*, Vol IV by Charles J. McCarthy, 1963.

24   See 'Douglas News'.

25   See 'Salute to Ed Heinemann' *Flight Test Historian*, issue No 1 May 1995, Edwards AFB, CA.

26   See 'The Life of Ed Heinemann', *Flight Test Historian, op cit.*

27   See *Ed Heinemann; Combat Aircraft Designer* by Edward H. Heinemann and Rosario Rausa, Annapolis, 1980. The authors state that that designed wingspan was 42ft (12.6m).

28   See *Dive Bomber! An Illustrated History, op cit.*

29   See *Ed Heinemann: Combat Aircraft Designer, op cit.*

30   For example, see Air Ministry report '. . .aircraft of clean aerodynamic design will reach too high a velocity to make recovery from 1,500 ft reasonably safe and certain . . .'. 'Dive-bombing technique with high speed aircraft of clean aerodynamic design', dated 2 April 1936. AIR2/1655/5/36709.

31   See 'The History of the Northrop Division' by Harry Jay Nichols, *Douglas News*, May, 1938.

32   See *Ed Heinemann: A Combat Aircraft Designer, op cit.* All Ed Heinemann's papers are held in collection by Ray Wagner at the San Diego Aerospace Museum library.

33   See Captain Vernon E. McGee, USMC, 'The Air Corps has conducted some dive bombing experiments with pursuit airplanes in recent years, but has never evolved any tactics for the employment of dive bombers as a class. At present there are no airplanes within the Army Air Force capable of being used as dive bombers.' *Dive Bombing*, Washington 1937.

34   See Lieutenant David B. Overfield, 'Dive bombing compared with bombing from level flight', Washington, 1939. He concluded that the dive bomber '. . . is superior in accuracy when the fire is directed toward precision targets such as bridges, trestles, cross-roads, single ships at sea etc.' By contrast, the horizontal

bomber was effective against the same precision targets '. . . only by formation bombing when one or more bombs *might* be placed on the objective by means of salvo fire.' On the merits of range, Overfield pointed out that a dive bomber working from a carrier base had unlimited range compared to a heavy bomber operating from a fixed land base, and was infinitely more versatile as its base could move daily and hourly with no let-up in operations.

35  *Ed Heinemann,: Combat Aircraft Designer, op cit.*, states 100 gallons (454l)!

36  *Op cit.*

37  See Peter B. Mersky, *U.S. Marine Corps Aviation; 1912 to the Present*, Annapolis, 1983.

38  *Ed Heinemann; Combat Aircraft Designer, op cit.*

39  See the forthcoming Aeroclassic title by the author, *The Curtiss SB2C Helldiver*.

40  Some sources state that these were for the French Navy, the *Aéronavale*, but there is no mention of them in John McVikar Haight, Jr's *American Aid to France, 1938-1940*, New York, 1970. The French *did* place orders with Douglas at this time, for 180 of the DB-7, the export version of the Army's A-20 twin-engined Attack bomber, known as the Havoc in the USA and the Boston in the RAF. The French Navy certainly took delivery of export Vindicators (the V-156) and had ordered 170 of the Brewster SB2A and 130 Vultee V-72 dive bombers also, specifying the Wright 2600 engine as the power-plant for both orders. See also: Le Général Paul Jacquin, *Memoir*, 19 May 1951.

41  See *Case History of A-24 Airplane Project*, Material Command, Wright Field, X-44185-2, 22 February 1945. Inter-office memorandum dated 3 July 1940 'Status of the Dive Bomber'.

42  See Chief, Plans Div. to Chief, Material Division, 'Dive Bombing', 3 June 1940.

43  See Chief, Mat. Div. to Chief of Air Corps, 'Re-Design of A-20 Airplane for Dive Bombers', 8 June 1940.

44  'Re-Design of A-20 Airplane for Dive bombers', *op cit.*

45  'Status of Dive Bomber', *op cit.*

46  See 'Joint Army and Navy Procurement Program', Mat. Div. to Douglas Aircraft Company, 13 July 1940.

47  See 'Procurement of SBD-2 Airplanes for the War Department', Mat. Div. to BuAer, dated 13 July 1940.

48  *Case History of the A-24 Airplane Project, op cit.*

49  'Procurement of SBD-2 Airplanes for the War Department', Mat Div. to BuAer, dated 19 July 1940.

50  Ed Heinemann wrote to Nick Williams on 19 July 1979: 'Was it ever called BANSHEE? I can't remember that, and neither can any of my friends who also worked with it.'

51  Memorandum War Department: to Colonel Volandt from Major P. W. Timberlake, dated 23 June 1940.

52  See: *Narrative of the 27th Bombardment Group*, edited by Captain James B. McAfee (private circulation).

53  *Narrative, op cit.*

54  See Daniel R. Mortensen, *A Pattern for Joint Operations: World War II Close Air Support North Africa*, Washington DC 1987, pp. 26–7.

55  See 'Additional Procurement of SBD-3 Airplanes for the Army', dated 7 March 1942.

56  See Towers to Arnold, dated 21 March 1942.

57  See 'U.S. Army Aircraft, 1908–46' by J.C. Fahey.

58  See memorandum Meyers to Arnold dated 26 April 1942 (CTI-596) and cost-plus-fixed-fee contract no 91397, dated 27 April 1942 from the Navy Department Bureau of Supplies and Accounts.

59  See confidential memorandum War Department to Joint Aircraft Committee, 'Manufacture of A-24 Type Aircraft by Douglas at Tulsa', (case no 2357) dated 30 April 1942.

60  See memorandum BuAer to Commanding General, AAF, Aer-PL-6-EX, dated 16 May 1942.

61  See memorandum, Lieutenant Colonel F. I. Ordway, Jr. Assistant Executive, USAAF, to Navy Department, Washington, DC (AFAMC-13) dated 21 May 1942.

62  See memorandum, Chief BuAer to Chief BuOrd (Aer-PRD-251-JL) signed by Lieutenant Commander A. F. Bonralie, USNR, dated 1 June 1942.

63  See letter 'A-24B Airplanes Correspondence Handling of' Douglas Aircraft Company, Inc, El Segundo to Commanding General AAF, Material Centre, Wright Field, Dayton, Ohio, dated 2 June 1942.

64  See memorandum 'Model RA-24B Airplanes, Contract 28716- History of', Foster Evans, project engineer to D. E. Dunlap (RA024B-D251-395) dated 4 December 1943.

65  See memorandum Colonel O. R. Cook, Chief, Production Engineering Section, to Commanding General AAF Material Command, Washington, DC dated 1 July 1942 (WTR.RE: 70–2).

66  See memorandum Foster Evans to D.E. Dunlap *op cit.*

67  See memorandum Lester to Seasums, 'A-24 Production', dated 26 April 1942 (AFDMA-4D)

68  See teletype message JH:RR,ng:3-3, dated 29 April 1943, Branshaw, Material Command to District Supervisor, Western Procurement District, Los Angeles.

69  See memorandum, Brentnall to General Inspector of Naval Aircraft, Wright Field, (RRR/vlk/70-2(F-21), dated 3 August 1943.

70  See memorandum from Colonel T. A. Sims, Deputy Chief of Staff, to Production Division, (CTI-I824) dated 9 March 1944.

71  *Ed Heinemann; Combat Aircraft Designer, op cit.*

72  *ibid.*

73  See Peter C. Smith, *Dive Bombers in Action* London, New York & Sydney 1985, and *Vengeance!* Shrewsbury & Washington 1986.

74  See service school lecture 'Douglas Model A-24 – Surface Controls' by Francis Hanback, El Segundo, TDC-9-7, M016685., *op cit.*

75  See service school lecture, 'Hydraulics' by J. T. Alexander, El Segundo, TDC 9–7, M016685, *op cit.*

76  See service school lecture 'Instruments and Radio' by E. J. Weitekamp, El Segundo, TCD-9–7, M016685, *op cit.*

77  See service school lecture 'The Normal Procedure in Starting the A-24 Engine' by Jack Lehman, El Segundo, TDC 9–7, M016686, *op cit.*

78  Ron W. Hinrichs to the author, 24 October 1996.

79  See *Dive Bomber* by R. A. Winton, London, 1940.

80  See *A Pattern for Joint Operations, op cit.*

81  See *Case History of the A-24 Airplane Project, op cit.*

82  This chapter is mainly compiled from eyewitness accounts given to the author, supplemented by reference to the *Manual of Air Tactics*, 'Rough Notes on Dive Bombing tactics', which was based on US Navy dive bomber tactics in 1942–4 (AIR23/5287); *Dive Bombing*, by Captain Vernon E. McGee, USMC, ACTS; *Dive Bombing Compared with Bombing from Level Flight*, by Lieutenant David B. Overfield, USN, 248.222–64; and *Dive Bombing* (AIR 23/5287). Very good personal eyewitness detail is contained in *Dauntless Helldivers* by Commander Harold L. Buell, USN New York 1992, and various editions of *The Hook*, The Tailhook Association, Bonita, Cal.

83  See Service School lecture 'Douglas

Model A-24 – Surface Controls' by Francis Hanbeck, El Segundo, TOC-9-7, MOI 6685, op. cit.

84  See Dickinson, Lt Clarence E. (in collaboration with Boyden Sparkes) *The Flying Guns; Cockpit Record of a Naval Pilot from Pearl Harbor through Midway*, New York, 1943.

85  See *The Big E* by Commander Edward P. Stafford, USN, New York, 1962.

86  The submarines were positioned, from east to west, as follows: I-76, I-68, I-69, I-70, I-71, I-72 and I-73. See *Sunk; the Story of the Japanese Submarine Fleet 1942–1945* by Moschitsura Hashimoto, London, 1954.

87  See Dickinson, *The Flying Guns op cit.*

88  See *The Flying Guns*, by C. E. Dickinson, New York, 1942.

89  See Dickinson, *The Flying Guns op cit.*

90  See *The Big E, op cit.*

91  See Dickinson, *The Flying Guns, op cit.*

92  See *The Big E, op cit.*

93  See David Brazelton, *The Douglas SBD Dauntless*, Leatherhead, 1967.

94  See Rob Stern, *SBD Dauntless in Action*, Carrollton, Texas, 1984.

95  See *They Fought with what They Had*, by Walter D. Edmonds, Washington, 1963.

96  See General Henry H. Arnold, *Global Mission*, New York, 1949, who claimed the solenoids were actually in the crates the A-24s were shipped in but were burned by those who unpacked them. In view of the lack of other parts, this does, however, seem questionable. General Brereton claims that the parts were known to have been missing in the States, and were to have been shipped out on B-17s, but never got there as these bombers were held at Hawaii. Whatever the truth, Davies' men had to make bricks without straw.

97  Most of this chapter is based on the official microfilm records of the 27th Bomber Group (Light), made available by the USAAF Historical Unit at Maxwell AFB, Texas and in the author's collection; but see also 'Special Order Number 21, HQ 5th Bomber Command, FEAF, Malong, Java, dated 25 February 1942, Major K. R. Krebs. Also consulted was the 'unofficial' *History of 27th Bomber Group op cit.*

98  *ibid.* See also official Japanese history, *Military History of World War - vol. - Naval drive to Dutch East Indies and Bay of Bengal*, Military History Department, Tokyo, 1969 and correspondence with the author, November 1996.

99  See Japanese Military History Department, Tokyo, volume and correspondence, *op cit.*

100  See Japanese Military History Department, Tokyo, 4th Destroyer

Squadron Battle Report 19 Feb–10 March 1942. Lt G. J. de Haas, of 3rd *Afdeling*, stated that one dive bomber placed a full hit, the others missed the target. Gerard J. Casius, 14 Nov 1980.

101  This section is mainly based on the 3rd Bomb Group Diary, and the 8th Squadron Composite History, Maxwell AFB, Alabama.

102  *ibid*

103  *ibid*

104  *ibid.*

105  *ibid.*

106  See *Ground Attack Aircraft of World War II* by Christopher Shores, London, 1977.

107  The attitude of both Kenney and his squadrons to dive bombers and dive bombing are perhaps typified by the following, reported in his memoirs. On a visit to the 3rd Bombardment Group (Dive) at Charters Towers, which had one squadron equipped with the A-24, they complained to him: 'The 3rd, which used to be the 3rd Attack Group back home, did low-altitude strafing and bombing work. They still wanted to be called an attack group, so I told them to go ahead and change their name. That organization had trained for years in low-altitude, hedge-hopping attack, sweeping in to their targets under cover of a grass-cutting hail of machine-gun fire and dropping their delay-fused bombs with deadly precision. They were proud of their outfit and they liked the name "Attack". Now the powers-that-be had changed their name to "Light Bombardment Dive" and they didn't like it. I knew how they felt. I had been an attack man myself, had written textbooks on the subject and taught it for years in the Air Corps Tactical School.' This explains a lot; thus dive bombing might be a far more accurate form of delivery of ordnance to the target than the so-called 'deadly precision' of the Attack concept, which had never worked in combat, but that was what they had trained for and where their hearts lay, not in dive bombing, and so that was that! See Kenney, George C. *General Kenney Reports*, New York 1949.

108  See 'A-24B Airplanes Correspondence Handling of', E25-2639, dated 2 June 1942.

109  See Memo, 'Contract AC-28716, Government Furnished Equipment', dated 1 July, 1942.

110  This excludes the sinking by the Nagumo Force dive bombers under Lt Cdr Egusa of the Royal Navy carrier *Hermes* off Ceylon on 9 April, as she was unable to strike back or even defend

herself as someone had ordered her to sea *without* her aircraft!

111  This chapter is mainly based on the *Combat Reports of Enemy Action* of VB2, VS5 and VB5; NARA, College Park, Maryland.

112  Some accounts assert that the Japanese Nakajima B5N 'Kate' torpedo bombers dropped 'Long Lance' torpedoes in this, and other attacks. This assertion is absurd, because the 24in (60cm) oxygen-fuelled torpedo was much too large a weapon (6,107lb (2,770kg), while an unladen Kate itself only weighed 4,643lb (2,106kg)!). The Long Lane was only used by destroyers and cruisers. The weapon used by the carrier-borne torpedo bombers was the 18in (45cm) Type 91, Mod 2 with a 450lb (204kg) warhead with a range of 2,000 yards (1,800m).

113  See *Dauntless Helldivers*, by Commander Harold L. Buell, New York, 1992.

114  For a detailed account of this battle, see Peter C. Smith, *The Battle of Midway*, Speldhurst, Kent, 1996.

115  See Marine Aircraft Group Twenty-Two, Second Marine Aircraft Wing, Midway Islands T.H., *Report of the Battle of Midway*, June 30, 1942, with preliminary phase from 22 May 1942. Dated 7 June 1942. (DoD DIR 5200.10, DARA, College Park, Maryland.

116  *Ibid.*

117  *Ibid.*

118  See *Major Lofton Henderson, A Memoir*, Office of U S Marine Corps, Washington, DC 17 June 1949 AG-1265-kps.

119  *Ibid*

120  *Ibid.*

121  *Ibid.*

122  See *Major Lofton Russell Henderson, a Memoir*, Office of US Marine Corps, 17 June 1949. AG-1265-kps.

123  Lieutenant Daniel continued to ride his luck at Guadalcanal where he survived being wounded, but nemesis finally caught up with him back home in the States when he was killed in a flying accident.

124  Incredibly, these brave Japanese pilots were described in some Stateside accounts as flying Messerschmitt 109s, as if it were not possible for Japanese Navy flyers to fight so well. Xenophobia taken to extremes. See Lieutenant Commander Joseph Bryan, *Mission Beyond Darkness*, New York, 1944 among others.

125  See 3rd Bomb Group, Operations, 3rd Bomb Group Diary and 8th Squadron Composite History, Maxwell AFB, *op cit.*

126  *Ibid.*

127  *Ibid.*
128  Richard K. Smith to the author, 13 February 1988.
129  See Robert Sherrod *History of Marine Corps Aviation in World War Two*, Annapolis, 1948.
130  So termed by the Americans because of the numbers of warships which were sunk in the almost nightly battles and which rested on the seabed there.
131  This chapter is mainly based on the combat reports of the squadrons involved, NARA, College Park, Maryland; but see also Miller, Thomas G. *The Cactus Air Force*, New York, 1969; Buell, Harold L. *Dauntless Helldivers*, New York, 1992, Sherrod, Robert, *History of Marine Corps Aviation in World War Two, op cit*, and White, Alexander S., *Dauntless Marine* Fairfax Station, Va, 1996.
132  Under the very able command of Rear Admiral Raizo Tanaka, Japanese destroyers ran in troops and supplies almost nightly, when losses among the slower troop transports proved prohibitive. Frequently ambushed by superior American naval squadrons, Tanaka's destroyers often proved their master in the night fighting, even though they lacked the sophisticated radar of the US ships. So successful was he at this job that even the Americans named him 'Tenacious Tanaka'. These troop runs were nicknamed the 'Cactus Express', or just plain 'Express' by the defending American forces on Guadalcanal, but this was too subtle for the US press which re-dubbed it as the 'Tokyo Express' as it was better 'copy'!
133  He was found by friendly natives and later managed to get back to Henderson Field.
134  See Buell, Commander Harold L. *Dauntless Helldivers, op cit.*
135  See Buell, *Dauntless Helldivers, op cit.*
136  See 'Remembrances of Guadalcanal' by James H. Cales, *The Hook*, Volume 18, August 1990.
137  See Buell, *Dauntless Helldivers, op cit.*
138  See Paul S. Dull, *A Battle History of the Imperial Japanese Navy*, Annapolis, 1978, page 216.
139  Some sources state only three.
140  Fact, not fiction; see Captain S. W. Roskill, *The War at Sea, Volume Two*, London, 1956, pp 236. The US Navy's aerial torpedoes were of poor quality for the first two or three years of the war, in stark contrast with the efficiency of the Japanese air-launched torpedoes.
141  See Stafford, *The Big 'E', op cit.*
142  See Dull, *Battle History of the Imperial Japanese Navy, op cit.*
143  See Sherrod, *History of Marine Corps Aviation in World War II, op cit.*
144  *Not* torpedoed or bombed. See Dull, *The Battle History of the Imperial Japanese Navy, op cit.*
145  See Sherrod, *History of Marine Aviation, op cit.*
146  See Dull, *The Battle History of the Imperial Japanese Navy, op cit.*
147  See Buell, *Dauntless Helldivers, op cit.*
148  Interestingly the US Navy SBD aircrew were relearning an old lesson already proven by their counterparts in the Royal Navy. Among the very first attacks made by Fleet Air Arm Blackburn Skua dive bombers from the carrier *Ark Royal* were against German submarines. Off the Orkney Islands, Scotland, in the very first days of the war, the Skuas had attacked U-boats at low level in the same way that the Dauntlesses attacked the Japanese submarines, and with the same lack of results. Even more humiliating was the fact that in a low-level attack one Skua was blown into the sea by the explosion of its own bomb, and the crew taken prisoner by the very U-boat they had been trying to sink! One Skua pilot told the author that bombing submarines with such a weapon was about as useful as throwing a tin of marmalade at them! See *Impact!, the dive bomber pilots speak*, London & Annapolis, 1981.
149  See Stafford, *The Big 'E', op cit.*
150  See Dull, Hara, Rohwer & Hummelchen etc.
151  See Buell, *Dauntless Helldivers, op cit.*
152  Accounts differ on the number of hits scored by the SBDs on *Ryujo*. Prof Samuel Eliot Morison, in *History of United States Naval Operations in World War II, Volume V, The Struggle for Guadalcanal*, Boston, 1951, states there were four to ten bomb hits; the *Ryujo's* commanding officer, Captain Tadao Keno, claimed that she avoided *all* the bombs except a near-miss, and that it was a solitary torpedo hit that sank her. Captain Tameichi Hara, commanding officer of one of the escorting destroyers, the *Amatsukaze*, recorded that 'Two or three enemy bombs hit the ship near the stern, piercing the flight deck . . .' and that ' . . .more bombs made direct hits . . .' See Hara, Fred Saito and Roger Pineau, *Japanese Destoyer Captain*, New York, 1961.
153  This vessel was later sailed to Japan where she and her sister ship, *Chiyoda*, were converted into light carriers. Both were sunk off Cape Engano in October 1944, during the Battle of Leyte Gulf.
154  See *Dauntless Helldivers, op cit.*
155  According to a press interview conducted with Eugene Burns, Lieutenant Strong recalled that there were '. . . about twenty planes parked on the forecastle (sic) . . .'. Burns, Eugene, *Then There Was One*, New York, 1944; but another account has it that 'There was just time to notice that both decks were empty . . .'. *The Big E, op cit.*
156  Although the anti-aircraft gunners of the *Enterprise* and the *San Juan* also claim a good number of these!
157  Morison, Professor Samuel Eliot, *History of United States Naval Operations in World War II, Volume II, Operations in North African Waters*, Boston, 1947.
158  See Captain S. W. Roskill *The War at Sea, Vol. III, Part I*, London, 1960.
159  *Ibid.*
160  See Peter C. Smith, *Task Force 57*, London, 1995.
161  *Ibid.*
162  See Hanson, Norman, *Carrier Pilot*, Cambridge, 1979.
163  See Sherrod, *History of Marine Corps Aviation, op cit.*
164  This chapter is based mainly on 'Report of Enemy Action, Midway Island', from the commanding officer, Marine Aircraft Group 21, dated 10 June 1942 (EV21/A16-3/rbs (0111). NARA, Washington, DC.
165  See *War Diary, Strike Command* 26 July 1943– 19 November 1943, US Marine Corps 33063.
166  See Sherrod, *History of Marine Aviation, op cit.*
167  See Captain Warren H. Goodman, USMC, *The Role of Aviation in the Bougainville Operations*, USMC Historical Monograph, Washington, DC.
168  See *Command and Employment of Air Power*, Army Monograph FM 100–20, 1943.
169  See Sherrod, *The Big E, op cit.*
170  See Requisition Form BAC/10832, NZSM/F244, 40, 521 NZ from F. W. Musson, British Air Commission, for Army Air Forces Action, dated 21 April 1943.
171  *Ibid.*
172  Meyers to Dayton, AFDMA-4Bm 5585, Ref LLI No 60, dated 27 April 1943.
173  Lt Col P. I. Doty, to Major Paul R. Blum, dated 3 May 1943.
174  Arnold to Material Command, technical executive, CR 130, dated 20 January 1944.
175  This method was almost identical to that used by Royal Navy Blackburn Skua pilots in the 1939–40 period as described to this author, and also by trainee RAF A-35 Vultee Vengeance pilots in India during 1943 in readiness for the Burma Front. These latter also

received initial training from experienced US Navy dive bomber instructors.

176 See Jenks, *Dive bomber, op cit.*

177 See Buell, *Dauntless Helldivers, op cit.*

178 See Stafford, *The Big E, op cit.*

179 *ibid*

180 See Lieutenant Oliver Jensen, USNR, *Carrier War*, New York, 1945.

181 From Sherrod, *History of Marine Corps Aviation, op cit.*

182 See Major Charles W. Boggs Jr, *Marine Aviation in the Philippines*, USMC monograph, Washington, DC.

183 See Aircraft Repair Branch, July 1942–May 1944. E. J. Chettle, General Foreman.

184 See Confidential Report, *Radio Call Signs*, dated 26 June 1943, VII Bomber Command APO 953.

185 See First Lieutenant L. W. Higbie, IO, Mission Report 531–3, *Strike Against Mille Shipping*, dated 24 December 1943, NARA NND-745005.

186 See First Lieutenant L. W. Higbie, IO Mission Report 531–4, *Strike against Mille Shipping and Ground Installations*, dated 24 December 1943, NARA NND-745005.

187 See First Lieutenant John G. Tinder, IO, Mission Report 531–5, *Mille*, dated 1 January 1944, NARA NND-745005.

188 See Captain Ross D. Thompson, *Rear Echelon Headquarters VII Bomber Command*, APO 963, dated 23 March 1944.

189 See Confidential Aircraft Status Report, 22 April 1944 to 28 April 1944.

190 See internal memo AFRDS to AFAMC - AFDMR, *A-24 Airplane*, R-4-2/cpw, dated 3 July 1942, NARA Washington DC.

191 See Memo AFRGS to AFDMR, *A-24 Airplane*, dated 9 July 1942, NARA Washington DC.

192 See TWX Teletype from Colonel O.R. Cook, to AAF Rep, Douglas Aircraft, El Segundo, SIB.BR.70-2, dated 14 July 1942. NARA Washington DC.

193 See Kenney to HQ Army Air Force, Telegram No A-262, dated 12 August 1942.

194 Author's emphasis.

195 See AFDMR to AFADS, *A-24 Airplane*, dated 14 August 1942.

196 See Colonel Robert W. Harper, to AFADS, *A-24 Airplane*, dated 19 August 1962.

197 See *Cost-Plus-a-Fixed Fee Supply Contract (Army Air Forces) War Department*, W 535 ac-28716 (8so7) AA-1 dated 1 December 1942, NARA Washington, DC.

198 See Memo Mat Cmd to Douglas Tulsa, *Contract AC-28716 A-24B Airplane Engineering Conference*, dated 16 November 1942, NARA Washington DC.

199 See memo from Douglas to Commanding General Material Center, Wright Field, Dayton, Ohio, *Contract W535 ac-28716 A-24B Airplanes*, B311-33, dated 24 December 1942, NARA, Washington, DC.

200 See Major Williams to Air Mat Div, Washington DC, *A-24 Douglas, Tulsa*, JHW/lwc, dated 1 February 1943.

201 See Brig Gen K. B. Wolfe, memo to Chiefs of Staff, *Request for Board Orders*, LFH:BGS:70–2, dated 19 March 1943, NARA, Washington DC.

202 See Colonel S. R. Brentnall, to Douglas, El Segundo, *Contract AC-28716 Model A-24B Airplanes*, SRB/ies/70–2, dated 22 March 1943, NARA, Washington, DC.

203 For example the A-25 Shrike by Curtiss, the A-35 Vengeance by Vultee, or Consolidated as it had become. And the Brewster Buccaneer or Bermuda.

204 See Brig Gen K. B. Wolfe to General Meyers, KBW:hmg: 70-A, dated 2 April 1943.

205 See Col D. Hutchins, Control Section, to Chief, Procurement Div, *Contract AC-28716 A-24B Airplanes*, WJA:vk:77-B-13, dated 4 May 1943, NARA, Washington, DC.

206 See Col Mervin E. Gross, to AC/AS, MM&D, *A-24 Production*, Col Gross:ctp/3030, Comment No 1, dated 10 July 1943, NARA, Washington, DC.

207 See memo Col S. T. Brentnall, to Major Rison, 'Curtailment of A-24 Production at Tulsa', LF:maw;70–10, dated 21 July 1943.

208 See Arnold to Mat Cmd, AFDMA-4D-631, dated 18 August 1943, NARA, Washington DC.

209 See teletype AFDMA-4G-65, Arnold to technical executive, dated 24 August 1943.

210 See Col T. A. Sims, to Production Div, *Modification of A-24B Airplanes*, TI-1550, dated 26 August 1943, NARA, Washington, DC.

211 Col T. A. Sims to Prod Div 'Removal of Turrets, Guns and Armour from A-24, A-25 and A-35 Series Airplanes', CTI-1462, dated 30 September 1943, NARA, Washington, DC.

212 Emphasis in original.

213 Arnold to tech exec AFDMA-4G 194, dated 25 October 1943, NARA, Washington, DC.

214 See transcript of telephone conversation Cook to Conant, *Cancellation of last 635 A-24s, 4:00 p.m. 29 October 1943*.

215 This was the Douglas SB2D Destroyer, under development at El Segundo. Only a few examples were ever completed before this project was also cancelled.

216 See Col O. R. Cook to General Meyers, assist chief of air staff etc. ORC:EKG:70–A, dated 29 October 1943, NARA Washington, DC.

217 See Col W. M. Morgan, Prod Eng Section to AAF rep, Tulsa, TOM/led-70–7, dated 1 November 1943, NARA, Washington, DC.

218 See Lt Col W. W. Wise to Mat Cmd, Wright Field, *Heaters for A-24 Airplanes*, ASC 452812 (ASCMS3X), dated 2 November 1943, NARA, Washington, DC.

219 See telegram comptroller, Matl Cmd to General Meyers, Material Div, RCS 5134 dated 3 November 1943, NARA, Washington DC.

220 See telephone conversation transcript, Cook to Cawthon, *A-24 cancellation at Tulsa*, timed at 5:12 pm, 4 November 1943, NARA, Washington, DC.

221 Telephone conversation transcript, Cook to Meyers, *A-24 Type Airplane*, 1:00 A.M. 4 November 1944, NARA, Washington, DC.

222 See Capt Carr to Douglas Aircraft Corporation, Tulsa, 87-14:HCW:ep, PD-T-6165, dated 16 November 1943, NARA, Washington, DC.

223 See telegram Arnold to Mat Cmd, Wright Field, GR 130, dated 20 January 1944, NARA, Washington, DC.

224 See Col Sims to Production Division, *Cancellation of 60 RA-24B Airplanes from the 'H' Program, Acceleration*, RIW:RAS;ms:3-3, CTI-1824, dated 9 March 1944, NARA, Washington, DC.

225 See AAF 'Aircraft Procurement Programs', (RC-301), dated 30 June 1944, filed at Historical Office, Material Command, Wright Field.

226 In fact, records show that three aircraft – AF nos. 42-54452, 42-54453 and 42-54454 – were delivered to Romulus on 1 September 1943.

227 Mr Barton N. Hahn to Nick Williams, dated 23 September 1985. I am indebted to Nick Williams for allowing me to use this interesting information.

228 According to W. D. Dickson, *The Battle of the Philippine Sea*, Annapolis, 1975. Combat reports and personal memoirs place it at 1610 or 1615.

229 This section is mainly based upon the Combat Action Reports of VB-10 and VB-16, NARA, Washington DC, but see also Rear Admiral J. D. Ramage, USN, Rtd, and Dave Crawley, ex-ARMl/c, 'A Review of the Philippine Sea Battle, 20 June 1945' reproduced in *The Hook*, August, 1990 edition; Stafford *The Big E, op cit*; and Dull,

*Battle History of the Imperial Japanese Navy, op cit.*

230 This was VB-14 from the *Wasp*, commanded by Lieutenant Commander J. D. Blitch. As a result of their attacks the oiler *Hayasui* was hit by one bomb and near-missed by two more, but survived. The oilers *Genyo Maru* (three near-misses) and *Seiyo Maru* were both damaged so severely that they had to be sunk by their own forces later.

231 And not only in these two instances: the US Marine Corps flyers had pioneered many aspects of dive bombing and close support of their own ground forces ever since 1919, in the Haiti, Dominica and Nicaragua and other small-scale campaigns.

232 Even the AAF itself War Department document *Command and Employment of Air Power*, FM100-20 July 1943, had stated that close support missions were '. . . most difficult to control, are most expensive, and are, in general, least effective. Targets are small, well dispersed, and difficult to locate.' But two years later an AAF Evaluation Board's findings, 'POA Report No 3, was confessing that: 'The above doctrine is in error.' It contrasted the Seventh Division's experience of working with both Army and Navy methods in the Pacific theatre, and came down heavily in favour of the latter, finding the Navy version of close support workable, effective, safe and well practised and rehearsed, while their own AAF methods were slated for having no system, lacking control, practice or rehearsal, and dangerous. Similar analysis of the AAF's attitude in the European theatre revealed the same shortcomings, see Daniel R. Mortensen, *A Pattern for Joint Operations: World War II Close Air Support North Africa*, Washington, 1987.

233 See Admiral William F. Halsey and J. Bryan III, *Admiral Halsey's Story*, New York, 1947.

234 See Sherrod, *History of Marine Corps Aviation, op cit.*

235 This chapter is based mainly on Lieutenant Colonel Keith B. McCutcheon's CMC report, *Close Support Aviation*, Washington, DC; copy in author's collection.

236 This total figure includes the six SBDs belonging to the two air groups' staff units, SMS 24 and SMS 32, which had three aircraft each on their strengths.

237 See memo, Lt H. C. Lynch, Material Branch, to Major C. W. Newhall, Jr, Munitions Assignment Committee, (Air), Case Nbr 202, dated 31 March 1943.

238 See memo, *Quantity and Description*, C6016V, dated 31 March 1943.

239 See requisition C-6016 (V), Captain L. H. Clarke, AC, China Defense Supplies Inc, to Lt Col P. I. Doty, AC, for Major Paul L. Blum, AC, dated 19 April 1943.

240 See Brigadier General B. E. Meyers, international officer for AAF, to Commanding General, Air Service Command, Patterson Field, Ohio, AFDMA-4B, WWR:drg 6767, dated 12 June 1943.

241 Lt-Cdr Smeeton to C R Fairey, 30 September 1941, Ref: 277-efh. (AVIA38/744)

242 Memorandum to Mr Fairey, BAC, from Lt-Cdr Smeeton, 2 October 1941 (AVIA38/744)

243 Lt Miller to C R Fairey, Ref: 303-mkb, dated 9 October 1941. (AVIA38/744)

244 C R Fairey to Smeeton, 18 October, 1941. (AVIA38/744)

245 See Pierre Rivière, 'Les Forces Aériennes de L'Atlantique, 1944/45', in *Le Fana d'Aviation* Paris 1983, and *Douglas SBD 'Dauntless'*, L'album du spotter, AviMag 746, Paris, 15 January 1979.

246 See Captain Eric Brown, *Wings of the Navy*, Shrewsbury, 1987.

247 This section is based on the following documents held at the *Marine Nationale, Service Historique*, Vincennes, Paris: Document MNII BB7bis 15 et 40: *Comptes-rendus d'activité de la Mission navale aux Etats-Unis en 1944 et archives de l'aéronavale*, Document 2DD7-276: *Manuel d'entretien du SBD-5 1943*, and *Avec les S.B.D. du G.A.N.2*, by *Enseigne de Vaisseau* Futaully, Saman, 1985.

248 SHAA 4 em bureau (Material Services) report, dated 25 February, 1944.

249 Letter from Jean Cuny to the author, 22 April 1985.

250 See Pierre Rivière, 'Les Forces Aériennes de L'Atlantique, 1944/45', in *Le Fana d'Aviation* Paris 1983, and *Douglas SBD 'Dauntless'*, L'album du spotter, AviMag 746, Paris, 15 January 1979.

251 M. Jean Cuny to the author, 22 April 1985.

252 See Document UVV 67: *Comptes-rendus d'activité des flottilles 3F et 4F pour la période de la guerre d'Indochine; Marine Nationale, Service Historique*, Vincennes, Paris.

253 See document 3BB2 Aero 28: *Base D'Hyères, Escadrille 54S, Comptes-rendus d'activité et correspondances pour la période 1945–1952, Marine Nationale Service Historique*, Vincennes, Paris; and V. A. R. Vercken, *Histoire succincte de l'aéronautique navale*, Ardham, 1993 (Cote 8 - 7340).

254 See 'Highly Prized 40's Plane Stolen From Lake Michigan is Recovered by F.B.I.', story special to the *New York Times*, undated.

# Index